the mass media and modern society

the mass media and modern society

SECOND EDITION

William L. Rivers
Stanford University

Theodore Peterson
University of Illinois
at Urbana-Champaign

Jay W. Jensen
University of Illinois
at Urbana-Champaign

RINEHART PRESS, San Francisco

To Fred Siebert,
teacher, colleague, and friend

Preface

Only six years have passed since the first edition of this book was published, but the world of the 1970s is starkly different from the one we were writing about in 1965. And although we wrote then, as now, primarily about the mass media, we find it necessary once again to take account of the broad context in which the media operate. Our conviction that the condition of the world affects the media and is affected *by* the media has grown stronger. The mass media did not grow up in a vacuum, nor do they perform in one. They emerged, grew, changed, and in some cases even died as a result of geographical, technological, economic, cultural, and other forces. To understand the media, then, one must look at them in their historical, intellectual, economic, political, and social contexts. What may otherwise seem the result of perversity, stupidity, chance, or caprice becomes understandable when one looks at the development of the media from such a perspective.

Some will say perhaps that this is a critical book. In a sense we hope it is. Surely we have not tried to gloss over the shortcomings of the media as we see them. It was not criticism in the sense of fault-finding that was uppermost in our minds as we wrote. Rather, we have tried conscientiously to make this book critical in the sense that it is an analysis of both the strengths and weaknesses of the media as they play their roles in society.

In writing this volume, we have benefited from the ideas of a number of friends and academic colleagues at Stanford, at the University of Illinois, and elsewhere, although we alone, of course, take full responsibility for whatever uses we have made of those ideas. It is impractical to name all the persons to whom we are indebted, but a few deserve special recognition. As students and co-workers of Wilbur Schramm, we have profited enormously from his perceptive insights, from his rare and broad perspective, and above all from his unmatched ability to synthesize findings relevant to communications from a half-dozen or more disciplines. Fred Siebert taught us a great deal about both the history and the philosophy of mass media in the political order. The ways in which each of these men has helped us, directly and indirectly, are beyond measure. We also give public thanks to Dr. Eleanor Blum, librarian in the College of Communications at the University of Illinois, Urbana-Champaign, who helped us to track down many sources and elusive facts.

Diana Winter, of Stanford, who typed the manuscript, was similarly helpful, and Charlene Brown was, as usual, a sharply perceptive critic.

W. L. R.

T. P.

J. W. J.

Stanford, California
Urbana, Illinois
January, 1971

Contents

Preface   vii

1   The Mass Media and the Challenge of Change   1

2   Communication and Society   21

3   The Media and Their Social and Economic Environment   37

4   The Intellectual Environment—Libertarianism   67

5   The Intellectual Environment—Social Responsibility   87

6   The Media and Government—The Early Experience   103

7   The Media and Government—The Modern Experience   125

8   Regulation of the Mass Media   145

9   The Economic Framework of the Mass Media   163

10   The Media as Informers and Interpreters   187

11   The Media as Persuaders   209

12   The Professional Persuaders   235

13 The Media, Entertainment, and American
    Culture   255

14 The Audiences of the Mass Media   277

15 Criticisms of the Mass Media   295

16 The Mass Media and the Future   317

   Bibliography   325

   Index   337

The Mass Media
and the
Challenge of Change

A good newspaper . . . is a nation talking to itself.
ARTHUR MILLER

In 1970 the Columbia Broadcasting System conducted a highly significant national survey of public opinion. Designed to reveal attitudes toward key provisions of the Bill of Rights, the survey indicated that a majority of adults in the United States seemed willing—even eager—to restrict certain basic freedoms. Fifty-five per cent said that, even in time of peace, newspapers, radio, and television should not be permitted to report some stories if government officials considered them harmful to the national interest.

The respondents were not speaking mindlessly for restricting all freedoms. Three out of four (seventy-five per cent) of them said that the government should never be allowed to hold a secret trial. And two out of three (sixty-six per cent) said that the police should not be allowed to enter a home without a search warrant, even if they suspect drugs, guns, or other criminal evidence to be hidden there. Clearly the respondents were weighing the freedoms guaranteed by the Bill of Rights—and deciding unmistakably that in certain cases the mass media should be controlled.

As the United States entered the 1970s, there were other signs that the public was disenchanted with the mass media. "Public criticism of the newspapers is the shrillest and most widespread I have seen in eighteen years" observed Wallace Allen, managing editor of the Minneapolis *Tribune*. "The public mood is uneasy, querulous, fearful." NBC News Director Reuven Frank wrote that the intellectual and upper mid-

1

dle-brow critics who had long excoriated television were now being joined by "the basic American audience, the most middle-class majority in history."

Some of the criticism of the mass media is no more than a reflection of troubled times. In a country that is often tight with tension when it is not wracked by violence, it is not surprising that the messenger should be blamed for the bad news he brings. This is not entirely irrational. Not only is there evidence that media reports sometimes inflame abrasive situations, it is also true that journalists rewrite and edit the news and decide which messages will be carried.

But if blaming the messenger for the message is responsible for many of the currents of criticism that are now washing over the mass media, it will not do to assign to this tendency all suspicions and doubts. In recent years a vast literature on media performance has been written. This literature indicates that much of the criticism is warranted.

THE "NEW" FIRST AMENDMENT

A large part of this book is devoted to the challenges and criticisms that confront mass communications. In this chapter, in which we are concerned primarily with basic changes, we explore the disenchantment with the First Amendment guarantee of a free press. "Congress shall make no law . . . abridging the freedom of speech, or of the press . . ." the First Amendment declares. United States Supreme Court decisions have interpreted the Fourteenth Amendment in a way that prohibit the states as well as the Federal government from abridging free speech or press. That seems simple enough, but thoughtful specialists in law and in mass communications who have been looking at the First Amendment from many perspectives suggest that the traditional view of a free press is short-sighted.

One of the most important perspectives is provided by Jerome Barron, Professor of Law at George Washington University, in an article titled "Access to the Press—A New First Amendment Right" (*Harvard Law Review*, 1967). Barron argues:

> There is an anomaly in our constitutional law. While we protect expression once it has come to the fore, our law is indifferent to creating opportunities for expression. Our constitutional theory is in the grip of a romantic conception of free expression, a belief that the "marketplace of ideas" is freely accessible. But if ever there were a self-operating marketplace of ideas, it has long ceased to exist. The mass media's development of an antipathy to ideas requires legal intervention if novel and unpopular ideas are to be assured a forum—unorthodox

points of view which have no claim on broadcast time and newspaper space as a matter of right are in a poor position to compete with those aired as a matter of grace.

. . . First Amendment theory must be re-examined, for only by responding to the present reality of the mass media's repression of ideas can the constitutional guarantee of free speech best serve its original purpose.

. . . Today ideas reach the millions largely to the extent that they are permitted entry into the great metropolitan dailies, news magazines, and broadcasting networks. The soap box is no longer an adequate forum for public discussion. Only the new media of communication can lay sentiments before the public, and it is they rather than the government who can most effectively abridge expression by nullifying the opportunity for an idea to win acceptance.

. . . What is required is an interpretation of the First Amendment which focuses on the idea that restraining the hand of government is quite useless in assuring free speech if a restraint on access is effectively secured by private groups. A constitutional prohibition against governmental restrictions on expression is effective only if the Constitution ensures an adequate opportunity for discussion. Since this opportunity exists only in the mass media, the interests of those who control the means of communication must be accommodated with the interests of those who seek a forum in which to express their point of view.

To summarize the gist of Barron's argument: The First Amendment's guarantee of a free press was meant to assure that every voice should be heard. But the interpretation of the First Amendment has granted real freedom only to the proprietors of the mass media. They may—and do—prevent some voices from being heard effectively by denying them access to the only channels that will reach a complex modern society. Thus we must have a "new" First Amendment, which can be accomplished by reinterpreting it to provide full access to the media.

Because we are likely to think first of access for disadvantaged minorities, it may seem odd to consider members of Congress in this category. And yet when one considers the power of the President to reach the American people, it is not difficult to imagine the opposition in Congress as disadvantaged. Senator J. W. Fulbright of Arkansas has made this point most cogently:

There is nothing in the Constitution which says that, of all elected officials, the President alone shall have the right to communicate with the American people. That privilege was a gift of modern technology, coming in an age when chronic war and crisis were already inflating the powers of the Presidency. . . . Communication is power, and exclusive access to it is dangerous, unchecked power. Television has done as much to expand the powers of the President as would a constitutional amendment formally abolishing the coequality of the three branches of government.

Senator Fulbright pointed out that the President can command a national television audience to hear his views on controversial matters in prime time, on short notice, at whatever length he chooses, and at no expense to the government or to his political party. But others who hold public office must rely on "highly selective newspaper articles and television news spots, which at most will contain bits and snatches of their points of view."

Broadcast Responsibility

Support for Professor Barron's argument has come from many quarters. The most interesting approach was advanced by Kenneth Cox, a member of the Federal Communications Commission (FCC). He granted that radio and television "must serve much more effectively than they have as forums for the discussion and resolution of the complex issues now facing us." But he pointed out that broadcast licensees, unlike the owners of the print media, are already required to grant a measure of access, especially because of the FCC "Fairness Doctrine." The key provision of the doctrine reads:

> That it is not enough for a licensee simply to be willing to broadcast opposing views if asked to do so, but that he has an affirmative duty generally to encourage and implement the broadcast of all sides of controversial issues—and that fairness in the presentation of any controversy will be difficult, if not impossible, of achievement unless the licensee plays a conscious and positive role in bringing about balanced presentation of the opposing viewpoints.

Commissioner Cox went on to suggest that newspapers should heed the example of broadcasting because

> . . . if the First Amendment has as a prime objective the creation of an informed public capable of conducting its own affairs, then certainly the Constitution guards the right of the public, as well as the publisher, in a free press. Whether this is yet the law, or ever will be in view of our long history of giving a highly preferred place to the press, I think it is good policy. It seems to me that the publisher, even though he does not use the public's spectrum, owes the same moral duty as the broadcaster to use his medium to help fashion a better society. If this poses new problems for him—as some broadcasters think [it] does for them—then this must be accepted because with opportunity and power goes responsibility. As a matter of logic

and law it has long seemed to me that Congress could—*if* it wished— constitutionally apply counterparts of our equal time and right to reply obligations to most newspapers, since they move in, or clearly affect, interstate commerce and since the public interest in their providing their readers with both sides of important questions is clear.

If all this seems cogent and well designed to enhance public enlightenment, one aspect is not yet clear. Exactly how would a right of access to the press operate? This is an easier question for broadcasting because so little broadcast time is devoted to news and public affairs. But while radio and television are primarily entertainment media, newspapers are primarily informative and are heavy with news and views. No one has addressed squarely the question of how to implement access to the columns of newspapers. How difficult it would be to draw rules for a right of access to newspapers is suggested by Clifton Daniel, associate editor of *The New York Times.*

Taking full note of the arguments of the proponents, Daniel pointed out that Professor Barron spoke of the press as having "an obligation to provide space on a non-discriminatory basis for representative groups in the community."

"Space! How much space?" Daniel asked.

He then reported that *The New York Times* in the preceding year had received 37,719 letters to the editor, at least eighty-five to ninety per cent of which were "fit to print." The *Times* had the space to print only six per cent. If all the letters had been printed—and every letter-writer may have thought he had a right of access—they would have amounted to eighteen million words and filled at least 135 complete issues of the *Times,* leaving no room for anything else.

"Non-discriminatory! Discrimination is the very essence of the editing process," Daniel stated. "You must discriminate or drown."

He pointed out that the *Times* receives between one and a quarter million and a million and a half words every day. The editors can print only a tenth of what is received. Noting that Professor Barron had suggested legal remedies for those who were denied access, Daniel reported that 168 bushels of waste paper, most of it rejected news, are collected and thrown away every day at the *Times.* "Do you imagine that the courts have the time to sort it all out? Do they have the time and, indeed, do they have the wisdom?

"Representative groups! What constitutes a representative group?" Daniel asked. "Who is to decide? I would say that representative groups already have access to the press. It's the unrepresentative ones we have to worry about."

Daniel then stated that it isn't easy for anyone with a cause or grievance to obtain space in newspapers and that in his opinion it should not be. "Nowhere in the literature on access to the press do I find any conspicuous mention of the hate groups . . . Must a Jewish editor be forced to publish anti-Semitism? Must a Negro editor give space to the Ku Klux Klan?"

Although he said that the problem has been exaggerated and the proposed legal remedies are either improper or impractical, Daniel admitted that there is a problem of access. But rather than turn to a reinterpretation of the First Amendment as a solution, he approvingly quoted devices suggested by press critic Ben Bagdikian:

(1) Start a new journalistic form: the occasional full page with a skilled journalist writing clearly and fairly six or seven ideas of the most thoughtful experts on solutions of specific public problems.

(2) Devote a full page a day to letters-to-the-editor, some days for random letters and others on a particular issue.

(3) Appoint a fulltime ombudsman on the paper or broadcasting station to track down complaints about the organization's judgment and performance.

(4) Organize a local press council of community representatives to sit down every month with the publisher.

THE RED LION DECISION

Ironically, whether such useful devices are incorporated into the machinery of mass communication may determine whether there will *be* a "new" First Amendment. As the Hutchins Commission of nearly three decades ago warned, if the mass media do not become more responsible, they will find that the First Amendment will be amended to enforce responsibility. Broadcasters—who have never enjoyed the freedom of the print media—have already seen the First Amendment reinterpreted in a way that dismays many of them. In 1969 they argued before the United States Supreme Court in *Red Lion Broadcasting Co. v. Federal Communications Commission* that the First Amendment protects their desire to use their frequencies continuously to broadcast whatever they choose and to exclude whomever they choose from ever using their facilities. But Justice Byron White wrote a majority opinion for the Court that held:

. . . as far as the First Amendment is concerned those who are licensed stand no better than those to whom licenses are refused. A license permits broadcasting, but the licensee has no constitutional right to be the one who holds the license or to monopolize a radio frequency to the exclusion of his fellow citizens. There is nothing in the First

Amendment which prevents the government from requiring a licensee to share his frequency with others and to conduct himself as a proxy or fiduciary with obligations to present those views and voices which are representative of his community and which would otherwise, by necessity, be barred from the airwaves.

THE AUTONOMY OF THE WORKING JOURNALIST

Will a decision like *Red Lion* also encompass the print media? We have no way of knowing until the United States Supreme Court addresses itself to an issue regarding access that involves newspapers or magazines or both. But there is another aspect of press freedom that springs from a similar impulse, and it, too, has strong First Amendment implications. It is so new that no convenient label has yet been attached to it, but we can speak of it as "the journalist's autonomy." This refers to the freedom of the journalist to write and edit news and opinion according to his view of the truth and the dictates of his conscience rather than according to the view of the truth or the beliefs—or the whims—of his employer. It poses this question: Is freedom of the press only the publisher's freedom? What about the journalist's freedom? In a formal sense the idea of the journalist's autonomy was born in Europe. Some Scandinavian editors have worked for years on long-term contracts that give them a free hand in running their papers, independently of the beliefs of the owners. In recent years reporters and editors who work for two of the leading French newspapers, *Le Figaro* and *Le Monde*, (the latter is one of the half-dozen best newspapers in the world), have won editorial control. Journalists on several leading West German newspapers and magazines have persuaded management to sign editorial statutes to assure that they will not be pressured to write articles that run counter to their consciences. Owners of the powerful German weekly *Stern* recently acquiesced to demands that the staff select the editor-in-chief and set editorial policy. In Britain and in Italy large groups of journalists are working to bring the conduct of the mass media under the control of working journalists.

In a much less formal sense than is suggested by the signing of editorial statutes and the like, journalists in the United States have been working toward autonomy for decades. They have been aided by the peculiar nature of their business: that it is the sole business guaranteed protection by the Constitution, and that the color of the public interest is upon it. For this and other reasons few owners today will attempt to order a journalist to write falsely or to slant a story—or try to persuade an editor to issue such orders. The professional ethic among journalists has grown too strong to allow many such owners to survive. But subtler pressures are sometimes apparent. For example, the newspaper reporter learns what kinds of stories are placed on the front page or otherwise given prominence; the radio or television reporter learns which of his stories are played up on the news show. Reporters in all the media get a message—sometimes erroneously—when their work is not published or broadcast.

How strong and widespread such subtle pressures actually are may determine how far the movement for autonomy will go in the United States. There are several signs that this may be one of the pivotal issues of the 1970s. Certainly *Columbia Journalism Review*, the best of the organs critical of journalism, is filled with articles by working journalists. *Chicago Journalism Review*, founded by a group of newspapermen in the bitterness that followed the 1968 Democratic National Convention, has been acidly critical of mass communications in Chicago. Perhaps most significant is the contract signed in 1970 by the Denver chapter of the American Newspaper Guild with the Denver *Post*, which provides for the appointment of a joint committee of journalists and management "to guarantee as far as it is able, constant honesty in the news and to raise standards of journalism ethics in the newspaper industry." The contract interests so many other chapters of the Guild that this may be the wedge whereby working journalists achieve a significant degree of control over the media.

THE MILITANT JOURNALISM

Still another challenge to conventional journalism has come from the so-called underground press, which began to flourish in the late 1960s. Some underground papers built circulations in the tens of thousands, among them the highly successful *Berkeley Barb*. In 1969 wrangling between the owner, Max Scherr, and his staff became public, to reveal just how lucrative such an operation can be. It also revealed that, like the capitalist men of the commercial press, some underground journalists are money-conscious. A large group of Scherr's helpers broke away and began to publish the Berkeley *Tribe*, but not before their negotiations to buy the *Barb* had reached figures in the hundreds of thousands. Thomas Pepper titled an article in *The Nation* (April 29, 1968) "Growing Rich on the Hippie."

It will not do to assign sweeping significance to the underground press. For every such publication that succeeds, ten die after a few issues. Sometimes they fail because they are undercapitalized. Some simply fall of their own weight as their founders discover that publishing is hard work. A great many underground newspapers and magazines begin as challenges to the established order, with some valuable muck-raking articles floating in a sea of four-letter words. Then, because few who produce such publications have any real interest in journalism, the muckraking thins out and comes to be based more on rebellion and emotion than on journalism.

Ray Mungo, one of the founders of Liberation News Service, which provides material for underground newspapers, has written:

> Lots of radicals will give you a very precise line about why their little newspaper or organization was formed and what needs it fulfills and most of that stuff is bullshit, you see—the point is they've got nothing to do, and the prospect of holding a straight job is so dreary that they join the "movement" and start hitting up people for money to live, on the premise that they're involved in critical social change blah blah blah. And it's really better that way, at least for some people, than finishing college and working at dumb jobs for constipated corporations; at least it's not always boring . . . that's why we decided to start a news service—not because the proliferating underground and radical college press really needed a central information-gathering agency staffed by people they could trust (that was our hype), but because we had nothing else to do.

At the same time it is important to recognize the real strengths of this new journalism. It is certainly a response to the inadequacies of conventional journalism. It has provided a forum for ideas that were not considered, or not considered adequately, in conventional media. The undergrounders have also provided a view of a different life style and have afforded different and valuable perspectives.

What this new journalism proves is that a vast distance stretches today between the conventional media and important segments of the public. There was a time when a newspaper or a magazine served its own small public. The circulation was relatively slender, but an editor spoke directly to the central interests of his readers, and he could usually count on their loyalty. Anyone who cherished another point of view might attack, and a publication that posed a threat might be destroyed—the abolitionist papers, for example—but most people simply subscribed to publications that squared with their own prejudices and idiosyncrasies.

When the conventional media became large and few, however, and editors were trying to corral mass audiences, separate voices could no longer be raised so readily in a free market place of ideas. Wilbur Schramm has commented:

> The small, numerous media, as we knew them in the eighteenth and nineteenth centuries, were representative of the people in their checking

on government; in fact, they *were* the people. But the larger and more centralized media have to some extent withdrawn from the people and become a separate set of institutions, parallel and comparable with other power centers such as business and government.

As Thomas Pepper wrote, the undergrounders have awakened journalism to "the fact that regular metropolitan dailies do not communicate with sub-cultures."

Many underground papers have succeeded in building close and enduring relationships with their readers, at least in part because they have revived the art of speaking to a relatively homogeneous audience. One important technique is to present news in a heavily subjective prose: "A growing revolt against the selfish and reactionary American Medical Association came to a head here," began an article in *Open City*, a Los Angeles paper. "Objectivity is a farce," said Thorne Dreyer of Liberation News Service, which provides information for many underground papers. Jeff Shero, former editor of *The Rat*, said, "We make our biases clear. That frees our writers to talk about their guts."

Perhaps the strongest challenge to conventional journalism is this "gut reporting" that is so central to the underground press. For there is a marked distaste in the world of the underground for the roots of journalism: the search for verifiable facts. This is in part a reaction against conventional reporting. Ben Bagdikian, national editor of the Washington *Post*, has pointed out that "trying to be a first-rate reporter on the average American newspaper is like trying to play Bach's St. Matthew's Passion on a ukelele: the instrument is too crude for the work, for the audience, and for the performer." This does not mean that Bagdikian favors the approach of the undergrounders. Instead, he supports interpretative journalism, which clarifies, explains, and places fact in a meaningful context and which is usually quite different from the emotional substance of the underground press.

It is nonetheless obvious that the free-wheeling reportage of the undergrounders is having an effect on conventional journalism. Reed Whittemore, the perceptive *New Republic* critic, has asserted that the "spirit of fact" has lost heavily in journalism. He cites, among other examples, a book by Ray Mungo, *Famous Long Ago*, which defends an underground paper's report of an event in Vietnam that did not occur, on the grounds that the story was "plain and unvarnished and human." The new journalism, according to Mungo, is: "tell the truth, brothers, and let the facts fall where they may."

Whittemore concluded that "many a journalist has decided to become a dramatist or novelist. Even if he hangs in there as a journalist . . . he aims at what people *might* have said or *should* have said.

In a responsible journalist's hands this is, still, thankfully, what they approximately said, but the shift nonetheless indicates a change in the climate of truth-gathering."

This is a fearsome challenge to the conventional press, especially since many of its young reporters envy the undergrounders' license to make sweeping judgments. For example, one wrote in a report on an Urban Coalition meeting: "Two factors motivated these men to discuss urban problems. One was a simple desire to cool the explosive situation in America's ghettoes. Of equal importance was the desire to tap a potentially rich socio-economic market." The latter point may be true, but the only evidence offered was the reporter's statement.

The influence of underground journalists will become especially frightening as their casual attitude toward the truth affects more conventional reporters. One editor, who was asked about a widely reprinted underground press story that reported riots and an alleged murder in Texas (actually, no one had been killed), replied offhandedly: "Well, the straight press didn't print anything, and we printed too much. It all balances out in the end."

THE OLD DAYS

All this is so foreign to what journalism has been in the United States that it is necessary to look at the old realities to understand the contrast. Consider, for example, some of the leading figures of earlier journalism.

In the fading years of the nineteenth century, a handsome, dashing newspaperman named Richard Harding Davis took the world for his beat. In clothes of the most fashionable English cut, he covered his assignments and found news where other reporters did not. He disguised himself as a burglar and hung out in shady dives to expose a robber band and get the full story of its operations for his paper. The best magazines bid for his manuscripts. He posed for Charles Dana Gibson's illustrations for the leading magazines of his day. At parties he traded conversation with such celebrities as Oscar Wilde, Mark Twain, Sarah Bernhardt, and Ellen Terry, and in the quiet elegance of Delmonico's, where dining was a ritual, he ordered dinners and wines with the discrimination of a continental gourmet. Leaving such comforts from time to time, Davis dashed off to cover the little wars that broke the tedium of the later Victorian age. When love came to him, he met the young lady's rebuffs with a characteristic flourish, handing to the messenger at his club in London a note for Miss Cecil Clark, Prairie Avenue, Chicago. The imperturbable Jaggers carried the message across the Atlantic, and in time, in the best story-book tradition, Miss Clark became Mrs. Richard Harding Davis.

In the years when Denver was growing from a raw mining town into the metropolis of the Rockies, its daily *Post* was owned by two flamboyant publishers, Harry Tammen, a former peripatetic bartender, and Frederick Bonfils, a one-time lottery operator. A story's sales value, not its significance, was their guide in judging news, and no cause was too minor for their newspaper to champion. When two children complained that a vendor had sold them a nickel's worth of rancid peanuts, Bonfils turned loose three reporters to expose "the peanut situation." The publishers got their readers into the proper spirit for Christmas by having a National Guard plane fly over the community with a huge neon-tube cross affixed to its underside. Tammen once hired a sports writer named Otto Floto because he had "the most beautiful name in the world"; and when Bonfils and Tammen became owners of a circus, they worked in the writer's name—Sells-Floto Circus—even though he owned no part of it. Using a composite of their own names, they named an elephant Tambon; and when Tambon died, Tammen sorrowfully had it stuffed and mounted in a large glass case outside his office.

For almost a quarter-century, until a day in 1918 when his own newspaper carried a headline saying that he was wanted for murder, Charles Chapin drove the staff of the New York *World* in his fanatic worship of "that inky-nosed, nine-eyed, clay-footed god called News." More heartless than any city editor in fiction, he fired reporters who missed getting a story by as little as a minute or two. "That," he once told the assembled city-room staff, "is the hundred and eighth man I've fired." One reporter, whom Chapin had warned not to return without his story, plunged into the icy East River to get an interview with a woman ambulance driver at Bellevue. After he was dragged from the river unconscious and taken to the hospital, someone thoughtfully telephoned Chapin to let him know that the reporter would survive. "Tell him that he's fired," Chapin replied. And then one night Chapin quietly murdered his wife, hung a "Do Not Disturb" sign on the door of the hotel suite in which the body lay, wandered through the city for hours, and finally gave himself up. His life thereafter was spent cultivating beautiful gardens on the prison grounds at Sing Sing, where he served out his sentence until his death in 1930.

Those men and scores of others just as colorful really lived. They live on today in books of reminiscences; in novels, movies, and comic strips depicting newspaper work; and in television dramas in which the reporter exposes corruption in city hall, solves a mysterious murder, and wins the pretty girl. It is unfortunate they bear so little relationship to reality today.

THE DEVELOPING JOURNALISM

The days of wild unrestraint were submerged in many changes. One was the technological-industrial revolution, which increased the size, speed, and efficiency of newspapers and changed them from small personal or party organs into vast, expensive, mass-produced, and generally impersonal social institutions. Newspapers became fewer; and they grew to be large enterprises, too costly to be jeopardized by irresponsible individualism. The success of a paper came to rest less upon the single performances of virtuosos than upon the aggregate performance of a whole staff of specialists. In short, the newspaper became institutionalized.

Another development certainly was a growing sense of responsibility. As journalism attracted an increasing number of men interested in raising the level of their papers and of the press as a whole, as it became good business for newspapers to consider the wishes of their audiences, and as local publishing monopolies raised the possibility of outside restraint, publishers began avowing a duty to the public as well as to their cash boxes. Journalism seems to have shared in the increasing awareness of social responsibility that has characterized American business generally since the start of the twentieth century.

Still another development was a change in the sort of person drawn to journalism. College-educated reporters and editors became more and more common, especially after the advent of the schools of journalism in the early years of this century. The American Newspaper Guild was founded in the 1930s in the hope of improving the professional status of newspaper workers. Even if the Guild has been more concerned with the material conditions of life than with professionalism, as its critics have charged, it certainly has contributed to stability among newspaper personnel.

Newspaper publishers, editors, and reporters have become more stable, sober, and responsible. Gone is the tramp newspaperman who, hearing of a job in Tulsa, would catch the next train without even bothering to pull the copy paper from his typewriter. The typical newspaperman today is a craftsman, often a highly specialized one, who does his own small part in turning out a mass-produced product. He ordinarily stays in one locality, raises a family, tries to pay off the mortgage on his house, and goes for long spells without covering a murder, let alone solving one.

It should not be surprising that recruiting this new breed has placed a stronger color of the establishment upon the press. The executive of a typical Midwestern daily with a circulation of between 20,000 and 30,000 has told how he chooses his staff members: "We pick people who won't be just reporters out on a story. They are representatives of the *Daily*. They come from average middle-class families. They are Midwesterners. They have imagination. They meet people well. We expect them to stay quite a while." A publisher in a small Southern city says that he tries to pay his staff members good salaries because he wants them to associate on an equal footing with the business and professional men of the community. And at least one Midwestern newspaper chain subjects all candidates for jobs to a battery of psychological tests, a procedure that would have appalled hard-bitten editors like Charles Chapin.

A similar change has come over the printers who set news into type. Once they were as colorful a breed as the reporters who wrote the copy they set. "In the days before typesetting machines and time studies, when steam beer went at a nickel a pint and railroads had not found all of the valleys," Paul Fisher has written in *Journalism Quarterly*, "in these days the American tramp printer had his time in the sun." In the bright years between Appomattox and Ottmar Mergenthaler's Linotype, tramp printers drifted across the land, their beds clean sheets of newsprint on the composing room floors. Some had taken to the road because of seasonal fluctuations in the industry, some because of financial or marital mistakes, some because of old age or alcohol. They would stay at a newspaper sometimes for a week, sometimes for a month, gratuitously sharing with editors their superior knowledge of fact and grammar and, with all who would listen, their contempt for reporters. When the Linotype invaded the composing rooms in the mid-1890s, nomadic typesetters such as "Old Slugs" Biggsby and "Muskogee Red" were driven into oblivion. Their departure was hastened no doubt by unionization of the graphic arts trades and the mass death of small weekly newspapers as urbanization made cities trading centers for ever-larger areas.

WHY COMMUNICATIONS?

The passing of foot-loose eccentrics from newspaper staffs is just part of the much larger story of the impact of technological and social change upon America's communications. Since World War II that change has given a new meaning to an old term—mass communications.

At one time *journalism* was an adequate term to describe the media of communication. That perennial authority, *Webster's New International Dictionary*, defines journalism: "The business of managing, editing, or writing for, journals or newspapers; also, journals, or newspapers collectively." Journalism, then, was a good word for describing the media in the years when most communications were carried on by magazines and newspapers.

Printed Journalism

And those years spanned a long period. The first mechanical device by which man could share his thoughts with others on an extended scale was the printing press—its invention almost at once broadened the outlook of the whole Western world. No longer did the reader have to decipher the cramped handwriting of manuscripts; instead, his eyes and mind could race along the printed page. With printing came a revival of classical learning, an end to the monopoly of knowledge by the exclusive few, the standardization of languages, and the growth of national literature. With it too came the birth of journalism.

This is not to suggest that journalism sprang full-blown into being once William Caxton had set up his press at Westminster in 1476. Although the newspaper had forerunners in broadsides and pamphlets, about a century and a half elapsed between the introduction of printing to England and the emergence of a regular periodical devoted to the dissemination of news. There were perhaps good reasons for the delay. Primitive means of communication made it difficult to gather and distribute news. Literacy was not yet diffused throughout the population. And not everyone could afford the products of the press. Printing itself was sometimes a dangerous trade, bound by restrictions.

The printed word was so important that it is doubtful that the modern nation-state could have emerged without it. For centuries it was largely through printed materials that common ideals, aspirations, traditions, and political allegiances were maintained over wide areas. The printed media alone performed the functions that society today expects all the media of communication to share. The printed media informed and enlightened the public, interpreted events and issues, challenged capricious authority, entertained the populace, persuaded the many publics toward a consensus, and, to a limited degree, brought together the buyers and sellers of goods and services.

The Widening Field

Then the communications revolution of the nineteenth and twentieth centuries brought the motion picture, radio, and television, which joined the printed media in spreading information, ideas, and entertainment. Both because of their electronic nature and because of the variety of ways in which they have carried out their functions, they have made *journalism* an obsolescent term for denoting all media.

Moreover, the communications revolution brought with it types of persuasive communication that scarcely fall within the traditional meaning of journalism. Advertising became an important adjunct of the marketing system; its persuasive function is not clearly covered by the word *journalism*. Nurtured by the utility companies, which believed that their monopolistic position could best be maintained by public satisfaction, public relations grew from a tiny infant in the late nineteenth century into a strong half-brother of advertising in the mid-twentieth. At its enlightened best, public relations brings the policies of institutions into harmony with the public interest and then extolls them. In doing so, it uses the media of communications—from which it has recruited many of its practitioners—but its manipulative intent puts it too beyond the meaning of journalism. The company-sponsored newspaper or magazine, the house organ—proliferated after World War II. It can be argued plausibly that the house organ also is not best described as journalism.

Mass Communication

Today one can more correctly speak of "mass communications" or "the mass media" than of "journalism" when referring to media other than newspapers and magazines. In a sense, of course, every communication uses some medium, is committed to some channel for transmission. The letterhead or sheet of notepaper in correspondence, the sound waves utilized in conversation—these are channels or media. But in mass communication, a whole institution becomes the message carrier—a newspaper, a magazine, a broadcasting station—and is capable of carrying its messages to thousands or millions of persons almost simultaneously. It is also affected by the problems that beset it as a social institution: control, government restriction, economic support, and the like—and we shall have much to say about these influences in later chapters.

The term *mass communication* has sometimes been defined in two ways: communication by the media and communication for the masses. Mass communication, however, does not mean communication for everyone. The media tend to select their audiences; audiences likewise select among and within the media.

Characteristics of Mass Communication

One of the most important distinguishing characteristics of mass communication is that it is mostly one-way. Seldom is there a quick or easy way for the reader, viewer, or listener to talk back, to ask questions, or to get clarification if he needs it. Second, it involves a good deal of selection. The medium, for instance, chooses the audience it wishes to reach. The *New Yorker* is aimed at a sophisticated, urban readership. *Successful Farming* is aimed at farmers in the richly agricultural Midwest. *The New York Times* and New York *Daily News* each seek different types of readers. Those on the receiving end, on the other hand, select among the media. They decide whether they will switch on the television set or pick up a book or newspaper. They choose what they want from the available content. They may listen to a television news program but switch to another channel when a quiz program comes on. They choose the times that they will use the media.

Third, because the media are capable of reaching vast, widespread audiences, there is actually a need for fewer media than there used to be. To transmit a message throughout the entire United States by the human voice alone, one needs the assistance of many, many speakers. But a single broadcasting network can reach millions of people at the same time. This has its parallel in the whole economic and social system. Under the American system of mass production, for instance, a relatively few manufacturers can turn out an astronomically large number of standardized products.

Fourth, to attract as large an audience as possible, the media are addressed to some mythical modal point at which the largest number of people cluster. It is seldom the lowest common denominator, but for many instruments of mass communication it is not quite up to middle range. City editors used to tell their cub reporters to write for "the guy who moves his lips when he reads." That man was the lowest common denominator of the newspaper audience. If he could understand the newspaper's stories, so could the better educated. According to readability studies, three-fourths of the American people—those with average education—can be expected to understand writing at the level of that in the slick-paper and digest magazines. Because the media are addressed to a mythical reader, listener, or viewer, they lose the intimacy of communications addressed to a single individual. A newspaper account of an event is vastly more impersonal than a letter from a friend telling about it.

Fifth, in mass communication the communicating is done by a social institution that is responsive to the environment in which it operates. As this book will indicate, there is an interaction between the media and society. The media not only influence the social, economic, and political order in which they perform, they are influenced by it. To understand the media properly, therefore, one must understand the society in which they exist. And to understand society, one must examine its setting, its major assumptions, its basic beliefs. All of which is to say that a knowledge of history, sociology, economics, and philosophy is necessary for a true understanding of the media.

THE MEDIA TODAY

As we begin to explore the social context in which the media operate, a brief overview of the condition of each medium today may be helpful, especially because the coming of television has altered the shape of mass communication.

NEWSPAPERS   Only a few years ago it was widely assumed that newspapers were dying. If they survived the competition with television, it was said, they would be weak and ineffectual—a minor medium. Such prophecies seemed safe, as metropolitan newspaper after metropolitan newspaper died, often suddenly. As the 1970s began, however, it became clear that the newspaper world had only been going through a realignment, though a severe one. While many of the giant papers were dying, others were surviving because they had developed strong ideals of service, and the suburban dailies were growing much stronger. Entering the 1970s, total circulation of dailies in the United States was pushing close to sixty-three million, an increase of nearly five million in a decade. The total number of dailies, 1,761, was about the same as it had been for twenty-five years. (The low point was 1945, when there were 1,749 dailies. The high point came in 1952, when there were 1,786.) Moreover, daily newspapers take in more advertising than radio and television combined, more than television and magazines combined, and almost as much as radio, television, and magazines combined. Newspapers take in nearly 30 per cent of the $20 million now spent annually on advertising.

MAGAZINES   Like newspapers, magazines have had to adjust to new conditions. And, again like newspapers, the giants have done much of the suffering. But as most of the big general weeklies and some of the general monthlies have disappeared, magazines that cater to special interests have become much stronger. Significantly, some of the greatest successes in publishing during the last twenty years are special-interest magazines: *Sunset, Yachting, Sports Illustrated, TV Guide,* and *Scientific American,* to name only a few. In a special report on magazines in its May 2, 1970, issue, *Business Week* pointed out: "More than 750 consumer magazines are now rolling off the presses—up almost 10 per cent from five years ago . . . For hunters and fishermen alone, there are now more than 60 magazines. For boaters and yachtsmen, there are 37, including *Yachting*, which carries more advertising (2,298 pages in 1969) than any other monthly consumer magazine." In the magazine world it is no longer the era of *Collier's* and the *Saturday Evening Post,* two old household words which died, and even *Life* and *Look* are in financial trouble. But the era of specialization is yielding healthy magazines.

BROADCASTING   Radio has had to move over for its more glamorous sister, television. It has done so by going local through a more decisive readjustment than was forced on either newspapers or magazines, and it may have been saved by the transistor. Network radio, which dominated many a household in the 1930s and 1940s, is almost dead. Radio stations—there are more than 5000 of them—not only are distinctively local, they reach for a share of the audience rather than the total audience. And many are making the kind of special-interest appeal that we associate with magazines. Many radio stations are profitable, but in the large metropolitan areas, where competition is fierce, station after station is hard put to hang on. The many radio stations must divide only $1.2 billion in advertising revenues, about a third as much as the relatively few television stations derive.

Television, which is still growing even though it already dominates much of the world of mass communication, seems likely to become much healthier. Although there are slightly fewer than 900 television stations in the United States, television advertising revenues went from $561 million in 1949 to $3.6 billion in 1969. There are soft spots; some advertisers have decided that television commercials are priced far beyond budget and reason. Nevertheless television advertising revenues are likely to grow. The great uncertainty in television is the future impact of technological change. What will be the effect of pay TV? of cable television?

FILMS   It is a curious fact that films, which are the object of so much of the fervor of youth in a country whose population is rapidly growing younger, are in deep trouble. In 1970 the Associated Press undertook a broad survey of the film industry; these are some of its findings: more than 13,000 behind-the-camera workers unemployed; combined losses of more than $113 million for five major film companies; only 118 screen-writers employed compared with 218 the year before. *Daily Variety*, the trade paper of the entertainment industries, summed up the gloom: "Never before has Hollywood seen such a crisis." Part of the reason for the Hollywood decline, of course, was that films were being made elsewhere—not only overseas but in cities across the United States. It is nonetheless true that despite the great surge of population in the United States, the box office gross in 1969 was 24 per cent below that of 1946—and it was as high as it was primarily because ticket prices were up. In number of movie patrons, 1969 represented an all-time low since World War II. Seventy-five per cent of those filmgoers were under thirty, perhaps because their elders were staying home to watch films on television.

BOOKS The contrast of films with books could not be sharper. Book publishing was for years a sedate business, as Paul Reynolds has pointed out:

> In the book world's halcyon days in the 1920s, trade book publishing was said to be a gentleman's occupation. A publisher sat at his desk, authors submitted manuscripts, the publisher selected what seemed to him the best, and contracted for them at modest dollar guarantees against conventional royalty rates. He published the books in a routine fashion, advertised them in a staid manner, sold them to book stores, and pocketed a reasonably certain profit. Rarely was the profit exorbitant. On the few occasions when he made a sale of subsidiary rights, the money involved was small and had little effect on his balance sheets.

All this began to change with the coming of paperbacks, especially as they became widely popular and as paperback reprint rights reached great heights—$500,000 for Truman Capote's *In Cold Blood*, $700,000 for James Michener's *The Source*. Book club rights—the minimum guarantee of the Book-of-the-Month Club is $75,000—have become another important factor. And despite the doldrums in which the film industry finds itself, film rights to best-sellers are sometimes more lucrative than paperback and book-club rights combined. The result has been such a boom that Reynolds has written, "Publishing has become a cold business."

American book publishers, who issue more than 35,000 titles a year, have become increasingly business-oriented not only because of the enormous profits to be made from best-sellers, but also because increased emphasis on education has made nearly all publishing—perhaps especially the publishing of textbooks—seem a blue chip. Many a publishing house has been swallowed up in conglomerates, and the old gentleman's occupation is now fiercely competitive—and profitable.

There is much more to say about the condition of the mass media, of course, and the remaining chapters will attempt to say it. For the moment, it is enough to be aware that the world of mass communication is continuing in a period of stark change.

Communication
and
Society

The human imagination can only bear a certain degree of
complexity. When the complexity becomes intolerable, it
retreates into symbolic images.

KENNETH E. BOULDING

Americans have come to take the mass media so much
for granted that it would be hard for most of them to imagine a world
without the media—without a morning paper; without *Time* magazine to
reveal just what the visiting dignitary whispered to the President; without
the *Reader's Digest* and its "unforgettable characters," medical marvels,
homely philosophy, and shining deeds; without Tom Jones, Mike
Nichols, James Reston, Walter Cronkite, Matt Dillon, Elizabeth Taylor,
and the Beatles—all creatures of the mass media.

Because so many Americans have taken mass communication so
much for granted, they have overlooked how important the media really
are. Few have considered the influence of the media on their ways
of thinking and acting or on the functioning of society. From time to
time, of course, some people have shown concern over the ways in
which the media affected their interests, likes, and dislikes. If broadcasting fare seemed overladen with trivia or if a rash of books or magazines
exploiting violence and sex seemed to threaten the morals of the young,
a few outraged citizens might speak out in protest. And sometimes a
few would applaud a newspaper for its expose of delinquency or of
graft in city hall, or praise a television station for its timely
documentaries.

Perhaps most Americans are still concerned at best only with
the immediate ephemeral effects of the mass media on their day-to-day
lives; perhaps they seldom consider the importance of a mass-communi-

cation system in a modern industrial society. Perhaps the majority still do not think about the unseen ways in which the media help to shape and sustain political, social, economic, and cultural life.

Yet there is some evidence that increasing numbers are aware, at least, of the impact of the media. In the 1970's there is a degree of sophistication in much of the lay criticisms which indicates that significant segments of the population have begun to think carefully about mass communication. This is not to say that all the criticisms of the concerned are cogent—indeed, we expect to show in later chapters that some are not—but we are encouraged by many of the insights. In this chapter we offer some other insights from those who have been thinking longer—and usually more deeply—about the fundamental nature of communication.

At the outset the terms *communication* and *communications* need clarification. Put simply, the difference is this: communication is the process of communicating; communications is the technical means used to carry out the process. Communication, then, is a central fact of human existence and social process. It is all the ways by which a person influences another and is influenced in return. The ways may be direct and personal, as when a teacher talks to a student, or indirect and impersonal, as when a tom-tom or a television station carries the message. Communication is the carrier of the social process; it makes interaction within humankind possible and enables men to be social beings.

On the other hand, the plural "communications" has a much narrower meaning. It embraces all the technical means of indirect or "mediated" communication, from tribal drums, smoke signals, and stone tablets to telegraphy, printing, broadcasting, and film.

Edward Sapir makes an important distinction between communication and communications: For him the singular form covers what he calls the primary processes—conscious and unconscious behavior that communicates. His four primary processes are language, gesture in the widest sense of the term, imitation of the overt behavior of others, and a large group that might be vaguely called social suggestion. He uses the plural communications to cover what he calls secondary techniques—the instruments and systems that help to carry out communication. Among these he lists Morse code, wigwagging, bugle calls, the telephone, and radio; he could, of course, have added thousands more: stylus, brush, reed pen, papyrus, parchment, paper, printing press, film, and television transmitter.

The distinction between the two words has real historical and sociological importance, Sapir thinks, for all mankind is blessed with the primary processes of language, gesture, imitation of behavior, and social suggestion, but only relatively advanced civilizations have developed sophisticated secondary techniques.

All secondary techniques have two things in common. First, even though they are physically different, their main task is to extend communication by language to situations in which face-to-face contact is impossible. Some of the techniques extend communication by gesture, or movement, as well: painting, sculpture, still photography, motion pictures, and television. Second, all the secondary techniques provide the indirect means by which the primary processes of imitation and social suggestion are carried out. Indirect they are; the telegraph and radio, for example, do not communicate by themselves; they can do so only when someone uses them to convey his symbols.

By creating, improving, and multiplying these technical means, man has virtually freed the communication process from the limitations of time and space. Man can communicate not only with his contemporaries but with unborn generations. He can be put in touch quickly with others in far-flung places. Moreover, the communications system has made it possible for acculturation to take place over great distances in parts of the world physically remote from one another so that societies take on similarities not shared by the peoples of regions adjoining them. Geographical contiguity has lost much of its importance. Today the "scientific community," which has no clear-cut location on the map, shares common values, attitudes, and beliefs. In general, so do the "democratic world," the "Christian world," the "totalitarian world," and so on.

The mass media, like the spoken word and the raised eyebrow, are simply aspects of human communication. They are technical extensions of speech and gesture, much as the shovel and pile driver are technical extensions of the human arm, but their capacity is such that the structure of society is fundamentally altered by their very existence. It is an obvious point, but it is often overlooked. People do not always recognize the fundamental relationship of the mass media to human nature and human society, and they often misread the role of the mass media in their lives. Many intellectuals, for instance, see the media as a kind of accidental by-product of technology that has been taken over by hucksters, propagandists, and manipulators. That view has some truth in it, but it neglects the objective relationships between the mass media and society, relationships that seem to exist quite apart from the motives and interests of owners, managers, editors, writers, and so on.

MAN AS SYMBOL MAKER

Traditionally philosophers have set man apart from other animals on the basis of his powers of reason. But another faculty distinguishes man from other animals—his ability to communicate by symbols. He is the one creature we know to react not only to his real physical environment but also to a symbolic environment of his own making. A hungry dog reacts to food by eating it. A man may react in the same way, but he may also have more complicated reactions, which depend on symbolic considerations: He may avoid some foods for fear of offending the deity; he may eat other foods for their reputed curative powers; he may even eat some foods, such as caviar, primarily for status.

What all this means is that man has an environment far different from that of other creatures. Most creatures live largely in physical environments. They receive stimuli; they respond to them. They have little or no sense of past or future; as Kenneth Boulding reminds us, a dog has no conscious idea that there were dogs on earth before he arrived and that there will be dogs here after he has gone. But man, by creating a symbolic world, has given reality a dimension known only to the human species. Between the mere stimulus and response of other creatures, he has erected a symbolic system that transforms the whole of human life and sets it apart from the life of all other animals. This distinctive mark of human life is not necessarily related to man's rationality (or to his irrationality, for that matter). It is a remarkable achievement that has taken man out of a merely physical universe and put him into a symbolic universe of language, art, and myth.

Man does not confront reality firsthand. Instead of always dealing with things themselves, as other animals do, man develops *ideas* about things. He so envelops himself in linguistic forms, in artistic images, in mythical symbols, or in religious rites that he cannot see or know anything except through his symbolic system. As Epictetus said, "What disturbs and alarms man are not the things, but his opinions and fancies about the things."

Reality, of course, contains all the things that reach man through his senses; but the framework and structure of reality are not something that man can touch or directly see. They are intellectual, and man can perceive them only indirectly through symbols. Animals react to outside stimuli either directly or not at all. Men, on the other hand, respond largely in a cerebral way, producing images, notions, figments of all sorts, as symbols for ideas about things. A cat may cower under a porch during a thunderstorm; only a man would interpret the storm as a sign of a god's wrath. For man the symbol-maker, then, the world is mainly a pseudo-world, a web of symbols, of his own making.

Yet his pseudo-world is not sheer fantasy. Even the mythologies of man, like mathematics, language, and the formula $E = mc^2$, are his rational and practical efforts to deal with experience. They are attempts to organize his sensations and to build up around them symbolic systems that give meaning to his existence.

Mass Media and Pseudo-environment

Walter Lippmann, in *Public Opinion*, which was published in 1922, painted an excellent portrait of the pseudo-environment. The objective world that man deals with, Lippmann said, is "out of reach, out of sight, out of mind." In his head, man makes for himself a more or less trustworthy picture of the world outside. Thus men behave not on the basis of direct and certain knowledge of the real world but on pictures they have made or derived from others. What a man does depends on those pictures in his head.

Public Opinion begins with the peculiar matter-of-fact power that informs all of Lippmann's writing:

There is an island in the ocean where in 1914 a few Englishmen, Frenchmen, and Germans lived. No cable reaches the island, and the British mail steamer comes but once in sixty days. In September it had not yet come, and the islanders were still talking about the latest newspaper which told about the approaching trial of Madame Caillaux for the shooting of Gaston Calmette. It was, therefore, with more than usual eagerness that the whole colony assembled on the quay in mid-September to hear from the captain what the verdict had been. They learned that for over six weeks now those of them who were English and those of them who were French had been fighting in behalf of the sanctity of treaties against those of them who were Germans. For six strange weeks they had acted as if they were friends, when in fact they were enemies.

Lippmann goes on to show how little the world as it really is conforms to the picture of the world that we carry in our heads. He defines our stereotypes:

For the most part we do not see first, then define; we define first and then see. In the great blooming, buzzing confusion of the outer world we pick out what our culture has already defined for us, and we tend to perceive that which we have picked out in the form stereotyped . . . That is why accounts of returning travellers are often an interesting tale of what the traveller carried abroad with him on his trip. If he carried chiefly his appetite, a zeal for tiled bathrooms, a conviction that the Pullman car is the acme of human comfort, and a belief that it is proper to tip waiters, taxicab drivers, and barbers, but under no circumstances station agents and ushers, then his Odyssey will be replete with good meals and bad meals, bathing adventures, compartment-train escapades, and voracious demands for money.

This internal picture-making process inevitably colors the messages that man gets from the world outside. Man uses stored-up images, preconceptions, prejudices, motivations, and interests to interpret the messages, fill them out, and in turn direct the play of attention and the vision itself. These interpretations and expansions become patterns, or stereotypes. And these stereotypes, Lippmann thinks, determine human action. Originally a stereotype was the plate made by taking a mold of a printing surface and casting type metal from it. According to Lippmann the minds of men are also poured into molds—their pictures of the world outside. The minds then reproduce ideas and react to stimuli according to the patterns of the molds.

Lippmann was writing only of the relationship between public opinion and newspapers. However, his concept can profitably be extended to all mass media. As a chief source of knowledge, the media provide people with messages from the outside world. People use these messages to form mental pictures of the world of public affairs.

The mass media can also be viewed as creating a kind of pseudo-environment between man and the objective "real" world. This view has important implications for the role of the media in society. For one thing the media have brought speed, ubiquity, and pervasiveness to the traditional role of communications. Therefore the media are sometimes seen as enveloping modern man in a kind of ersatz reality. For another thing, as a means by which the dominant institutions exercise social control, the media are widely regarded as so imbuing the public with the prevailing values and beliefs of their culture that society is in danger of becoming stagnant. The fear is that because the commonly accepted pattern goes unchallenged, people will behave toward one another in almost ritualistic fashion and that their lives and institutions will become fossilized.

Historian Daniel Boorstin has suggested a refinement of the idea of the pseudo-environment. In *The Image* he has written: "Now the language of images is everywhere. Everywhere it has displaced the language of ideals." Boorstin is chiefly concerned with what he calls "pseudo-events"; in fact, the subtitle of his book is "A Guide to Pseudo-Events in America." He characterizes the pseudo-event as follows:

> It is not spontaneous, but comes about because someone has planned, planted, or incited it. Typically, it is not a train wreck or an earthquake, but an interview.
>
> It is planted primarily (not always exclusively) for the immediate purpose of being reported or reproduced . . . Its occurrence is arranged for the convenience of the journalist. Its success is measured by how widely it is reported.
>
> Its relation to the underlying reality . . . is ambiguous.

Usually it is intended to be a self-fulfilling prophecy. That is, to say that something is true, or to act as if it were, leads to the general belief that it is true.

A plan to create a new image through pseudo-events was disclosed by *Newsweek* in 1966 when it unearthed a confidential memorandum from an old government hand to then-Vice President Hubert Humphrey. The memo, entitled "You and the Media," ran:

> Your character and personality are being shown to the people in only one way: through the spoken and written word. You are always thought of . . . primarily as a talker and writer . . . Other facets of yourself ought also to be considered for public understanding. They also ought to add up to a totality approximating your complete self.
>
> You might consider two streams of concern that run strongly through your life:
>
> (a) The reverence and love of life:—the people, family, staff, the wounded, the sick, the hungry, the poor, the dispossessed, the victims.
>
> (b) The defense of life:—the fatherly, brotherly and personal concern that life be preserved, defended, shielded . . .
>
> These two tumbling courses run steadily down through the stream of your life . . . During the next years, they will sweep you into a position of even graver consequence to the world. But they must be given a public portrayal that is more honest and open and rounded than the picture of the talker-writer . . .
>
> The missing elements of yourself must be put back in the picture. They are you in physical action: moving, acting, visiting, climbing, worshiping, hunting, fishing, sailing, boating, hobbying, reading, studying, thinking, sitting, gazing, looking, working, shirt-sleeving, gardening, flying and cooking.
>
> Doing these things will automatically broaden the selection of clothing and the flat image of the correctly dressed gentleman will be enriched by views of the hard-nosed worker, the rough-and-ready woodsman, the cool and steady sailor, the overalled miner, the un-stuffed-shirt statesman.

Despite the effort to present himself as "the hard-nosed worker" and "the cool and steady sailor," Hubert Humphrey lost the Presidential election in 1968—though narrowly. The man who won it, Richard Nixon, was the beneficiary of subtler efforts to create a positive image through pseudo-events. Joe McGinnis has analyzed the campaign in *The Selling of the President 1968*, a book that reveals the depth of the cynicism with which strategists try to manipulate events. Nearly every appearance Nixon made during the campaign was contrived. How this was arranged is suggested by a memo written by one aide about Nixon's television appearances, describing the "question and answer" programs:

> We open as if we'd walked in late, in the middle of. a question. As Nixon starts to answer, a voice-over announcer identifies the program and a super comes on (suggested titles: "Hotseat"; "Nixon on the spot"; "Nixon speaks up on what's getting you down"; "Dialogues with Richard Nixon"; "Straight talk"; "Nixon in New Hampshire"; etc.). The group is identified. And for the rest of the period, the program is simply an informal unrehearsed question and answer session between Nixon and the group. The setting will be casual and the mood easy. There will be humor, seriousness, provocativeness, controversy and sincerity. The plan would be to tape 20 or 30 minutes of discussion, then edit it down to the most interesting five minutes. Questions would be planted to make sure that the issues we want discussed would be brought up.

COMMUNICATION AS THE BASIS FOR HUMAN SOCIETY

Because man can create symbols, he has powers that other animals do not have: the power to communicate complex intentions, meanings, and desires and, therefore, the power to change the forms of social life. Communication is thus the carrier of the social process, which depends upon the accumulation, exchange, and transmission of knowledge. Without communication man could achieve only the most primitive knowledge, and no social organization—primitive or otherwise. Without communication human society would remain static, grounded in instinctive behavior, not much different from the societies of other animals.

John Dewey once remarked that communication is "of all affairs the most wonderful." In Dewey's view society not only continues to exist *by* communication; in a sense it originated *in* communication. For obviously communication was necessary before people could band together into society, necessary for all the adjustments and understandings that society demands of its members and for reaching the agreements without which society would disintegrate. By communication man maintains his social institutions, each with its values and ways of behaving, not only from day to day but from generation to generation.

MASS MEDIA AND SOCIETY

In every society, from the most primitive to the most complex, the communication system performs four broad tasks. Harold Lasswell had defined three of these as: surveillance of the environment, correlation of the components of society in responding to the environment, and transmission of the social heritage. Wilbur Schramm has used the simpler terms: watcher, forum, and teacher. Schramm and others add a fourth task: entertainment

Every society has its watchers, who provide other members with information and interpretation of events. They survey the environment, so to speak, and report on the threats and dangers as well as on the good omens and opportunities. A watcher may be the elder in the tribe who complains that the younger generation is showing less and less respect for ritual or the foreign correspondent who reports political tension in the Middle East.

In deciding what to do about the threats and opportunities, society uses its communication system as a forum. Because its ways are always changing, society needs some way of reaching agreement on what those changes will be. Without agreement there may be a breakdown of social organization. Although troubled times may allow no consensus, through the discussion carried on via its communication system, society usually settles upon the direction of change so that individuals and groups act together as a community. Simple societies may reach their consensus from face-to-face discussion, complex industrial ones may rely largely on the mass media.

Society also uses its communication system as a teacher to pass the social heritage from one generation to the next. As the system can be compared to the tribal council or the New England town meeting in its function of correlating responses to the environment, so it can be compared to the institutions of home, church, and school in its task as teacher.

Charles Wright of the University of Pennsylvania suggests that another "function of mass-communicated entertainment is to provide respite for the individual which, perhaps, permits him to continue to be exposed to the mass-communicated news, interpretation and prescriptions so necessary for his survival in the modern world." In discussing television, Gary Steiner suggests that entertainment is an essential function that not only amuses but also provides palatable learning situations.

Communications and Cultural Change

Communication systems are also a force for bringing about cultural change. Harold Adams Innis, a Canadian economist who became a communication theorist, believed that the technology of communication was central to all other technology. As James Carey of the University of Illinois has pointed out:

Innis argued that the available media of communication influence very strongly the forms of social organization that are possible. The media thus influence the kinds of human associations that can develop in any period. Because these patterns of association are not independent of the knowledge men have of themselves and others—indeed, consciousness is built on these associations—control of communications implies control of both consciousness and social organization . . . Innis argued that various stages of Western civilization could be characterized by the dominance of a particular medium of communication.

Christianity exploited the advantages of parchment for maintaining the old order. The durability of parchment gave the Church a means of preserving a nucleus of ideas over many centuries; the scarcity of parchment limited the guardianship of those ideas to a few and for a long time left the Church relatively free from challenge or dissent. Innis pointed out that the secular state, on the other hand, used cheap paper for disseminating knowledge widely, thus challenging the traditional order and extending control over large areas.

When faced with barbarian invasions and the ambitions of the kings and princes, the Church tried to maintain a monopoly of knowledge, stressing stability and continuity through dependence on a limited body of scriptural writings in Latin. The Church's control of ideas and opinions helped it to defend itself against ideological challenge.

However, Innis theorizes, the Church's monopoly over knowledge was gradually destroyed in the competition for men's minds that followed the increased use of paper and the renaissance of classical learning, especially Greek science and philosophy. The invention of printing and increasing supplies of cheap paper supported the Reformation and the growth of vernacular literature, both of which became important in determining the character of the new nation-state.

The industrial revolution and the application of steam power to the printing and paper industries were similarly important. They profoundly influenced the rise to power of the middle class and the emergence of liberal democracies in western Europe and America. Indeed, contemporary forms of society, democratic or totalitarian, would not have been possible without high-speed presses and electronic media for rapid communication with large numbers of people over vast areas.

As Carey has made clear, whereas Innis saw communication technology as principally affecting social organization and culture, his disciple, Marshall McLuhan, who is also a Canadian, sees its effect on sensory organization and thought as most significant.

McLuhan holds that in the Electric Age, which was first established with the invention of the telegraph, a network of electric circuitry was built which now links the world in a web of instant awareness. In effect, the world has become a global tribe.

McLuhan agrees with Innis that man, when he discovered movable type, did not merely find a new tool for mass-producing communication; he changed his own essence. McLuhan builds on this to suggest that in the age before the alphabet, the ear was dominant in communication—hearing was believing. Then the new medium of the phonetic alphabet and the beginning of reading forced a change to a new sensory balance centered in the eye. The invention of movable type and the vast spread of literacy required that man begin to comprehend in linear, connected fashion, taking one thing after another in slow progression. When the Electric Age annihilated space and time, the new media—especially television, which involves all the senses simultaneously—took over from print. From such beliefs McLuhan derives his aphorism "the Medium is the Message," which simply means that society is shaped more by the media through which men communicate than by what they communicate. That is, print itself is more important than anything or everything that has ever been printed. Television is more important than anything or everything shown on television.

McLuhan has filled several books with elaborations of these ideas, and the mass media are only a part. Indeed, he speaks of "media" as all the "extensions" of man—including automobiles, clothing, clocks, and a wildly disparate collection of other items. His ideas about changing eras are taken to the point of holding that the linear sense that developed in response to movable type is directly responsible for the assembly line and for the Newtonian and Cartesian philosophies of the universe as a mechanism in which it is possible to locate a physical event in time and space. The all-at-once Electric Age, McLuhan believes, explains why football, in which everything happens at once when a play starts, is slowly submerging baseball, which is a one-thing-at-a-time, linear sport.

One need not accept all McLuhan's scattershot speculations—he calls many of them "probes" rather than theories and serenely refuses to try to substantiate them, saying "I explore, I don't explain"—to consider his central idea provocative, and even useful. If the medium is not the message, it is quite obviously something more pivotal than a mere tool for multiplying audiences. If it is not possible to find hard evidence to prove or disprove the theory, McLuhan's thought at least causes us to wonder whether the instruments of mass communication have the power to alter man.

Communications as a Means of Social Interaction

On the one hand, communication systems make for stability, since they always tend to purvey the values and beliefs of the society in which they operate. Media content in the United States, for example, is colored by traditional values. On the other hand, communication systems also bring about change, since they are one means by which the existing order is challenged. Thus, on the one hand, they tend to maintain the status quo and, on the other, to disrupt it.

As an institution a communication system has much power in its own right. It also is a means by which other institutions make their power felt. Its ability to spread messages to multitudes of people over large territories makes the system a source of power, no matter what information and ideas it carries. By influencing what the system sends out, other institutions attempt to use it for their own ends.

It is the link to politics and industry that inflames the activist young and brings epithets about the "Establishment media." Just how important politics and industry are will become evident in later chapters, which show in some detail how the rise of democracy and the industrial revolution helped to shape the mass media in the United States. However, politics and industry in turn are influenced—sometimes decisively—by the communications system. The growth of the mass media in the United States greatly affected the development of American political institutions and the American form of mass production. It is doubtful that any modern form of political organization could have developed without the conquest of time and space by the mass media.

The Media and Social Control

Some theorists, who are not willing to go as far as Innis and McLuhan in assigning extraordinary power to the media, nevertheless consider mass communications a strong agency of social control and an arm of the ruling order of society. This is a sharp break with libertarian theory, which saw the press as freeing men from the tyranny of ignorance and inherited superstition and as thus enabling them to govern themselves by right reason and individual conscience. The new theory does not necessarily deny the traditional importance of the press in public enlightenment. But it does give a new angle of vision for looking at the media without regard for what they *ought* to be and do.

Social control by the mass media is so extensive and effective that some observers believe it to be the chief characteristic and function of the media. For instance, Joseph Klapper sees the "engineering of consent"—a term for the process of social control—as the most significant feature of the mass media. Attempts to engineer consent are neither new nor limited to those with sinister motives, of course. One function of communications has always been to engineer consent, which is necessary for stable society. But never before, according to some social scientists, has there been engineering on such a vast scale, with the media working in such unison that there is little counter-engineering.

The media have brought about a change in the types of social control. Paul Lazarsfeld and Robert K. Merton are among those who see coercion as giving way to subtle persuasion through the mass media. "Increasingly," they say, "the chief power groups, among which organized business occupied the most spectacular place, have come to adopt techniques for manipulating mass publics through propaganda in place of more direct means of control." Even the ruling powers in totalitarian societies such as the Soviet Union and Communist China have made this change, although they continue to use the more direct methods of organized violence and terror as well.

Mass Media as an Adjunct of the Industrial Order

Whether big or little, the mass media in America are businesses; they are oriented to marketing; they are, as George Gerbner has said, "the cultural arm of American industry." This is the primary fact about the mass media in the United States. One must understand this fact to grasp the essential meaning of the media and their relationship to the American social order.

A similar understanding is necessary for analysis of the Soviet communication system. To grasp the essential meaning of the Soviet mass media and their relationship to Communist society, one must first recognize that the Soviet communication system is an arm of the political order, as it is in any authoritarian society.

In the United States the industrial order, which directly and indirectly controls the mass media, is concerned largely with preserving the status quo. It does not wish to encourage revolutionary changes in a social system that provides it with abundant freedom and benefits. It has no more interest in doing so than the ruling political order in an authoritarian society has in furthering dissent. To that end it seeks to intensify and mold certain existing tendencies of the system, to nurture sanctioned values and beliefs, and to sharpen public attitudes and desires so as to produce particular actions in the market place. The media are an important means of realizing those objectives.

This is not to say that business interests have conspired to control the policy and content of the mass media for their own selfish ends. This point is worth emphasizing. Deliberate, organized, and calculated propaganda in support of the existing system and against social change is insignificant. There is no plot, no cabal, no organized effort to preserve the status quo, but the media serve the industrial order nonetheless.

The strategic policy and the bulk of content of the mass media work toward engineering consent in favor of the existing order because commercial control of the media and the resulting need to please the largest possible audience virtually assure that they will. The media operator seeks to saturate the market he has cut out for his product in order to hold down his unit costs and, if he accepts advertising, to justify high rates for space or time. To attract a huge following, the media must stick to majority views, reflect prevailing values, and reinforce the primary assumptions of the social order. The more completely their content reasserts the form and character of existing society, the more efficiently the mass media perform as an adjunct of the industrial order. To depart from the popularly sanctioned path is often to invite economic disaster.

For at least two reasons, some observers agree, the American mass media are "exquisitely fitted to turn the status quo into social law," to use Klapper's phrase. One reason is that the media operate in a democracy grounded upon public opinion—a public opinion that countless special pleaders of all sorts wish to shape. Another is that the media are directly and indirectly controlled by commercial interests, which have increasingly used persuasion to reach their goals.

The Obstinate Audience

Not all observers are convinced that the social control exercised by the mass media is as extensive and decisive as the appraisal of Klapper, Lazarsfeld, Merton, and others seem to imply. And these dissenters include many who nevertheless speak of the media in fearful tones.

Louis Wirth, for instance, somewhat uneasily acknowledges the citizen's increasing dependence on the mass media for knowledge and guidance. Yet he says that the high degree of consensus already existing in society lends the media much of their apparent effectiveness. The media, he says, operate in situations already prepared for them in the social process. It is easy to get the "mistaken impression that they or the content and symbols which they disseminate do the trick."

Richard T. LaPiere, in his *Theory of Social Control*, carries the argument further. He sees membership in small, primary groups—the family, church, and intimate circle of friends—as more influential in determining an individual's values, attitudes, and behavior than any influences of the media. People come to the media seeking what they want, not what the media intend them to have. Because there are so many media and media units, people have considerable choice. They have their defenses up; they defend their strongly held beliefs. Because of their distance from the media, they tend to put great reliance on their own social groups and their own advisers. Interpersonal channels of information function side by side with mass media channels, filtering messages from the mass media. Because each individual is embedded in networks of interpersonal communication, the success of a message from the mass media depends on whether the relevant social environment or network favors or opposes the message—and whether more than one social network is competing for authority.

The mass media become especially powerful when those who use them are able to build close and influential relationships with their audience. In the 1930s Father Coughlin used radio to build a following that can be described only as personal. Many dictators in our own time feel that control of the media is essential to their power and continuing influence. The birthday and "get well" cards that some people send to entertainers they do not know, and even to cartoon and fictional characters, are evidences that personal attachment can build up through the media.

Mass communication media can and do effect change, particularly when many of them agree. Imagine all those with pivotal roles in all the media agreeing to present the information and develop the psychological dynamics that would persuade the American people to adopt one point of view—toward the war in Vietnam, toward race relations in the United States. There indeed would be a possibility of dramatic change.

In the absence of such an unlikely agreement, we must consider the power of the mass media not as a tidal wave but as a great river. It feeds the ground it touches, following the lines of existing contours but preparing the way for change over a long period. Sometimes it finds a spot where the ground is soft and ready, and there it cuts a new channel. Sometimes it carries material that helps to alter its banks. And occasionally, in time of flood, it washes away a piece of ground and gives the channel a new look.

It seems clear enough that the mass media have been and will continue to be important in transforming contemporary social life. Succeeding chapters will tell how they became "mass" and thus more formidable instruments of communication than man had ever known before, how social and intellectual forces have shaped them, how they have been accommodated to the American system of private enterprise, and what, according to democratic theory, Americans think they ought to be and do.

The Media and Their Social and Economic Environment

Newspapers are the schoolmasters of the common people.
That endless book, the newspaper, is our national glory.
HENRY WARD BEECHER

In Colonial America newspapers first sprang up in seaports, the early communication centers, where news was available from ship, stage, and post; from sailors, travelers, and people coming to market. As trading centers the ports were most likely to provide sources of advertising. As population centers they had the greatest potential audiences to support newspapers; more than that, because the ports were social and cultural centers, the audiences were likely to welcome newspapers. Perhaps most important, the seaports were political centers, where the governor lived and the council convened. There the publisher might augment his income by doing public printing or find financial support by aligning with one of the political factions.

For good reason, too, the early publishers were often postmasters. From the government's viewpoint, postmasters made good publishers. Their views were likely to be those of the ruling group and, as political appointees, they could be held in line. Moreover, the postmaster, who was visited by travelers and had access to incoming papers, was in a good position to gather news; and his franking privilege enabled him to hold down the cost of distributing his paper.

The times as well encouraged the birth of the newspaper. As the eighteenth century opened, the Colonies were firmly established. People had more time to read, and the school systems were providing new audiences for the press. Trade had developed sufficiently to justify newspapers as economic enterprises.

Three major forces, which had a tremendous effect upon social, economic, and political institutions, molded this early American communications system. These were the rise of democracy, the industrial and technological revolution, and urbanization. In the years following the Civil War, these forces have gathered momentum enough to influence virtually every aspect of American life, including the media.

RISE OF DEMOCRACY

The rise of democracy helped to create the great middle class, which has largely dominated American culture and whose tastes, interests, and demands have shaped our communication system.

In America in the nineteenth century, government by the elite gave way to government by the masses. For the first time in modern history, a large part of an adult population achieved effective power to choose its own rulers and to direct the destiny of the nation. Awakened to his political power by the Revolution, the common man began to concern himself with public issues that had previously been settled for him by others.

Universal Suffrage

Even after the Revolution the older states denied the ballot to a substantial part of the population. Most of them limited voting to adult property-owners or taxpayers and set high requirements of property ownership for eligibility to hold public office. But several conditions worked to give the common man the ballot.

People in the new agricultural states admitted to the union between 1789 and 1840 were more alike in wealth and social status than those in the original colonies. No wealthy ruling class dominated those states, as it did the older ones, and their constitutions were more liberal. They generally granted adult white males not only the right to vote, with few or no restrictions, but also the right to hold public office. The new states sent a growing number of representatives to Congress, and these states became increasingly influential in determining Presidential elections. In time politicians from along the seaboard had little choice but to yield to the rising democratic spirit.

At the same time class differences were breaking down in the eastern states. Political equality there was fostered by a growing political consciousness among the farmers, by the labor parties and trade unions springing up in the industrial cities, and by the tide of immigrants who were acquiring citizenship.

Gradually the states along the seaboard altered their constitutions to drop or lower the property requirement for voting. By mid-century, adult white males generally could vote without holding property. After the Civil War, women renewed their agitation for suffrage. They won local gains in some states and then eventual victory in 1920, with the Nineteenth Amendment. Meanwhile, the franchise had been extended to the Negro—although in some areas much more in theory than in practice.

As voting became a universal right, popular rule was strengthened by still another development. The spread of democracy broke down the restrictions that had limited the right to hold public office to men of wealth or to men with certain religious qualifications.

Free Universal Education

As the democratic movement surged forward, so did a cause closely tied to it, free universal education. Although popular education was a cause of chagrin to the taxpayer, it was an issue that could unite the liberal and the conservative factions. Liberals saw in free universal education a concomitant of universal suffrage, for only an educated populace could be counted on to govern itself wisely and to put forth candidates worthy of public office. Conservatives saw it as a means of making the great mass of people less prone to the radical ideas of demagogues. By 1860 the principle of free public education was well established in most of the northern states and in a few of the southern ones.

The big gains in popular education came after the Civil War, when the high school became an American institution. Between 1870 and 1890 the proportion of children attending school increased from 57 to 72 per cent, and the number of illiterates dropped from about one person in five to about one in ten. By 1910 only 7.7 per cent of persons age ten or older were illiterate, with the figure for the white population only 4.9 per cent.

After the Civil War, colleges too entered a period of growth. Federal subsidies stimulated growth of the state universities, and wealthy benefactors such as Leland Stanford and John D. Rockefeller helped to establish and support private colleges. Higher education, like the ballot, became available to women as well as men. The state universities opened their classrooms to both sexes, and the strong current of women's suffrage helped to create such colleges as Radcliffe and Bryn Mawr.

INDUSTRIAL AND TECHNOLOGICAL REVOLUTION

Between the end of the Civil War and the opening of the new century, industrialization and mechanization hit American with the force of revolution. In those years the nation shifted from an agrarian to an industrial economy. The impact was so great that a man of George Washington's time probably would have been more at home in the Holy Land in the days of Jesus Christ than in America in 1900. By the concluding years of the nineteenth century, railroad tracks were binding the nation together with steel. In 1869 the Union Pacific, pushing west from the Missouri River, met with the Central Pacific, building from San Francisco. For the first time one could cross the continent by rail.

Those tracks traversed a land rich in natural resources—coal, oil, ore, lumber—and rich in farmlands only partly tilled. Adventurous men saw the fortunes to be made in converting that raw bounty of nature into salable goods, and a swelling population stood ready to develop those resources. Between 1870 and 1900, fed by a swift stream of immigrants who poured into the country from all over the world, the population of the nation approximately doubled. Of the more than 11,500,000 foreign-born who flocked to American during those years, some five million arrived in the 1880s.

The number of industries of all types shot up from 140,000 in 1860 to more than 500,000 in 1900. In the sixty years from 1850 to 1910, the average manufacturing plant increased its capital more than thirty-nine times, its number of wage earners nearly seven times, and the value of its output more than nineteen times. Partly to feed the furnaces that made that expansion possible, miners dug out ten times as much coal in 1900 as they had in 1865; and between those years the estimated national wealth increased fourfold.

Mass Production

Behind those figures lay a system of production geared increasingly to standardized mass consumption. In 1798 Eli Whitney used division of labor to turn out firearms with interchangeable parts. In the mid-nineteenth century, Samuel Colt pushed this principle further than any manufacturer before him.

When industry after industry adopted mass production techniques, the assembly lines of America spewed forth a profusion of all sorts of products for the consumer. In time some economists warned the consumer that it was his duty to consume in order to maintain the level of the economy. For production was geared to mass consumption; if the consumer faltered, the wheels of industry slowed down.

Mass production also inevitably meant a standardization of product. Aiming at a mass market, the manufacturer could not afford to take into account the wishes of a small minority. The individualist who wanted an automobile painted in a checkered pattern of heliotrope and orange with leopard-skin upholstery could not count on the automobile makers of Detroit to supply it.

Furthermore, mass production necessitated changes in the system of marketing. Before the industrial and technological revolution hit with full force, in the days before railroads had spun their web over the land, the manufacturer produced for local consumption. His market was a local area—his own community or region. The system of retailing made brand names relatively unimportant. Grocers weighed out sacks of flour for their customers from a large barrel, and druggists poured perfume from a big jug on their shelves. Mass production and its need for mass distribution helped to change all this.

The conception of markets changed from areas to people—to consumers living anywhere. The manufacturer detected a need common to a large number of people and set about filling it. Advertising could make people aware of the product; the burgeoning transportation system could carry it to retailers anywhere in the nation. In the late nineteenth century manufacturers and retailers began to see the advantages that packaged goods had over those sold in bulk. As packaged goods replaced bulk goods, the brand name and the trademark became important assets, identifying the product in the mind of the consumer and giving the manufacturer control over a share of the market. The manufacturer of Evergreen Soap, for instance, had a firm hold on the patronage of every consumer who swore by his product and would accept no other.

Inevitably advertising became the handmaiden of mass production and mass marketing. When production was little above the subsistence level, manufacturers had no great need to sell potential buyers on the benefits of their goods. Nor were elaborate advertising campaigns necessary when distribution was chiefly local or regional. The small newspaper notice, the handbill, the shop sign generally sufficed. But as manufacturers turned from local markets to national ones, they needed some inexpensive form of salesmanship. They needed, too, some way of impressing a particular brand name on the consumer's mind. Advertising was well suited to those tasks, and its development, as we will see, had manifold effects on the media.

Concentration of Power

With industrialization came concentrations of economic power in almost every field. As profits flowed back to them, the industrial leaders had to reinvest their money if they were to earn a return on it. Thus Andrew Carnegie, who had made a fortune in manufacturing iron, branched out into railroads, Great Lakes shipping, mining, and steel. Paradoxically competition itself often seemed to encourage concentration of control. A manufacturer who found that the high cost of raw materials put him at a competitive disadvantage, for instance, might buy control of their sources. Or a manufacturer whose competitve position was shaky might combine with others in his industry to dominate the market.

For a time, people quietly accepted unrestrained exploitation of natural resources and a supra-government run by financial and industrial barons who put private gain high above common good. The blessings of industrialization were so rich and so many that for a while they discouraged public interference with a magic system that had brought them. Eventually, however, Americans cried out in protest against the greed and arbitrary power of what seemed a new feudal order. The Interstate Commerce Act of 1887; the Sherman Anti-Trust Act of 1890; the Populist movement of the early nineties; the crusades conducted for the workingman by the metropolitan newspaper of the late nineteenth and early twentieth centuries; the muckracking movement among magazines for the decade after 1902—all were manifestations of popular indignation at the excesses of big business.

URBANIZATION

The rise of the city followed rapidly in the wake of the industrial and technological revolution. When the nineteenth century opened, America was still a rural nation. Only five towns had populations of more than 8000 in 1790—Boston, New York, Philadelphia, Baltimore, and Charleston—and their combined population of under 135,000 accounted for only about 3 per cent of the nation's total. Even thirty years later only thirteen towns had populations of 8000 or more.

But as the century wore on, as factories attracted uprooted farm laborers and as steamships carried more and more imigrants to American shores, an increasing number of persons settled down to life in the cities. When Lincoln became President, New York and its environs already comprised a metropolis of more than a million inhabitants.

The most rapid growth in urbanization came in the last two decades of the nineteenth century, when the number of towns and cities with populations of 8000 or more doubled. So did their total population, which jumped from 11 million to 25 million. By 1890 about one-third of the population was living in communities of 4000 or more. By the 1920s, it was clear that agricultural America had been supplanted by urban America.

REDISTRIBUTION OF INCOME

The rise of democracy, industrialization, and urbanization were all apparent before the twentieth century opened. In the new century a fourth development also made some impact on the media. It was a redistribution of income, which narrowed the extremes in purchasing power and heightened the role played by the mass market. Even today, of course, some Americans live in bleak poverty, many, many more in want; but gone is the immense chasm that separated rich and poor when the new century opened.

In the single year 1900, when the dollar bought considerably more than it does today, Andrew Carnegie had a personal income of $23 million—all of it free of income tax. The average workingman took home somewhere between $400 and $500 a year. If he could find work— and the odds were that he would be idle several months a year—the unskilled laborer could hope for the standard $1.50 for a ten-hour working day. His annual income was less than $460 in the North, less than $300 in the South. Thus, as Frederick Lewis Allen has pointed out, Carnegie's annual income was at least 20,000 times greater than that of the average workingman.

Such disparities had largely disappeared by the mid-twentieth century. The graduated income tax, the coming to power of the labor unions, a changed attitude of business toward its public responsibilities, laws establishing minimum wages and fair employment practices, rising productivity, and full employment born of the war—all contributed to the emergence of a large, moneyed middle class.

EFFECTS ON THE MEDIA

The media, like other American institutions, changed under the impact of the rise of democracy, the industrial and technological revolutions, and the rise of the cities.

When common men got the ballot, they became self-governing individuals with a strong stake in government and, with varying degrees of intensity, took an interest in public affairs. The press became an important means of keeping the political system in operation. It also became a source of education, new cultural values, and entertainment for the workingman. The influx of foreign-born and the spread of free education both helped to enlarge the audience of the media. The technological revolution changed communications from craft to industry. As in other fields the machine took over many of the tasks once performed by man. Clattering Linotypes replaced the printers who had once set all type by hand from the job case. Automatic presses replaced the crews who had once fed paper onto inked forms a sheet at a time. Photoengraving meant an end to the painstaking process of reproducing drawings by engraving them on wooden blocks, and color presses liberated the hundreds of women who had once tinted magazine illustrations with brushes.

As the technological revolution increased the size and efficiency of the printed media, it brought into being the new media, motion pictures, radio, and television. Electricity, harnessed for power in factories and transportation, was the foundation of radio and television from the start and of the motion picture after its first groping years.

Urbanization brought together the multitudes who made possible the large circulations of newspapers and magazines and, in later years, made up the huge audiences of local broadcasting stations. As cities grew in size and number, more and more of them could support daily newspapers. Improved communications enabled the big dailies to expand their coverage and to win over readers once served by smaller papers. The big became bigger—the more so as high fixed costs brought about suspensions and mergers.

THE BUSINESS OF JOURNALISM

In 1897 Lincoln Steffens, that keen analyst of American institutions, took a long look at newspaper journalism across the United States and shared with the readers of *Scribner's* just what he had found. He reported that the executive heads of some two-score great newspapers, talking shop the previous spring, had referred to their properties as factories and had likened the management of their editorial departments to that of department stores. "Journalism today is a business," he wrote with a little of the awe of discovery.

And indeed it was. Joseph Pulitzer and William Randolph Hearst had clearly emerged as industrial capitalists of the press. They were demonstrating, even as Steffens wrote his article, that the newspaper could not only market news, it could manufacture it as well. Hearst's reporters were tracking down criminals and building circulation as a result. Journalism had become a business in no small measure as a result of the forces discussed above, forces that brought a new content to the media, changed the way in which they earned their keep, increased their efficiency, standardized their products and made those products available to an ever-increasing number of Americans.

DEMOCRATIZATION OF CONTENT

One important effect was what might be called democratization of content. Newspapers, magazines, and books once addressed themselves to a small circle of educated, well-to-do readers. But in time education and economic well-being spread as political power had spread, from the elite to the population at large; so did use of the media. The printed media geared their contents to the common man's tastes, and their prices to his purse. Movies, radio, and television, arriving after the democratic movement had achieved victory, appealed to a mass audience from the start. The tastes and interests of the great majority of that audience came to determine the fare that the media served and the ways in which they served it.

Newspapers

In the early nineteenth century the newspaper turned from a small upper-class readership to a popular mass audience. After the American Revolution the majority of newspapers were mercantile or political publications for well-to-do businessmen and politicians. But as education came to the small shopkeeper, mechanic, artisan, and farmer, and as immigrants swelled the populations of the growing American cities, publishers saw a new market for their newspapers. They aimed at that new and expanding audience, and they changed the content accordingly.

In September, 1833, a young printer named Ben Day turned out the first issue of his New York *Sun* on a hand press. Day sold his paper for a penny, a price in sharp contrast with the six cents publishers typically charged. He counted on a mass demand to bring him his financial return, despite a low profit margin, and he cannily concentrated on the street sales made possible by urbanization.

While the six-penny papers served their readers prolix stories of heavily political cast, Day wooed his audience with short, bright items about police-court doings, executions, suicides, wonders and marvels of the world, and local trivia. By 1835, when steam-driven presses were helping him turn out enough copies to meet the demand, Day was boasting that his *Sun* had a circulation of 19,360: "the largest of any daily newspaper in the world." After Day had shown that it could be done, other publishers leveled their newspapers at the audience he had tapped.

Street sales, made possible by the growth of the cities, were important from the time of the penny press onward. Competition for the coins of the newspaper-buying public led at times to sensationalism and to speed rather than to completeness in coverage of the news. Newspapers increased their emphasis on local news, human interest copy, crime reports. From about the time of the penny press, no doubt as a result of the agitation for women's rights, editorial copy slanted toward women's interests bulked large in newspaper fare. James Gordon Bennett, who in his New York *Herald* gave the inexpensive newspaper a wider appeal than other penny papers did, created the idea that the newspaper is primarily a purveyor of news, not of editorial opinion.

In 1883 Joseph Pulitzer bought the New York *World* and introduced a new journalism that served readers generous helpings of human interest, gossip, sensation, and scandal. What Pulitzer did was to revive the sensationalism of the penny press and to present it with greater skill and better technical execution. His reporters, masquerading as inmates, wrote sensational exposes of conditions in jails, hospitals, and asylums; they were ever alert to witness incidents which, by a bright reportorial style and piquant headlines, could enliven the paper. But, in addition, Pulitzer gave his readers complete coverage of the news of the day and a liberal editorial policy, which championed the cause of the workingman against the aristocracy of wealth and social position. His *World* crusaded, for instance, against graft and for a better reception of immigrants at Ellis Island. It sponsored drives, and contributed its own funds, to provided the poor with free Christmas dinners, summer excursions, and medical aid. Human interest and sensation were simply the bait necessary to lure readers, Pulitzer said, so that they could be exposed to the significant news and editorials.

Pulitzer's formula was well calculated to win him a large following. Technological advances had made mammoth circulations feasible, and urbanization had created the potential audience. New York's population increased 50 per cent in the decade of the 1880s, and many of the newcomers were the immigrants who streamed to America in unprecedented numbers in that decade. Transported to a strange world, lonely and helpless, the immigrants turned first to their foreign-language newspapers for reassurance, comfort, aid, and escape. In Europe newspapers, had been priced beyond their means; village gossip had told them all they had needed to know. But in this unfamiliar land the foreign-language newspapers, by keeping immigrants in touch with the old country and helping them to adjust to the new, converted them to newspaper reading. From the foreign-language papers, they sometimes moved on to the English-language dailies. Their sons and daughters, scorning a foreign tongue, were quick to accept the American dailies.

Pulitzer knew his audience well. He had worked for a German-language newspaper in St. Louis and perhaps, as Oscar Handlin has suggested, his skill in making the *World* attractive to a second generation of German-Americans contributed to its success. Dailies of the new journalism to which the *World* gave birth took on some of the characteristics of the immigrant press in their emphasis on entertainment, their willingness to help and advise their readers, and their identification with the welfare and emotions of immigrant groups.

At its extreme the democratization of the newspaper led to sensationalism. Ben Day's *Sun* is still remembered for one of the greatest newspaper hoaxes of all time, a series of stories by Richard Adams Locke which described life on the moon in straight-faced but thrilling detail. Pulitzer's new journalism was based on sensation, which was rationalized as a means of gaining readers for worthier material. Sensationalism reached its height in the circulation wars of the 1890s. In 1895 William Randolph Hearst, confident that he had mastered the techniques of mass journalism on the West Coast, bought the New York *Journal* and challenged Pulitzer's *World*. The unprincipled race for circulation that followed gave America its era of yellow journalism, marked by extravagant use of pictures; campaigns that championed the underdog with perhaps more cynicism than altruism; screaming headlines in oversize type, sometimes in bright color; manufactured and fraudulent news; and lurid Sunday supplements. The jingoism that permeated the *Journal* and *World*, according to even so careful a historian of the press as Frank Luther Mott, was probably responsible for touching off the Spanish-American War. Hearst sent a famous illustrator, Frederic Remington, to Cuba to draw war pictures. Remington cabled: "Everything is quiet. There is no trouble here. There will be no war. Wish to return." Hearst responded: "Please remain. You furnish the pictures and I'll furnish the war."

Another debasement of the newspaper's democratization led to the gaudy era of tabloid journalism in the 1920s when, as someone once remarked, "Sin sold for two cents a day." The tempo of life in America went into high gear after World War I. The postwar period was a time of speeding automobiles, faster trains, distance-eradicating airplanes; a time of frenetic dancing to the jazz that had come up the Mississippi from New Orleans; a time in which many Americans frantically sought to enjoy their new prosperity and to forget their disillusionment about politics and world affairs.

Into this setting came the tabloid. Its smaller size, its generous use of pictures, its emphasis on brevity and brightness all made it well suited to the reader on the run. It identified itself wholly with the masses from the start, and its formula was compounded of such elemental ingredients as birth, death, sex, and violence. Its photographs were often faked, retouched, and in appallingly bad taste; its stories were frequently ghost-written accounts in the first person; its headlines were cynically written to fetch coins: "He Beat Me—I Love Him," "I Am a Merry Gold Digger But I Don't Take Pay," and "Valentino Poisoned," with a smaller line of qualification, "Broadway Hears Doctors Deny." The tabloids demonstrated that the newspaper could compete with other amusements, which had expanded to include movies, radio, phonograph records, and dance bands and marathons.

The Modern Magazine Emerges

The change from a class audience to a popular audience came to magazines about a half century later than it did to newspapers. The modern magazine of low price, popular appeal, and large, national circulation emerged in the last decades of the nineteenth century. By then such fruits of democracy as popular education had resulted in a potentially large reading audience, which magazines could serve. Machines had freed man from many irksome tasks and had given him the leisure time in which to read. The technological revolution had brought about the high-speed presses and other equipment that publishers needed to reach large audiences; a network of railroads had begun to permit distribution over a vast territory. But more than that, large-scale advertising was emerging as manufacturers sought to sell their mass-produced products across the entire land, and the magazine became a national medium for reaching the growing body of consumers.

Magazines were an established American institution. Andrew Bradford published the first magazine in America in 1741, a few days before Benjamin Franklin launched the second. But even as late as the Civil War, magazines were short on advertising, short on circulation, and short in life span, and few of them ventured any great distance from their places of publication.

Even in 1890 the magazines leading in prestige and circulation—*Harper's*, *Century*, and *Scribner's*—were directed at a minority of the population, the well-bred society of culture and means. They were edited, as the late Fredrick Lewis Allen once put it, for

> the educated man, the philosopher, who is at home not merely in his own land and his own age, but in all lands and ages; from whose point of perspective the Babylonian seal-workers are as interesting as the Pittsburgh steelworkers; who lives not merely in the world of food and drink and shelter and business and politics and everyday commonplace, but in the timeless world of ideas.

Their content was remote from the lives and interests of the great bulk of the population. Flipping through the pages of *Atlantic* and *Harper's* readers of the early 1890s encountered such articles as "The Social Side of Yachting," "Along the Frontier of Proteus's Realm," and "A Successful Highwayman in the Middle Ages."

In the 1890s S. S. McClure, Frank Munsey, Cyrus Curtis, and a handful of other publishers revolutionized magazine publishing. They saw that an audience numbering in the hundreds of thousands wished inexpensive reading matter. They saw also the important role that advertising was beginning to play in the American economy. They brought the content of their magazines into harmony with the tastes and interests of the great and growing middle class. Gone were articles of esoteric appeal. Instead, *Munsey's* and *McClure's* ran articles about athletics at Harvard, "the horseless age," the modern war correspondent, the writers of popular songs, cattle brands of the West, a man who supplied zoos with wild animals, and personages in the public eye. Edward W. Bok made Curtis' *Ladies' Home Journal* one of the first magazines to achieve a circulation of a million by giving his women readers practical advice on the business of running a home and rearing a family, by trying to elevate their standards in art and architecture, and by crusading against public drinking cups and patent medicines.

Publishers cut the prices of their magazines to what the average American could afford—prices that meant selling their publications for less than the cost of production. Frank Munsey put *Munsey's* on sale in 1893 for ten cents, a price so low that the major magazine distributors refused to handle it and he had to deal directly with retailers. Later Curtis sold his *Saturday Evening Post* for five cents, which did not even pay for the paper on which it was printed.

But the popular content and the low prices attracted readers by the tens of thousands. Advertisers paid handsomely to reach them. What the publisher lost from the sale of copies, he got back in revenues from the advertising his large circulation attracted. As the redistribution of income narrowed the extremes in purchasing power, the great middle class became the market for mass-produced goods; this was the readership toward which magazines generally were aimed. Publishers sought not just large numbers of readers, they also sought homogeneous groups of readers—groups tied together by common interests or by a common trade or profession—so that the magazine advertiser could reach the particular consumer group most likely to be interested in his product.

Books

Today the book remains the least democratic of the mass media, reaching, according to some estimates, perhaps 35 per cent of the adult population. As foreigners are fond of observing, Americans simply are not book readers. And there is some truth in their generalization that while Europeans are readers of books, Americans typically are readers of periodicals. It is perhaps significant that fewer than a dozen of the 1,761 daily newspapers in the United States carry regular book-review supplements.

Hellmut Lehmann-Haupt, a historian of book publishing, has pointed out that in America books are somewhat dependent on the more powerful periodicals press; in contrast this dependence does not exist in Europe, where books have their own traditions, older and more substantial than those of periodicals. He has found a clue to the different attitudes Europeans and Americans take toward books in the different purposes for which printing was originally used on the two continents. In Europe, he says, printing was started in long-established communities as a cheap and easy way of duplicating the literary heritage of the classical and medieval world from the accumulated wealth of manuscripts. In America, on the other hand, printing became almost at once an important force in the colonization and westward expansion of the nation. He adds: "The European press primarily nourished thought: the American, action. In Europe printing from the very beginning meant 'books,' in America almost from the start, 'newspapers.'"

Even so, books turned from a restricted class audience to a wider popular one, much as the newspapers and magazines did. In England the book-reading public shifted from the upper class to the middle class in the eighteenth century. By the middle of the century, the intellectuals and wits were no longer writing for their own little coteries. Instead, middle-class novelists such as Richardson and Fielding were writing for a middle-class audience, many members of which liked to think that they were improving themselves while they were being entertained. By the latter half of the century, literacy—and the reading of books—had penetrated to the working class. The new reading public was still small compared to the mass reading public of today but large compared with that of previous periods. With that change in audience seems to have come a tendency to read more exclusively for pleasure and relaxation than in the past, a tendency that contributed to the development of the novel and to the craze for novel-reading that swept England toward the end of the eighteenth century.

Until late in the nineteenth century, much of what Americans read came from England—that is, the words did, although the books did not. Books published in England were not protected by copyright in this country, and American publishers found it more profitable to reprint English books without paying royalties to the authors than to take a chance on American writers. One result was that cheap books for the masses in this country exceeded those in England. Even after the middle of the nineteenth century, when cheap reprints became common in England, American publishers could bring out those same books in New York as new offerings at twenty-five or fifty cents.

The audience for books in the American Colonies was restricted by limitations of various sorts: the comparative lack of printing facilities, the exigencies of establishing a way of life in a new land, the lack of widespread education. While the Colonists evidently regarded books highly, books were hard to come by for the average man. The books the Colonists favored were, for the most part, serious or utilitarian works; there was little demand for books designed chiefly for entertainment or amusement.

Although the audience grew after the Revolution and the popularity of the novel in England was reflected in this country, it is doubtful that the average American could afford any sort of library until the 1840s. Up until then, well-printed books in cloth or leather bindings were expensive and, with few exceptions, sold only in small editions. Cheap paper and faster presses helped to bring about a revolution in book publishing in the 1840s. Publishers not only brought out inexpensive periodicals laden with the most popular English novels but also published frequent "extras" or "supplements," which enabled the masses to buy this form of book from newsboys on the streets for twenty-five cents or less.

Thereafter, although there was a market for high-priced books, the inexpensive book was a part of the American publishing scene. Dime novels, cheap library sets, reprints, paperbacks all helped to satisfy the demand for inexpensive reading.

The first two recent revolutions in the dissemination of inexpensive books came in 1939 when three publishers formed Pocket Books, Inc., to bring out twenty-five-cent paperbound reprints. Their success led other publishers to try paperback publishing, and the firms tapped thousands of retail outlets never before used for books—newsstands, drugstores, cigar counters, supermarkets, train stations, bus depots, airline terminals, post exchanges. In its first twenty-five years, Pocket Books, Inc., alone published three thousand titles with total sales of a billion copies.

The second came in the early 1950s with the introduction of the so-called quality paperbacks. They were priced higher than the early paperbacks, but their major difference was their appeal to highly educated readers, some of whom had remarkably esoteric tastes.

Another dimension of service was added to paperbacks in the 1960s. While conventional publishers were still devoting many months to production, some paperback houses were bringing out volumes close on the heels of the news—so close they might be called "newsbooks." The process of writing, editing, and producing such volumes soon became so refined that when four students at Kent State University were slain early in May, 1970, a paperback describing the killings was available before the end of the month.

In both England and America books changed from a medium for the cultured few to one for the great middle class. Some authors continued to address themselves to a small audience of intellectuals, and their books remain an exceedingly important medium for the introduction of new ideas and for transmitting the cultural heritage. But many more writers gear their output to more popular tastes, thus making books also a medium of mass entertainment.

The Electronic Media

The electronic media—movies, radio, television—have histories differing sharply in some respects from those of the printed media. Products of the industrial and technological revolution, the electronic media first appeared when the democratic movement was full-blown and when urbanization had brought together multitudes whom they could address simultaneously.

For those reasons the electronic media were democratized from the start and have always appealed to popular rather than to class audiences. Unlike the printed media they require that their viewers or listeners attend to them in a single body; indeed, one characteristic of either radio or television is instantaneous transmission. This evening we can pick up a copy of Plato that has lain undisturbed on a library shelf for the past ten years and read it in utter solitude. But if we switch on the television set too late, our favorite program is gone forever, and the millions who viewed it have become occupied with something else. Soon, however, the home video tape will change all this.

Technology, the nature of the electronic media, and the hard facts of economic support dictated almost from the start a need for a mass audience for movies, radio, and television. Even a short, unpretentious movie or radio program is expensive to produce, requiring the services of many specialists: writers, producers, directors, performers, engineers, and technicians of many types. To spread its cost over a large base, its producer inevitably must address a mass audience.

The movies were plebeian from their inception. Originally they were little more than peepshows in penny arcades. In New York gay blades of 1894 could step up, one at a time, to squint into a battery of machines that amazed them with snatches of vaudeville acts, boxers in brief fistic encounters, dance bits, and short slapstick routines. When those jerky peepshow shorts were joined with the magic lantern, whole audiences could view a movie at the same time. *The New York Times* for April 24, 1894, reported the first public showing of motion pictures— two blondes "doing the umbrella dance with commendable celerity," the surf breaking against a beach, an allegory, a burlesque boxing match. "So enthusiastic was the appreciation of the crowd long before this extraordinary exhibition was finished that vociferous cheering was heard," it reported. "There were loud calls for Mr. Edison, but he made no response."

Almost at once the movie became a popular addition to the bills of variety shows in vaudeville houses. Traveling carnivals and amusement parks pitched black tents where the curious could watch movies. In 1903 Edwin S. Porter filmed *The Great Train Robbery*, the first movie with a story, although its plot was rudimentary. Two years later the film was a hit at a small theater that had been opened in Pittsburgh with movies as its only attraction. In quick imitation other small nickelodeons sprang up—five thousand within a year.

Most of the nickelodeons were established in large cities where there was a high concentration of foreign-born—a concentration fed by the immigration movement then at high tide—for the film was a form of amusement that recent arrivals to this country could afford and comprehend. The early silent movies were heavy on pantomine. Even if an immigrant could not translate the elementary subtitles, he could follow the plot, which transported him momentarily from his humdrum job and from the difficulties of adjusting to this strange land. It did so at a price he could afford; admission was a standard five cents, a small price for such entertainment.

An air of disrepute hung over the movies in those nickelodeon days. In an advertisement in the St. Louis *Republic* in 1910, one exhibitor commented on "the general known prejudice against the motion-picture theater," and in 1914 respectable people were a little surprised that a poet—Vachel Lindsay—should take the movies seriously enough to write a book about the art of the films. The development of the motion picture was retarded in part by restrictions on its length. David Wark Griffith, developing the art of storytelling with film, was impatient to spread his techniques over more than a single reel. His backers grudgingly allowed him to go two reels—about twenty minutes' showing time—but no more, on the grounds that longer films would bore and fatigue audiences. An independent operator named Adolph Zukor was under no such restraint. He imported a four-reel French film play, *Queen Elizabeth*, starring the famous Sarah Bernhardt. Playing at the Lyceum Theater in New York in 1912, *Queen Elizabeth* attracted and impressed a fashionable upper-income audience, which would never have patronized the nickelodeons. Zukor was convinced that the motion picture was capable, like the legitimate stage, of offering audiences a full evening's entertainment, and he went on to produce longer films of his own under the slogan, "Famous Players in Famous Plays." Griffith also gave impetus to the development of the feature film, breaking with his employers and striking off independently to film the epic, *The Birth of a Nation*. It opened at the Liberty Theater in New York in March, 1915, at a two-dollar admission.

Meanwhile, as the audience for the motion picture expanded,

theaters moved from laboring-class districts into middle-class neighborhoods. Their accommodations became more comfortable, their décor more fashionable, their names more appealing or exotic, the prices of admission higher.

For a time the novelty of the movie itself brought many persons into the theaters. Each big production converted more of them to the movie-going habit. Paul Rotha, film producer and critic, has said: "During this period, therefore, from about 1912 until 1920, the very marvelling of the general public, watching every new film with mouths agape, was sufficient for the studios to become established on a practical basis, capable of mass production." By the time the novelty had begun to wear thin, movie-makers had begun to feature individual actors and actresses, and the star system became entrenched. Charlie Chaplin, Mary Pickford, Douglas Fairbanks, Francis X. Bushman, Beverly Bayne—their names alone were enough to fill theaters across the nation.

As the motion picture grew up, the costs of film production mounted. The new stars, who were valuable properties, commanded high salaries. As studios chose locations other than rooftops and city streets for shooting scenes; as artificial lighting replaced the sun; as scripts took the place of directors' and cameramen's improvisations; and as equipment and techniques underwent refinements, more and more dollars were needed to complete a feature film. To get the greatest return on their outlay, movie-makers tried to turn out films that would appeal to the widest possible public.

Similarly commercial broadcasting from its inception aimed at a mass audience. For a time curiosity alone held listener's ears fast to the crackling headphone of the early receivers and brought the family together around the spluttering loudspeakers. But eventually curiosity was not enough. Then advertising moved in to sponsor the various programs and to make mass appeal necessary. A person could listen to only one program at a time; each advertiser wanted potential customers to listen to *his* program, and he wanted them in multitudes. By 1929 radio had begun to develop its star system, as the movies had earlier, and famous entertainers from vaudeville and Hollywood headed for the microphones of radio. To keep listeners clustered around their sets, producers of the 1930s filled the air with variety hours, comedy shows, and dramatic programs. Shows became more elaborate; an advertiser who once had wooed listeners on a budget of $25,000 a year now sometimes spent ten times that on a single star-studded variety show, employing a staff of hundreds. Americans made the star performers their darlings, and in everyday conversation echoed the taglines of their favorite comedians. Listening to Edgar Bergen and Charlie McCarthy became a Sunday evening ritual in millions of homes, and in some circles a person who was not abreast of the latest doings of Amos and Andy was a social oddity.

CHANGE IN SUPPORT

Publishing newspapers or magazines and broadcasting via radio or television is expensive. Over the years three major sources have been tapped singly or in combination. One has been subsidy by government, political party, religious denomination, labor, industry, philanthropic foundation, or some special interest group. Another has been the customer, who pays not only the cost of production but enough in addition to give the owners a profit. The third has been advertising, the sale of space or time.

With industrialization, the advertiser emerged as the man who indirectly pays the bills of the most substantial part of our communications system. In effect, he rents an audience. Mass production and mass distribution required mass selling to bring together the buyers and sellers of goods and services on a nationwide basis. Urbanization confronted retailers with the necessity of reaching a growing local consuming public. The redistribution of income enlarged the market, fattened the consumer's pocketbook, and helped to convert luxuries into necessities. Advertising came to be the economic foundation of the newspaper, magazine, and broadcasting industries.

Some of the media do get their money from other sources, of course. The customer ordinarily pays the bill for movies and books. Subsidy provides the support for the entire house-organ press. And while advertising is the chief source of revenue for periodicals and broadcasting, there are numerous exceptions. A number of radio and television stations are subsidized by colleges, for instance, and philanthropic friends often help to make up the deficit of such magazines of opinion and comment as the *New Republic* and *Nation*. In the recent past there has been one fairly protracted experiment with a metropolitan daily that accepted no advertising, *P M*, which Marshall Field published in New York from 1940 to 1948.

Advertising, however, became the lifeblood without which most periodicals and broadcasting operations could not exist, and its development profoundly altered the role of the periodical publisher. In an earlier day the publisher of a newspaper or magazine was essentially the manufacturer of a product. He produced it as inexpensively as he could, and he took his profits from the difference between cost and selling price. True, some newspaper publishers also sold their editorial services to a party or faction, but once partisan journalism had declined, the publisher's big job was manufacturing a product for the reader. Advertising changed everything. The publisher became a dealer in both a product and a service. His product, as always, was a newspaper or magazine; his service was giving advertisers the opportunity to reach a large or carefully screened body of consumers with their sales messages. Thus advertising converted the newspaper and magazine—and later broadcasting—into adjuncts of the marketing system.

Support in the Past

Colonial newspapers seem to have depended primarily on their readers for revenue, although the income from notices inserted by merchants and traders was by no means negligible by the mid-eighteenth century. In the political warfare after the Revolution, the subsidized newspaper came to be almost typical. Especially in the bitter political struggle between the Federalists and anti-Federalists in the early nineteenth century, newspapers drew some of their support from political factions and were frankly biased organs of views rather than news. From the time of the penny press onward, however, advertising became increasingly counted on to replace a newspaper's other sources of revenue, and by the early 1900s some critics were complaining that commercialism dominated the entire news and editorial operations of the American newspaper.

Although advertising was of growing importance to magazines after the Civil War, it did not really begin to alter the nature of the industry until the 1890s, when the national magazine of popular appeal, low price, and large circulation emerged. Well into the second half of the nineteenth century, many publishers refused or limited advertising because they thought it detracted from the dignity of their publications. They ran advertisements where they would be most unobtrusive, and they treated advertising people scornfully. A young advertising agent, George P. Rowell, once approached the publishers of *Harper's Weekly*, a magazine in which he had been placing advertisements for his clients, to learn its circulation. The publishers were so shocked by his impertinence that they turned down his next batch of advertisements. Fletcher Harper refused $18,000 offered by a sewing machine manufacturer for the back page of *Harper's* for a year. Harper thought the advertisements unworthy of his magazine, and he wanted the space to promote his own books.

Few of the magazines that accepted advertising actively sought it. One that did was *Century*, a magazine of prestige which circulated among well-to-do, well-educated readers. Its aggressive attention to advertising in the 1870s and 1880s has been credited with helping to break down the resistance of other leading magazines to carrying advertisements. In the 1890s Frank Munsey, as mentioned earlier, hit upon what has since become standard publishing practice. He sold his magazines for less than cost to win readers and took his profits from the advertising a large circulation attracted. As Munsey and his followers demonstrated how much money was to be made from this practice, publishers joined the scramble for circulation and advertising.

Pioneer broadcasters regarded radio mainly as an instrument for the widespread dissemination of culture. Owners of receiving sets could support radio by paying an annual license fee, some thought, and manufacturers would profit handsomely from the sale of sets and other equipment. Advertising support was not ignored; rather it was positively denounced. Even the advertising and broadcasting trade press carried articles warning of the harm that advertising could work. The April 27, 1922, issue of *Printers' Ink*, the advertising trade weekly, declared that radio advertising would offend a great number of persons. "The family circle is not a public place," it observed, "and advertising has no business intruding there unless it is invited." That same year *Radio Broadcasting* magazine complained about the advertising, some of it indirect, which already had begun to invade the ether:

> Concerts are seasoned here and there with a dash of advertising paprika. You can't miss it; every little classic number has a slogan all its own, if it is only the mention of the name—and the shrill address, and the phone number—of the music house which arranged the program. More of this sort of thing may be expected. And once the avalanche gets a good start, nothing short of an Act of Congress or a repetition of Noah's excitement will suffice to stop it.

Not everyone was critical. When William H. Rankin, head of a New York advertising agency, heard a theater orchestra on his son's homemade crystal set, he was at once impressed by the potentialities of radio as an advertising medium. Before recommending it to his clients, Rankin tested its effectiveness by buying time on WEAF in December, 1922, to give a fifteen-minute talk on advertising. The response to his talk included a $500,000 contract to handle the advertising of a new client, whose product Rankin immediately began promoting in a thirteen-week series of talks. Within weeks Rankin was using radio as a means of extolling the products of other clients. His agency has been credited with being the first to use sponsored radio programs as advertising. Other agencies and their clients also recognized the possibilities of radio; broadcasters quickly saw the great commercial potential that lay in abandoning their dreams of cultural enrichment and dedicating themselves to building up audiences for the advertiser's sales pitch. In a few years the listening public had largely ceased questioning the desirability of using the air waves to sell products. By the time television came along, commercial sponsorship of broadcasting had become so ingrained in the system that any other means of support seemed beyond serious consideration.

SPECIALIZATION OF FUNCTION

Caught up in industrialization and technological change, the communications industries in the nineteenth century began to use the division of labor techniques that were making possible mass production in other industries. Specialization was a concomitant of the growing size and increased efficiency that came to characterize the media in the twentieth century, helping to bring about a standardized product in communications as it did in the manufacture of automobiles and soap and refrigerators.

The Media

The one-man newspaper gave way to the newspaper manned by scores of specialists, each of whom made his particular contribution to its production. In 1835, when James Gordon Bennett started his New York *Herald*, he tramped the sidewalks for news, penned many of the stories that gave his paper its bright personality, managed the paper's business affairs, and even waited on customers at a desk consisting of a plank laid over two barrels. Most newspapers of that time depended little on regular reporters. The editor covered what local news he could and filled the rest of the paper with telegraphed news, items from his correspondents and clippings from exchanges. By the 1890s the staffs, in number and in specialization of duties, were similar to what they are now. Specific persons were charged with specific tasks, such as supervising the reporters, handling telegraph news, covering sports and women's interests, writing literary and dramatic criticism.

So it was with the other media. In his autobiography, *King of Comedy*, Mack Sennett tells of the first movie he made on his arrival in Hollywood in 1912. Thirty minutes after getting off the train he and his co-workers saw a Shriners' parade on Main Street, too impressive a free spectacle to pass up. He sent one of his workers to a department store to buy a doll that could pass as his star actress' baby and a shawl for a headdress. With just those props—and the parade—he improvised a script, cast it and filmed it on the spot. He needed only a few additional scenes and closeups shot in his small studio to tie the film together. Thus Sennett performed many of the tasks that were later to become the province of specialists. He was script-writer, property man, producer, director, and assistant cameraman.

Specialization invaded broadcasting as well. A radio program became not the creation of one man but the result of complex interactions among packagers of talent, producers, directors, script-writers, performers, announcers, and musicians. Network news commentators no longer prepared their own scripts. Instead they read the work of their writers, who in turn depended on the network's own news-gathering facilities and other sources.

Advertising

The advertising agency, which serves all media, also underwent a series of mutations, which enlarged and specialized its functions. When Volney Palmer created the first advertising agency in the early 1840s, he and his followers were little more than space brokers. Those early agencies simply bought large blocks of space in newspapers and magazines and sold it in smaller units to advertisers. Neither the cost nor the selling price of space was standardized, and the agencies performed no services for advertisers beyond making space available.

After 1900 advertising agencies underwent a period of consolidation. Advertising and agency rates became standardized, and agencies began to take on new functions on behalf of the advertiser, such as copywriting and layout, media selection, and pioneer market research. Conducting research for their clients in which the techniques and findings of the social sciences were applied became an ever more important task of agencies in the twentieth century.

Today the advertising agency occupies an important and specialized position between advertiser and media. On the one hand, the media recognized the unique position of the advertising agency by allowing it to deduct a 15-per cent commission from the standard or "card" rate on the advertising it places. This commission forms the basic income of an agency, although it also charges advertisers fees for collateral services. An advertiser who wishes to work directly with a medium pays the full card rate; he saves nothing by circumventing the agency. On the other hand, the advertiser recognizes the unique position of the advertising agency by assigning it responsibility for planning an advertising program, creating the ads and placing them in the media most effective for the purpose. The advertiser may go far beyond that in making the agency his ally in his entire sales and marketing program. He may have the agency handle research involving his product, market, and individual advertisements; he may even call on the agency for help in developing a new product, creating its trademark, designing its package, and advising on its distribution.

INCREASED EFFICIENCY

When President Abraham Lincoln delivered his Gettysburg address on a November day in 1863, he had the attention of about 15,000 persons at most. When Franklin D. Roosevelt spoke to the nation over the radio shortly after the Japanese attack on Pearl Harbor in December, 1941, he was heard by some 62 million adults out of a possible 90 million. And in 1965 President Lyndon B. Johnson spoke simultaneously to TV viewers in the U.S. and in Europe, his message relayed by a space satellite 22,300 miles above the earth. Thus did the new electronic media that came with America's industrialization enlarge a speaker's audience. They enabled man not only to communicate directly with multitudes but to do so instantaneously.

So, too, did the industrial and technological revolution increase the efficiency and speed of the older printed media. Before technology had borne such fruit as high-speed presses, Linotypes, telegraph, and railroads, newspapers were low in news volume, low in circulation, and costly to the reader. The screw-type press of Gutenberg, modeled on the wine press, gave way in the early nineteenth century to the iron Columbian press, which was operated by a system of levers but which, by today's standards, was capable of a very limited rate of output. In 1825 American newspapers began to install steam-driven cylinder presses, which could print 2000 copies an hour, and a few years later some newspapers were using double-cylinder presses, which could turn out twice that many copies. The steam-driven press eventually gave way to the electrically powered rotary press, capable of spewing out 20,000 or more impressions an hour.

No longer need a newspaper be restricted in size because of slow printing operations. High-speed presses meant large circulation, which, in turn, was a factor in reducing unit costs through the principles of mass production.

The new technology brought increased timeliness in news coverage. Transmission of news and pictures to newspapers was accelerated by the steamship, telegraph, camera, and photoengraving process. In the early nineteenth century England was thirty-six days away from America, but the regular steamship runs after 1838 shortened the time to less than three weeks, then to two. After the Civil War the transAtlantic cable put American in almost instant touch with Europe.

Even domestic news was slow in reaching print. In the War of

1812, news that New Orleans had successfully resisted the British reached New York a month after Jackson's victory. Five days after New Yorkers learned that New Orleans had withstood attack, they heard that a peace treaty had been signed in London—signed two weeks before the battle at New Orleans.

Editors used a number of ingenious methods for speeding the gathering of news. Some sent reporters by fast boat to incoming ships to gather news from abroad and to speed back with it. Some had swift pony express service between key cities. Daniel Craig earned a good living by meeting the incoming ships off Boston, summarizing whatever news from abroad he could collect, and hastening it to his clients by carrier pigeon. His system soon spread to Philadelphia and New York, where James Gordon Bennett offered Craig $500 for every hour that his *Herald* received the news ahead of its competitors.

None of those methods could compare with the telegraph, however. In its issue of May 25, 1844, the Baltimore *Patriot* ran a short telegraphic dispatch about an action by Congress, the first wire story to appear in an American paper. Two years later a column of telegraphic news briefs was a staple in all New York dailies. The amount of wire copy increased, and so did the number of papers carrying it, when the first really cooperative news-gathering agency was formed in 1848. In time the press agencies expanded the coverage of individual newspapers. The telegraph made it possible for press agencies to flash news to papers moments after an event had happened. The newspaper could take the entire world for its beat and cover it immediately.

One spur to the adoption of more efficient methods of news-gathering and newspaper production was the Civil War. Public interest in the war was intense; readers wanted to know what happened yesterday, not two or three weeks ago. Out of competition newspapers were forced to send corps of reporters and artists into the field. To issue the news promptly despite the exigencies of war, papers substituted machines for men wherever possible. The war forced *The New York Times* to buy additional presses, for instance, and to adopt the process of stereotyping—casting whole pages from papier-mâché matrices.

The spread of photoengraving in the latter part of the nineteenth century made the reproduction of artwork in newspapers and magazines faster and less expensive than it had been by such earlier means as woodcuts, zincographs, and steel plates. In the days when woodcuts were still an important means of reproducing art, some nineteenth-century magazines, in their fight to speed production, assigned several artists to one illustration, each artist engraving one small portion of the whole. When all the pieces were engraved, they were assembled into a single illustration. Photoengraving, of course, was a far less laborious, far less costly process, and it brought artwork to publications that had previously not been illustrated. Pictorial journalism gained in immediacy with the development of the portable camera, the flashbulb, and the camera that could photograph in natural light. Wirephoto, first used regularly in 1935, made possible the transmission of photographs from one distant point to another in a matter of minutes.

The efficiency of trains, planes, and trucks enabled publishers to put copies of their publications into the hands of readers soon after they had rolled from the presses.

STANDARDIZATION OF PRODUCT

A comparison of the large metropolitan dailies on any given day reveals that their similarities are more striking than their differences. By and large, most of them are alike in size, format, and general appearance. They use similar systems of headlining their stories, and many stories are written to a common pattern—summary lead atop an inverted pyramid structure which presents the facts in order of decreasing importance. Many papers are much alike even in the national and international news they carry and in the relative play they give it.

Magazines too have become standardized, within groups. There are strong similarities of content, style, and format among fashion magazines, for instance, or weekly news reports, or literary quarterlies.

Such standardization of product was perhaps an almost inevitable consequence of the impact on the media of industrialization, mechanization, urbanization, and the redistribution of income. The media changed from crafts to industries—to industries utilizing the techniques of mass production. Efficiency required some standardized method of writing the script, the news story, the magazine article. Competition for a mass market required that the media aim at some low common denominator of interest and ability to absorb their messages. There are exceptions, of course—and perhaps the book and film industries offer more exceptions than other media—but it is generally true that mass communication can no more afford to accommodate the tastes of the individualist than could the automobile makers of Detroit. The necessity of pleasing the majority contributed to a conservatism in the realm of ideas which has characterized the mass media generally in the twentieth century.

Newspapers

Caught up in the industrial and financial expansion that followed the Civil War, newspapers underwent a transition from personal ventures to corporate enterprises. The great editors whose papers were organs for their personal views and whose names were familiar to their readers became a vanishing breed. On large papers and even on many small ones, the editor became a hired hand, aided by a paid staff; the newspaper itself became an impersonal institution which objectively reported the news and anonymously editorialized about it.

There were good reasons for the shift from personal to corporate journalism. The growth of cities made possible large circulations, which required huge outlays in equipment and high operating costs. The demands of readers for efficient and expanded services added to the cost. The corporation could raise the money with greater ease and run the risks with less jeopardy then the individual entrepreneur. Corporate journalism, however, encouraged a mass-produced, standardized product.

So did the newspaper chain. The seeds of newspaper chains were planted in America when Benjamin Franklin, helping printers go into business as editors and publishers, became a partner in at least a half-dozen newspapers. However, chains really flowered in the late nineteenth century when consolidation and trusts were commonplace in virtually every field. William Randolph Hearst piled holding upon holding, and Frank Munsey recklessly bought, merged, and killed newspapers in an unsuccessful attempt to realize his dream of a great national chain of papers run from a common headquarters. Between 1878 and 1917, E. W. Scripps and Milton McRae started twenty-seven newspapers and bought another five as links in their chain. Although there were exceptions, chain newspapers tended to be standardized in editorial policies, in appearance, or both.

While the press associations, such as Associated Press and United Press, enlarged the coverage of individual newpapers, and while syndicates offered papers a variety of features they could not otherwise afford, both these services increased standardization. The dailies subscribing to the wire services gave their readers essentially the same account of events. And those accounts were written to a standard formula—summary lead and inverted pyramid—which discouraged the individualist.

Magazines

When magazines fervently embraced advertising in the late nineteenth century, they became inextricably joined to the marketing system. Content was the bait with which the publisher coaxed an audience to his magazine—an audience of consumers valuable to the advertiser for its size, homogeneity, or both. After a publisher had struck upon a happy balance of content which attracted the desired readers, he was reluctant to change it. Hence every issue of a given magazine tended to be similar to many others.

Such standardization of content was a natural outgrowth of the quest for a popular market and the mass production necessary if a magazine was to compete successfully for that market. Well into the nineteenth century, when magazines were still generally edited for the elite few, an editor could remain an aloof arbiter who chose what he liked from among the contributions of aspiring writers. However, the editor of a mass-produced magazine tailored to the interests of a specific popular audience could not count on filling it with stories and articles selected from chance contributions. The types of material he used and the distinctive handling his writers gave it determined the editorial personality of his magazine, and it was this personality that caused readers to buy. Thus an increasingly large proportion of magazine content came to be planned by the staff. Walter Hines Page demonstrated the feasibility of such planning during his tenure as editor of the *Forum* from 1887 to 1895. He astounded his colleagues by jotting down a table of contents months in advance of publication and then scouting out writers qualified to produce the articles he wanted. Today the major magazines have adopted Page's basic idea of editorial planning. On many publications the staff originates ideas for a high percentage of the features the magazine carries. Some of the ideas are assigned to established free-lance authors who research and write the articles. Others are developed by staff writers. In either instance, with only a few exceptions, the net effect is standardization.

Imitation also contributed to the standardization of magazine fare. When a publisher succeeds with an original publishing idea or with an adaptation of an old one, competitors rush to bring out imitations in order to get a share of the market. In 1922 a young man named DeWitt Wallace brought out the first issue of a modest little magazine that summarized what he considered the best articles from the magazines of the day. He called it the *Reader's Digest*. Readers were soon flocking to it. Other publishers brought out imitations. Eventually, a whole new category of magazines—the digests—sprang up. Similarly other new categories arose as imitators aped successful new ventures: the fact detective magazines, the confession magazines, the news magazines, the picture magazines, the men's adventure magazines.

Other Media

Standardization of content and technique became a characteristic of the other media as well. Movie producers, by capitalizing on what they thought to be peaks of public interest, brought forth cycles of movies on a particular theme—gangster films and lavish musicals in the 1930s, for instance, neorealistic films in the postwar 1940s, surfing films in the 1960s, motorcycle films in the early 1970s. Often motion pictures simply reiterated the content of the printed media. Gambling millions on a single picture, producers tried to reduce their risks by filming stories that had already proved their success in magazines or books or on the stage. "I think it's a legitimate attitude considering the economics of the industry," Ernest Lehman, a veteran script-writer, told *Variety*. "I can understand the position of the producer. He has seen how it played previously and knows what the critics have said. If he has to go with an original, he's not sure what he's getting."

Moreover, the movie script was developed according to a conventional formula. There was small room for the experimentalist, the individualist. "There's no room in motion pictures for writers who want to write for themselves," Lehman said. A writer who wants to express himself had "better go off to some other field where millions of dollars are not riding on his personal aspirations."

On November 1, 1926, the National Broadcasting Company was formed—in time to broadcast the 1927 Rose Bowl Game. Thereafter three or four major networks contributed to the standardization of broadcasting by feeding the same programs to thousands of local stations. Even if the listener had a choice of rival networks, he was likely to get essentially the same fare on each—one soap opera or another in the morning, for instance, or one variety show or another in the prime evening hours.

Television settled comfortably into the rut of standardization which radio had already plowed. It was as imitative as magazines and movies. A successful program of any type bred a rash of others, a point well illustrated by the large number of quiz shows, domestic comedies, and Westerns of the 1960s.

Standardization of media fare worried some serious students of the communication system. Standardization encouraged conformity, they warned, and posed a threat to the free flow of information and ideas essential to a democratic society.

The Intellectual
Environment
Libertarianism

4

The theory of a free press is that the truth will emerge
from free reporting and free discussion, not that it
will be presented perfectly and instantly in any one
account.

WALTER LIPPMANN

The mass communications system in America, like that
in other lands, has been shaped to some extent by its intellectual environment. The ideas dominant in a society shape its institutions just as surely
as do the social and economic forces. The communications system in
the United States performs as it does to some degree because of our
concept of freedom and our theory of what communications should
be and do.

It will not do, however, to assign to ideas and to the intellect
the sole responsibility for shaping our communications system. Freedom
of the press was gained as much because of contending interests as
because of philosophy, by factions, in England and in America, struggling
for their own ends. In many cases the philosophers appeared quite late,
after the battle was all but won, to rationalize and consolidate the gains.

During the American Revolution there was no freedom of
expression in the Colonies. There was freedom to hail the Patriot cause,
but there was a summary silencing of anyone who questioned that cause
or advocated another course. After the war the states made no attempt
to rid themselves of the seditious libel laws on their books or even
to amend them.

When the American tradition did emerge, it came about from
the bitter interaction of contending interests, each working for its own
protection, first in the controversy over adopting a Bill of Rights, then

in the furor over the Alien and Sedition Acts of 1798. As it turned out, the tradition went far beyond the conventional thinking of the eighteenth century, and it had respectable philosophical arguments to sustain it.

Some fifty-five years ago Charles Beard, in *An Economic Interpretation of the Constitution,* contended that the Constitution owed far less to abstract concern about rights than to the self-interest of the men who drafted it. Recently Professor Leonard Levy, in his *Legacy of Suppression,* has cogently developed the thesis that the generation that adopted the Constitution, the Bill of Rights, and the early state constitutions did not believe in a broad scope for freedom of expression, especially in political matters. He concluded that there is good reason to believe that the Bill of Rights was more the chance product of expedience than the happy product of principle.

The Bill of Rights resulted from the contest between the Federalists, who favored a strong national government, and the Antifederalists, who preferred a league of more or less independent states. Antifederalists held that since the national government had only enumerated powers, it had no authority to regulate the press. They considered a Bill of Rights essential to protect the interests of the individual states. Such a bill would prevent the central government from imposing any restrictions on speech and the press. It would reserve to the states the power to regulate free expression.

The traditional restraints that had plagued English and Colonial publishers disappeared from the American scene. The press was virtually free of controls, and there was no immediate prospect that they would return. To be sure, publishers at times spoke as if the specter of repression haunted them. If Congress proposed increasing the postal rates, if a state legislature considered altering the requirements for publishing legal notices, publishers sometimes sounded as if the republic were in peril. But what concerned them most about such moves was the threat to the profitability of their enterprises rather than any interference with their freedom to speak.

It is important to remember that the libertarian philosophy discussed in the following pages was at least equally balanced by self-interest in shaping the American communication system.

To understand the communication system of any society, one must know what the society expects of it. What are the system's functions? How much freedom does it have? What do we mean by freedom anyway? The answers to these questions come only after one has looked at the basic assumptions the society holds. What view does the society take of the nature of man? What does the society regard as the ideal relation between man and the state? What is the society's idea of truth?

Sooner or later, then, the study of a communications system leads to questions of philosophy.

The system in the United States has a strong English heritage, for the Colonists copied the institutions and culture of England. They modeled their newspapers and magazines on those in the homeland. To keep their press in line, they imported the controls that were used in England. When they revolted, they justified their action by citing their rights as free-born Englishmen. And when, under their newly won freedom, Americans developed a theory of the press, they borrowed liberally from thinkers in England and in Europe.

LIBERTARIAN PHILOSOPHY

In the seventeenth century there was emerging a new conception of the nature of man and of his relationship to the state. Scientific and geographic discoveries broadened minds and vistas. The rising commercial class disputed the privileges of the nobility and challenged the supremacy of the monarch. The old order was crumbling. When the century began, the authoritarian order seemed secure; when it ended, the Crown was subordinate to Parliament, and liberalism was in the ascendancy. The eighteenth century provided the laboratories in which the tenets of liberalism were put to practical test.

Libertarian Government

From the theorists of the seventeenth and eighteenth centuries came the libertarian philosophy that underlies the American democratic form of government. That philosophy conceived of the world as a vast perpetual-motion machine, going timelessly on according to the laws of nature. The libertarians believed that man is a creature guided by reason, not by passion or narrow self-interest. By using his reason, he could discover the laws of nature which govern the universe, bring his institutions into harmony with them, and so build a good and just society.

Men, the libertarians thought, are born with certain natural rights, which limit the hand of government and demand protection for the individual's liberty and property. Although tyrants might temporarily abridge these rights, no one can properly take them away, for they are as much a part of the divine scheme as the laws under which the universe operates.

According to the libertarian view, men, in their natural state—

before they voluntarily joined together to form governments—existed perfectly free and equal. But in that state of nature, their enjoyment of their rights was in constant danger, since the individual was at the mercy of his domineering fellows, who could deprive him by force of his liberty and property.

So, by common consent, men form governments to secure their natural rights. The best way that government can ensure those rights is by leaving the individual as free as possible. The best government, then, is that which governs least. When government fails to protect the liberty and property of its citizens, it has failed in its purpose; and it is the right and duty of the people to establish a new government which does enable them to enjoy their freedom.

The libertarians saw truth as deriving not from authority but from the intellect of men. Man is not to be led and directed toward truth; he is to find it himself with the reason with which he is endowed. With the free play of his intellect, he can discover the all-embracing truth which unifies the universe and the phenomena in it.

As Carl L. Becker has remarked, modern democracy offers long odds on the capacity and integrity of the human mind. It assumes that man is not only a rational being but a moral one. If man is to be free from all but the most necessary of restraints, his moral sense must enforce those obligations to his fellow men that are not specifically covered by law. Human perfectibility, natural rights, and natural reason, then, are three of the key points in the libertarian philosophy.

What is the nature of man? Man is a creature who is guided by reason. He is disposed to seek truth and to be guided by it. What is the ideal relationship between man and the state? Man should be governed only with his own consent. The state, by keeping its power at a minimum, should preserve but not infringe upon man's natural rights. What is the nature of truth? Truth is not the monopoly of the few in power, but it is discoverable by all men using their natural intellect; it is the key to understanding the natural order of things so that man can form a harmonious society.

Libertarian Theory of the Press

Those same answers are the base on which the libertarian theory of the press was erected. Let us briefly summarize the theory.

In libertarian theory the press must have a wide latitude of freedom to aid men in their quest for truth. To find truth through reason, man must have free access to information and ideas. Out of the fare the press serves him, he can, by employing his intellect, distinguish truth from falsehood. He finds some truth hidden amid falsehood, some falsehood hidden amid truth. Yet over the long pull, if man is faithful to his reason, truth will emerge from the unrestrained interplay of information and ideas. Social change will come, then, not from force but from a process of discussion and persuasion.

Since, according to libertarian theory, free expression carries built-in correctives, there need be few restrictions on what men may speak and write. The great majority of men are moral creatures who will use their freedom responsibly in an honest desire to find truth. One need not worry about the small minority who may abuse their freedom by lying and distorting. Others will find it profitable to expose them—and the lies and distortions will be shown up for what they are since all information and ideas are put to the powerful scrutiny of reason. Therefore, it is unnecessary to exact responsibilities in exchange for freedom; most men will assume them without being asked, and the remainder can cause no great harm. Charles Beard was quite correct in saying that under the Constitution freedom of the press originally was "the right to be just or unjust, partisan or non-partisan, true or false, in news column and in editorial column."

Censorship before publication is an evil for at least three reasons under libertarian theory. First, it violates man's natural right to free expression. Second, it could enable tyrants to perpetuate themselves in power and to make the state a foe instead of liberty's protector. Third, it could temporarily hinder the quest for truth by throwing off balance the delicate process by which truth ultimately emerges. If man is to discover truth, he must have access to all information and ideas, not just those fed to him.

Governments operating under libertarian theory have permitted some restrictions on expression. They have sanctioned libel laws to protect the individual from defamation. If a person is defamed, he may seek recompense in the courts—after publication. Governments also condone laws regulating obscenity, although there is confusion over just what constitutes the obscene. The theory has even permitted mild sedition laws. Those limitations, however, staked out wide boundaries to the area of free expression.

SHAPERS OF THE TRADITION

The libertarian theory of the press, as it developed abroad and in America, drew on the ideas of more men than the few whose names are commonly associated with it. However, some had reputations that gave greater prestige to their teachings; some did a better job than their contemporaries of expressing the ideas current among the thinkers of their times. Therefore, we can chart the unfolding of libertarian theory by summarizing the contributions of just a few of those who shaped it.

John Milton

After the Puritans had fought their way to power in the civil wars that tore England in the turbulent seventeenth century, they perceived, as British monarchs had before them, that regulating the press was one means of stifling dissent and maintaining authority. One method was licensing books, pamphlets, and papers. In 1644 a few pamphleteers raised their voices against such regulation, and the most powerful voice was that of the poet John Milton, who had run afoul of authorities with a tract on divorce. His *Areopagitica* has since become regarded as a classic defense of a free press.

Although the *Areopagitica* can be summarized in many different ways, it offers three major arguments against licensing. One is that licensing is the evil child of evil parents. Licensing was invented by the Roman Catholic church, an anathema to the Puritans, and used to prohibit anything the Church found unpalatable. Second, licensing is impractical. It simply will not work. It assumes infallible and incorruptible censors; and if such men could be found, licensing would be a waste of time and wisdom. Licensing is not broad enough to control the minds of men, since it merely regulates the current output of the press. To do the job effectively, one must also censor everything printed in the past, cut the bad parts out of good books, and strictly regulate all activities of the citizens. Therefore, licensing cannot keep the truth from winning out in the end. In the meantime, however, it can do great harm by making citizens feel that their government does not trust them and by stifling free inquiry.

That point leads to Milton's third reason: Licensing hinders man's search for truth. Truth will win out in any free and open encounter of ideas, Milton said; the surest way of suppressing falsehood is to have it refuted. But licensing discourages the writing and the arguing, the knowledge in the making, which help men to find truth. It affronts learning, spells an end to teaching, and makes ignorance a virtue.

Perhaps the most effective argument Milton could have used on the Puritan authorities of his day was that licensing is impractical. His most philosophical argument, however, was that truth arises from the free and open encounter of ideas. And this is Milton's most significant contribution to the libertarian theory of the press. What the main stream of the theory absorbed was his idea of the "self-righting process," the idea that free expression carries its own correctives. Grant all men the freedom to express themselves. In the clash of ideas that ensues, the true and sound will triumph over the false and unsound. Falsehood may seem to win out temporarily, but if the government does not weigh the balance in favor of either side, truth will be the victor in the end.

Viewed from the twentieth century, Milton's idea of press freedom was narrow. He was the product of his age, although his *Areopagitica* transcended it, and it is unfair to criticize him for sharing the beliefs of his times instead of our own. Nonetheless, the freedom that he advocated was negative, a freedom from government restriction; indeed, his chief concern was simply an end to licensing. He believed that the government should prohibit certain types of publications—blasphemy, atheism, libel—and punish offending printers.

Moreover, Milton put narrow limits on who should be allowed to write without hindrance. He would have denied free expression to those who disagreed with him on fundamentals—Royalists, for instance, and Catholics. In short, he would have denied freedom to anyone who challenged the primary assumptions of public order as it existed in 1644. Superficially at least, his idea of press freedom resembles that of the present-day Soviet state, which forbids criticism of the basic assumptions of communism but does permit some criticism of how the work of the party is carried out.

Milton seems to have accepted man's rationality. Yet one cannot help feeling that he was defending free expression for only the educated few, not the masses, and that his freedom applied only to serious books and discussion, not to the newsbooks, broadsides, and polemics that abounded in his time.

Milton gave the *Areopagitica* a strongly religious cast. Unlike later shapers of the tradition who justified free expression as a natural right, Milton justified it on religious grounds. God—a Puritan God—desired men to have a free press so they could discover truth.

That truth for Milton was something outside of man, an expression of a higher law—the will of his Puritan God. Man once had it, then lost it:

> Truth indeed came once into the world with her divine Master, and was a perfect shape most glorious to look on; but when he ascended and his Apostles after him were laid asleep, then strait arose a wicked race of deceivers, who . . . took the virgin Truth, hewd her lovely form into a thousand pieces, and scatter'd them to the four winds.

From that sad day onward, friends of Truth tried to pick up the scattered pieces so as to reconstruct the whole.

For Milton, then, the stream of libertarian theory was narrow; freedom of the press meant little more than an end to licensing so that men could discover the will of a Puritan God. It may seem anti-climactic that the *Areopagitica* had little effect in its own day and that Milton himself later became a government licenser of newsbooks. Yet neither circumstance detracts from the significance of Milton's contribution to libertarian thought. If one reads the *Areopagitica* as a defense of serious books, not of ephemera, his becoming censor does not necessarily reflect a violation of principle. His *Areopagitica,* ignored in its own time, provided a major concept—that of the self-righting process—when libertarians in the eighteenth century broadened the stream of theory.

Newton, Locke, and Smith

In expanding the boundaries of freedom in the eighteenth century, libertarians drew heavily on the works of three men, none of whom wrote specifically about the press. The orderly nature of the universe, natural law, natural rights, the rationality of man, and the hands-off role of government were ideas expressed by Isaac Newton, John Locke, and Adam Smith and were used to justify curbing the authority of the state and making the individual paramount.

Unifying work done in physics and astronomy, Isaac Newton in 1687 gave man a new picture of the universe. In that picture, as we saw when discussing libertarian government, the universe was an orderly machine, timeless, unchanging, running on according to certain discoverable laws of nature.

Building on Newton, John Locke gave libertarians their picture of man and his relation to government. Locke, in vindicating the scientific achievements of his age, set out to show that all knowledge comes from experience, from the senses. While the human intellect does have limits, its powers are great enough to secure happiness for mankind. He proved to the satisfaction of libertarians that man is distinguished by his capacity for creative thought.

In his essays on civil government, which provided ringing phrases for the American Declaration of Independence, Locke advanced a system of natural rights. Like Newton's discoveries, these rights rest on the unchanging laws of nature. Men in a state of nature are free and equal with certain inalienable rights. They form government by their own consent to protect those rights, and a government that does not protect them has violated its purpose and should be dissolved in favor of one that does.

The libertarian theory of the press took two of its vital propositions from Locke: the rationality of man and free expression as a natural right. Man's rationality became inextricably bound up with the self-righting process of Milton. By putting all discussion, spoken or written, to the powerful test of reason, man could discover truth. Newton had given a glimpse of the majestic truth that man could discover—the enduring laws of nature. Mortal man could discover those laws, bring his institutions into harmony with them, and thus found an earthly paradise of justice and order.

Free expression became accounted one of man's natural rights, and no one has the authority to deprive him of it. Indeed, it is the right on which all other rights depend, for if men are free to speak their minds, they can rally support whenever the government acts unjustly or arbitrarily.

In 1776 Adam Smith showed how economics fits into both Newton's orderly world and Locke's system of natural rights and self-government. He contributed two more propositions to the libertarian theory of the press.

One was that government should assume a negative role in man's affairs, should take a position of laissez faire or "hands off," lest it upset the delicate workings of nature's laws. The idea was an appealing one to libertarians, who had long eyed the government as the chief threat to freedom. Here was good reason why the press should be obliged to make its own way in the market place. Here too was good reason why the government should not sponsor media of its own in competition with private media.

Smith's second contribution was his theory that as each person works for his own gain, he serves the welfare of the community. The libertarian press has applied this idea in various ways. The idea lies, for instance, behind the remark of the editor who said that his readers vote for his newspaper with their coins every time he brings out a new issue. According to this line of thought, the press is accountable to the public, and the public controls the press in its own interests by the choices it makes. If a newspaper, magazine, or broadcasting station serves what people regard as the public interest, they will give it their patronage, and it will flourish. If it fails to serve the public interest, they will not patronize it. In consequence, it will wither and die. By working for his own personal gain, then, the publisher or broadcaster automatically gives the public the sort of media it wants and needs. Smith's idea also can be used to justify the publication of virtually anything. The argument can be put something like this: Helping to find truth is in the public interest. Many ideas and much information are needed for the discovery of truth. What I publish for my own personal profit serves the cause of truth and hence the public interest.

Mansfield and Blackstone

Even in the eighteenth century, when the libertarian movement came to full flower, some shapers of the libertarian tradition held views of press freedom almost as narrow as Milton's. Two such men—Lord Mansfield and Sir William Blackstone—were responsible for this basic principle: The government shall not restrain the press before publication.

Lord Mansfield sat as chief justice on the King's Bench in England from about 1750 to 1790. He held that the government does not have the right to suppress any material before it is published. However, it does have the authority to punish publishers of material which causes damage, as determined by the common law and Parliament. The publisher is free from censorship before publication; he may publish whatever he wishes, but must bear full responsibility for the abuse of his freedom.

Mansfield's ideas were picked up by Sir William Blackstone, a jurist influential in setting the law of his day. He worked them into his famous *Commentaries*.

By libertarian standards both men had a narrow view of press freedom. They granted law-makers the authority to decide what materials constituted abuses and to set the punishments for offenders. In effect, then, they gave law-makers the authority to decide what should be published. Under such a system the government could easily stifle ideas. It could simply declare the publication of certain materials an abuse of freedom. Or it could make penalties so severe that fear of punishment would discourage publishers from bringing forth certain ideas.

What has survived of the libertarian theory of the press is the basic principle that there should be no censorship before publication. The courts have continued to uphold that principle, sometimes with references to Blackstone.

Camden and Erskine

By giving the legislature a strong control of the press, Mansfield and Blackstone were at odds with a growing and influential body of libertarians who believed in a minimum of government. Lord Camden and Sir Thomas Erskine were among the Englishmen who had adopted Locke's philosophy of man's reason and natural rights. They broadened libertarian theory by arguing that the power of the government to interfere with the press should be severely restricted. Across the Atlantic their position was shared by Thomas Jefferson, an important figure in shaping the bent of ideas about press freedom in America.

Camden and Erskine believed that the authority of government is limited by natural law and natural rights. Because free expression is a natural right, the government should not restrict the press either before or after publication, so long as the material is aimed at peaceful change. Even to save itself, the government should not interfere with any publication that would change the existing order by peaceful means or by appeal to the intellect. Here the scope of freedom is far, far broader than that pleaded for by John Milton, who would have spared the existing order from public questioning.

Thomas Jefferson

In America Thomas Jefferson also had an optimistic faith in man's reason and a pessimistic distrust of government. He wrote no unified work on the press, but his letters are full of scattered references to it. From them one can piece together his idea of press freedom and the role of the press in a democratic society. His beliefs arose quite naturally from his political philosophy.

Like the philosophers of the Enlightenment, Jefferson believed that the universe had been created in accordance with some orderly plan. Men had been given reason so that they could discover that plan and bring their lives and institutions into harmony with it. He put strong faith in the rationality and morality of mankind; men are good unless ignorance or bad institutions corrupt them. Because men are essentially reasonable, because they have certain natural rights, they should have a minimum of governing. But even under the best form of government, Jefferson knew, those in public office may become so corrupted by power that they will stifle the freedom of the people. Therefore, the citizens must be alert to any attempts to curtail their liberty.

The role of the press followed from that picture of man and the state. As Jefferson saw it, the press has two major functions: to enlighten the public and to safeguard personal liberties.

"The press," Jefferson wrote in 1823, "is the best instrument for enlightening the mind of man, and improving him as a rational, moral, and social being." Democracy places a heavy burden on the individual citizen. Self-governing, he must be enlightened in order to govern himself wisely. The press is an important auxiliary of government as the means of giving the citizen the facts and ideas he needs for proper self-government. Jefferson himself summarized this viewpoint in an oft-quoted passage from a letter to Edward Carrington:

> The basis of governments being the opinion of the people, the first object should be to keep that right; and were it left to me to decide

whether we should have a government without newspapers or newspapers without a government, I should not hesitate a moment to prefer the latter. But I should mean that every man should receive those papers, and be capable of reading them.

The press should also be a check on government, Jefferson thought. The freedom of the individual is the core of democracy, but even a democratic government can trample the rights of its citizens. An important function of the press, Jefferson believed, is to safeguard personal liberties, to serve as a watchdog who sounds the alarm whenever individual rights are threatened or infringed. As a result public officials who rule despotically can be deposed peaceably by public opinion instead of violently by revolution. The role of the press as watchdog was on Jefferson's mind when he wrote to George Washington in 1792:

> No government ought to be without censors; and where the press is free, no one ever will be. If virtuous, it need not fear the fair operations of attack and defense.

To perform as enlightener and as watchdog, the press must have the widest possible freedom, and that Jefferson granted it. Like Erskine and Camden he believed that the government should not hinder the press, even to save itself. He apparently did favor libel laws to protect individual citizens from unwarranted attack. At first he seems to have thought that private citizens should have the right to sue for libel but that public and political figures should not have such protection; by 1803, however, he seems to have favored extending the same libel protection to public figures. Even so, his theory imposed only the barest of restraints on the press.

The Eighteenth-century Libertarians

The concept of freedom of the press held by Jefferson, Camden, and Erskine was the predominant one in the late eighteenth century when the American Constitution was being written. Although eighteenth-century libertarians sometimes differed on minor points, they agreed on fundamentals. How had they changed libertarian theory since Milton?

The libertarians had changed the basis of press freedom. While Milton had justified freedom of the press as the will of God, they justified it as an inherent, natural right of man.

They had broadened the concept. Indeed, in the late eighteenth century libertarian theory was as broad as it was ever to become before the problems and complexities of the twentieth century narrowed it once more. While Milton had seen press freedom as simply freedom from licensing, the libertarians saw it as an absence of government interference in virtually every form. Milton denied free expression to those who disagreed with him on fundamentals. Not so the libertarians; for them, freedom meant the right to question even fundamentals. The form of government itself was not to be spared from questioning, and the state could not intervene even to save itself. As we have seen, Milton approved of restrictions on certain types of content—atheism, for example, and blasphemy. The libertarians, with their strong faith in reason, permitted publication of virtually everything, although they did sanction mild sedition laws, libel laws, and laws regulating obscenity.

They had a different conception of the truth, which free inquiry was intended to disclose. While Milton equated truth with the will of a Puritan God, the libertarians saw truth as a revelation of the laws that governed the operation of the harmonious universe.

John Stuart Mill

Although some restrictions were imposed on the press before and during the Civil War, the libertarian tradition strongly predominated in the United States throughout the nineteenth century; viewpoints of all sorts were tolerated, even those that questioned or attacked the beliefs of the majority.

Shortly after mid-century, an English scholar contributed two new ideas to libertarian thought. In his essay "On Liberty," John Stuart Mill justified free expression not on the basis of natural rights but on the grounds of utility. He emphasized that the government, the traditional enemy of liberty, was not the sole threat to individual liberty, that the majority might tyrannize the minority, the majority might stifle minority thought.

For Mill liberty is the right of the mature individual to think and act as he pleases so long as he harms no one else by doing so. Harm to others is the sole justification for restraint. For its own protection society may try to advise, instruct, and persuade the individual; it may, indeed, ostracize him. But it may not restrain him for his own good.

Mill grounded his case for freedom not on natural rights but on utilitarian principles. All human action, he said, should aim at creating the greatest happiness for the greatest number of persons. This happy state will come about most surely if the individual is free to think and act as he pleases. The individual needs freedom to bring his capabilities to their fullest flower, Mill argued; and as each individual flourishes, society as a whole benefits.

Four major arguments underlie Mill's case for free expression. First, if we silence an opinion, we may be silencing the truth. Second, a wrong opinion may contain a grain of truth necessary for finding the whole truth. Third, even if the commonly accepted opinion is the whole truth, people will hold it not on rational grounds but as a prejudice unless they are forced to defend it. Fourth, unless commonly held opinions are contested from time to time, they lose their vitality, their effect on conduct and character.

Fighters for liberty commonly regard the government as their chief enemy, Mill said, and think that they have won the battle when they have thrown off the yoke of government. Yet the majority can tyrannize just as surely as government by imposing its collective opinion on the individual:

> There needs protection also against the tyranny of prevailing opinion and feeling; against the tendency of society to impose, by means other than civil penalties, its own ideas and practices as rules of conduct on those who dissent from them; to fetter the development, and, if possible, prevent the formation, of any individuality not in harmony with its ways, and compel all characters to fashion themselves upon the model of its own.

Oliver Wendell Holmes

Libertarian theory was somewhat narrowed by Justice Oliver Wendell Holmes of the Supreme Court, who believed that some limits must be set to the free expression guaranteed by the Bill of Rights. Determining just where the limits should be drawn, he thought, involves a fine balancing of the rights of the individual and the protection of society.

Like Milton and the eighteenth-century libertarians, Holmes saw the interplay of ideas as the way to truth. But his truth seems to have been a pragmatic one. Since the majority of reasonable men can be counted on to choose whatever is best for them at a given time, they will choose truth. The truth they seek, Holmes seems to have said, is not a unified, cohesive whole that explains all of nature and human affairs. Rather they choose a succession of little truths—"whatever proves itself to be good in the way of belief," as William James put it—in a continuous process of refining, maturing, and perfecting. Truth, then, is that which endures.

Free expression provides men with the divergent opinions that are necessary if they are to decide what is best for them. It is, moreover, a good safety valve in democratic society.

Yet government must protect the majority as well as the minority, Holmes thought, so it must draw some line between what it permits and what it does not. Speech is sometimes a form of action and, if criminal, should be punished. What matters is not whether the words in question are mere theory or actual incitement. What matters is the circumstances. Words allowed at one time under one set of circumstances might not be allowed at another time under a different set. "The most stringent protection of free speech would not protect a man falsely shouting 'fire!' in a theatre and causing a panic," he wrote in the case of *Schenck v. United States,* and he added: "The question in every case is whether the words used are in such circumstances and are of such a nature as to create a clear and present danger that they will bring about the substantive evils that Congress has a right to prevent."

The "clear and present danger" doctrine sets as wide bounds to freedom as possible while allowing the government to protect itself in emergencies. The danger must be urgent, the possibility of harm immediate. Although the doctrine has been cited less often in recent years, it has been one test by which the courts have judged most attempts to restrict freedom of expression.

LIBERTARIAN FUNCTIONS

According to F. S. Siebert in *Four Theories of the Press,* the mass media, in original libertarian theory, had two major tasks. The first was to inform; the second was to entertain. Eventually, a third—advertising, or sales—developed as the press sought financial independence.

Basically, of course, the underlying purpose of the media is to help discover the truth, to assist in the successful working of self-government by presenting all manner of evidence and opinion as the basis for political and social decisions, and to safeguard civil liberties by providing a check on government. In sum, then, libertarian theory seems to recognize at least six social functions: public enlightenment, servicing the economic system, servicing the political system, safeguarding civil liberties, profit-making, and providing entertainment. No one medium is responsible for all these, of course; they are the functions of all the media working together. By looking at how libertarian theorists defined these functions and how they expected them to be carried out, we get a picture of what libertarians thought the media should be and should do.

Libertarian theorists universally regarded public enlightenment as a major function of the press. From the time of Milton, they saw the press as an important partner in the search for truth. The press can feed man the information he needs to formulate his own ideas; it can stimulate him by presenting the ideas of others. The press, in short, is one of the most pervasive and inexpensive of educators.

Akin to that first function of the press is the second—servicing the political system. Democratic government places heavy responsibility on both the citizen and the press. To govern himself wisely in congregation with others, the individual citizen must be aware of the problems and issues confronting the state and of their possible solutions and consequences. In a government resting on public opinion, then, the press furnishes the people with the information and ideas they need for making sound decisions.

The third function of the press—safeguarding civil liberties—stems quite naturally from the second. The idea of individual autonomy is the heart of libertarian theory. John Stuart Mill expressed the idea this way: "The only freedom which deserves the name, is that of pursuing our own good in our own way, so long as we do not attempt to deprive others of theirs, or impede their efforts to obtain it. Each is the proper guardian of his own health, whether bodily, or mental and spiritual." As each individual pursues his own good in his own way, as he freely develops his capacities, libertarians thought, society would be enriched.

But the individual's freedom is threatened. The libertarians generally regarded government as the traditional and chief foe of liberty; even in democratic societies, those in office might use their power capriciously and dangerously. Therefore, libertarians assigned to the press the task of maintaining a constant check on government, of playing the watchdog to warn the public whenever personal liberties are endangered. Jefferson especially made much of this point, writing in 1816: "The functionaries of every government have propensities to command at will the liberty and property of their constituents . . . Where the press is free, and every man able to read, all is safe." All is safe because the press can arouse the citizenry against the offenders. For, as he wrote a few years later, "This formidable censor of public functionaries, by arraigning them at the tribunal of public opinion, produces reform peaceably, which otherwise must be done by revolution." The press, then, must protect not only its own freedom but the freedom of all citizens.

Libertarian ideas on economics lend strong justification to the fourth function of the press—making a profit. According to libertarian theory, only a free press, operating under a private-enterprise system as conceived by classical liberal economists, can enlighten the public, service the political system, and safeguard civil liberties. Only a free press, beholden neither to government nor to any faction in society, can serve the cause of truth and, ultimately, the rights of individuals and the public interest. Therefore, if the press is to be free to present views and information without fear or favor, it must be a private, independent business enterprise. This line of thought has been used also to justify large communications units, including monopolies and chains and cross-media empires. The argument is that a large prosperous organization can better withstand pressures than a small marginal one.

Today, according to disciples of traditional libertarian theory, a free people should strongly resist the government's entry into the communications field. Media owned outright by the government would be more interested in perpetuating the party in power than in encouraging a free trade in information and ideas. Media subsidized by the government would threaten the autonomy of privately owned communications. Moreover, with no compulsion to earn a profit, media of either type would have an unfair economic advantage over the traditional commercial press. Therefore, they would inhibit the operation of the self-righting process inherent in a competitive market of ideas and opinion.

In linking press autonomy with profit-making, libertarian theory has borrowed freely from Adam Smith's concept of "the invisible hand" in classical economics. In the economic market place, each individual working for his own gain ultimately contributes to the wealth of all. In the market place of knowledge, each individual freely expressing his ideas and opinions furthers the inevitable emergence of truth. Public benefit is virtually guaranteed by the profit motive, which results in a press finely geared to the wants and interests of the community. As the late George Sokolsky once expressed it, "The battle for circulation becomes a battle for the truth." His explanation of that remark is in the best libertarian tradition:

> Some newspapers and some journalists may become subservient to base purposes but in a competitive system, the truth will out. What one seeks to suppress, another will publish. The error of one reporter is corrected by another. The fallacy of one editor is made right by another editor. The attempt to serve some private cause is exposed by a competing newspaper or news service.

By serving his own personal interest in making a profit, then, the publisher, as if by deliberate intent, gives the community the sort of newspaper it wants and needs.

Contemporary critics of libertarian theory have challenged this. Instead of the invisible hand at work, they see a sort of Gresham's law of journalism, under which bad publications tend to drive out the good. For, they argue, a press system devoted to the irresponsible pursuit of profit results not in publications serving the wants and needs of the community but in publications ill equipped to meet the demands of a complex industrial society. The saving point in traditional theory— which most critics disdain—is the libertarian's contention that man is essentially moral; that if the pursuit of profit does not result in responsible journalism, the publisher's innate moral sense eventually will cause him to provide it.

Servicing the economic system, the fifth function of the press, is intimately bound up with the task of profit-making. It became an accepted function of the media with the rise of modern advertising. From its infancy the American press to some degree served the economic system. Colonial newspapers carried information in their news columns about commerce and shipping; in their advertising columns they carried announcements of merchants and traders. Mercantile dailies, newspapers devoted to specialized commercial information and announcements, were an important segment of the press even after Ben Day and his followers began turning out in the 1830s mass-oriented papers heavy with human interest.

However, as industrialization brought mass production and mass distribution, the media became linked more than ever to the economy and its operation. As always the media report happenings in the business and industrial world, but today they do it on an unprecedented scale. For some sixty million readers some two thousand business, technical, and trade publications cover new ideas and new developments in the specialized areas they serve. General newspapers and magazines carry an impressive load of material about business and economic affairs. Perhaps even more important, through advertising the media play an important role in bringing together the buyers and sellers of goods and services. By doing so, according to C. H. Sandage, they contribute to a high level of consumption, help to allocate the nation's resources, stimulate product variety, and help to make possible prices that are favorable to consumers.

Based on the assumptions of eighteenth-century thought, libertarian theory had to be modified as the media developed. But even today it is a powerful factor in the formulation of policy of public communication. Conceiving of free expression as a natural right essential to individual autonomy and of a free press as indispensable to that prerequisite of a free society, and showing a strong faith in the rationality and essential goodness of men, libertarian theory takes for granted the existence of a self-righting process inherent in a free and open market place of knowledge and opinion. Its ultimate and morally persuasive appeal is to a transcendental order of values. Truth (the will of God or the laws of nature) is discovered by rational, moral men in the contest with falsehood. Freedom lies in the knowledge of truth and in living in accordance with the book of nature (or the word of God). The center of libertarian attention is the individual. The freedom of the press is a universal, personal right. The right to publish is subject only to individual reason and conscience and to the minimal restraints of a free society composed of autonomous individuals with similar and equal rights. Comprehensive and impressive in stature, libertarian theory helped to order the development and shape the character of America's contemporary media of mass communication.

The Intellectual
Environment
Social Responsibility

Although libertarian ideas still guide thinking about the press system in America, a new theory is emerging. Called the social-responsibility theory, it rests on this proposition: Whoever enjoys freedom has certain obligations to society. The mass media are guaranteed freedom by the Constitution and are therefore obliged to perform certain essential functions. To the extent that the media assume those obligations, libertarian theory will suffice. If the media are remiss, other agencies, including government, must make them live up to their responsibilities.

This new theory has arisen as critics in recent years have challenged the adequacy of the libertarian theory of the press and the accuracy of its description of man and society. They have questioned not only the performance of the press but also the underlying assumptions of libertarian theory regarding the nature of reality, man, society, and freedom. The revolution in ideas wrought by Darwin with his theory of evolution, Einstein with his theory of relativity, and Freud with his theory of the unconscious has undermined the very foundations of libertarian theory. The ideas of evolution and modern physics have challenged the Newtonian picture of the universe as a timeless, unchanging order. Modern psychology, with Freud and behaviorism, has laid siege to the fortress of rationalism. Contemporary political science, attacking the tradition of natural law, has declared the doctrine of natural rights

87

to be merely a persuasive slogan of an outmoded ideology. Economists and social scientists, questioning the radical individualism of libertarians, have raised doubts about even the possibility of a free and open market place of either commodities or ideas. The self-righting process has been widely rejected as a notion without foundation in reality; and free exercise of the individual will has been forcefully attacked as often harmful to the community.

Moreover, critics assert, certain social forces and certain developments within the media themselves have so altered the environment of public communication that the media cannot be and cannot do what libertarian theory prescribes. Most critics cite the three forces described in Chapter 3—the rise of democracy, the economic and technological revolution that produced America's modern industrial culture, and the continuing urbanization of American life. Some mention the development of markets for mass consumption of the mass-produced and the development of modern advertising, publicity, and public relations for the exploitation of those markets. All those factors, the critics say, have so transformed the character and functions of the media that much of traditional libertarian theory is either obsolete or misguided.

GRAFTING NEW THEORY ONTO OLD

Like its predecessor the social-responsibility theory is a composite of ideas. In one sense its ideas, beliefs, and values have been grafted onto the roots of traditional theory. For instance, social responsibility accepts the libertarian functions of enlightening the public, servicing the political system, and safeguarding civil liberties. However, it reflects the belief that the media have not performed those tasks as capably as they should in a modern industrial democracy. The social-responsibility theory also accepts the functions of servicing the economic system, providing entertainment, and making a profit; but it would subordinate those tasks to the more important ones of promoting democratic processes and public enlightenment. Thus the social-responsibility theory accepts the six social functions traditionally assigned to the media. However, it does not accept the ways in which some owners and operators have interpreted those tasks or the ways in which the media in general have fulfilled them.

In another sense the social-responsibility theory is quite new. Its major premise is that freedom, including the freedom of the press, cannot be defined apart from a responsibility for its exercise. The media, which enjoy a protected and privileged position under American laws and customs, have an obligation to society to carry out certain essential functions in a complex, modern industrial democracy. If the media assume their responsibilities and make them the basis of operational policy, remedies may be unnecessary to ensure the fulfillment of contemporary society's needs. But, as some social-responsibility theorists warn, in the areas where the media do not assume those responsibilities, other social agencies, including government, must see that the essential tasks of mass communications are carried out.

The First Amendment to the Constitution made no demand that publishers accept responsibility in return for their freedom, and the framers of the Constitution intended no such demand. To them, as to all libertarians of the time, freedom of the press meant the right to be true or false, fair or unfair. The aim was to promote untrammeled discussion, tempered only by reason and conscience. There was no need to exact responsibility, for the system carried its own built-in correctives. In the free play of ideas and opinions open to the inspection and judgment of rational men, truth would inevitably arise victorious, and society would inevitably progress.

The twentieth century, however, has brought a gradual shift away from that radically individualistic conception of freedom of the press. Somewhere between the bitter partisanship of the early press and the ostensible objectivity of modern communication, faith diminished in the happy notion that unrestrained liberty, coupled with man's reason and conscience, would assure a press adequate to society's needs. Some readers began to demand higher standards of press performance, threatening to enact legislation if the media did not meet those standards. In part as a response to these criticisms, publishers began to link responsibility with freedom. And, over the years, a remarkable change took place in the media's definition of free expression.

A NEW DEFINITION OF FREEDOM OF THE PRESS

Today publishers and broadcasters commonly speak of "the public's right to know" and "the responsibility of the press." This amounts to a shift in the theoretical foundation of freedom of the press from the individual to society. What was once looked on as a universal, personal right to free expression is now described in terms of public access, of the right to know.

It is hard to say exactly when publishers began to link responsibility with freedom. In the early days when publishers were mainly printers who ran newspapers as sidelines, they could scarcely be expected to give much thought to the ethics of journalism. And in later years when editors were frankly partisan and wedded to political interests, they could scarcely be expected to put the public interest above their own. By the middle of the nineteenth century, however, some newspapermen like Horace Greeley thought the newspaper should ignore the trivialities of the penny press and the political bondage of the partisan press. The newspaper should not be politically neutral; it should not serve any political party or faction; it should furnish political leadership by setting the public good above party allegiance. At mid-century, too, there were men like Henry Raymond of *The New York Times*, who thought that the newspaper should be free of party but not of principle, that it should give its readers the broadest possible coverage, and that it should actively promote the community welfare. Later in the century men like William Rockhill Nelson of the Kansas City *Star* saw the newspaper as an aggressive force for community betterment. In all those views there were traces of a growing sense of social responsibility.

In the twentieth-century, professions of public responsibility have become more numerous and more explicit. Increasingly publishers have spoken of the duties imposed on the press by its growing professional spirit and its important role in the progress of society. In 1904 Joseph Pulitzer took nearly forty pages of the *North American Review* to defend his proposal for a college of journalism. But, as more than a plea for journalism education, his article asked publishers to place duty to the public above duty to the counting room.

> Commercialism has a legitimate place in a newspaper, namely, in the business office . . . But commercialism, which is proper in the business office, becomes a degradation and a danger when it invades the editorial rooms. Once let a publisher come to regard the press as exclusively a commercial business and there is an end of its moral power.

Journalism needed moral and courageous men to give newspapers their ideals; for as Pulitzer put it, "Without high ethical ideals a newspaper not only is stripped of its splendid possibilities for public service, but may become a positive danger to the community."

As the decades passed, other publishers reminded their fellow journalists in similar words of the responsibilities that went with freedom. As newspaper ownership became increasingly concentrated and as the number of competing dailies declined, editors and publishers spoke of the special responsibilities of ownership in one-newspaper communities. In time movie-makers and broadcasters, too, picked up the theme of public responsibility.

Codes of Performance

This sense of responsibility has been represented by codes setting ethical standards for the media. In 1923 the American Society of Newspaper Editors, a national organization, adopted its Canons of Journalism, which call upon newspapers to act with responsibility to the general welfare, truthfulness, sincerity, impartiality, fair play, decency, and respect for individual privacy. The canons are more attuned to libertarian theory than are the codes of the motion-picture and broadcasting industries. The newspaper, some three centuries old when the code was adopted, was deeply attached to the liberal movement of the seventeenth and eighteenth centuries which led to the battle for press freedom. The newspaper canons share the libertarian's faith in the rationality of man and in his ability to find truth and to distinguish right from wrong by the power of his reason and the dictates of his conscience. The canons also share the traditional faith that the self-righting process will operate in a free market place of knowledge and opinion. What is new in the canons is their acknowledgment that freedom of the press carries a responsibility to the public welfare.

In contrast the codes of broadcasting are spiritually attached to the emerging values and beliefs of the social-responsibility theory. They reflect not only the intervening changes in intellectual and social climate but also the dark cloud of government intervention and regulation. The radio code of 1937 and the television code of 1952—both of which have been amended extensively—were written under conditions of existing government regulations, which required them in any case to perform "in the public interest, convenience, and necessity." These codes see broadcasting industries as devoted primarily to producing entertainment, although they do make some references to educational functions. The codes also reflect the changing image of man as not altogether rational in his behavior and as highly susceptible to moral corruption. The broadcasting codes are largely concerned, as a matter of social responsibility, with promoting public morals and conforming to accepted standards of good taste in programming and advertising. Only as if by afterthought do they deal with promoting democracy by enlightening the public.

The movie code, which was written in 1930, was merely negative, and set minimum standards of acceptability, not of responsibility. Then, late in the 1960s, movie-makers began to ignore most of the provisions. The industry amended the code to emphasize a system of rating movies to prevent the very young from attending movies designed for adults.

All this attention to codes and rating systems, of course, is a sharp break with libertarian theory. It is in much closer harmony with the assumptions and goals of the social-responsibility theory.

The Commission on Freedom of the Press

Changing attitudes of newspaper owners and managers toward the functions and operations of the media reflect a general drift in the direction of collectivist conceptions of reality, of man, and of society. However, not until 1947, with the report of the Commission on Freedom of the Press, were those attitudes and conceptions organized into what amounts to a new, integrated theory of the press. The commission, a group of distinguished private citizens headed by Robert M. Hutchins, conducted its studies with money provided by Time, Inc. and Encyclopaedia Britannica, Inc. Social-responsibility theory is spelled out in *A Free and Responsible Press*, compiled by the commission as a whole, and in *Freedom of the Press: A Framework of Principle*, written by William T. Hocking, a commission member.

Most publishers and broadcasters criticized the social-responsibility concept defined in those volumes. However, the concept is significant for two reasons: It reflects a conviction that contemporary thought and the conditions of modern society have outmoded libertarian theory. And it suggests a direction that future thinking about the press may take. Already, despite disavowals, much of the theory has found its way into the ideology and behavior of the mass media.

The commission listed five things that contemporary society requires of the press. Together they provide a new conception of what the media should be and do, as well as a measure of their performance. Ironically these requirements did not originate with the commission; it drew them largely from the professions and practices of the most responsible of those who operate the media.

Truth and Meaning in the News

The first requirement of the media in contemporary society, according to the commission, is that they provide "a truthful, comprehensive, and intelligent account of the day's events in a context which gives them meaning." The media should be accurate; they should not lie. Moreover, they should identify fact as fact and opinion as opinion and should separate the two as much as possible. In simpler societies, the commission says, people could often compare accounts of events with other sources of information. Today they can do so to only a limited degree. Therefore, it is no longer enough to report *the fact* truthfully—as, for example, an accurate account of a statement made by a politician. It is now necessary to report *the truth about the fact*—presumably the motives and interests of the politician and the political situation in which he made the statement.

The media themselves appear to agree with the commission's dictum that they should be accurate and should separate news and opinion. Most newspapers try to adhere to the principle of objective reporting and to relegate expression of opinion to the editorial page. Quite apart from the newspapers' growing sense of professionalism, of course, economic considerations have led to the development of objective reporting. The omnibus newspaper, which seeks to attract everyone and to alienate no one, has found in the technique of reporting events and ideas without comment or interpretation a way to have its cake and eat it too. But philosophical principle was also involved. By separating news and opinion, by giving opposite sides of an issue, by reporting without comment what happened or what was said, the newspaper saw itself as helping the self-righting process by making it easier for the reader to discover the truth. Broadcasters took much the same view of their interests and responsibilities. Newscasters, depending heavily upon wire-service copy turned out according to newspaper standards, seldom violate the principle of objectivity deliberately. There are exceptions, of course, just as in the newspaper columns. But most newscasters, when they do make comments on the news, are careful to label them as such and to separate them from straight news.

With respect to the commission's demand that the media tell the "truth about the fact," the situation is somewhat different. Many newspapers and broadcasting stations are reluctant to go beyond telling what happened or what was said. To give the reader or listener the facts necessary to an understanding of the *why* would be to run the risk of introducing bias and distortion into the straightforward account of events as they happened, of statements as they were uttered. In addition, to give the background of events and put them into context can be costly, not only in manpower and time but in audience reaction. The major elements of the newspaper's market might not find the "truth about the facts" palatable, even if it were attainable. Nevertheless, increasingly, many media leaders are promoting "interpretative" and "depth" reporting. In public-affairs reporting, interpretation is widespread.

Common Carrier of Ideas

A second requirement of the media, says the commission, is that they serve as a forum for the exchange of comment and criticism. What this means is that the media should regard themselves as "common carriers" in the realm of public discussion, even though not subject to the legal obligations of such common carriers as railroads. The commission does not expect the media to give space or time to everyone's ideas; but without giving up their own proper function of taking a stand, they should, as a matter of policy, carry views contrary to their own.

Behind this requirement is the concentration of media ownership in fewer and fewer hands. The individual citizen finds access to the facilities of public expression more and more difficult. Therefore, the media must act as a common carrier of viewpoints that otherwise might not find public circulation.

On this requirement, too, the media seem to agree with the commission—even if they oppose the prescription for access to the media proposed by Jerome Barron (cited in Chapter I). For example, Norman Isaacs, former managing editor of the Louisville *Times,* has written: "The one function we have that supersedes everything is to convey information. We are common carriers. The freedom of the press was given for that purpose—and that purpose alone." Another newspaperman, Grove Patterson, defined one of the social responsibilities of the press as making sure that "newspapers are representative of the people as a whole and not of special interests." The failure of some editors, publishers, and owners to make their papers truly representative of the people lies in their erroneous belief that freedom of the press belongs to them alone, he said, and added, "A free press is vastly more than a meal ticket for publishers."

Broadcasters, too, speak in their code of exerting every effort to ensure equality of opportunity in the discussion of public issues. The television code suggests that stations "give fair representation to opposing sides of issues which materially affect the life or welfare of a substantial segment of the public."

The media, of course, could be expected to oppose laws compelling them to accept all applicants for space and time or any move by government to regulate their rates. Likewise they could be expected to oppose anyone who demanded, as a right, that they disseminate his ideas. Broadcasters fought bitterly against the necessity to carry commercials against cigarettes—and later the ban on cigarette advertising. Commercial motives in these cases were at least as important as principles. But in principle and in broad practice, especially in recent years, the media accept the commission's conception of their role as common carriers of news and views. This makes sense on two counts. It helps the media to appeal to as many people as possible in their audiences. And it helps them to circulate ideas that would not otherwise gain access to a mass audience.

In 1970 CBS President Frank Stanton announced a revolutionary concept based on a recognition that any President of the United States carries an authority, a prestige, and a visibility that give him crushing advantages over his political opposition. Stanton pointed to the rising curve of appearances of the last four Presidents on prime-time network television during the first eighteen months of their administrations: Eisenhower, three times; Kennedy, four times; Johnson, seven times; Nixon, fourteen times. Clearly, Stanton said, under Nixon the advantages of the Presidency "have been pressed to an unprecedented degree." Stanton applauded the "direct and unfiltered access" of the President to the people, pointing out at the same time:

> But if the words and views of the president become a monolithic force, if they constitute not just the most powerful voice in the land, but the only one speaking for a nationwide point of view, then the delicate mechanism through which an enlightened public opinion is distilled, far from being strengthened, is thrown dangerously off balance. Public opinion becomes, not informed but instructed, and not enlightened, but dominated.

To avoid this danger, Stanton said, CBS had developed a concept of "Loyal Opposition." This meant that the network and its affiliated stations would allow the principal opposition party free network time to present its views. He did not specify how often time would be made available, but he did say that he and his colleagues had considered offering the time to members of the House and Senate who represented the opposition party, but then had ultimately decided that the offer should be made to the national committee.

It is not yet clear how great an impact this will have on national politics, but political television is so obviously influential that the effects are likely to be profound. Certainly the plan for making time available to the party that does not hold the Presidency is in keeping with the requirement that the mass media serve as a national forum.

A Representative Picture of Society

The third requirement is that the media give a representative picture of the various groups that make up society. That is, they should portray accurately all social groups and not perpetuate stereotypes. Media performance in this area has been tragically weak. The commission urged that the media take into account each group's values and aspirations as well as its weaknesses and vices.

Philosophical reasons for such policy are difficult to find in libertarian theory, which assumed and approved of social as well as intellectual competition, of the conflict of group interests and wills. Reasons for this policy may be readily found, however, in the ascendant twentieth-century conceptions of man, of society, and of freedom. For these conceptions emphasize social equality over personal liberty, foreswear the ruptures caused by social competition, and seek to socialize individual interest and will.

Clarification of the Goals of Society

The fourth requirement offered by the commission is that the media present and clarify the goals and values of society. The commission does not suggest sentimentalizing and manipulating the facts to create a rosy picture. Rather it asks for realistic reporting of the events and forces that work against social goals as well as those that work for them. The media are an educational instrument, perhaps the most powerful one we have; therefore, they must "assume a responsibility like that of educators in stating and clarifying the ideals toward which the community should strive."

Putting aside the question of whether educators would agree, media practitioners seem to accept this requirement with little hesitation. Despite isolated objections from time to time, the media meet this requirement quite naturally. True, their content is in conflict regarding goals and values, especially in the political and economic areas. But the majority show a strong tendency to close ranks when the traditional goals and values of society are at stake. In fact, many who are dissatisfied with what seem to be the goals of American society argue that the media are altogether too eager to support the traditional values.

In general, most news columns, editorial pages, magazine articles, radio and television shows, and feature films tend to support and reinforce the accepted goals and values of society. Whether the values expressed in the underground press and other instruments of challenge and dissent will ever replace some of the majority values is not yet certain. But there are strong reactions against sudden change: There is the natural tendency of men to conform, and there is also the practical necessity of pleasing the customers. But some influence can be attributed to honest, more or less independent belief in the commonly accepted goals and values of American society. In any event both the principle and the practice encouraged by the commission's recommendation clearly run counter to the radical individualism and competitive ethos of the libertarian tradition.

Full Access to Information

The final requirement that the commission urges is that the media provide "full access to the day's intelligence." The citizens of a modern industrial society, the commission says, need a far greater amount of current information than people needed in any earlier time. Even if the citizens do not always use all the information they get, the wide distribution of news and opinion is essential to government carried on by consent. Moreover, information must be available to everyone because leadership changes so often and so freely that any citizen may suddenly find himself holding the power of decision.

Media leaders surely agree. They are eager, for economic reasons, to reach as wide an audience as possible, but they also accept the obligation that the social-responsibility theory imposes of maintaining what the commission calls "freedom of information." As the media sought to conquer larger and larger markets and became more and more imbued with a sense of social responsibility, the idea that the public has a *right* of access to information, a basic right to be informed, became a foremost tenet of editors, publishers, and broadcasters.

This social-responsibility doctrine represents a break with traditional thinking in two ways. First, libertarian theory assumed that full access to the day's intelligence would be the natural consequence of a free and open market place of knowledge and opinion. No provision was made for guaranteeing the flow of information when individuals chose to be silent. But of what benefit is the right of free expression without full access to the information that ought to be conveyed? Hence, the media see themselves as active agents in breaking down the barriers of secrecy and silence. The American Society of Newspaper Editors, the journalism fraternity Sigma Delta Chi, and other professional groups have formed committees to champion the public's right to know and to help open up the sources of news at all levels of government. Such respected journalists as James Reston, James Pope, and Erwin Canham have warned repeatedly of the dangers to democratic government of censorship by suppression of information.

Second, libertarian theory saw the media as instruments of individual—as opposed to public—will and interest. In principle no person was barred from either acquiring or using the media for individual ends. Indeed, libertarian theory encourages the selfish use of the media on the assumption that conflict in ideas, as in society, is of itself good. Today, however, the media are more and more seen as instruments of public, rather than individual, will and interest. With their operation and ownership resting in fewer and fewer hands, the media are exhorted to act as agents not of the individuals who own and manage them but of the public, which bestows freedom.

What we have said here may seem to be lavish praise for the media. We do not argue that a sudden burst of human kindness is transforming mass communication from free-swinging libertarianism to social responsibility. Indeed, we suspect that just as the free press grew as much out of the clash of contending interests as out of philosophic ideals, social-responsibility theory is growing as much out of fear as out of high-minded principle. The threat of action by citizen and government has motivated some media operators to more responsible performance.

Moreover, we do not argue that all the media are socially responsible by any standards other than their own. Although spokesmen for the media talk of socially responsible performance, many critics say that the media are largely responsible to the Establishment and to traditional goals; and this argument has some validity, but we can gain an insight into what it represents by recalling the anecdote about the parson, the geologist, and the rancher who were gazing upon the Grand Canyon for the first time.

"One of the wonders of God," said the parson.

"One of the wonders of science," said the geologist.

"What a hell of a place to raise a cow!" said the rancher.

It does not satisfy those who are acidly critical of the media to point out that there are many views of responsible performance, many perspectives on responsibility. But what is important is that media leaders now speak of their responsibilities as often as they speak of their rights. Whereas those who would change the media once had to persuade publishers and broadcasters that they had responsibilities, they now need only argue what those responsibilities are. The difference is significant.

MEDIA COUNCILS

To help the media interpret and fulfill their social responsibilities, mass media councils may be widely established in the United States, as they have been in Europe. As the 1970s began, about a dozen local councils were operating in cities across the United States. Although some served only newspapers, a few were concerned with all the local media. All the councils had a similar function: to meet periodically—usually monthly or quarterly—to assess the performance of the media and to advise responsible representatives of local newspapers and broadcasting stations how council members thought the media could improve performance. Often the meetings were more educational for the council members than for the media; some citizens began to learn for the first time what the mass media are and what they are designed to do in a democratic society.

European nations have used media councils for decades. Sweden formed the Press Fair Practices Commission in 1916 to serve as an intermediary between press and public. About fifteen other European nations have since set up councils or courts of honor, with the British Press Council probably the most famous and successful. In most of Europe, the council is considered as a protector of freedom of the press and as a channel for dialogue between the newspaper and its readers. J. Edward Gerald of the University of Minnesota has characterized the effective overseas press council:

(1) It is a private body designed to ward off government pressures upon the press.
(2) It operates as a buffer between the press and the public and between the press and the government.
(3) Its membership is composed of balanced representation of the community and the media.
(4) It has no statutory power and relies on public support after reporting its deliberations and decisions.
(5) It appears to function best in nations where newspapermen avoid all forms of extremism.

In the United States the first suggestion for press council operations seems to have originated in the 1930s with Chilton R. Bush, then head of the Department of Communication at Stanford. He conceived the notion that a newspaper could strengthen itself and its community by establishing a council of citizens who would offer criticisms and suggestions. He developed the idea and promoted it among publishers.

In 1950 William Townes, then publisher of the Santa Rosa, California, *Press Democrat,* decided to try it. Townes chose the members of his "Citizens' Advisory Council" to represent community interests, such as labor, agriculture, education, city government, business, and to include a few outspoken critics of his policies. After telling the council members at the first meeting that he alone would decide publishing policies, Townes emphasized that he would welcome criticisms and suggestions. After a hesitant period at the beginning of the first meeting, the members engaged in lively discussions. Townes spent most of his time listening. It was not even necessary for him to defend his paper against its harshest critic, a judge who had been asked to serve on the council because he was known to oppose the paper, for the other council members were quick to challenge unfounded criticisms. Until Townes left Santa Rosa, he kept the council in operation and said it had helped him to improve his paper. *Editor & Publisher,* the trade weekly of the newspaper business, commented in 1951:

. . . On the practical side, this particular newspaper reports that Council meetings revealed several important stories that had not been covered. And Council members felt free to visit the newspaper offices thereafter, something many of them might not have thought about previously.

This is an experiment in getting closer to the community which strikes us as valuable. The good points out-weigh the bad, and if conducted properly and regularly can only result to the benefit of the newspaper.

Nonetheless the press-council idea languished in the United States until 1967. It was then that Ben Bagdikian became president of the Mellett Fund, one of the smallest foundations. The Fund was established with a bequest from Lowell Mellett, who had been editor of the Washington *Daily News*, an adviser to President Franklin Roosevelt during World War II, and a syndicated columnist. Part of his estate went to the American Newspaper Guild, and he directed that the money be used to encourage more responsible performance by the press without infringing First Amendment freedoms. He specifically mentioned the hope that his bequest could be used to establish "a relationship between the people and the press whereby full responsibility for its behavior would be met by the press."

These words led Bagdikian to suggest to the Mellett Fund Board that the $40,000 it had in 1967 be used to support university researchers who would establish local councils. A series of small grants led to council experiments in small cities in Oregon, California, and Illinois, and to the setting up of media councils in Seattle and St. Louis. These, in turn, stimulated other councils that were not the direct result of Mellett Fund grants. Some of those who participated in the Mellett Fund councils became enthusiastic proponents of the idea and helped to encourage the establishment of councils in other cities. Robert W. Chandler, editor of the Bend, Oregon, *Bulletin*, the first editor to agree to participate in the Mellett Fund program, was instrumental in convincing newspapers in Hawaii to set up a council. It began operating in 1970. Later, Minnesota newspapers set up a statewide council.

How far the council idea will spread, and whether it will lead to regional councils—or even to a national council—is not yet certain. At this point it is clear only that councils can serve a distinctively valuable purpose in bringing representatives of the mass media together with the public.

EDUCATION FOR RESPONSIBILITY

That schools and departments of journalism and communication have been deeply involved in many media councils is a measure of their expanded role and suggests their attention to the need for socially responsible media. In their early years the schools concentrated largely on supplying the demand for newspaper staff members. Today the best of them provide a professional education, not merely technical training—and many have substituted in their titles "communication" or "communications" to reflect broader and deeper concerns. Most of them give students an overview of the entire range of human communication even as they place their primary focus on the mass media.

Nearly all the schools have broadened their offerings to include more than preparation for newspaper work. Their graduates now go into public relations and public information and take positions with broadcasting stations as script-writers, announcers, newscasters, directors, or producers. Still others make careers on magazines—general, technical, trade, professional, company-sponsored—as writers and editors, often after starting as editorial assistants. Some graduates, combining journalism with a speciality, have gone into agricultural journalism, home economics journalism, and medical journalism. Some go into positions in many phases of advertising; with agencies as copywriters, layout specialists, researchers; with retail stores and mail-order firms; with newspapers; broadcasting stations; and magazines, both general and specialized. In short, the schools of journalism and communication have come to serve all the media.

In the past twenty years graduate as well as undergraduate instruction has, in some cases, reflected a broadening of outlook. Few schools offered academic instruction beyond the master's level before World War II. The University of Missouri awarded its first doctorate in journalism in 1934, to be sure, and a few other institutions offered a journalism minor in combination with a doctorate in some other field, such as political science.

Since World War II about twenty schools have established doctoral programs in communication. Most of these programs have attempted to apply the methods and disciplines of the various social sciences to the basic problems of communication. They cover such areas as the communication process, the philosophy of communication, policies and structures of communication systems, and public opinion and attitude formation.

Similarly communication research has flourished during the last twenty-five years. Before World War II there was comparatively little research, and only a handful of men associated with schools and departments of journalism had earned national stature as scholars. For the most part research in the mass media was left to those in other disciplines—political science, psychology, sociology, for example—who became interested in communication problems as an outgrowth of their other studies. As Wilbur Schramm has observed, communication was a crossroad where many passed but where few tarried. Today some schools that are unable to afford elaborate research departments have at least one staff member whose primary assignment is research. And a few schools or colleges support research centers, among them Stanford, Michigan State, the University of Minnesota, and the University of Illinois. Most of these are dedicated to an interdisciplinary approach to the problems of both interpersonal and mass communication; staff members, who may represent such academic specialties as anthropology, economics, linguistics, psychology, and sociology, have a professional commitment to communication research.

Most of the educational programs for undergraduates demand that no more than twenty-five per cent of the student's time be devoted to journalism courses, thus allowing him the full scope of a broad education. Journalism and communication students now have the opportunity to learn about the responsibility as well as the skills of the mass media while studying the arts and sciences as well.

Education for Mid-Career Journalists

Opportunities for working journalists to return to the campus for special studies began in the 1930s with the Nieman Fellows Program at Harvard. For decades there was little more than that. Then in the late 1960s the Ford Foundation made grants to Stanford, Northwestern, Columbia, and the Southern Regional Education Board to establish educational opportunities for other working journalists. Programs of study ranging from three-day seminars to a full academic year are operating successfully. Many of those who have participated in these programs argue that such programs are essential if the mass media are to meet the challenges of the 1970s and beyond. It is doubtful that a communication system that can truly be termed socially responsible is possible without education that will help the journalist obtain a wider view of the world.

The Media
and Government
The Early Experience

Do you gentlemen who control so largely public opinion, do you ever think how you might lighten the burdens of men in power—those poor unfortunates
weighted down by care, anxieties, and responsibilities?
LINCOLN to a correspondent

One day in 1690, a printer in a Boston printing shop, using a deerskin swab tied to the end of a stick, inked some forms of type, screwed down the wooden platen on a wooden press, and pulled off a copy of Benjamin Harris' *Publick Occurrences*. That was the first newspaper attempted in the American colonies. A two-column affair of four pages, one of them blank, it was dedicated to recording "Memorable Occurrences of Divine Providence."

Anticlimactically, *Publick Occurrences* died with its first issue. Its quick death resulted from ideas then current about the press. The paper offended authorities, presumably with a story about brutalities committed by Indian allies of the Colonial military forces. The authorities responded by forbidding publishers to bring out printed materials without first getting permission from the government. Such censorship rested on the right of colonial governors to control the press on instructions from the British crown. It was consistent with a firmly established idea about the press: It should be controlled to serve the interests of the government in power.

This is much more than a mere incident from history. It is central to understanding the American experience. For a prime consideration in assessing the role of the mass media is the heavy hand of official authority.

The need for newspapers in the new land was clear, but their growth was severely retarded by the attitude of government. Although the Colonies were originally established by trading companies and other independent groups, the trend was toward making them royal wards. Strong control over the press was exerted by governors and other authorities. Since the Puritans governed Massachusetts Bay, the first two presses in the Colonies were controlled by the church and turned out religious tracts and official printing. An effort to set up commercial papers in the middle of the seventeenth century resulted in a law providing for a board of three members to license the press and to examine all material before publication. In Philadelphia, where the Quakers were firmly in control, the first publisher was William Bradford, who published laws and almanacs—and showed everything to the authorities before publication. Then in 1689 he published a speech by a critic of Quaker policies. Although he was acquitted by a jury, Bradford's presses were for a long time kept in custody.

Not until 1704 was a publisher, John Campbell, able to establish and maintain a private paper of continuous publication. His *Boston News Letter* succeeded only because Campbell promised never to offend the government.

The colonists controlled the press by methods that had been used in England, although even there some were losing their effectiveness. The threat of prosecution for treason seems to have been a potential but little-used instrument; however, the Colonists did import one strong English control: a ban on reporting the meetings of Parliament. This method seems to have been much used; and sessions of the Colonial legislatures were closed to the newspapers.

Threat of prosecution for seditious libel as a means of control also was imported from England to the Colonies, where it was administered by Colonial courts. In general, seditious libel was any published material that, without lawful justification, cast blame on any public man, law, or institution established by law. Its scope was wide, and truth was no defense. In this country seditious libel was resisted earlier than it was in England. Juries, as in the case of John Peter Zenger in 1735, refused to bring in verdicts of guilty. While their reluctance did not change the law, it reduced the effectiveness of seditious libel as a means of control. Seditious libel probably was no serious threat to Colonial editors after about 1735.

Taxation, used as a means of control in England, was never imposed extensively on the newspapers in this country. It was tried, primarily as a means of obtaining revenue, under the Stamp Act of 1765, but it met with strong resistance.

THE PRESIDENTS AND THE PRESS

One revealing way to look at the relationships of the media and the government is to consider how this country's leaders have treated the media. Let us devote some attention to the men—especially those who became Presidents of the United States—whose careers tested their beliefs in freedom of the press.

The role the framers of American democracy foresaw for the press bears some resemblance to the way the system has actually worked. But that may be less a tribute to the vision of the founding fathers than it is a commentary on their attempts to subvert it. For if anything is clear about press-government relationships throughout our history, it is this: in theory, America's leaders have wanted a free and independent press as a check upon government; in practice, they have wanted no such thing.

The theory is quite clear. By carefully refraining from setting up an official information system within the government, and especially by granting freedom to the press in the First Amendment, the founders asserted their belief that an independent information system is central to democracy.

How greatly the founding fathers valued the theory of a free press is suggested by George Washington's ringing, "Sir, *concealment* is a species of misinformation." So convinced was General Washington of the value of the press that he issued a plea to patriot women asking that they save all available material for conversion into paper for printing.

James Madison was as emphatic, and a good bit more philosophical in viewing the role of the press: "Knowledge will forever govern ignorance. And a people who mean to be their own governors must arm themselves with the power knowledge gives. A popular government without popular information or the means of acquiring it, is but a prologue to a farce, or a tragedy, or perhaps both."

All this was the laudable theory. The government would carry on its actions; a free and independent press would report, comment on, and investigate those actions. The only trouble was that those who propounded the theory were unable to live with it. The result has been fascinating interplay between America's leaders and the men of the press. At times in our history, government and press have been the most savage adversaries imaginable, and at other times they have been such sweethearts that much of the press has been incorporated into the machinery of power.

The gap between theory and practice has been apparent from the beginning.

Washington and Jefferson

The Constitutional Convention of 1787 was held in secret. One day a delegate carelessly mislaid his copy of the proposals. It was found and turned over to George Washington, the President of the Convention. Washington appeared to ignore it, but as the meeting was adjourning for the day, he stated grimly: "Gentlemen, I am sorry to find that some one member of this body has been so neglectful of the secrets of the convention as to drop in the state house a copy of their proceedings, which by accident was picked up and delivered to me this morning. I must entreat gentlemen to be more careful, lest our transactions get into the News Papers and disturb the public response by premature speculation."

Secrecy in government soon took on the color of doctrine. One of the most enduring official concepts, Executive Privilege, was established in 1792, when a committee of the House of Representatives was investigating the "St. Clair Disaster," one of the most resounding defeats in battle in American history. Major General Arthur St. Clair's troop, which was camped at the headwaters of the Wabash River, was attacked by Indians and lost six hundred men. The House committee called for the original letters and instructions bearing on the expedition. Washington and his Cabinet rejected the request and replied:

> We had all considered and were of one mind 1. that the House was an inquest and therefore might institute inquiries. 2. that they might call for papers generally 3. that the Executive ought to communicate such papers as the public good would permit, and ought to refuse those the disclosure of which would injure the public.

But Washington was eager for the public to read news that reflected credit on his Administration. He said to Alexander Hamilton regarding the Farewell Address: "The doubt that occurs at first view is the length of it for the News Paper publication . . . All the columns of a large Gazette would scarcely, I conceive, contain the present draught."

Realizing that they cannot win popular support without a communication system, and having no such system in the government, officials have always sought to use the press. For decades their method could be best designated as "the party press." When one faction established a newspaper as its party organ, another retaliated by imitation.

While a member of President Washington's Cabinet, Jefferson led the opposition to Hamilton's Federalists, who had already established the *Gazette of the United States* at the new capital in Philadelphia. Eager to develop an editorial voice for anti-Federalism, Jefferson tried to enlist Philip Freneau, a talented journalist who had become famous as "the Poet of the Revolution."

Freneau declined the first offer. Lamenting the rejection, Jefferson revealed in a letter to Madison how much favoritism he was ready to bestow on an editor who would echo Jefferson's own views: "I should have given him the perusal of all my letters of foreign intelligence & all foreign newspapers; the publication of all proclamations & other public notices within my department, & the printing of all laws . . ."

Later the itch for a newspaper that would speak for him led Jefferson to woo Freneau by letter again: "The clerkship for foreign languages in my office is vacant; the salary, indeed, is very low, being but two hundred and fifty dollars a year; but it also gives so little to do as not to interfere with any other office one may chuse . . ."

The sinecure lured Freneau. He established the *National Gazette,* which immediately became the loudest anti-Federalist voice and the most incisive critic of President Washington. The attacks were "outrages on common decency," President Washington protested. He questioned Jefferson closely regarding Freneau's reason for coming to Philadelphia. Jefferson replied that he had lost his translating clerk and had simply hired Freneau to replace him. "I cannot recollect," Jefferson told Washington, "whether it was at that time, or afterwards, that I was told that he had a thought of setting up a newspaper." In any case, Jefferson pointed out, he could control his employee in the clerkship, but Freneau was a free agent in editing the *National Gazette.*

Washington did not ask that Freneau be fired, but he could not control his anger. Jefferson described a scene that developed during a Cabinet meeting shortly after Freneau had published a scalding satire:

> The President was much inflamed, got into one of those passions when he cannot command himself, ran on much on the personal abuse which had been bestowed on him, defied any man on earth to produce one single act of his since he had been in the government which was not done on the purest motives, that he had not repented but once the having slipped the moment of resigning the office, and that was every moment since, that *by God* he had rather be in his grave than in his present situation. That he had rather be on his farm than be emperor of the world and yet they were charging him with wanting to be king. That *that rascal Freneau* sent him three of his papers every day as if he thought he would become the distributor of his papers.

Jefferson seized the publicity initiative as soon as he became President-Elect in 1800. The Nation's Capital was being moved from Philadelphia to Washington, and Jefferson persuaded young Samuel Harrison

Smith to set up his newspaper shop there by luring him with printing-contract patronage. It was a blatant exercise of news management, but there was a reason for it. Jefferson was so vilified by the opposition press that he once suggested editors categorize the contents of their papers under four chapters: Truths ("The first chapter would be very short"), Probabilities, Possibilities, and Lies.

The party press dominated political journalism from the beginning of the Jefferson Administration. The President had other favorites—he once wrote to William Duane, editor of the wild *Aurora*, asking for "an exact list of the prosecutions of a public nature against you, & over which I might have controul"—but Smith's *National Intelligencer* was the dominant source of Presidential news. It was an efficient system. There were no Presidential press conferences and no Presidential interviews. Other editors were forced to rely for information on partisans like Smith.

How effectively such tactics worked is suggested by the success of the party organ, the *National Intelligencer*, when Jefferson became President. The editor of a rival newspaper, the *United States Telegraph*, announced that he had hired a Washington correspondent:

> We congratulate the readers of the *United States Telegraph* upon an arrangement by which the editor is able to obtain earlier, and he trusts *more full and accurate* information of the proceedings of Congress and the measures of government, than can be had from the Washington papers. We have hitherto been obliged to depend principally upon the *National Intelligencer* for reports of the proceedings of Congress; a paper which is conducted with very considerable ability, but with very little candour, inasmuch as the wishes of the president and his particular friends must be consulted in whatever representations are there made . . .

The minimal value of out-of-Washington newspaper correspondents in the country's early days is suggested by the fact that the *Telegraph's* man lasted only a few months. He could report on Congress, but could find no avenue to the Presidency, and he was soon reduced to reading the *National Intelligencer* to determine what Jefferson was up to.

None of the next three Presidents—James Madison, James Monroe, or John Quincy Adams—could manage the news as astutely as Jefferson. Madison and Monroe, however, did continue to use the *National Intelligencer* as party organ; Adams used a new paper edited by Peter Force, the *National Journal*. Adams revealed the extent of his control over the paper in this entry in his diary: "P. Force called to say that Mr. McLean, the Postmaster-General, was desirous of publishing in the *National Journal* an article in answer to a published letter addressed to him by J. Binns in the Democratic Press. I told him I could have no objection to this . . .."

Andrew Jackson

Presidential control of information reached its zenith under President Andrew Jackson. He subscribed to twenty newspapers, dictated to almost as many, and led "King Mob" to the Capital and elevated journalism to a visible force in government. Despite its power the earlier status of journalism had been suggested by William Cullen Bryant: "Contempt it too harsh a word for it, perhaps, but it is far below respect." But this image was to change quickly. In the judgment of historian James Schouler, "Jackson was the first President who ruled the country by means of the newspaper press."

President Jackson surrounded himself with newspapermen, among them Amos Kendall, an able Kentucky editor who became the leader of the "Kitchen Cabinet." One Congressman later said of him, "He was the President's thinking machine, his writing machine, aye, and his lying machine." Another newspaperman, Duff Green, had proved his friendship for Jackson during the Presidential campaign by fabricating a story that President and Mrs. Adams had had premarital relations. Jackson asked Green to "remove to Washington and become the organ of the party."

Green's *United States Telegraph* was the first Jacksonian organ, and for a time it served the President well. But Green developed a strong liking for the ambitious and magnetic John Calhoun. Administration leaders urged the President to replace Green. Always fiercely loyal, the President would not, but Kendall persuaded him to bring in Francis P. Blair to establish another Administration paper, the Washington *Globe*.

Jackson was never content to have only one organ grinding his tune. For a time there were fifty-seven journalists on the government payroll, and both Green's *Telegraph* and Blair's *Globe* carried the Administration line. But it was soon apparent that Blair was to be *the* official spokesman. A rival editor described him as "one who must be believed when professing to act by *authority*." Only six weeks after the establishment of the *Globe*, there was no doubt that Jackson would be a candidate for re-election; Blair had written: "We are permitted to say that if it should be the will of the nation to call on the President to serve a second term in the Chief Magistracy, he will not decline the summons."

Blair visited the White House almost daily, usually bringing a jug of milk from his farm at nearby Silver Spring. He and Jackson would lounge and drink and discuss Administration policy and *Globe* strategy. They shared the direction of both. Back in his office, Blair would translate the President's ideas into fiery editorials. In the White House an assistant who came to the President with a sticky problem was likely to be directed to "Take it to Bla'r" or "Give it to Frank Bla'r—he knows everything."

Anti-Jackson factions feared the cruel hook of Blair's satire. In time they learned to fear his devious system for spreading the influence of his paper. Blair would write pro-Jackson essays and editorials, plant them in small rural newspapers, then reprint them in the *Globe* as "indications of public opinion."

The Congressional Dilemma

Meanwhile Congress, which had opened its doors to the public in 1795, found it far more difficult to use the press. Dominant factions maintained a degree of control by awarding printing contracts to key Washington papers and by holding secret sessions. But the leaders were never able to shroud entirely the fishbowl of Congressional debate. For years reporters prowled about the Senate chamber at will, many of them taking down minute-to-minute stenographic accounts. In this atmosphere only the most adept Congressmen could compete in the area of public opinion with Presidents who were adroit at managing the news.

It was almost impossible for a member of Congress to promote a clear national image. Even Henry Clay—daring, magnetic in debate, a thin, molten figure before a crowd and a man greatly gifted at exciting intense personal enthusiasm—could not fight through the network of newspaper animosity and draw enough of the people to him to win his golden ambition, the Presidency. For a Senator might find his speech described by a friendly reporter as "full of marrow and grit, and enunciated with a courage which did one's heart good to hear. No mealy-mouthed phrases . . . but strong and stirring old English, that had the ring of true metal." But then another newspaper would publish a savage description: ". . . a soft, catlike step; a keen, snaky eye; a look and address now bold and audacious, and then cringing and deprecatory; his whole air and mien suggesting a subdued combination of Judas Iscariot with Uriah Heep."

To add to the complications, some of the correspondents of that time were eminently bribable. One critic charged that the principal mission of correspondents in Washington was to negotiate terms with "those who stand in need of newspaper assistance." With the President controlling some and bribing others, it was no wonder that independent Congressmen found it difficult to put together a coalition of newspaper support that would allow them to move out of their provincial constituencies and onto the national stage.

Decline of the Party Press

Significantly the end of the era of Presidential government and the beginnings of Congressional government began with a change in the press, which came soon after the Jackson Presidency. His successors—Van Buren, Harrison, Tyler, Polk, Taylor, Fillmore, Pierce, and Buchanan—were seldom able to manage either the press or Congress. There was little they could do; Presidential control of the news was gradually eroding. Powerful dailies had grown up in many cities, and now their editors were sending probing reporters to Washington. By 1841 James Gordon Bennett, publisher of the New York *Herald*, was spending $200 a week to maintain a corps of Capital correspondents that was abler than the entire staff of any newspaper published in Washington. Bennett himself, who had earlier been a Washington correspondent, conducted the first recorded Presidential interview, a conversation with Martin Van Buren. The dyspeptic commander of the powerful *Herald* was not a man a President could ignore.

The Associated Press also contributed to the decline of tightly controlled Presidential news by establishing its first Washington correspondent in 1843. When the colorless Presidents who followed Andrew Jackson named their party organs, these little Washington dailies and weeklies were powerless in competition with the Washington bureaus and the AP reports. It was a situation made to order for the stentorian editors of nineteenth-century America.

Abraham Lincoln

Two events of 1860 dealt the death blow to the party press. The Government Printing Office was established, all but destroying the printing-contract patronage that fed so many Washington newspapers—and President-Elect Lincoln arrived in the capital. Lincoln listened civilly to several editors who tried to persuade him that their papers should be his official journals. Then he rejected all offers. This was altogether characteristic of his shrewd approach to shaping opinion through the press. Lincoln refused to adopt an Administration organ because he saw that the Washington papers were impotent and because he realized that tying himself to one newspaper would restrict his dealings with others. He owed political debts to many a publisher, having used the press from the beginning of his political career—even working anonymously as a correspondent for the *Sangamon Journal* while serving in the Illinois Legislature.

He was most deeply in debt to Joseph Medill of the Chicago *Tribune*. Their relationship dated back to 1854, when Lincoln appeared personally at the office of the *Tribune* to pay four dollars for a subscription. Medill met Lincoln then and, over the years, came to think of him as a great man. When the debates with Stephen Douglas made Lincoln famous, Medill circulated through Congress a ringing letter endorsing Lincoln for President. He pushed his candidate so relentlessly in the *Tribune* that Lincoln himself was disturbed. "See here," he said to Medill, "you boys got me up a peg too high. How about the Vice Presidency—won't that do?" Medill was adamant: "Now it is the Presidency or nothing."

As one of the founders of the Republican Party and the publisher of its strongest newspaper, Medill was in a unique position to promote Lincoln. He persuaded other party leaders to hold the nominating convention in Chicago in 1860, then took over the pivotal arrangement himself. He distributed all the available spectator seats to Lincoln's supporters and manipulated the delegate seating so that those who favored William H. Seward could not affect the votes of the undecided.

Medill confessed later with satisfaction.

It was the meanest trick I ever did in my life. New York was for Seward . . . It followed that the New York delegates were seated at one end of the vast hall, with no state for a neighbor that was not hopelessly for Seward. At the other end of the hall, so far away that the voices of the Seward orators could scarcely be heard, was placed Pennsylvania [the most important of the doubtful states]. Between Pennsylvania and New York were placed the Lincoln delegates from Illinois; also those of Indiana and New Jersey.

Medill himself sat with old friends in the Ohio delegation and tried to win them for Lincoln. At the end of the third ballot—before the totals were announced—it was clear that Lincoln was still three and a half votes short of the nomination. Medill coaxed an Ohioan: "If you throw Ohio to Lincoln, Salmon Chase can have anything he wants." Ohio switched four votes from Seward to Lincoln, and the nomination was in hand.

It is an unfortunate fashion in historical writing to picture Lincoln at bay, the press bent on bringing him down. And it is easy to find slashingly negative comments on his great speeches, the First and Second

Inaugural and the Gettysburg Address, in the partisan journals of that time:

> New York *Express:* The President holds out, except in words, mere words, very, very little of the olive branch . . .
> Richmond *Enquirer* . . . couched in the cool, unimpassioned, deliberate language of the fanatic.
> Trenton *American:* It is very evident . . . that he feels all the perplexity of his position and his incompetence to shape his own course.
> Hartford *Times:* This wretchedly botched and unstatesmanlike paper . . .

But it is also easy to find examples of high editorial praise for the same addresses:

> Philadelphia *American:* Its language is so direct, its tone so patriotic, its honesty so unmistakable, that all will feel the earnestness of its author and the significance of his words.
> Buffalo *Republic:* . . . certainly one of the most important addresses ever issued from Washington.
> New York *News:* . . . an able and statesmanlike document.
> Washington *Star:* . . . a state paper of great force and reasoning.
> New York *Courier & Enquirer:* The address is a noble one . . .

The truth is that in a time of a strong and savage press—a time of unavoidable and deep controversy for the American people—Lincoln came off quite well, largely because of his own insight. He knew the extent of the political power that resided in the great editors of the mid-nineteenth century, and he pointed out: "In this and like communities, public sentiment is everything. With public sentiment, nothing can fail; without it, nothing can succeed. Consequently, he who moulds public sentiment goes deeper than he who enacts statutes or pronounces decisions."

Lincoln was especially sensitive to the criticism of the greatest editor of the time, Horace Greeley of the New York *Tribune.* Greeley was often critical; the President was usually conciliatory. Lincoln once asked a Washington correspondent for the *Tribune* why the impatient Greeley—who often wanted what the President wanted, but faster—could not "restrain himself, and wait a little." The answer was noncommittal. The President sighed, "Well, I don't suppose I have any right to complain. Uncle Horace is with us at least four days out of seven."

Lincoln went to surprising lengths to win Greeley's cooperation. For a time the *Tribune* had a secret inside line to the White House.

The President would give information to Robert J. Walker, a special adviser in the Department of the Treasury, and Walker would pass it on to Greeley "for the use or guidance of the *Tribune*." Later, when the Civil War campaign of 1864 began and Greeley's editorial tone became sharp, Lincoln wrote to him: "I have been wanting to see you for several weeks, and if I could spare the time I should call upon you in New York. Perhaps you may be able to visit me. I shall be very glad to see you." There was no response. Lincoln turned to a mutual friend, praising Greeley and expressing regret that he had not named the editor postmaster, adding that he could have the position if Lincoln was re-elected. The editorial tone of the *Tribune* promptly became more favorable.

Lincoln also went far out of his way to placate the arrogant James Gordon Bennett, whose New York *Herald* was influential in Europe as well as in the United States. The President sent an emissary to Bennett—an editor named Thurlow Weed, who had a profound sense of political journalism. Weed persuaded Bennett to slant his editorials in Lincoln's favor. Later, when a *Herald* reporter who had been refused a pass down the Potomac by Secretary of the Navy Gideon Welles went over Welles's head to the President himself, Lincoln was in haste to oblige; he wrote Bennett a "private and confidential" letter of apology.

None of this should suggest that Lincoln made the basic mistake of surrendering to the powerful editors. He granted many of their requests and demands, but just when it appeared that he had capitulated, he would refuse a favor and ignore their editorials. Few editors realized how subtly Lincoln used them. The celebrated Emancipation Proclamation, for example, was as much a publicity weapon as it was a declaration of the national conscience, a fact that is emphasized by Lincoln's own account of having issued it two months after it had been written:

> Things had gone from bad to worse, until I felt that we had reached the end of our rope on the plan of operations we had been pursuing; that we had about played our last card, and must change our tactics, or lose the game. I now determined upon the adoption of the emancipation policy . . .

None of the nineteenth-century Presidents after Lincoln could match his subtle command of the press. During the period from Lincoln's death to the beginning of the twentieth century, there were many centers of press power over the United States, and no public official could hope to master public opinion for long. When Greeley made his try for the Presidency, he met such fierce opposition from some of his fellow journalists that he said later that he was sometimes uncertain whether he was running for the Presidency or the penitentiary.

The power of the press was still scattered in many clusters across the nation as the era of Theodore Roosevelt began. As Colonel Roosevelt, firing the horseless "Rough Riders" into their dash up San Juan Hill, TR had demonstrated how a leader with a flair for drama could over-shadow the comic-opera flavor of an absurdity like the Spanish-Ameri-can War. (Years later, Roosevelt himself commented, "It wasn't much of a war, but it was the best war we had.") As Governor of New York, he had promoted his many causes through twice-a-day meetings with the small corps of Albany correspondents. Then he was maneuvered into accepting the Vice-Presidency, where the Old Guard of his own Republican Party was happily certain his political career would die. But President William McKinley was assassinated in 1901—"Roosevelt luck," one of his despairing detractors called it—and TR, who had been chafing in the tranquillity of presiding over the United States Senate, was suddenly thrust into his sternest test as a shaper of public opinion.

The new President fixed shrewdly on two important facts. First, the great press associations, which served many papers of varying politi-cal persuasions, had been forced during the latter part of the nineteenth century to develop "objective reporting" so that any paper could safely use any story. Except for the few remaining yellow journals, the giant dailies that used dispatches from their own reporters in Washington had been shamed into reporting most political news with relative impar-tiality. The partisan publishers were relying largely on acid editorial pages to shape opinion. That was ideal for the theatrical Roosevelt, who knew quite well that a strong President can promote an indelible image through the news, whatever the editorials may say about him.

Second, the Age of the Reporter had been ushered in by romantic figures like Richard Harding Davis and by Lincoln Steffens, Jacob Riis, and the other "muck-rakers"—a term Roosevelt himself had coined—with the result that some of the power that had resided in the thundering editors and publishers back home was passing to the correspondents on the scene. The political reporters of TR's day were much more inde-pendently powerful than the newspaper "agents" of nineteenth-century Washington.

And so Theodore Roosevelt set about managing the news more adroitly than any President before him. The thrust of his method was high-level press agentry: both courting the correspondents and com-manding them. One day he saw a small group standing outside the gates interviewing departing visitors and ordered an anteroom set aside for reporters. This became the White House Press Room. He developed a subtly effective press conference, long before Woodrow Wilson estab-lished it on a formal basis, by regularly calling in the three correspon-dents whose reports were most widely circulated: David Barry of the

New York *Sun's* Laffan Agency, Charles Boynton of the Associated Press, and Ed Keen of the Scripps-McRae Press Association (now United Press International). Everything the President said was off the record, which allowed him a maximum range of comment and no responsibility for anything they used. The day Keen joined the group, Roosevelt loosed an especially virulent view of his own party's Old Guard, then made the system clear to the newcomer with: "If you even hint where you got it, I'll say you are a damned liar."

Roosevelt's press relations were always a fascinating mixture of apparent impulsiveness and tight control. He was, one correspondent wrote, "the master press agent of all time." He sometimes gave reporters the run of the White House and often overwhelmed them with news. When Lincoln Steffens had completed his exposés of corruption in municipal and state governments and turned to Washington, he was given open access to the Executive offices and a daily appointment with Roosevelt at the barber's hour. "I always came into the room," Steffens wrote, "primed with a question that I fired quick; and he went off." But one thoughtful correspondent, Charles Willis Thompson of the New York *Times*, has written,

> He was never interviewed, in any proper sense. He gave out many statements, some of them in the form of interviews, and sometimes, too, he was actually interviewed, but in such cases he always dictated the form the interview should take . . . he never said one word more than he had decided to say. Impulsive? The thousand reporters who have tried to catch Roosevelt off guard and make him say something he did not expect to say will laugh. . . .

William Howard Taft

It was one of the perplexities of American politics at the beginning of the Administration of William Howard Taft that he did nothing to win the Washington correspondents. Ponderous but genial, Taft was TR's hand-picked successor, with a full opportunity to learn from Roosevelt. Moreover, Taft had once worked as a reporter in Cincinnati and, when serving in Roosevelt's Cabinet, had been the favorite news source of many correspondents. While he was Secretary of War, they developed the habit of "going Tafting" every afternoon at four o'clock, and he often helped them dig news out of other Executive departments. An unguarded spokesman in those days, Taft sometimes had to be protected from himself. Once, when Taft had been especially outspoken, Arthur Wallace Dunn of the Associated Press urged him "to place the injunction of secrecy on us" to prevent "disastrous consequences to yourself." Taft was grateful then and again when he became the Republican Presidential nominee in 1908 and saw that many correspondents were passing up stories that might have hurt his chances. But his new relations with his old friends were forecast on Inauguration Day. Several correspondents called at the White House to pay their respects. A secretary said that Taft would not see them then and was not likely to be seeing them very often in the future.

Much later it became clear that this was no simple case of a new President going high-hat. To put it plainly, Taft was afraid. Always envious of Roosevelt, he knew that he could not match TR's confident command, and so he took the worst possible course—doing nothing. Archie Butt, who was an aide to both Roosevelt and Taft, wrote:

> There are a good many leaks about the White House. Neither the President nor his secretary gives out anything of real interest, nor do they understand the art of giving out news. In consequence, the papers seek their information from whatever source they can find and therefore print rumors which, if printed a month ago [during the Roosevelt Presidency] would have resulted in a clean sweep of the Executive offices. Not able to find out much of the political intentions of the President or his Cabinet, they are turning their attention to the class of news known as bedroom politics . . .

Into the vacuum came that which Taft feared most—criticism. TR, dismayed by his successor's floundering, prepared for what some correspondents termed "The Return from Elba." And for a time Taft's chief pleasure was reading the New York *Sun's* lampoons of Roosevelt. He would not even look at the critical papers. One night in 1911 when he asked for the New York papers and Mrs. Taft handed him the *World*, he snapped, "I don't want the *World*. I have stopped reading it. It only makes me angry."

"But you used to like it very much," said Mrs. Taft.

"That was when it agreed with me, but it abuses me now, and so I don't want it."

"You will never know what the other side is doing if you only read the *Sun* and the *Tribune*," she rejoined.

"I don't care what the other side is doing," Taft said.

It is easy to suspect that the turbulent Presidential politics of 1912, which had Taft opposed for re-election by TR as well as Woodrow Wilson, are a monument to his bewilderment about the network that forms public opinion.

Woodrow Wilson

Wilson's Presidency began with loud applause from the Washington press corps. Wilson inaugurated the formal Presidential press conference and announced this credo: "I, for one, have the conviction that the government ought to be all outside and no inside. I, for my part, believe that there ought to be no place where anything can be done that everybody does not know about . . ."

It was a laudable theory, but those correspondents who had experienced the shrewd manipulations of Theodore Roosevelt wondered whether a President following Wilson's policy of "pitiless publicity" could compete effectively with a Congress operating outside this enlightenment.

Wilson was not naturally suited to the public relations role he had established for his Administration. Actually, he was warm and human, a lover of vaudeville who once confessed that he also liked fishing, baseball, wrestling, and such intimate sports as running to fires behind clanging engines, gossiping with policemen on their beats, reading grisly crime stories, and watching dogs fight in the street. But none of this came across to the public. Wilson was outwardly a cold man, whose only excitements were intellectual. His phrases were stiff: "Open covenants, openly arrived at," "a little group of willful men," and the like. His approach to the Presidency was unrelaxed. He shielded his family from publicity and went to extravagant lengths to avoid informal pictures of himself. Photographers were not allowed on the White House grounds and were rebuffed when they sought to picture the President playing golf. Annoyed by their persistence, Wilson's Secret Service chief seemed one day to acquiesce, took them out to a "shack full of knotholes" near one of the greens where the President would be putting, and crowded them in. When their eyes became accustomed to the darkness, the photographers found that there were no knotholes and the door was padlocked. The President played undisturbed—and many a voter continued to think of Wilson as the epitome of austerity.

Meanwhile, the National Press Club, which at that time had rooms over Affleck's Drug Store, was becoming an informal home for Congressmen as well as correspondents. Great powers—among them Senator Thomas Gore of Oklahoma and Senator Boies Penrose of Pennsylvania—were letting their hair down in antic Press Club debates like the one that examined the question, "Resolved: That bow-legs are a greater menace to navigation than knock-knees." Later fourteen Senators and Representatives engaged fourteen correspondents in a spelling bee at the Press Club, and won. It was a time of growing comradeship between the men of the press and the men of Capitol Hill.

Many reporters retained their high regard for Wilson, but he soon demonstrated that he was not really willing to practice his theory of pitiless publicity. Like Taft he was supersensitive, and he blamed the correspondents for reporting criticisms of his Administration voiced by Congress. Resentment grew in the press corps when it became known that the President was, in private, a harsh critic of the reporters. "I am so accustomed to having everything reported erroneously," Wilson told Senator J. W. Stone of Missouri, "that I have almost come to the point of believing nothing that I see in the newspapers." He gradually withdrew into a shell of persecution. Press conferences were more widely spaced; then, as the United States was drawn into World War I, they were no more.

When Wilson returned to the publicity front after the war, the press corps demonstrated how strong it had become. Wilson was straightforward in promoting his League of Nations; Congress and some of the correspondents were not. Columnist Ray Tucker has described the way a small group of correspondents

> . . . conspired hourly with the "irreconcilables" and performed service far beyond the call of newspaper duty. They tipped off most of the Congressmen to Wilsonian statements and maneuvers, and started Congressional counterattacks before the War President could unlimber his orators. They wrote phillipics for the Borahs, Johnsons, and Reeds, cooked up interviews . . . carried on research into the League's implications, dug up secret material. Their dispatches bristled with personal hostility to the League, and carbon copies which they distributed to pro-Wilson writers affected even the latter's supposedly favorable articles. The covenant was defeated by the Senate press gallery long before it was finally rejected by the Senate.

It is easy, and perhaps right, simply to condemn the correspondents. But David Lawrence, Wilson's best friend and most devoted admirer in the press corps of the time, suggests that the President was largely at fault for his bad relations with the press. "They constituted a series of misunderstandings and unfortunate clashes," Lawrence has written. "The growing tendency in recent years in America to anticipate the news and to discuss future events or the processes by which conclusions are reached, were deeply resented by Mr. Wilson. His theory was that nothing in news until it was completed."

Harding and Coolidge

The Harding era was epitomized by the Pulitzer Prize chronicle of corruption written by brilliant, erratic Paul Y. Anderson (who was later to descend into an emotional whirlpool and commit suicide). First, Anderson's reports in the St. Louis *Post-Dispatch* pushed the Senate into a full-dress investigation of Teapot Dome. Then, during the hearings, he and other correspondents supplied many of the searching questions used by Senators Thomas Walsh and Burton Wheeler to cut through evasions in the testimony of Administration officials. In the end Warren Harding's name became almost synonymous with Presidential ineptitude.

This was, in a way, a surprising denouement. Harding, an Ohio newspaper publisher and United States Senator who liked being around reporters, was protected better by the press during his early days in the White House than any other President. He began well by restoring the press conference to the place it had during the early months of the Wilson Presidency. If he was a bit pompous in answering questions during the formal conferences, he won the correspondents with warmth and an openly friendly feeling after hours. He was an attractive man—"No one ever looked more Presidential," one reporter wrote—who privately confessed his limitations; he told the correspondents that he knew he could not be the greatest President but that he wanted to be the best loved.

Unfortunately Harding did not always know what he was talking about. He had been in office only a short time when he was asked during a press conference whether the Four Power Pacific Pact drawn up during the famous Washington Conference for the Limitation of Armaments involved the protection of the Japanese Islands. The President said that it did not. Actually it did, and Harding's answer raced around the world, creating an international sensation. Secretary of State Charles Evans Hughes, his chin whiskers bristling, rushed to the White House to get an official correction. Then he prevailed upon Harding to agree that only written questions submitted well in advance of press conferences would be answered. It was a crushing backdown for a President who was warmest and most expansive in talking to newspapermen.

Toward the end, as the correspondents and the Congress revealed more of the scandals of his subordinates, Harding seemed to withdraw from life. He died in 1923, leaving a memory of a man who had only gradually become aware that he had surrounded himself with thieves.

The Administration of Calvin Coolidge was a frustrating time for the Washington press corps. It is doubtful that Coolidge, the inert beneficiary of national prosperity, could have been affected by anything. He presided over a time of repose, napping often and boasting of sleeping soundly for eleven hours every night. It was dismaying for reporters on the lookout for an angle. As Leo Rosten put it, "The most striking characteristic about the new President was his lack of a striking characteristic."

Although the President was a little huddle of a man—Coolidge conquering the tense and controversial times that enveloped his successor is almost unimaginable—it is also true that he calculated his actions. Much later he revealed in his autobiography that a kind of philosophy dictated his tight-lipped image:

> Everything that the President does potentially at least is of such great importance that he must be constantly on guard . . . Not only in all his official actions, but in all his social intercourse, and even in his recreation and repose, he is constantly watched by a multitude of eyes to determine if there is anything unusual, extraordinary, or irregular, which can be set down in praise or blame.

Coolidge did little, and many correspondents simply ignored him. Raymond "Pete" Brandt of the St. Louis *Post-Dispatch* said that his group "never covered Washington in the 'Twenties. We covered the Senate. You wasted your time downtown." Those who were responsible for covering Presidential news inadvertently built the image of a man of strength and silence. Henry Suydam, who was then a correspondent for the Brooklyn *Eagle,* has written that President Coolidge would observe laconically, "with respect to a certain bill, 'I'm not in favor of this legislation.' The next morning Washington dispatches began as follows: 'President Coolidge, in a fighting mood, today served notice on Congress that he intended to combat, with all the resources at his command, the pending bill, etc.' "

Thus did the correspondents divert themselves in the quiet days of the Coolidge Era.

Herbert Hoover

The press corps reawakened during the Administration of Herbert Hoover, and for a time it mastered both President and Congress. It had been the custom in the Senate since the time of George Washington for reporters and spectators to leave the chamber during votes on Presidential nominations. But Paul Mallon of the United Press and his assistant, Kenneth Crawford (later a columnist for *Newsweek*), decided to destroy the system. They began checking with friendly Senators after the executive sessions and publishing the secret roll-call votes.

In 1929 President Hoover sent up to Capitol Hill a highly controversial nomination: Senator Irvine Lenroot of Wisconsin to be a federal judge. The senatorial votes on Lenroot's nomination were certain to affect the elections in a number of states in 1930; the Senate took extraordinary precautions to ensure secrecy. But Mallon made his usual rounds afterward and published the complete senatorial box score, which showed that several Senators had been talking one way in public and voting quite another way behind closed doors. Mallon was subpoenaed and questioned sharply by a Senate committee, but he would not reveal the sources of his information. The Senate gave up and has since virtually abolished executive sessions, having gone into executive sessions fewer than a dozen times in the last four decades.

Hoover's own relations with the correspondents were a carbon copy of Taft's. As Secretary of Commerce under Harding and Coolidge, Hoover had been the best news source in Washington, and he and the correspondents formed a mutual-aid society. Hoover gave the reporters what Paul Y. Anderson described as "a perfect gold mine of graveyard stuff"; and the reporters gave Hoover a national stature that no Secretary of Commerce since has been able to attain. Gradually, Anderson has written, newspaper editors and the American people came to believe "that Hoover knew more about the affairs of government and the actual condition of the country and the world than any other man in the administration." Hoover entered the White House on a wave of respect and liking—and promptly changed. Instead of continuing his impartial news policies, he began to play a few favorites among the correspondents—Mark Sullivan was a particular pet—and he did it so blatantly that they became known as "trained seals."

One Sunday afternoon when Hoover was relaxing at his mountain retreat on the Rapidan, news of a sudden development sent him racing back to the White House at sixty miles an hour—dangerous speed on the Virginia roads of those days. The White House correspondents, who were not allowed to stay at the camp, were at an inn several miles away and learned of Hoover's trip too late to catch up with him. But the next day *The New York Times* carried a front-page story on the President's breakneck run to the White House. Convinced that there had been a leak from his staff, Hoover ordered the Secret Service to investigate. Then it became known that Turner Catledge of the *Times* had simply worked a problem in arithmetic involving the distance covered and the time consumed in making the trip and had written the story merely to emphasize the foreign-affairs emergency—but Hoover's fury strengthened in the correspondents their growing belief that the President had become a sour and resentful man.

Through much of his Presidency, Hoover's relations with the men who covered his actions were strained and humorless. The President invited publishers to the White House to complain about their Washington men and caused several correspondents to be transferred or fired. When leaks from his disenchanted subordinates reached print, Hoover announced that "only such news as is given out through the stated channels of the executive offices should be printed by the newspapers of the country." This was actually an effort to cut down on the leaks, but it had the clear implication that the Chief Executive should rule the press as well as his Administration.

Finally, unable to exert any control, Hoover resorted to clumsy lies. He required that press conference questions be submitted twenty-four hours in advance. Then, when he bypassed these pointed questions and was asked about them, he would say that he had not received them.

The most damning incident came in 1931, when Hoover denied knowledge of a letter from Governor Franklin Roosevelt of New York on negotiations with Canada for a St. Lawrence waterway project. Roosevelt promptly announced that he would make public his copy of the letter. Then Hoover admitted that the letter had been received but denied that he had denied knowledge of it and denied that there had been any negotiations. At that point many of the few friends he had left in the Washington press corps deserted him.

When panic grew after the Great Crash of 1929, Charles Michelson, a former New York *World* correspondent who had become publicity director of the Democratic National Committee, fired broadside after broadside at the hapless Hoover. Considering the President's ragged relations with the men who wrote about him day by day, it is not at all surprising that, having the option of using Michelson's charges or ignoring them, the reporters played them up. In Hoover's abortive re-election campaign of 1932, crowds booed him, men ran into the streets to thumb their noses at him, and the most widely repeated remark ran, "If you put a rose in Hoover's hand, it would wilt." The President became morose. He said not a word to his successor as they drove to the Capitol on Inauguration Day.

The Media
and Government
The Modern Experience

There aren't any embarrassing questions—just embarrassing answers.

CARL ROWAN

Modern political persuasion began with Franklin Roosevelt. Leo Rosten describes Roosevelt at his first press conference:

> His answers were swift, positive, illuminating. He had exact information at his fingertips. He showed an impressive understanding of public problems and administrative methods. He was lavish in his confidences and background information. He was informal, communicative, gay. When he evaded a question, it was done frankly. He was thoroughly at ease.

Henry M. Hyde, one of the oldest and most respected of the correspondents, termed it "the most amazing performance the White House has ever seen." At the end the correspondents applauded spontaneously—for the first time in Presidential history.

Eventually, however, Roosevelt's instruments of persuasion seemed to deteriorate. He was occasionally waspish during press conferences, assigning low percentages of accuracy to columnists with national fame, labeling two reporters as dunces and inviting them to stand in the corner, paying tribute to the educational value of radio and movies and ignoring newspapers—all in public. Arthur Krock wrote that the Roosevelt Administration used "more ruthlessness, intelligence and subtlety in trying to suppress legitimate unfavorable comment than any I know."

But Raymond Clapper, the most respected columnist of the time, pointed out that the working press judges Presidents as men, not as archangels. If the reporters were only 60 per cent for the New Deal now, he wrote, they were still 90 per cent for the President personally. Clapper gave specific reasons for Roosevelt's continuing high standing with the press corps: Their personal contacts were usually pleasant and intimate; Roosevelt's press conferences were almost certain to yield live news; the correspondents admired the President's political skill and craftsmanship, and even when they disagreed with his purposes, they generally believed in his sincerity, courage, and readiness to experiment. Finally the Rooseveltian theme of rescuing the forgotten man was a powerful lure for those who had investigated the real conditions of the American society.

The value of Clapper's insight became clear early in 1936. Several Republicans were jockeying for the opportunity to oppose Roosevelt in the Presidential election. Leo Rosten asked the correspondents: "Of the current candidates for President, who is your choice?" Roosevelt received fifty-four votes. His closest opponents, Governor Alfred Landon and Senator Arthur Vandenberg, received eight votes each.

Too little has been made of this, and too much of the "Fireside Chats." The President was stunningly effective over the radio—those full, confident tones that John Dos Passos called "the patroon voice, the headmaster's admonishing voice, the bedside doctor's voice that spoke to each man and to all of us." But there were few Fireside Chats: four in 1933, two in 1934, one in 1935, one in 1936. Roosevelt actually preferred to reach the people through the Washington correspondents. During that four-year period, when the President appealed to the people over the radio exactly eight times, he held three hundred and forty press conferences.

More should be made, too, of Roosevelt's shrewd use of his own expressive features. The thirties, one photographer has said, "marked the opening of a golden era for Washington cameramen. Roosevelt had a perfect sense of the dramatic and unusual." Newspaper and magazine editors clamored for any shot of that mobile and animated face. On occasion Roosevelt punished the newspapers for opposing him by restricting pictures. In 1935 he furiously banned all pictures for a short period because a birthday photo that was snapped when he had taken off his glasses and was rubbing his eyes had been captioned, "President Ponders Farm Problem."

As a rule only one kind of picture of the polio-crippled President was forbidden: He was never to be photographed in pain or discomfort. Once, with dozens of photographers around him, Roosevelt fell full-length on the floor. Not a picture was taken.

Otherwise anything went. The President was shown eating hot dogs, munching peanuts at a baseball game, kissing his wife when she returned from a tour, playing with his pet scotty, and—especially in the days immediately before he ran for a fourth term, when rumors were persistent that he was a very sick man—with his big jaw thrust forward, cigarette-holder clenched in his teeth at a jaunty angle.

There was much more to Roosevelt's domination of the news. At least part of the success of his Administration sprang from the work of his press secretary, Stephen Early. Unlike Herbert Hoover's inept and hesitant press men, Early was a seasoned wire-service reporter, who was given, according to another Presidential assistant, "one of the most important voices in the government." He not only worked with the President but also presided over a large and growing apparatus of public relations and information that was spread throughout the federal departments and agencies. The Roosevelt Presidency marked the firm establishment of government by publicity.

Federal press agentry had begun in a small way in 1910. Some of the members of a Congressional committee looking into the operations of the Census Bureau had been startled when the director confessed that "for about six months now we have had a person whose principal duty is to act as what might properly be called, I suppose, a press agent." This had been Whitman Osgood, a former reporter whose work had been thoughtfully disguised under the title "Expert Special Agent."

Soon after this disclosure, members of Congress themselves had begun to hire assistants whose principal duty was to act as what might properly be called press agents. Congressmen had always emphasized publicity, but it had been personal and somewhat erratic; Senator Pat Harrison of Mississippi was given to reminding his staff nervously, "Every day we don't get in the papers is a day lost." Congress had begun to fear that public-relations expertise in the Executive branch would help make the President dominant. And so in 1913 a bill had been passed, providing: "No money appropriated by this or any other Act shall be used for the compensation of any publicity experts unless specifically authorized for that purpose." The immediate target had been President Wilson, and the proviso had hampered him and his successors. But during the Roosevelt era it was little more than an invitation to subterfuge. Executive departments and agencies hired no "publicity experts"; they took on specialists in "public information" and "editing."

In the mid-thirties the fighting became intense, and a bit petty. Senator Vandenberg proposed that Senate approval be obtained before any Executive agency could use color printing in annual reports. Senator Harry Byrd of Virginia headed an investigating committee that turned up 270 public-information employees under the President's control.

Others were hired, one correspondent wrote, even as Byrd made his report.

All in all, by putting adroit emphasis on government publicity and by catering, cajoling, and lecturing the Washington correspondents in 998 press conferences, Franklin Roosevelt managed the news more artfully than any other President before him.

Harry Truman

It was not in FDR's successor to be either artful or devious. Harry Truman was so open and obvious that even the correspondents who respected his crusty strength sometimes found it difficult to remember that they were questioning the President of the United States. As Douglass Cater has observed, the language of a reporter tends to take on the flavor of the Chief Executive he questions. Truman's meetings with the Washington press corps resulted in some of the testiest press conference prose in history.

> REPORTER: Could you tell us anything about your conference with the Secretary of State and the Secretary of the Treasury?
> TRUMAN. No, it's none of your business.
>
> REPORTER: Would that mean, sir, that you would shake up the individual civilian end, service heads of the Navy Department, if this fight continues?
> TRUMAN: Not necessarily. I think it would work itself out. Just wait a little.
> REPORTER: I'll bet you two to one.
> TRUMAN: I'll take you on that. I'll take you on that.

Almost everything Harry Truman said emphasized his one great quality as President: he was positive. If he had an abrasive personality, and if he sometimes seemed to suffer from an inability to think consecutively, he always gave the impression of believing devoutly in himself, in his friends, and in his program. And his hardheaded and repetitious emphasis on his beliefs made news. He spoke, as one reporter put it, "the language of Main Street, and Main Street understands it—even to the grammatical errors and slurred words." The editorials were overwhelmingly against him, but a columnist who had no great admiration for President Truman noted sagely that the President had demonstrated one endearing quality: "He has more guts than a fiddle factory."

Specialists in the ghostly science of political measurements have laughingly criticized the press by listing all the newspapers and magazines opposed to Truman in 1948, adding up their circulation figures, and capping it all with a triumphant number: Truman's two million-vote margin over Thomas E. Dewey. This seems convincing enough as common-sense evidence, but it takes account only of *editorial* opposition to the President, ignoring the hurdy-gurdy, news-making campaign, in which Truman captured the information initiative.

While Dewey, the confident Republican nominee, was holding vaguely that "our streams must abound with fish," Truman attacked "the do-nothing Eightieth Congress." Only the most violently partisan newspapers gave their splashiest headlines to Dewey's platitudes. Most of the others, including a great many that promoted Dewey in long-winded editorials, played up Truman's salty speeches on page one. This is not necessarily paradoxical; some Republican publishers have an appreciation of news values that transcends their biases, and the counting-house mentality that afflicts others told them that "our streams must abound with fish" would not sell newspapers.

Throughout the campaign of 1948, Dewey, unaware that he was running way behind, seemed satisfied with his resounding victories on the editorial pages. Truman, who, like Roosevelt, often paid tribute to working reporters in the same breath he used to damn their publishers, preferred the news victories on the front page.

The focus on Truman the man was so relentless during his seven years as President that few noticed what was happening to the publicity apparatus he had inherited from Roosevelt. One who was alarmed by it was Congressman Christian Herter of Massachusetts, who wrote: "During the recent session of Congress our federal bureaucracy revealed itself as the most powerful and potentially the most dangerous lobby of all. It fought, bureau by bureau, every Congressional move to curb its innate desire to expand. Backed by its vast, tax-supported propaganda machine . . ."

By the end of Truman's Presidency, the machine had doubled. The Executive branch had 3632 employees working in the "Information" and "Editorial" Civil Service classifications, plus an unknown number whose titles were "Deputy Assistant Secretary for Public Affairs," "Administrative Assistant," "Executive Assistant to the Assistant Secretary," and the like. Senator Byrd, despairing of trying to decide who should stay and who should go, simply called for a general reduction of 25 per cent, hoping that such a cut would result in "more news and less bull from the federal publicity mill." Characteristically President Truman ignored him.

Dwight Eisenhower

How astute press agentry can overwhelm the Washington press corps is best revealed by the Eisenhower Presidency. And although it is doubtful that the President himself was responsible for many of the shrewd ploys made on his behalf, it is a mistake to assume that he was altogether unaware of the publicity methods used. Eisenhower had served for decades in the United States Army, where the struggle for status is often fierce and where the stakes are huge for an officer who can create a favorable image. In regard to military custom, it is revealing to cite the difference between an editorial as it was originally written for a military newspaper controlled by General Douglas MacArthur and the same editorial as it actually appeared in that paper. The writer, who apparently did not know of the rivalry between Eisenhower and MacArthur, wrote the version that appears at the left. The published version, as edited by officers more sensitive to MacArthur's wishes, appears at the right:

The words of General Eisenhower Tuesday at a dinner honoring the men of Russia, Britain, and the United States who fashioned victory in Europe illustrate something fundamental about this war.

The words were spoken by a man who commanded the most powerful, the most destructive army ever put on the field by the western allies. Yet not a single line extolled the glories of war . . .

The words of American generals, who along with their Russian and British colleagues, helped fashion victory in Europe, illustrate something fundamental about this war.

The words were spoken by men who commanded the most powerful, the most destructive armies ever put on the field in Europe. Crowds in London, in Paris, in Washington, in Chicago, in Los Angeles thronged to pay tribute to their achievements. Yet, in none . . .

When the Eisenhower Administration took over in 1953, it inherited most of Truman's publicists, who were secure in their Civil Service positions. Not trusting them with the Republican merchandising, Eisenhower's lieutenants added their own men. During Eisenhower's first four years, Executive information personnel nearly doubled: In 1957 the Civil Service Commission listed 6878 "Information and Editorial Employees." The increase continued during the second term, and Christian Herter, who had been aghast at the size of the Truman Administration's propaganda machine, eventually became Eisenhower's Secretary of State and presided unprotestingly over one of the largest cogs in that machine.

"Press agent" is too weak a word to describe the Eisenhower Administration's chief publicist, James Hagerty, just as the description of Hagerty by another correspondent as "the best Republican President who was never elected" is too strong. But Hagerty certainly demonstrated how a canny PR man creates an image for his employer.

Hagerty often made subtle decisions about which stories should involve the President. The news of the first successful United States satellite was released not from the launching site but from Augusta, Georgia, where the President was vacationing. Later, when White House reporters asked where they could learn whether an Army satellite that had been fired that morning had gone into orbit successfully, Hagerty answered, "If it is in orbit, we will have an announcement." A correspondent who had grown wise in the ways of the press secretary then asked whether the White House would release the news if the satellite failed. "No," Hagerty replied. The satellite did not orbit. The Army announced the failure.

Eisenhower's many vacations were common knowledge, but Hagerty blunted the edge of criticism by making it appear that each trip away from Washington was a working vacation. Once, when the President was golfing in Augusta, the press secretary announced the appointments of three ambassadors. The decision to appoint them had been made three weeks earlier, and the nominations were not to be sent to Congress until ten days later, but Presidential news was scarce, and Hagerty always aimed to keep Eisenhower on the front pages. It worked. Later in Augusta, Hagerty announced that Secretary of Labor James Mitchell would visit the President to discuss a bill protecting labor welfare funds. The bill had been introduced in Congress four months earlier, but the President again made the headlines.

Eventually all the correspondents who covered the White House during the Eisenhower Presidency became aware of Hagerty's methods, but there was little they could do. As Russell Baker, the perceptive "Observer" columnist of *The New York Times* pointed out,

> Hagerty's enduring contribution to the White House was his demonstration of how to exploit the weakness of the American newsgathering system for the promotion of his boss . . . If editors demanded a Presidential story a day, it follows that reporters will be found to satisfy them one way or another. On days when there is no news, they will poke around darkened rooms, look under the carpet, or start staring at the west wall and adding two and two in news stories. When that sort of thing happens, the White House is in trouble. Hagerty prevented this by seeing to it that there was rarely a newsless day. If there was no news, he made a little.

John Kennedy

In the spring of 1963, a newspaper publisher who had just received the latest Gallup Poll showing the country's attitudes toward its President exclaimed bitterly: "I just can't understand it. We've *ex-*

posed Kennedy. We've shown that he's been failing and lying to the American people . . . And yet they're making a god of him!

It was an understandable reaction, and not only because the publisher had been a whole-souled supporter of Richard Nixon. President Kennedy had just experienced the winter of his deepest discontent. His administration was failing the task it had set for itself in Laos and Vietnam. It had failed to get the country moving, while adding hugely to the national debt. Perhaps most important, government officials had admitted that, to put it gently, they had told less than the truth about the Cuban crisis of October, 1962. The whole orchestra had fallen downstairs at once; the critics were in full cry. And yet less than one fourth of the American people—exactly 24 per cent—disapproved of the way John F. Kennedy was performing as President.

A full view of the facts deepens the paradox, especially in view of the Administration's heavy-handed guides to reporting the Cold War. Secretary of Defense Robert McNamara set the tone shortly after he began his rule at the Pentagon. He had this plaintive question for correspondents who were revealing flaws in American weaponry: "Why should we tell Russia that the Zeus developments may not be satisfactory? What we ought to be saying is that we have the most perfect anti-ICBM system that the human mind can devise." That McNamara was simply arguing for false reports became clear when, shortly after suggesting that correspondents describe the Nike-Zeus program glowingly, he scrapped the program.

Then came the abortive Bay of Pigs invasion in 1961, only three months after Kennedy's Inauguration. Reporters were told at the height of the invasion that 5000 patriotic refugees were penetrating Cuba, when, in fact, a force of 1400 was involved. Like McNamara's guideline on Nike-Zeus, this was designed to mislead the enemy by misleading everybody.

In August, 1962, Senator Kenneth Keating of New York made his sensational charge that Russia was arming Cuba. In October he said that the Russians were building intermediate-range ballistic-missile sites for Castro. But White House, State Department, and Defense Department officials held that there was nothing to Senator Keating's charges. Only when the build-up in Cuba had gone so far that President Kennedy announced a quarantine on Cuba and issued an ultimatum to Russia, only then did the Administration admit that Keating had been right all along.

News management, and mismanagement, did not mar the Kennedy image for this simple reason: John F. Kennedy was one of the most sophisticated shapers of public opinion in Presidential history.

Kennedy's information policies were complicated—and sometimes contradictory—but their thrust was not to be found in the blunders of the beleaguered Defense Department. The center of information was the White House, and there the policy was the precise reverse of censorship. Never before had Washington correspondents been given so full a view of the President and the Presidency—they were invited to feel with Kennedy the crushing responsibility, and to be enveloped in the aura, of the greatest center of leadership in the Western world.

The value of this policy springs from the fact that a stark view of the Presidency is overwhelming. Talking to a President who has charm and toughness and keen intelligence, few newsmen will fail to admire him. More than anything else, the open White House enabled Kennedy—who had the awesome responsibility of deciding when or whether the world would end—to become the dominant source of news, explanation, and opinion.

Only a Washington correspondent who covered it during both the Eisenhower and Kennedy administrations can fully appreciate how profoundly John Kennedy revolutionized the reporting of the Presidency. The single innovation of the Eisenhower Presidency was the televised press conference, and these Eisenhower required to be filmed, so that they could be edited before release. In contrast, live television coverage of Kennedy's conferences was only one of many innovations.

Before 1961 the White House had been largely a closed preserve. Information was usually channeled through the President's press secretary, and some White House correspondents never so much as met some of the President's chief assistants. The almost invariable reply of Eisenhower assistants who were asked for interviews was "See Hagerty." One correspondent who arranged an interview with a Presidential speechwriter without going through the press secretary was so elated that he telephoned his editor to say, "I broke around behind Hagerty!" The important news was not the substance of the interview but the fact that he got one.

When Kennedy took over in 1961, correspondents wandered through the White House offices in such numbers that they created a traffic problem.

President Kennedy's staff did much to influence favorable press coverage, but the President was his own most effective promoter. He practiced personal salesmanship with the *élan* of one accustomed to establishing the rules of the game. Franklin Roosevelt granted one exclusive interview, to Arthur Krock of *The New York Times*. Harry Truman granted one, also to Krock. In both cases the storm of protest blowing up among other correspondents was so violent that neither President ever again granted such an interview. (Anne O'Hare McCormick of the *Times* spoke to Roosevelt privately and obtained authoritative views, but she produced nothing that could properly be described as an interview story. Krock has written that Truman granted one other exclusive interview but required that the source be veiled.) Eisenhower observed the protocol. But Kennedy, from the beginning, made such a fetish of giving exclusive interviews that his press secretary, Pierre Salinger, once observed that he often had to go to the President's office to get to see the White House correspondents.

Kennedy, James Reston wrote, broke every rule in the book:

> When he came into the White House, he was warned by his newspaper friends about all the wicked ways of the press, particularly their jealousy and their hostility toward anyone who gives special advantages to any individual reporter.
>
> The President indicated how seriously he took this warning at the very beginning of his Administration. After his Inaugural Ball, he suddenly showed up at Joseph Alsop's house . . .
>
> A few days later he drove around to Walter Lippmann's house for a talk, went to dinner at the house of Rowland Evans of the New York *Herald Tribune* and later had his old friend Charles Bartlett of the Chattanooga *Times* up to Hyannis Port for the weekend.
>
> When some of the President's associates asked the President whether this was wise, he took the original view that reporters were also members of the Human Race, and added that he proposed to see anybody he liked and even some reporters he didn't like.

Reston warned his fellow correspondents of the lure of the new order: "It is hard to go into that House that means so much to us historically and not be impressed with it and with the terrible burdens the President has to carry. How could you help but be sympathetic? Once you become sympathetic it becomes increasingly difficult to employ the critical faculties." Yet Reston himself, who had once boasted that he had never talked alone with a President during twenty years in Washington—having feared, he explained, that he might get "tied up"—yielded often to the lure of exclusive Presidential interviews. It is doubtful, however, that Reston, an exceedingly tough-minded man, got tied up for long.

Lyndon Johnson

The only law requiring that Presidents hold press conferences, Arthur Krock once observed, is the political law of self-preservation. Nothing better illustrates the point—or makes it more obvious that Presidents use the mass media for their own ends—than the stark difference between the press conferences of John Kennedy and Lyndon Johnson.

Kennedy was slender, handsome, magnetic, with a quick mind and an articulate tongue. He was ideally equipped for the mass conferences staged in the State Department auditorium—an auditorium so large that, to give the impression of a packed house, the television cameras were placed not at the rear but at the halfway point, with the correspondents crowded in between the cameras and the President. In the words of one correspondent, "Kennedy glittered—he positively glittered—up on that platform. No wonder he wanted live television!"

Johnson, whose political acumen in this instance curbed his ego, knew better than to match himself against the fresh memory of Kennedy's performances. Johnson is attractive in person, but he is also earthy, with more than a strain of vulgarity. In the company of sophisticates, he sometimes becomes aware of his cattle-and-tumbleweed manner. He once asked a friend, "When are you going to help me wipe this tobacco stain off my jaw?"

The kind of press conference Johnson preferred was apparent from the first. Two weeks after he became President, twenty-five of the regular White House correspondents went to the office of Press Secretary Pierre Salinger for what had been announced as a routine briefing. Suddenly they found themselves ushered into the President's office. It was a highly informal conference. Navy mess attendants served coffee; the President sat in a cushioned rocking chair at the head of two semicircular couches; the correspondents sat on the couches, sipping coffee and asking occasional questions to further the rambling flow of Johnson's conversation.

Ten days later Johnson held another surprise press conference that was almost as informal as the first. Then, during an extended work-vacation at the LBJ Ranch in Texas, he held no fewer than four impromptu conferences, one of them beside a haystack, another at a party given by the correspondents. He became wildly experimental. There was a conference in the old White House theater, another in the spacious East Room, another on the south lawn. The conferences became mobile: seven laps around the White House grounds. They became expansive: the reporters' wives and children were invited. Finally the Baltimore *Sun* asked somewhat plaintively, "Will the next press conference be tonight, tomorrow, or next week? Will it be held on horseback? In the White House swimming pool? Will the public be invited and the press excluded?"

The great value for Mr. Johnson of his spur-of-the-moment press conferences was that he faced only the White House correspondents, avoiding questions from the specialists who cover the rest of Washington—specialists who do not have a vested interest in remaining on good terms with the President. Another was that the intimate atmosphere of small conferences discourages embarrassing questions. The Bobby Baker case was at the height of interest during Johnson's first weeks as President, yet he was asked nothing about it during his first two meetings with the press. Perhaps the chief value for the President is that he can control an informal conference. Instead of submitting himself to a half hour of questioning in the Kennedy-type conference, which is controlled by the correspondents, the President can start and end as he likes. The importance of this factor became evident one Saturday two months after Johnson took office, when a rumor ran through the press corps that another impromptu conference was likely. By two-thirty that afternoon, more than a hundred reporters were milling about. The President waited until five to call them in. He alluded to the fact that he had heard complaints about "quickie conferences" and invited questions with what sounded like a warning: "I never enjoy anything more than polite, courteous, fair, judicious reporters, and I think all of you qualify." Then, after responding to a tentative question, he swerved into the Bobby Baker case and explained that his own involvement was innocent. Before the correspondents could pin down his exact relationship to Baker's deals, the President turned and walked out.

Not until his hundredth day in office did he schedule a traditional mass conference, after which James Reston commented: "President Johnson achieved his major objective in his first live television press conference: He survived."

It is not surprising that Johnson favored intimate, face-to-face meetings. Up close Johnson was overpowering. Ted Lewis of the New York *Daily News* has pointed out: "Johnson is formidably ingratiating— in private or semi-private gatherings. He easily dominates any group where he can look a man in the eye, grab lapels, poke chests, and talk about what happens to be on his mind."

Richard Nixon

Richard Nixon's strategy for relations with the mass media became apparent during his successful Presidential campaign of 1968. James Reston made clear what that strategy was:

> His television performances are masterpieces of contrived candor. He seems to be telling everything with an air of reckless sincerity, but nearly always in a controlled situation, with the questioners carefully chosen, the questions solicited from whole states or regions, but carefully screened.
>
> He is now complaining publicly about how he and Mr. Agnew are misrepresented in the columns of the New York *Times*, but he has been refusing to be questioned on the record by editors of the

Times and most other major newspapers ever since the very beginning of the campaign.

Mr. Humphrey and Mr. Wallace submitted to questions by CBS, but Mr. Nixon sent tapes of replies made in his carefully prepared broadcasts. And his refusal to debate Mr. Humphrey on television is merely one more incident in a long campaign of packaged broadcasts . . .

Another Reston column of about the same period pointed to an attitude that has afflicted Nixon throughout his career in public life:

Mr. Nixon has had more than the normal share of trouble with reporters, because, like Lyndon Johnson, he has never really understood the function of a free press or the meaning of the First Amendment.

Ever since he came into national politics, he has seemed to think that a reporter should take down and transmit what he says, like a tape recorder or a Xerox machine. He has learned to live with interpretive journalism more comfortably in this campaign [1968] than he did in the campaign of 1960, but he still suffers from this old illusion that the press is a kind of inanimate transmission belt which should pass along anything he chooses to dump on it.

When he became President, Nixon demonstrated the accuracy of Reston's judgments. He did not often submit himself to the adversary relationship of the news conference. Indeed, during his first two years in office, he averaged less than one meeting with the Washington press corps a month, about one-third as often as his three immediate predecessors. He preferred to go on national television with statements and not to respond to questions.

Unfortunately for the credibility of the Nixon Administration, reporters soon began to fix on its methods. When they were misled, they would quote Nixon's campaign attacks on the credibility gap of the Johnson Administration: "It's time we once again had an open Administration—open to ideas from the people and open in its communications with the people—an Administration of open doors, open eyes, and open minds."

But Nixon the President said in 1970: "Our plan to end the fighting in Vietnam as rapidly as possible consistent with achieving our basic objective of self-determination for the South Vietnamese people is well under way . . . Because of the need to maintain the security of this plan, certain information included in recent budgets does not appear this year."

By mid-August of 1969, so much doubt had arisen that *Newsweek* published a long catalogue of cases proving that Nixon's "open administration" was "suffering from an advanced case of closed doors."

There were signs, too, of a rebirth of the tough stance many reporters had adopted years before. After watching the Administration bow in quick succession to the American Medical Association, the American Pharmaceutical Association, and the Automobile Manufacturers Association—actually reversing decisions already made—one journalist remarked that Nixon would be in trouble with working reporters for a reason that has always been at the root of his policies: "He worries too much about the problems of people who own yachts."

One point of contention was the Nixon Administration's flouting of the Freedom of Information Act. Born as a result of years of lobbying by the press, and finally passed in 1966, the Act was designed largely to short-circuit the kind of secrecy so evident in the Eisenhower Administration. After Eisenhower wrote a letter to his Secretary of Defense commanding him not to present certain testimony before Senator Joseph McCarthy's investigating subcommittee on the ground of Executive Privilege, nineteen other federal agencies began to withhold information from the press, Congress, and the public on the same ground. Moreover, a section of the Administrative Procedure Act of 1946, which had been designed to make more information available, was actually being used by many Eisenhower appointees to conceal information.

Several members of Congress, led by Representative John Moss of California, began working in 1955 to write the Freedom of Information Act. By 1966 both houses of Congress had passed it, but it had been through the Congressional mill, and every lobbyist and government official who had a stake in concealing information had fashioned his own loopholes. Though not all of them succeeded, the law is nevertheless burdened with *nine* exemptions, some of them so broad and vague that they obscure more than they define. The one saving factor is that instead of requiring that the seeker of information prove his "need to know" before information is released (which was the old rule), officialdom is required to demonstrate a "need to withhold." Here the Administration ran into increasing trouble. For Nixon, like Eisenhower, chose to divorce himself for long periods from the day-to-day actions of government, failing to communicate not only with press and public but with his own officials as well. In the vacuum created by this aloofness, decisions were left to officials who do not know how far they can go or how much they can say.

Some tried to fashion their own loopholes. The commander of the Military District of Washington, D.C., attempted to withhold a letter that pressured liquor lobbyists and wholesalers to provide free drinks for 1200 guests at an Army party. His justification was the first exemption to the Act, which protects National Security Information.

Late in 1969 it became apparent that Vice President Spiro Agnew was to be the Administration's champion in its battles with the mass media. The first speech was delivered little more than a week after President Nixon attempted to explain his Vietnam policy on national television. Agnew's basic complaint was that liberal TV commentators had muted the effect of Nixon's address during the half-hour discussions that immediately followed the President's speech. Agnew's speech was vintage Nixon, emphasizing James Reston's point that Nixon believes the news media should act as an inanimate transmission belt, carrying anything he chooses to dump on it. In this case the networks had acted as a transmission belt carrying what Nixon had to say, and in a live broadcast. But the television reporters were hardly inanimate. It was this that aroused Agnew's—and Nixon's—ire.

There is rich irony in all this. For the "instant analysis" by the network reporters that seemed to Agnew so reprehensible was born, in part, of complaints from Richard Nixon and his friends. This can be traced back to June, 1957, when CBS broadcast an interview with Nikita Khrushchev, who was then the Soviet premier. So outraged were Eisenhower Administration officials that Khrushchev had been allowed to speak directly and at length to the American people that broadcasters, ever mindful of their precarious relationship to the federal government, took the advice of the most influential television critic, Jack Gould of *The New York Times*. He suggested that CBS had "many able and thoughtful commentators" and that "they should have been used immediately to analyze Khrushchev's words." Thus began the system of instant analysis that would cause Mr. Agnew such anguish.

Nonetheless Agnew's attack was effective. While his words were still reverberating, President Nixon appeared on national television for one of his infrequent news conferences. Immediately after the conference the commentators and analysts for commercial television appeared, talked at length, and said nothing. Instead of supplying the usual background information on the President's words and the closely reasoned analyses of those words, the commentators simply cited what Nixon had said.

What the television men should have been doing was demonstrated strikingly the next day by Tom Wicker of *The New York Times*. In response to criticism of reporters, Wicker asked: "What of the responsibility of Presidents to inform the American people accurately and fully?" He then cited the President's statement that the Marines had built this year "over 250,000 churches, pagodas, and temples" for the people of Vietnam and reported that the Marines had actually built 117 churches and 251 schools. The President misled the people again, Wicker said, when he answered a question about Laos by saying that there are no American "combat troops" there. In fact, as Wicker made clear, this was true only if one interpreted "combat troops" to mean those who fight on the ground. "There are Air Force pilots who drop bombs, and plenty of CIA agents and Army personnel who organize, train, accompany, and support native armies."

Wicker's catalog of President Nixon's misleading statements went on, but that is enough to demonstrate the point. Such revelations seemed only to excite new efforts to counter criticism from the media, especially television. It soon became known that White House staff members were carefully monitoring and judging television news shows. They even rated the networks:

> Most fair to the Administration: CBS (51 per cent of the time). Least fair: NBC (40 per cent). In the middle: ABC (41 per cent).
> Most favorable to the Administration: ABC (29 per cent of the time). Least favorable: NBC (15 per cent). In the middle: CBS (24 per cent).
> Most unfavorable: NBC (44 per cent of the time). Least unfavorable: CBS (25 per cent). In the middle: ABC (29 per cent).

NBC, according to the judgments of White House staffers, is the only network that "periodically becomes crusading and generates news tending to reflect unfavorably on the Administration." Reuven Frank, president of NBC News, commented, "My reaction to all this noise is that we ought to be doing more of it. I view it as a compliment."

Another dimension of news from government was revealed shortly after President Nixon sent American troops into Cambodia in 1970. So bitter was the reaction from the nation's campuses that the Administration decided to counter it by inviting expressions of opinion from any American who wanted to call the White House. Early one morning United Press International (UPI) reporters in New York made four calls to the special White House number that had been set up to record the votes for or against. Two UPI reporters who announced that they wanted to cast votes favorable to the President's action were switched immediately to someone who answered "White House." The other two callers, who said that they opposed the President's action, never got past the switchboard. The calls ran:

> UPI—"I'd like to register a vote for the President."
> WHITE HOUSE—"Yes, you certainly can."
> UPI—"This is the White House, I hope."
> WHITE HOUSE—"Yes, where do you live?"
> UPI—"New Jersey."
> WHITE HOUSE—"All right, thank you very much for your call."
>
> UPI—"Listen, are you taking votes?"
> WHITE HOUSE—"No, I'm not taking votes. Are you taking votes?"

UPI—"I'd like to register a vote against President Nixon."

WHITE HOUSE—"You're way late, where have you been?"

UPI—"You're not taking votes?"

WHITE HOUSE—"I'm not taking any votes and haven't been taking any votes."

UPI—"I'd like to register a vote for President Nixon's policy, please."

WHITE HOUSE—"You certainly can. Can I have your name, please?"

UPI—"James Coburn, Weehawken, New Jersey."

WHITE HOUSE—"I'll take a message if you want to give me one. Give it to me."

UPI—"I don't want to say too much except that I am thoroughly in agreement with everything the President has said."

WHITE HOUSE—"Okay, James, and we really appreciate that now, and I can tell you that he does too. Thank you very much."

UPI—"I understand you are taking votes and I'd like to say I'm against the President and Vice President Agnew too, and the policy. Can I register that please?

WHITE HOUSE—"You want to vote on the President?"

UPI—"Yeah, I'm against the President and against what he has been saying."

WHITE HOUSE—"This poll is being taken on the extension of troops into Cambodia and not on whether or not you're against the President."

UPI—"I'm against the extension of troops into Cambodia and against any more American troops going anywhere in southeast Asia."

WHITE HOUSE—"Where are you calling from?"

UPI—"New York City."

WHITE HOUSE—"From New York. Well, this office is closed here in Washington, it's almost six o'clock."

THE COSTS OF GOVERNMENT PR

As such incidents make clear, officialdom is far from defenseless in its combat with the news media. Results are sometimes rigged, as was clearly the case in the example above. And, whereas favorable reactions to Presidential decisions are usually reported ("Overwhelming; 10 to 1 for the President"), unfavorable ones are quite often not reported on the ground that the staff has had no time to tabulate the results.

The importance of favorable reporting is emphasized by the expenditure to achieve it. The federal government spends more than $400 million a year on public relations and public information. In fact, the federal Executive spends more on publicity, news, views, special pleadings, and publications than is spent to operate the entirety of the Legislative and Judicial branches. All together, federal expenditures on showing and telling American taxpayers are more than double the combined costs of news-gathering by the two major United States wire services, the three major television networks, and the ten largest American newspapers.

Some of this activity is designed to suppress information rather than to disseminate it. This became clear in 1970 when reporters disclosed that tens of thousands of Americans had long been engaged in combat in Laos, that about four hundred of them had been killed or were missing, and that the United States had spent more than a billion dollars in Laos—all in secret.

Vietnam is an especially revealing laboratory for studying government information. American and South Vietnamese officials have been trying for nearly a decade to persuade reporters, and through them other Americans, that the cause is just and that "We've got Charley on the run." Many have become so dedicated to this kind of persuasion that they are totally indiscriminate in deciding whom to persuade. In 1969 even Secretary of Defense Melvin Laird, next to the President the leading spokesman for the war, was taken in by a staged event. On one of his regular visits to Vietnam, Secretary Laird was treated to a 5000-man "mobile assault operation" carefully planned to seem fierce while attacking nothing. The operation was first scheduled to take place in another area, but the site was changed the day before Laird's visit because, an officer admitted, "one of our units had encountered enemy action." The operation went its harmless way, with Secretary Laird looking on from a helicopter above.

Some government persuasion at every level—city, county, state, and federal—has such a foundation of deception. Much more often, however, reporters and the public are misled by well-meaning officials who are so committed to their own policies and programs that they cannot view their own information policies from a wider perspective.

Speaking to the National Broadcast Editorial Conference in 1970, Senator Alan Cranston of California, a former journalist, made clear his dissatisfaction with television coverage of government. Some of the prescriptions he offered for improving it apply to the other media as well:

> Every instance of interference with the press by the Administration should be well publicized. The first few subpoenas to newsmen went unnoticed for several weeks last year because each publication and television network thought that it was alone and said nothing.
>
> There should be a national privilege law for newsmen.

Subpoenas damage a newsman's ability to gather news and should be issued only under carefully predetermined circumstances.

The proceedings of the House and the Senate should be open, within reasonable limits, to radio and television. And the House should follow the Senate's lead and open committee sessions. It is absurd to argue that the electronic media should cover government and then make it impossible for the media to use its primary tools.

There should be more commentary on television—especially commentary at the local level. It's one thing for a network commentator to appear on national television and discuss how an event effects the Nation. It is something quite separate, and equally important, for a local commentator to appear on local television and discuss the local effects of the same event.

News programs should be enlarged and there should be more time for explanation and background during the show. Several educational television stations are experimenting with an hour-long format that resembles a news meeting between an editor and a group of reporters. The results of the experiments have been very encouraging. I should think that a similar format might well be adapted to commercial television.

All newsmen should stay skeptical of politicians and government. Thousands of public relations men in Washington are cranking out press releases, manufacturing "news" and creating snazzy images for their bosses and agencies. As a result, the need for a skeptical, objective and thorough press corps is greater than ever.

Regulation
of the
Mass Media

> . . . freedom of the press is not an end in itself but a
> means to the end of a free society. The scope and
> nature of the constitutional guarantee of the freedom
> of the press are to be viewed and applied in that light.
>
> FELIX FRANKFURTER

In one of the Sunday sections which it devotes to reflective reporting, *The New York Times* printed not long ago a story headed, "It's Getting Hard Really to Libel Anyone in Public Life." The writer, Richard Phelps, analyzed several United States Supreme Court decisions and reported that the mass media are now substantially free of fear that public officials—or even those who do not hold office but qualify as "public figures"—can successfully bring libel action. It is possible for a public official or a public figure who has been defamed to recover damages, but he must prove that the defamation was a *calculated* lie, or that it reflected a reckless disregard of an effort to ascertain the truth.

This is a significant measure of the freedom the mass media enjoy, a freedom they enjoy in common—the electronic as well as the print media. We shall see in this chapter that the media do not share all the same freedoms equally.

To help develop a broad understanding of regulations that affect all the media, we sketch here the central freedoms and restrictions. This section owes much to the thought of Marc Franklin, Professor of Law at Stanford.

145

DEFAMATION

For centuries reputations were valued so highly that one who made false statements subjecting another to hatred, ridicule, or contempt, or caused him to be shunned, was required to compensate for damages. The reputations of private persons are, of course, still prized, and usually protected. But in the past two centuries the law has increasingly protected speech—sometimes regardless of its truth or falsity. Thus legislators, judges, and high executive officers are absolutely privileged to express themselves within the scope of their official duties, and when the media report their words, they, too, can escape suits for defamation.

Similarly the media enjoy a qualified privilege—"qualified" because sincerity is required—to comment on literary and artistic works. A critic's opinion of a work may be devastating, but it is protected.

In 1964 the United States Supreme Court extended protection in *New York Times Co. vs. Sullivan.* An advertisement in the *Times* that allegedly attacked an elected official of Montgomery, Alabama, included some defamatory inaccuracies. It is important to point out here that a communication medium may be held accountable if it prints or broadcasts defamation in an advertisement. In such cases the medium is usually sued, because it is likely to have more money than the advertiser. The Alabama courts, though holding that criticism of public officials was privileged, would not protect false criticism. The United States Supreme Court decided that this ruling unduly restricted the right to criticize government officials and hence violated the First Amendment. Professor Franklin has written:

> The balance articulated by the majority was that in such a case speech, although false, must be protected unless the speaker deliberately misstated the facts or recklessly disregarded the question of truth or falsity. In subsequent cases the Court has maintained its refusal to protect deliberately false defamatory speech, saying that such speech does not further rational discussion and is not a legitimate political weapon in our society . . .

PRIVACY

The doctrine of privacy began to develop in 1890 with arguments that the mass media be barred from communicating stories about events affecting ordinary citizens. In the early twentieth century, that argument provided a basis for holding the media liable for invasion of privacy. More recently the courts have increasingly held that the public's interest in learning about fellow citizens should be elevated. This is nearly always the case where the subject is a politician, a noted entertainer, or an artist, and where the subject is voluntarily or involuntarily involved in a newsworthy event.

In one case a onetime child prodigy named William Sidis was featured in a *New Yorker* article. Repelled by the publicity that had smothered him when he was a child, Sidis sued on the ground that his privacy had been invaded. But the court ruled, in effect, that he had been a public figure and still was.

FREE PRESS-FAIR TRIAL

If the mass media are free to print almost anything because of the protection of the First Amendment, can a defendant in a widely publicized criminal case receive the fair trial he is promised by the Sixth Amendment? That is the basic issue in a controversy that has for several decades involved spokesmen for the mass media and spokesmen for the bar. At the center of this issue, of course, is the possibility that a juror or a prospective juror may become biased by reports delivered through the mass media. Courts once tried to solve this problem by holding the media in contempt when they explored such questions as whether the defendant had confessed or had taken a lie detector test or had a prior criminal record. All such reports were deemed to injure the defendant's chance for a fair trial. But the focus now is on restraining communication by lawyers and law enforcement officials so that the media do not receive information that may damage the defendant.

The question of television in the courtroom has been answered this way by the United States Supreme Court: Given the present state of television technology and public reaction to the medium, a defendant's rights—at least in notorious cases—is violated by televising his trial over his objections.

The heart of this issue was summarized by United States Supreme Court Justice Tom Clark in a majority decision in the case of a swindler named Billie Sol Estes:

> These initial hearings were carried live by radio and television, and news photography was permitted throughout. The videotapes of these hearings clearly illustrate that the picture presented was not one of judicial serenity and calm to which petitioner was entitled. Indeed, at least 12 cameramen were engaged in the courtroom throughout the hearing taking motion and still pictures and televising the proceedings. Cables and wires were snaked across the courtroom floor, three microphones were on the judge's bench and others were beamed at

the jury box and the counsel table. It is conceded that the activities of the television crews and news photographers led to considerable disruption of the hearings. Moreover, a venire of jurymen had been summoned and was present in the courtroom during the entire hearing but was later released after petitioner's motion for continuance had been granted.

. . . Pretrial can create a major problem for the defendant in a criminal case. Indeed, it may be more harmful than publicity during the trial for it may well set the community opinion as to guilt or innocence. Though the September hearings dealt with motions to prohibit television coverage and to postpone the trial, they are unquestionably relevant to the issue before us. All of this two-day affair was highly publicized and could only have impressed those present, and also the community at large, with the notorious character of the petitioner as well as the proceeding.

NATIONAL SECURITY AND SECRECY

The media are usually involved only peripherally in cases in which free expression may result in the violent overthrow of government. Most often such cases involve a single speaker whose words may be deemed to suggest a "clear and present danger." In recent years, the United States Supreme Court has tended to turn from the "clear and present danger" test to a balancing approach first espoused by Judge Learned Hand of the United States Court of Appeals. Hand said that in each case the courts "must ask whether the gravity of the 'evil' discounted by its improbability justifies such invasion of free speech as is necessary to avoid the danger."

Another aspect of national security is access. As many spokesmen for the media point out, freedom to report may be meaningless if journalists cannot gain access to information—especially government documents and meetings of public bodies. They complain that security is used as a cloak to hide documents that should be made available and to close the doors to meetings that should be open.

Congressional committees and state and local governing bodies often go into executive sessions to keep their transactions secret. About a third of all meetings of Congressional committees are secret—some of them at the request of Executive branch officials who are to testify, notably in hearings involving foreign or military policy.

The increasing trend toward secrecy in government—at local, state, and federal levels—has resulted in counterthrusts from the mass media. Journalists have formed freedom of information committees in nearly every state to work for open documents and open meetings. Most such committees try to persuade the state legislatures to pass open-meeting laws like those in Florida, California, and Illinois.

GOVERNMENTAL NEED FOR INFORMATION

The need for access to information is a two-edged sword. Often government itself needs information, and officials have a weapon, the subpoena, which can be used to require a citizen who has information to appear and divulge it. Until recent years this power only infrequently affected the mass media directly. But in 1969 and 1970 federal officials in search of information regarding both civil rights activists and opponents of the Vietnam War began to subpoena journalists by the score and to require them to furnish notes and tape recordings of interviews and to supply the names of interviewees.

Such tactics brought an immediate reaction from all the media. Keeping some sources confidential has been a historic privilege that many journalists had taken for granted. Professor Franklin has written:

> Sixteen states have passed statutes recognizing this privilege, but in other states courts have found no common law basis for it, and efforts to give the privilege constitutional status, making it binding on all states, have failed. Despite the claim that this privilege would enhance freedom of the press by opening gateways to more news, the courts demand identification of sources even if this discourages persons from giving stories to newsmen, or, more likely, forces newsmen to accept imprisonment for contempt of court in order to keep sources confidential. Judicial skepticism may be based on ignorance of any professional standards, such as presumably govern churchmen, the bar, and the medical profession, that would keep newsmen from fabricating stories that need not be substantiated.

COPYRIGHT RESTRICTIONS

Because it is not often necessary for journalists to quote at length from copyrighted material, the laws protecting an author's works seldom affect journalistic practice. This is especially true because the courts have decided that copyright protects the concrete expression of ideas and facts—the exact words an author has used—but not the ideas or facts themselves. Thus, one may paraphrase with reasonable safety ideas or facts that have been copyrighted. Courts have also developed a "fair use" exception, whereby critics and scholars may take excerpts of reasonable length from copyrighted works in order to discuss and illustrate.

There is more concern for the copyright laws, of course, among those in the media whose chief function is providing entertainment rather than news and public affairs. The supply of good stories for films and television programs never meets the demand—nor does the supply of jokes and songs. The danger of encroaching on copyrighted stories is acute. At least once a year a suit is brought claiming that a famous humorist or composer has stolen the ideas of an unknown.

OBSCENITY

Professor Franklin calls this "a prohibition in search of a rationale." It is an acute judgment, for the government's interest in defining the obscene and removing it from constitutional protection is not clear. Does obscenity induce criminal and antisocial conduct? No proof has been offered. (The state's power to protect children to a greater degree than adults has long been evident, and perhaps no rationale is necessary for shielding children from what is termed obscene. Here, we are concerned with the shield for adults.)

The protection of the moral fabric of the community is often an implicit justification for banning what is thought to be obscene. Thus, obscenity is linked to the prohibition of private sex practices that the state defines as perverted. Thus, too, the ban on the obscene is linked to the protection of the American flag. A magistrate who was sentencing seven demonstrators involved in a flag-burning made clear that protecting the moral fabric of the community was his prime purpose when he said that although he could not teach anyone to love and respect the flag, he was "determined that they will respect the rights of others who do respect the flag."

Professor Franklin has written:

> Some have looked in the area of privacy to justify obscenity controls and have argued that the real objection is not to the material itself but rather to blatant sales promotion. This approach would put voluntary private sexual practices and discreetly circulated written matter beyond the reach of the law. The focus on this view then is essentially a variant of the time, place, and manner regulation. If the "moral fabric" justification is unacceptable, a focus on privacy would make irrelevant the impact on the public of mere awareness of the existence of disconcerting ideas unless that impact were linked directly to antisocial behavior. One observer has utilized the privacy approach to spotlight the interest of the recipient or consumer; he is willing to reject all claims of the seller to freedom of communication and con-

cludes that obscenity is really proscribed because it is viewed as "sin," an echo of the "moral fabric" argument. He then concludes that the punishment of sin is beyond the scope of our temporal law and is an invasion of the expanding interest in the privacy of the individual—at least so long as he keeps these matters to himself.

If we assume that there is some significant governmental interest that justifies prohibition of obscenity we must then define "obscenity"—though of course our definition might vary with the justification accepted. In its first effort, in 1957, the Supreme Court said that obscene material "deals with sex in a manner appealing to prurient interest" as well as being "utterly without redeeming social importance."

Subsequent cases have shown the difficulty of applying this standard and Justice Stewart was driven to concede that the term covered only "hardcore pornography," which he cannot define although he says he knows it when he sees it. While laymen may agree with this view, it is awkward for a judge to be unable to articulate principles or criteria to support his decision.

In the *Ginzburg* case the Supreme Court found obscene the advertising that was designed to sell the allegedly pornographic literature. Thus a distinguishing characteristic of the obscene became a suggestive and salacious sales pitch. The emphasis then began to fall on the circumstances surrounding sale and distribution rather than the words themselves. It is difficult to know how long the Court will pursue this line. It had hardly been established when the salacious became so central in much of American art and entertainment that Ginzburg's offense—judging either the advertising or the basic literature—was made to seem quite mild.

REGULATION OF ADVERTISING

Ginzburg, New York Times v. Sullivan, and many other cases make it clear that advertising is subject to court action, but there are other restraints. Indeed, according to the Advertising Advisory Committee to the Secretary of Commerce, more than twenty different federal agencies exercise some kind of control over advertising. The most important are the Federal Communications Commission, the Alcohol and Tobacco Tax Division of the Internal Revenue Service, and especially the Federal Trade Commission (FTC). They enforce legislation against advertising that is judged fraudulent, deceptive, or misleading; an unfair method of competition; or injurious to public safety or health.

The advent of "consumerism," the movement of outraged citizens to make business and industry live up to their warranties, promises, and other responsibilities, has put increasing pressure on these agencies to perform more capably. They have responded, but the appointment of a Special Assistant to the President for Consumer Affairs in the White House, the disclosures of Ralph Nader and his helpers, and the swelling ranks of consumer groups suggest the response has been inadequate.

There is evidence that the media themselves ban more advertising than do the regulatory agencies. A TV commercial for Stax, a hair preparation, showed a man and a woman caressing each other's hair with evident pleasure. Three stations canceled the commercial. *Advertising Age* recently commented, "There have been a couple of pretty suggestive television commercials and one or two moderately sexy ads in recent years, but on the whole advertising has been singularly strait-laced in comparison to almost anything. If you doubt this, compare the advertising content of television with the humor content of TV shows, or the advertising pages of any newspaper or magazine with the editorial content of the same publication."

In fact, the advertising departments of many publications and broadcasters are quicker to censor advertising than the news departments are to censor their fare. Thus, the Chicago *Tribune* will not accept ads that use such superlatives as "lowest prices," but the *Tribune* bills itself as "The World's Greatest Newspaper." The *Tribune* advertising department will not accept horoscope ads, but the news department runs a daily horoscope. The advertising department of the Denver *Post* inked in a higher bodice on a picture of an actress; the news department carried the same picture, untouched, on the same page.

DIFFERENCES IN REGULATION

If the media stand equally before the law in some cases, they stand at different levels in others. While our theories of freedom were evolving, the major media were the printed ones. The electronic media of the twentieth century—movies, radio, and television—brought new problems. How much freedom should be granted to media that appeal less to man's critical faculties than to his suggestibility? How much freedom should be given media that have entertainment, not information and discussion, as their chief objective? And how much freedom is it possible to grant to media, like radio and television, which are limited in number by the availability of channels?

To consider these questions, let us look first at the print media (briefly, because many of the preceding chapters have focused on print), then in greater detail at the electronic media.

The Print Media

As long as a publisher shows a decent respect for a few laws, he may do what he likes with his newspaper. If he opposes the Democratic candidate for President, the candidate's name can be stricken from the paper. If he hates golf, he can instruct his sports editor to forget that the game exists. If he visualizes thousands of little circles of family readers being offended by photos revealing the sex of naked animals, he can have his art department use an airbrush appropriately. The Democrats, the golfers, and the artists on his staff may rebel, readers may protest, a rival paper may thrive as a result, but the publisher's power in such cases is unmistakable.

This kind of freedom is available, too, of course, to publishers of magazines and books. As some of the observations above make clear, the print media are not entirely free of legal restrictions. Every society restricts free expression to some degree—usually with at least four basic controls: a law designed to protect individuals or groups against defamation, a copyright law to protect authors and publishers, a statute to preserve the community standard of decency and morality, and a statute to protect the state against treasonable utterances. It should be noted that two Justices of the United States Supreme Court, Black and Douglas, argue that the First Amendment means *literally* what it says. Black held in *Ginzburg v. United States*, "I believe that the Federal Government is without power whatever under the Constitution to put any type of burden on speech and expression of ideas of any kind." Justice Douglas wrote in *The Right of the People:*

> The First Amendment does not say there is freedom of expression provided the talk is not dangerous. It does not say there is freedom of expression provided the utterance has no tendency to subvert. . . . All notions of regulation or restraint by government are absent from the First Amendment. For it says in words that are unambiguous, "Congress shall make no law. . . ."

Government encroachment protested by many leaders of the print media is that directed at commercial practices. A successful suit was brought under antitrust laws against monopolistic advertising practices of the Kansas City *Star*. In other cases government has sought to require newspapers to pay newsboys a minimum hourly wage. The papers resisted successfully, arguing that the newsboys were "independent merchants" who actually bought papers from the publisher and sold them to subscribers.

Perhaps the most important commercial case was brought under antitrust laws against the Associated Press. The AP, which is cooperatively owned, had long protected its members by refusing to sell its service to their competitors. The new Chicago *Sun*, competing in the morning field with the Chicago *Tribune*, was unable to obtain AP service, and its suit became pivotal. That the *Sun* supported Franklin D. Roosevelt against the Roosevelt-hating *Tribune* added emotional overtones. Robert Lasch described the struggle:

> Almost to a man, the publishers of America interpreted the filing of this action as a foul assault against the First Amendment, and with frightening unanimity exerted all their power to impress upon the public that point of view.
>
> "We see in this, not the end perhaps, but surely the greatest peril, to a free press in America," said the Detroit *News*. From the citadel of its monopoly position in a city of 600,000, the Kansas City *Star* cried: "This is the sort of thing that belongs in the totalitarian states, not in a free democracy." "In the event of a government victory," said the New York *Daily News*, "the press services of the United States will be under the thumb of the White House."
>
> These were not extremist positions. They represented a fair sample of the opinion handed down by the press. . . .

In retrospect the press outcry seems a bit silly. The government won the case, the *Sun* got AP service, the White House did *not* put its thumb on the wire services, no newspaper was restrained or censored. The question was commercial: whether a news service could be withheld from some newspapers for competitive reasons.

In 1970 a similar question was resolved by the Congress of the United States in favor of newspapers. The "Newspaper Preservation Act" exempts from the antitrust laws any joint newspaper operation in which one paper can show it was failing at the time the joint agreement was adopted.

Now the press is fighting another battle with government decisions that come much closer to infringing concepts of freedom. Again the antitrust laws are pivotal. The question is whether, as the numbers of large metropolitan newspapers diminish, the remaining giants should acquire suburban papers in the same area. The Department of Justice has stepped into several such acquisitions, objecting that competition is diminished. It is not yet certain that the government will be able to establish guidelines for ownership to which the press must adhere, but magazine and book publishers are watching the developing battle between newspapers and government with keen interest, and some fear that a formula that will prevent wholesale acquisitions and mergers may be established. Obviously this is a question related not so much to historical concepts of freedom as it is to the press as a business institution.

Like the other instruments of mass communication, the newspaper is a business enterprise as well as an informative public service. As Zechariah Chafee observed, it is like a combination, in one organization, of a college and a large private business, the one devoted to educating the public, the other to making money for a few owners. This is an awkward combination, and yet it must be maintained. Newspapers must be economically strong so that they can remain independent of the government and report on it; yet we must expect an unusual kind of responsibility from newspaper owners. For the free expression of ideas they have been granted is broad. In *Winters v. New York,* a case involving the right to public accounts of crime and violence, the Supreme Court made it clear that entertainment is also protected:

> We do not accede to appellee's suggestion that the constitutional protection for a free press applies only to the exposition of ideas. The line between the informing and the entertaining is too elusive for the protection of the basic right. Everyone is familiar with instances of propaganda through fiction. What is one man's amusement, teaches another man's doctrine.

Clearly government regulation is sharply limited when the highest court construes freedom so broadly.

Films

Motion pictures in the United States have never enjoyed the breadth of freedom granted the printed media. For more than a half a century, a number of states and municipalities have had official movie censorship boards.

Chicago was among the first in 1907. Then came New York in 1909, Pennsylvania in 1911, and Kansas in 1913. The Pennsylvania law set the pattern from which most subsequent censorship laws were designed. No movie film could be shown in Pennsylvania without the approval of the state board of censors. The United States Supreme Court in 1915 upheld the Pennsylvania law—and similar laws in Kansas and Ohio—as a reasonable exercise of state police power.

Censorship of the movies seems to have been tolerated for a number of reasons. From their beginnings the movies were looked on primarily as an entertainment medium. In their infancy they were linked with vaudeville houses, where they sometimes rounded out the bills; as they matured, they became associated with the legitimate stage. In England, where much of libertarian tradition developed, the theater was regarded as an institution quite properly coming under government control on political and religious as well as moral grounds. The excesses of the film industry in the United States immediately after World War I created a climate of opinion favorable to restrictions. Producers tried to outdo one another in luring the public with risqué titles, lurid advertisements, and passionate love scenes. The stars themselves became involved in a succession of highly publicized off-screen scandals. Public pressure for governmental regulation was strong, and the movies had no tradition of freedom to prevent it.

Except for a few isolated instances, the young motion-picture industry itself did little fighting to enlarge its freedom. Aiming at a mass market, the major producers were much more interested in giving the public what it wanted than in championing the right to dissent. They cooperated with both official and unofficial censors, and they tried to keep screen fare antiseptic by a voluntary production code.

In *Treasury for the Free World* Darryl F. Zanuck stated:

> The fear of political reprisal and persecution . . . has prevented free expression on the screen and retarded its development. The loss has not been merely our own. It has been the nation's and the world's. Few of us insiders can forget that shortly before Pearl Harbor the entire motion picture industry was called on the carpet in Washington by a Senate committee dominated by isolationists and asked to render an account of its activities. We were pilloried with the accusation that we were allegedly making anti-Nazi films which might be offensive to Germany.

Similar pressures have been exerted in every time of tension during the lifetime of the motion-picture industry, especially during the early 1950s, when McCarthyism was rampant. Blacklists of suspected Communists among actors, writers, and directors were circulated through studios. The listed actors and directors could not work; some of the writers prepared scripts under other names. When an Academy Award was announced for a script written by one Robert Rich, no one came forward. "Rich" was actually Dalton Trumbo, a blacklisted writer. The power of the blacklist lasted for almost two decades.

But censorship by states and municipalities has influenced film content more strongly than any federal action. Film-makers have had a long history of conflict with states. For example, a film was banned in Ohio in 1937 because "the picture encourages social and racial equality, thereby stirring up racial hatred . . . the above doctrines are contrary to the accepted codes of American life." A documentary film on the Spanish Civil War was banned by the Pennsylvania Censor Board, with the suggestion that the film would be acceptable if the words "Fascist," "Nazi," "Italian," "Rome," "German," "Berlin," and others were deleted. Such experiences lead to anticipatory censorship, with film-makers themselves judging the political winds in each period of American stress and often producing their films accordingly. It is not so much that they fear the results of court action; taken to the highest level, films usually win legal tests. But until they win, the result of banning may be financial failure.

In 1952 the Supreme Court, in *The Miracle* case, moved motion pictures a step closer to freedom by ruling that a state may not ban a film on the censor's conclusion that it is sacrilegious, that motion pictures come under the protection the Constitution gives the press, and that their importance as an organ of public opinion is not lessened by their preoccupation with entertainment. But the court interpreted the Constitution as not authorizing absolute freedom to show every kind of movie at all times and places. Since sacrilege was the sole standard involved in *The Miracle* case, the court did not pass on other standards whereby states could ban films.

The 1952 decision established that the movies are entitled to the protection of the First Amendment, an important victory, which was consolidated and extended in later cases. Two years later the court held that New York could not ban *La Ronde* and in 1955 that Kansas could not ban *The Moon Is Blue*. In 1959 it rejected a ban that New York had imposed on a movie version of *Lady Chatterley's Lover,* which the censors said seemed to advocate immoral ideas. Justice Potter Stewart remarked that the Constitutional guarantee is not confined to majority opinions: "It protects advocacy of the opinion that adultery may sometimes be proper, no less than advocacy of socialism or the single tax."

In recent years the film industry has been bolder in testing the limits of indecency. Two feature films, which began playing in theaters across the United States in 1966, illustrate this point strikingly. *Who's Afraid of Virginia Woolf?* was a pioneer in its use of realistic dialogue: "Jesus" or "Christ" is used (irreverently) seventeen times; "God," "God damn," or "Lord" is used forty-four times; "damn," seven times; "hell," three times; "bitch," twice; "bastard," eight times; and "son of a bitch" or "S.O.B.," seven times. In comparison all other risqué films shown in first-run theaters in the United States prior to "*Who's Afraid of Virginia Woolf?*" were hesitant and tentative. The other film, *Blow-Up,* was similarly a pioneer. By comparison with it, nudity and sex scenes in other pictures seemed hesitant and tentative; nothing so unabashed had been shown in first-run theaters. A new spirit of tolerance was developing. Americans soon found a growing number of erotically candid quality films, by American as well as foreign producers, being made available to them.

As the 1970s began, it looked as though nearly all the taboos were dead. Only the few "family movies" failed to carry earthy dialogue or nude scenes or both. Explicit scenes of sexual intercourse were playing in neighborhood movie houses.

Broadcasting

In the early 1920s, when commercial broadcasting was in its infancy, one new radio station after another began sending its signals into the airwaves. The only laws regulating broadcasting then were those designed for radio telegraphy, and they were powerless to prevent chaos. Cacaphony filled listeners' earphones and speakers as amateurs cut in on the programs of professional broadcasters, as ships' radios punctuated musical programs with the dots and dashes of Morse code, as commerical stations tried to crowd competitors from their wavelengths.

The broadcasting industry turned to government for help in bringing some order from all the confusion. The eventual result was the Communications Act of 1934, which created the Federal Communications Commission to regulate broadcasting in the "public interest, convenience, and necessity."

The FCC is made up of seven members, each of whom is appointed for seven years by the President of the United States. Their terms expire at different times, so that no President is likely to appoint all the commissioners. Only four of the seven may be members of the same political party. These provisions of the Communications Act were designed to protect the Commission against partisan politics. They have succeeded, but not completely. Dean Burch, who was appointed Commission Chairman by President Nixon in 1970, remarked, after an FCC decision that was not to his liking, that the expiring terms of two FCC members would soon enable the President to appoint commissioners with more favorable attitudes.

Although the FCC has other duties—regulating military and police communication, transcontinental telephone and teletype, and, increasingly, CATV and communication satellites are among its many responsibilities—the chief public focus falls on commercial broadcasting. Congress gave the FCC the authority to license stations, to assign wavelengths, to decide hours of broadcasting for various stations, and to suspend or revoke the licenses of stations not serving the public interest. These are the kinds of decisions that make the FCC controversial.

On the one hand, the Commission is a regulatory agency. Its authority to regulate broadcasting stems from the assumption that the airwaves belong to all the people. A broadcaster may use the airwaves only under license after showing his qualifications for serving the public interest. The FCC decides to award a license partly on the basis of a proposed program schedule submitted by the applicant. And although a license may be renewed at the end of its three-year term, it may also be suspended or revoked if the FCC decides that the broadcaster has failed to serve the public interest—or if he has failed to live up to the promises in his original proposal. Rarely, however, has the FCC revoked a license.

On the other hand, the FCC is also a judicial agency, for it has been given the power to decide what constitutes the public interest. The scope of its judicial powers, however, is yet to be determined. The law specifically forbids the FCC to censor broadcast content, apart from such items as profanity, obscenity, and information about lotteries. Yet, since it is charged with making sure that stations operate in the public interest, the FCC has taken the position that it must necessarily concern itself with over-all program content. Broadcasters have argued that any interference with content runs counter to libertarian principles and that the FCC should do no more than regulate frequencies.

To what extent the FCC may concern itself with the over-all performance of stations has never been settled conclusively by either Congress or the Supreme Court. The Supreme Court has indicated that broadcasting is protected by the Constitutional guarantees of free expression. But it also has upheld the government's right to regulate the use of the airwaves and to decide the composition of the traffic on them. As Chapter I made clear, the FCC does have the power to require broadcasters to adhere to the "Fairness Doctrine," which opens the airwaves to dissident voices.

In 1970 the FCC began to tighten the obligations of the "Fairness Doctrine" by requiring that broadcasters who present a series on controversial issues, or who editorialize, invite specific spokesmen to state contrasting views. Except for the first program in a series, the licensee would no longer be permitted to rely solely on an announcement offering time to anyone with a contrasting view. The spirit of the requirement, Commission spokesmen said, is that a broadcaster "who should be as outspoken and hard-hitting as he wishes in presenting his view of an issue should be equally vigorous in getting the other side before the public."

Not long after that decision was announced, however, the FCC considered several complaints that armed forces recruitment broadcasts present only one side of an important public issue. A typical complaint was that "when such a large segment of our population is vehemently opposed to our military involvement in Vietnam and the foreign policy that it represents, the advocacy of the benefits and advisability of volunteering or enlisting in the military as opposed to seeking a deferment or exemption definitely constitutes a controversial issue of public importance." All those who complained stated that their local stations had refused their requests for free air time to present opposing views. The Commission majority decided that the complaints were not justified. But Commissioner Nicholas Johnson said:

> Today one branch of the Federal Government ignores the orderly complaints of its citizens and rules that another branch of that same government, the U.S. Army, can propagandize without preserving for the young their First Amendment right of self-defense. The Army and Marine Corps will be permitted to harness all the seductive merchandising talents of Madison Avenue to persuade draft-age young men to enlist in the armed forces. . . . To put it bluntly, the majority has held that the young people of this nation must find their path to the Fairness Doctrine in the streets. I dissent.

The Commission's vacillating on the Fairness Doctrine is fairly typical. Like all regulatory agencies, the FCC is often friendly with the institutions it regulates. Commissioner Johnson has rounded up this record of FCC actions:

> —The FCC once decided that a radio station proposing thirty-three minutes of commercials per hour would be serving the public interest.
> —It permitted the wholesale transfer of construction permits from one licensee to another, prompting the Special Investigations Subcommittee of the House Interstate and Foreign Commerce Committee to conclude in 1969: "The Commission apparently confused its role as guardian of the public interest with that of guardian of the private interest."
> —The FCC approved a license transfer application for a station that quite candidly conceded it proposed to program no news and no public affairs at all.
> —When presented with charges that a Southern station was engaged in racist programming, the FCC first refused to let the complainants participate in the case, then found that the station's performance entitled it to a license renewal. Even technical violations get little attention. Recently the Commission refused to consider revoking the license of a station whose owner, it was charged, had ordered his engineer to make fraudulent entries in the station's log book, operated with an improperly licensed engineer, and whose three stations had amassed eighty-seven other technical violations over a three-year period.
> Violations of the most elementary principles of good business practice don't arouse the Commission to action. Recently the FCC examined the record of a station guilty of bilking advertisers out of

$6,000 in fraudulent transactions. The local Better Business Bureau had complained. The station was already on a one-year "probationary" license status for similar offenses earlier. The result? The majority had no difficulty finding the station had "minimally met the public interest standards," and it therefore renewed the license.

As this record suggests, it is nearly always true that when broadcast licenses come up for renewal every three years, licensees can count on favorable Commission action. Thus it was a shock to WHDH-TV (Channel 5 in Boston) when the FCC denied it a renewal in 1969 and awarded the license to another group of Boston businessmen. That brought challenges in large cities across the United States, as group after group sought to demonstrate that licensees had not been operating in the "public interest, convenience, and necessity." Then broadcast lobbyists went to work on Capitol Hill. Soon more than one hundred bills had been introduced in the House and Senate to protect licensees. The most important, the bill introduced by Senator John Pastore of Rhode Island, would have virtually eliminated the possibility of a successful challenge. It would not allow the FCC to entertain an application for an existing channel until the Commission itself had first found that the licensee had not lived up to his responsibilities (which, considering the small FCC staff, is highly unlikely). Moreover the bill required that the FCC rely almost wholly on the licensee's report of his own performance. It may not matter whether this bill or one like it becomes law. It is clear that the FCC will deny license renewals only in the most extreme cases—usually to break up a concentration when a single proprietor or a group owns a newspaper and broadcasting facilities in one market.

And yet it is sometimes true that vacillation rather than weakness is characteristic of the FCC. Even as it was granting license renewals almost automatically in 1970, the Commission was announcing a rule that would limit network domination of prime-time programming. Designed to promote diversity in programs, the rule prohibits network affiliates in the fifty largest markets from accepting more than three hours of network programming from 7 p.m. to 11 p.m. (6 and 10 p.m., Central Time) after September 1, 1971. "Our objective," the commissioners reported, "is to provide opportunity—now lacking in television— for the competitive development of alternative sources of television programs so that television licensees can exercise something more than a nominal choice . . . "

At about the same time the FCC announced such revolutionary plans to restructure patterns of ownership that *Broadcasting* magazine headlined its report "Major Moves to Rip Up Broadcasting." One decision barred the owner of any full-time station—AM, FM, or TV—from acquiring another station in the same market. Moreover the Commission announced that it was proposing a rule to break up existing combinations of radio, television, and newspapers in the same market. Only AM-FM radio combinations would be allowed. Owners would be given five years to reduce their holdings in a single market to an AM-FM combination, a television station, or a newspaper. A Commission staff member explained that this rule was designed to "promote diversity of programming and viewpoints that might have an influence on public opinion, and to promote competition among the media." All this was a response to the increasing criticisms of heavily concentrated media ownership. Tabulating cross-ownership figures in 1969, the Commission found that 256 newspapers were jointly owned by broadcast licensees in the same city. It was also found that 68 communities had only one commercial radio station owned by the only daily newspaper and that of 666 commercial television stations 160 were affiliated with daily newspapers.

Such actions lead broadcasters to speak of the FCC in tones that are fretful when they are not fearful. The trade journals of radio and television—especially *Broadcasting*—are heavy with denunciations of what the FCC has done or what it may do. All this is evidence that, however essential commission regulation of broadcasting may be, regulating communication in a society that grew from libertarian roots can never be wholly acceptable.

9

The Economic
Framework
of the Mass Media

We can no longer distinguish the ad from the entertainment, the front cover of the national magazine, in
which an actor poses to plug his film, from the back
cover, in which an actor sells cigarettes and indirectly
also plugs a film. Television shows with groups of celebrities are a series of plugs (for books, records, night-
club appearances, movies) interrupted by commercials.

PAULINE KAEL

Early in 1970, with the television season half over, NBC
was so far ahead in the ratings that employees wore bright yellow but-
tons proclaiming "Happiness Is Being No. 1." Over at rival CBS, which
had been first in the ratings for fourteen consecutive years, Mike Dann,
Senior Programming Vice President, was planning "Operation 100,"
which meant that in the hundred days that were left of the 1969–70
season, Dann hoped to overtake and pass NBC.

He had had recent experience at coming from behind. Exactly
a year earlier NBC had been well ahead in the ratings at the halfway
point. Dann's desperate juggling of programs and schedules had brought
CBS almost even with NBC toward the end of the season. Much depended on the ratings of a CBS special, *Cinderella*. Dann sent a plea
by wire to the managers of all the more than two hundred stations
affiliated with CBS, hinting that his job was riding on success. "And
how you promote *Cinderella* will tell me something about your personal
feelings toward me." It worked. Cinderella was highly rated, and, at
least by its own figures, CBS won the season (NBC figures showed
a tie).

163

And so it was that in the middle of the 1969–70 season Dann and his aides were able to plan 104 changes in CBS programs and schedules. The most important was to rerun the movie *Born Free* one Sunday evening and have Dick Van Dyke introduce it. So heavy was the promotion that the showing gave *Born Free* the third highest movie rating in television history (after *Bridge on the River Kwai* and *The Birds*).

When it was all over, CBS claimed another victory—and again NBC demurred, claiming *its* season had begun earlier and ended earlier than that of CBS.

If all this is not meat for the critics who complain about the bizarre and counterfeit character of mass media entertainment, one of Mike Dann's comments, which reveals his regard for the viewing fare he presents, should be. Appearing at a meeting of CBS affiliates, he was asked what the new season would bring. "Same old crap as last year," he responded.

Nothing could more sharply point up the great economic reality in mass communication: Renting audiences to advertisers sometimes leads media executives to manipulate audiences as well as serve them. The object of manipulation, of course, is to win the widespread attention that lures the dollars of advertisers.

THE INSTITUTION OF ADVERTISING

Few observers have analyzed advertising—the strongest structure in the economic framework of mass communication—more acutely than David Potter, professor of history at Stanford. In *People of Plenty*, he points out that:

> . . . advertising is not badly needed in an economy of scarcity, because total demand is usually equal to or in excess of total supply, and every producer can normally sell as much as he produces. It is when potential supply outstrips demand—that is, when abundance prevails—that advertising begins to fulfill a really essential economic function. In this situation the producer knows that the limitation upon his operations and upon his growth no longer lies, as it lay historically, in his productive capacity, for he can always produce as much as the market will absorb; the limitation has shifted to the market, and it is selling capacity which controls his growth.

What this kind of emphasis on consumption means, Potter suggests, is that the radio and television programs and newspaper and magazine articles "do not attain the dignity of being ends in themselves; they are rather means to an end; that end, of course, is to catch the reader's attention so that he will then read the advertisement or hear the commercial, and to hold his interest until these essential messages have been delivered."

If this view is the correct one, surely the judgment made in *A Study of Four Media,* published by the Alfred Politz Research Company, is also correct in its flat assertion that "the delivery of an audience for the advertiser is the fundamental function of any medium." These views suggest the force of economic reality, but there are, of course, other perspectives. Although most of those who work in the mass media must think always of large audiences, it is doubtful that any writer of a news story or magazine article, any reporter for a radio or television news program, or even any director of a situation comedy ever weighs the possible effect of his work on the advertiser's ability to sell another Chevrolet or another case of Pepsi.

Audiences: Class or Mass?

Let us try to focus on the economic realities from the broad perspective afforded by examples and cases. The story that began this chapter—the battle for ratings between CBS and NBC—seems to us to offer an important insight into the struggle for sheer numbers in the television audience. But the case is not really that simple. For Mike Dann had hardly finished congratulating himself on what he conceived to be his 1970 victory over NBC when his superiors shocked him with some abrupt decisions. For the next season they vetoed some of the high-rated shows on Dann's schedule in favor of other programs aimed at smaller but more affluent and better-educated audiences. Not long afterward, Dann left CBS to work for the Children's Television Workshop.

Similarly, in 1968, thousands upon thousands of subscribers to the *Saturday Evening Post* got unflattering letters asking them to end their subscriptions. The trouble was that they just were not affluent enough for the *Post,* which hoped to save itself by cutting its circulation of some six million by about half.

Those dropped could take some comfort in the fact that, in the imprecise mass-hacking of the *Post's* subscription list, the discards included Gardner Cowles, chairman of the company that publishes *Look,* whose salary was $100,586; Winthrop Rockefeller; and Marvin Ackerman, the president of Curtis Publishing Company, who ordered the cuts in the first place.

That a magazine publisher expects to improve his finances by lopping off three million subscribers suggests how curious is the economics of the mass media. Publishers and broadcasters have shown considerable imagination, along with some downright foolhardiness, in assembling consumer audiences that they think advertisers will pay to reach. Some have been enchanted by sheer numbers. The *Reader's Digest* has collected an audience of nearly 40 million Americans interested in its medical marvels, anthropomorphic tales, and unforgettable characters. *Life*, even before it offered asylum to the subscribers banished from the *Saturday Evening Post's* list, had an audience of almost 33 million, which it liked to describe to advertisers as "mass-class," breathtakingly large and impressively affluent. Since literacy is not a prerequisite for viewing, television, of course, has a tremendous potential for collecting vast numbers of consumers at a given time.

Some media sift and screen consumers for the advertiser. By their content they bring together people with common tastes, interests, jobs, hobbies and so on. Because content that attracts some people repels others, the medium has a tidy, like-minded audience ready for the advertiser. In one recent year, for instance, publishers launched such specialized new magazines as *Weight Watchers, Surfing, Government Photography, Musical Electronics, Psychology Today for Physicians* and *Happier Marriage and Planned Parenthood.*

It is from renting their audiences to advertisers that newspaper and magazine publishers—usually—and commercial broadcasters—always—make their profits. The price a subscriber pays for a publication is usually just a qualifying fee. Although this price may fall far short of the cost of production, it tells the advertiser that the subscriber is interested in the publication. Sometimes a publisher will entice subscribers with a cut-rate qualifying fee—a bargain subscription offer. Thus, about 88 per cent of the new subscribers to *Life* in one six-month period paid less than the posted rates. In defiance of the usual laws of economics, then, a publisher of periodicals buys blank paper dearly and sells printed paper cheaply.

Since a publisher ordinarily loses money on a subscriber unless advertisers will pay to reach him, high circulation and low advertising volume threaten disaster. What the *Saturday Evening Post* was trying to do then, should be obvious. It was purging its lists of those it thought to be undesirable subscribers in order to concentrate on wealthy consumers in the top markets. It could cut its production costs. And, it hoped, it could charge advertisers a premium for reaching those readers with money to spend on Lincoln Continentals, Chivas Regal and vacations in Bermuda. But the scheme did not work—probably because it came too late—and the *Post* died. In the late 1960s and early 1970s, however, other publishers were reassessing their circulation practices.

Look announced that it was cutting back by 1.25 million to 6.5 million circulation.

Broadcasting requires no qualifying fee, of course, once the radio or television set is bought. To give the advertiser some idea of how large an audience he is getting for his money, broadcasters use several audience rating firms—among them Nielsen and Trendex.

Is Advertising Essential?

Not all media depend on advertising. There is nothing inherent in the nature of the media that requires them to depend on advertising for the large share of their income. Newspapers survived without any great amount of it for two or three centuries, and so did magazines. Books and motion pictures have never depended on advertisers. In many parts of the world, the media today put nowhere near the reliance on advertising support as in the United States. Even television, which in the United States is dominated by advertising, has other means of support in some countries.

Indeed, when radio sets began to make their entry into American homes, there was little thought that broadcasting would become married to advertising. Quite the contrary, there was a feeling that it should be protected from commercialization. Even David Sarnoff, who later became chairman of the Radio Corporation of America, saw broadcasting as a public institution free from commercial taint.

Printers' Ink, a voice of the advertising business, held in 1923:

> Any attempt to make radio an advertising medium . . . would, we think, prove positively offensive to great numbers of people . . . Imagine the effect, for example, of a piano sonata by Josef Hoffman followed by the audible assertion, "If you are under forty, four chances to one you will get pyorrhea." "Pickle Bros. are offering three-dollar silk hose for $1.98." Exaggerated, no doubt, yet the principle is there. To break in upon one's entertainment *in his own house* is quite likely intolerable, and advertising as a whole cannot be the gainer by anything of the sort.

Even if the mass media did not depend on advertising, however, it is doubtful that their content would be drastically different. Virtually all of the media are under pressure to saturate the market they have chosen for their product. This compulsion to maximize their chosen audience may have been encouraged by the growth of advertising, but mainly it has been a concomitant of mass production.

For any medium many of the costs of doing business are fixed. However, once the medium passes the break-even point, it may pile up profits rapidly. So even a medium without advertising strives for an audience large enough to take it past the break-even point and deep into the realm of profit.

But a large audience may influence what a medium carries and what it does not. To attract and hold its audience, a medium ordinarily cannot risk alienating any substantial part of it, so it usually stays close to the tastes, interests, and values of the great majority.

Consider *Reader's Digest*. From its founding in the basement of a Greenwich Village speak-easy in 1922 until April, 1955, it carried no advertising whatsoever. If advertising is the corrupting influence in mass communication, *Reader's Digest* should have been a cultural monument during the first 33 years of its life. Free from the taint of the advertiser, it should have been an enlightened, sophisticated, literate, courageous magazine. It was not. And the fact that it was trying to please more than ten million readers was pivotal.

Or consider most Hollywood movies. They have been criticized for being bland and superficial and depicting a dream world. Their content is what it is not because of domination by advertising—they have never counted on advertising for support—but because movie-makers consider the bland, the superficial, and the dreamlike good box office, the sort of fare that will fill seats in the Rialto and Orpheum.

Financing Educational Broadcasting

Educational broadcasting has long been the poor relation. With no advertising revenues, many of the early educational radio stations depended for support upon the universities or school districts to which they were tied. The pattern has been the same for many educational TV stations. By comparison with the affluent world of commercial broadcasting, ETV lives hand to mouth. In some cases the educational television stations have been unable to fill all the air time they were allotted.

Support for educational broadcasting has come from a wide variety of sources and from ingenious fund-raising ideas. Some stations that are not licensed to school districts have received school funds for making special broadcasts. Listeners and viewers have, in effect, become subscribers to educational radio and television, paying monthly or annual fees to help support stations. Although advertising is prohibited, companies may sponsor programs as a public service, and a few do. Foundation executives, many of them appalled by the standards of commercial broadcasting, have given millions to educational broadcasting. Several stations derive a substantial share of their annual budgets from auctions. They give over hours of air time to auctioning items donated by merchants and viewers as well as more imaginative prizes, such as having lunch or dinner with William F. Buckley, Jr., for which some viewers have paid thousands. KQED-TV of San Francisco raises more than $300,000 a year with its auction.

Years of effort have failed to put educational broadcasting on a more stable footing. But by the early 1970s it appeared that a combination of foundation largesse and Congressional appropriations might at least establish a viable educational network. In 1970 National Educational Television and a New York noncommercial station, WNDT-TV, announced the joint formation of the Educational Broadcasting Corporation (EBC). McGeorge Bundy, president of the Ford Foundation, said that the consolidation will "create the most comprehensive and best-financed public television production center in the United States." Thanks largely to the Ford Foundation, with a strong assist from the Corporation for Public Broadcasting, EBC began life with $20 million. Individual stations, however, are likely to continue to have to scratch for funds.

Advertiser Influence

It is true that advertising permeates the atmosphere in which most of the media are created. No editor or publisher, no producer or director, is ever completely unaware of the advertiser standing sternly in the background. Likewise, advertising permeates the atmosphere in which most of the media are received. It is a ubiquitous, persistent and often annoying competitor for the attention of reader or viewer, who, conditioned by salesmanship, often looks for it in even the most virginal of content.

The extent to which the media suppress or shape content at the request of the advertiser is difficult, if not impossible, to measure. The hand of the advertiser is discernible behind some of the content of newspapers and magazines, but what is more often discernible is the hand of an ingratiating editor or publisher, who wishes to impress advertisers with a demonstration of a certain harmony of interests.

Thus, there is often more than a chance correlation between the restaurants advertised in some publications and the restaurants recommended in their dining columns. And the editorial matter on the real estate and homemakers' pages of newspapers often plays a merry obbligato to the advertising. Not long ago *True* magazine carried an article saying that there is no proof that smoking causes cancer. The article was promoted in advertisements, and thousands of reprints were distributed. The author was employed by a public relations firm that represented the tobacco industry. *Life* was accused of killing an article that charged the oil industry with sabotaging the developments of shale oil for fear it would compete with crude oil. The author, a *Life* staff member, said the article was suppressed to pacify the oil industry, which advertises heavily in Time Inc. magazines. The editors replied that they killed it because it was an inadequate reporting job. The author secretly sold the article to *Harper's,* and his superiors fired him from his job with *Life. Reader's Digest* ordered Funk and Wagnalls, a book publishing firm it acquired in 1965, not to bring out Samm Baker's volume, *The Permissible Lie,* because it was critical of advertising and not in harmony with the magazine's philosophy. When the kill order came through, copies of the book were already printed and awaiting distribution. World Publishing Company took over publication of the book.

Nonetheless several factors have helped to diminish the influence of advertisers on editorial policy. One is the declining number of competing newspapers. Today, when most cities have but a single daily newspaper, the individual advertiser often needs the local newspaper as much as the newspaper needs the advertiser.

The rise of public relations as handmaiden of advertising, especially since the mid-1930s, has made the more blatant forms of editorial pressure somewhat anachronistic if not downright superfluous. Today industries, businesses, government agencies, religious institutions and even universities employ specialists to protect their images and their interests. Such subtle forms of persuasion as staging events, creating institutes and foundations, and guiding the flow of news at its source are probably at least as effective as blunt pressure on publishers and broadcasters.

Some publications, in fact, turn down advertising they find offensive or unlikely to be effective. The separation of the editorial and advertising sides of the *New Yorker* is so sharp that A. J. Russell, Jr., who retired as president in 1968, scarcely knew Harold Ross, the founding editor, although their tenures overlapped by more than twenty years. Russell had risen to his position on the advertising side of the magazine, where he saw little of Ross. He remarked a little wistfully, "I met him once a year at the *New Yorker* birthday party and on one or two occasions, but I didn't ever call him Harold. He didn't like to be talked to in the elevator, so I couldn't say 'Good morning.'"

Broadcasting is quite another matter. There advertising influence has generally been greater than among the printed media. In the most affluent days of radio, advertisers and their agencies dominated the networks. They themselves put together their programs and simply rented network time and facilities to beam them into the home. And so it was in the early days of television. However, all that has changed. Now the networks own an interest in almost all the programs offered during prime viewing hours, and multiple sponsorship of programs has become commonplace.

If television sometimes appears to be "a collection of hollow men trying to fill a vacuum tube," in Leon Gerry's description, it is not just because it cannot afford to offend any substantial number of viewers, although that is a part of it. Since the networks are competing with one another and with magazines for advertising revenue, they also cannot afford to offend their advertisers. The very form of television drama is governed by advertising. Writers must fashion scenes not only to meet the needs of plot but also to provide breaks for commercials.

Substance, too, is governed by advertising considerations. The chairman of the Writers Guild of America, testifying at FCC hearings, said that "sponsors' fear of an unknown" contributed to the death of original TV drama. Rod Serling has told how advertising considerations affected the entire treatment of his TV play based on the story of Emmett Till, a Negro boy from Chicago who was murdered in Mississippi. In Serling's version, the entire cast was white. At the insistence of the advertising agency, he had to move the locale from the South to New England, delete every suspected Southern colloquialism from the dialogue, and delete all references to Coca-Cola because it was "a Southern drink." Said Serling: "When the show finally hit the air, it had been so diluted and so changed . . . that the central theme I had my characters shouting about had become too vague to warrant any shouting."

In a drama about the Nuremburg trials, the word "gas" was blipped as a cause of death in Hitler's concentration camps because the sponsor was an association of gas interests. In a Chrysler program about the Civil War, all references to President Lincoln were deleted because he had the misfortune to bear the same name as a competing automobile. And on the Chevy Show no one ever could ford a stream.

THE STRUCTURE OF THE NEWSPAPER INDUSTRY

The creation of mass markets, which only large and costly units could efficiently service, led inevitably to a contraction of ownership in many cities and towns and thus to the development of newspaper chains. The high point in the number of newspapers published in the United States came in 1909, when there were 2600 daily publications. Thereafter consolidation became the dominant theme.

In the first half of the twentieth century, more than 2000 new daily newspapers (including those changing from weekly to daily) were started. But, during the same period, 1947 daily newspapers suspended publication or became weeklies, 547 disappeared through merger or consolidation, and at least 302 local combinations took place. At the same time the number of newspaper chains increased from 3, publishing

62 newspapers, to 70, publishing 386, with more than two-fifths of the daily and one-half of the Sunday circulation. In the 1950s there were scarcely more than one hundred cities with competing daily newspapers. In twenty-five years the percentage of one-publisher, or monopoly, cities rose from 57 to 92. In ten states there was not a single city with competing daily newspapers. In twenty-two states not one city enjoyed competing Sunday papers.

As the 1970s began, the nation's nearly 200 chains owned half of the 1760 dailies. Less than 4 per cent of the cities in the United States had competing newspapers.

According to journalism historian Frank Mott, consolidation of newspapers is not a strictly recent tendency; it can be found in all periods. But since World War I, the skyrocketing cost of newspaper publication has been a strong influence in accelerating the tendency to consolidate. Typesetting machines, high-speed presses, engraving plants, and other expanding mechanical facilities have meant not only increased operating costs but constantly larger investment. Melville E. Stone established the Chicago *Daily News* in 1876 with a few thousand dollars capital, and twenty years later Adolph S. Ochs was able to acquire *The New York Times* for only $100,000. But after the turn of the century, prices of daily newspaper properties rose to million-dollar levels. Stone's *Daily News*, for example, sold for $13 million in 1925. In 1963 two Omaha dailies were sold for $43 million, and in 1967 Newhouse Newspapers bought the Cleveland *Plain Dealer* for $53.4 million. Knight Newspapers paid $55 million for two Philadelphia papers in 1969.

Entry and Survival

In the typical American town in earlier days, more newspaper publishing ventures were attempted than the economy could support. Some newspapers—for example, those founded solely as voices of political parties or other interest groups—went out of business simply because they could not win general community support. Others were founded by men who went into the business apparently on the assumption that to make money it was only necessary to "buy newsprint white and sell it black." They soon discovered that, aside from the problems of editing a mass medium, such factors as the rigid advertising and circulation rates made newspaper publishing a dubious enterprise at best. For the new entrant today the problems are even more formidable.

Both in procuring their raw materials and in marketing their products, newspaper publishers exhibit the familiar behavior of monopoly and oligopoly. As buyers they use the customary pressures for keeping down costs; as sellers they maintain rigid advertising and circulation rates, discriminate by rate differentials, and practice block selling of space in morning and evening newspapers in combinations. The typical newspaper pays out for newsprint roughly one-third of its revenues, which is just about what it receives in circulation revenue. Practically all newsprint is sold in carload lots under long-term contracts, mostly to large publishers. Those who cannot afford carload lots get their newsprint from jobbers, brokers, and paper merchants at open-market prices, which are sometimes higher by 10 per cent or more than the carload rates.

Procuring syndicated features and wire services is no less difficult for the new entrant. The syndicated feature business is dominated by four major companies: AP Newsfeatures, King Features, NEA Service, and United Features. Most franchises provide for exclusive territories. Furthermore package selling enables large publishers to buy up rights to more features than they print. Oligopoly is likewise a chief trait of the two wire services.

The new newspaper is confronted in many markets by chain organization. Chains, especially of large newspapers, have certain special advantages: Notably they make wider use of editorial and feature writers; it is easier for them to obtain new funds from the capital market; they engage in block merchandising of space to national advertisers, in centralized and large-scale research, and in bulk purchases of newsprint, ink, and equipment; they are better able to make maximum use of specialized technical and managerial services.

In sum, except in certain burgeoning suburban markets and in situations in which a publisher can take advantage of photoreproduction and cold type, the daily newspaper business is essentially a "closed" industry. As a great many unconventional papers are proving, however, technological advances now make it possible to establish a slender weekly or monthly with very little capital. The weekly *Texas Observer* and the monthly San Francisco *Bay Guardian* prove that such publications can be valuable as well.

THE STRUCTURE OF THE MAGAZINE INDUSTRY

The modern magazine succeeded as a mass medium chiefly because of its original role as an adjunct of the marketing system. Like the newspaper, it was able, over the years, to appeal to an expanding range of tastes and interests. But, unlike other media, most magazines were designed for homogeneous audiences or special-interest groups. And, in contrast to the newspaper, their circulation was nationwide. Thus, although many magazines were directed to specialized audiences, magazines in general developed as a mass medium in the sense that they appealed to large numbers in a national market that cut across social, economic, and educational class lines.

Early in the twentieth century, some magazine publishers, notably those of pulps and digests, derived their income from a small unit profit on a high turnover of copies instead of from advertising. Still others relied on trade associations, fraternal organizations, and professional groups to make up any deficit. But with the rise of national advertising, the great majority—both in numbers and circulation—were closely bound to the marketing system. In effect, magazine publishing became fundamentally a matter of the publisher's deciding on a consumer group that advertisers wished to reach, devising an editorial formula to attract and hold that group, and then selling advertisers access to it.

In terms of *originating* a market for the advertiser, the relationship of magazines generally to their audiences is quite different from that of other media. Some magazine publishers have first developed a publication and then let both readers and advertisers seek out the magazine. But the typical magazine follows a less risky strategy. It devises an editorial formula that can be counted upon to attract a homogeneous and relatively small special-interest group; then, it assembles advertisers who want to address that audience.

Entry and Survival

Today a relatively few circulation leaders dominate the consumer magazine industry. But taken together, American magazines reflect virtually every shade of thought and opinion, virtually every interest, of their readers. And, despite the fierce competition and the uncertainties, magazine publishing on a small scale is perhaps the communication most accessible to the new investor. What counts most is the idea. If the entrepreneur has a fresh idea for a magazine, there are likely to be persons willing to finance it. If he can sustain his magazine while seeking acceptance by readers and advertisers, there is always some chance that he will achieve a modest success. And there is a remote chance that he will wind up in the company of the giants.

The ease of entry into the magazine industry, in contrast to the formidable obstacles encountered in newspaper publishing, broadcasting, and motion pictures, explains why the industry today is dotted with relatively small units, small staffs, and modest offices with little equipment. The magazine publisher ordinarily does not invest in presses and equipment, but instead lets out his printing on contract. A publisher who does not wish to compete with the large-circulation leaders can still launch a successful magazine on a million dollars or so—a comparatively small sum for starting a national medium. Some that began as regional publications started with far less. The *Rolling Stone* was begun with less than $20,000 and was first aimed at San Francisco Bay Area readers. Then it expanded to national distribution even while it limited advertising to "sincere" products. Survival, however, is a different matter. Factors that make it easy for one publisher to enter the industry make it easy for competitors to enter, also. Successful magazines invariably breed imitators, for the publisher cannot hide the formula for his success, forced as he is by the nature of publishing to exhibit his best ideas in public. Then, too, readers are fickle and it requires a particular genius to anticipate changes in tastes and interests before they are reflected in declining circulation.

Although the magazine industry has hundreds of relatively small circulation producers, a few large publishers account for a high percentage of total magazine circulation and of the advertising money spent on the medium. But they are not necessarily the most profitable.

In 1969 *Life*, which had a circulation of 8.5 million, took in $153 million from advertising. *Time*, its sister publication, was second with $95 million. But *Life* lost $10 million because of the high cost of producing and distributing 8.5 million copies. *Time*, which had a circulation about half that of *Life*, made a profit. *Look*, third on the list with $77 million in advertising revenues, announced in 1970 that it was getting out of the numbers race it had long run with *Life*. In 1970 *Look* executives announced that they not only would reduce circulation, but would concentrate on serving the nation's top sixty markets—and would reduce ad rates. A four-color page in *Look*, for example, was reduced from $55,500 to $48,500. Later, *Life* announced that *it* would reduce circulation.

THE STRUCTURE OF THE BROADCASTING INDUSTRY

The rise of radio as a big and costly purveyor of news and entertainment, and thus a full, fearsome competitor, began in 1920 with the broadcasting by station KDKA of the results of the Presidential election. The economic objective of the industry during this period was not revenues from broadcasting but profits from the sale of receiving sets. Many groups pioneered in broadcasting but with no clear idea of how they were to cover costs. David Sarnoff of the Radio Corporation of America has been quoted as arguing at the time that radio deserved endowment "similar to that enjoyed by libraries, museums, and educational institutions." He believed, according to Gleason Archer in his *Big Business and Radio*, that "Philanthropists would eventually come to the rescue of a hard-pressed industry."

Radio Goes Commercial

Sponsored programs were first broadcast experimentally in 1922 on station WEAF. Thereafter they developed rapidly—though not without protests from government officials and the public. For example, at the First Annual Radio Conference in Washington, Herbert Hoover, who was then Secretary of Commerce, declared: "It is inconceivable that so great a possibility for service . . . be drowned in advertising chatter."

When Congress finally recognized the confusion and passed the Radio Act of 1927, the broadcasting industry began to develop its four main contemporary characteristics: submitting to legal and administrative control by a system of federal licensing, providing mass entertainment, acting as an adjunct of the marketing system, and concentrating its operational control in network organization.

Three million radio sets were available to listeners who tuned in to the radio coverage of the 1924 Presidential election. The newspapers' fear of radio as a competitor for mass markets seemed unjustified, despite radio's spectacular advance as an advertising medium. In 1929 newspapers carried a record $160 million worth of advertising as compared to radio's $40 million. However, with the Depression of the 1930s and the impact of World War II, radio's percentage of total advertising volume rose steadily from 3.9 per cent to a peak 15.7 per cent at war's end, while that of newspapers fell from 33.1 per cent to 30.9 per cent. Magazines, too, suffered heavy losses in percentage of total revenues.

Radio, unable to get the news from the press associations and under attack for pirating copy from newspapers, undertook to gather news itself. The Press-Radio Bureau, established in Washington in 1934, had 245 subscribers. Five new services jumped in. Finally in 1935 the United Press and International News Service obtained permission from the American Newspaper Publishers Association to sell full news reports to stations. With the collapse of the newspapers' organized efforts to curtail news broadcasting, radio was entering maturity. The Associated Press, a newspaper-owned cooperative, joined the competition in 1940 and eventually made radio stations eligible for associate membership. The number of stations jumped from 605 in 1935 to more than 2500 in 1955, and advertising volume climbed to more than $500 million. In 1969 there were more than 5000 radio stations, which brought in advertising revenues of $1.2 billion.

Concentration of Ownership

The history of radio (and television) illustrates both the trend toward concentration in the mass media generally and its persistence despite traditional antitrust sentiment. The Radio Act of 1927 and the Communications Act of 1934 gave the government power to protect against monopoly in broadcasting that it has never had with respect to publishing. The Federal Communications Commission's *Report on Chain Broadcasting,* published in 1941, revealed in stark detail the extent of the controlling interests and contractual arrangements of the two major networks, National Broadcasting Company and Columbia Broadcasting System. Although the FCC ordered the dissolution of the RCA empire, and although the Blue network was sold (to become the American Broadcasting Company), the major radio networks continued to grow steadily. Indeed, some of the pressure on broadcasting today comes from the U.S. Department of Justice as well as the FCC. Broadcasting has become so concentrated that it runs afoul of antitrust laws. In 1969 there were four radio networks with more than 1350 station affiliates.

Network Domination

As television stations began to take form after World War II, their owners scrambled to affiliate with the four national networks that dominated the industry. By the summer of 1955, there were 432 television stations, including 13 noncommercial educational stations. More than half of them were served by only three networks—ABC, CBS, and NBC. And, in September of that year, control was further concentrated as the fourth major network, DuMont, ceased operations. This development moved Frieda B. Hennock, a former FCC commissioner, to state that the major networks maintained a "life and death control over TV." Quoting the president of Crosley Corporation, she warned that networks "seem increasingly inclined to consider individual stations as push-button operations, automatic outlets which cater to programming networks' desires." She called for an "immediate, vigorous network investigation (by Congress) to get at the monopolistic grip" exercised over stations, advertisers, programming, and talent "owing to the monopoly of scarcity created by the networks." The three major networks are now affiliated with more than 600 TV stations. (NBC has 213, CBS has 192, and ABC has 159 primary and 96 secondary affiliates.)

As the conquest by air of the nation's mass markets brought television programs into most American homes, the costs of broadcasting became enormous. To get even the smallest television station on the air requires an investment of between $500,000 and $1 million in building and equipment. A medium-size station represents an investment of more than $1 million. The costs of programming are also impressive. When the Astronauts on Apollo 11 landed on the moon in July, 1969, it cost the networks an estimated $11 million in expenditures and lost revenues to cover the spectacle. Production costs of a 60-second black-and-white commercial were $12,595 in 1969, and that figure did not include talent, music, agency commission, or time charges. To put a one-minute commercial on NBC's *Laugh-In* cost nearly $65,000 in time charges.

Television Gobbles Up the Advertising

Although television required development of new and costly advertising techniques, the growth of the TV advertising dollar has been spectacular from the outset. In 1946 no advertising was carried by the six television stations then existing. But, despite the temporary FCC freeze on the processing of license applications in 1948, by January, 1950, the number of stations had reached 98; there were more than 4 million receiving sets in American homes; and the volume of advertising exceeded $170 million. The following year TV's advertising volume nearly doubled; by 1954 it topped $800 million, or 10 per cent of the money spent in all media combined, and in 1955 it passed the $1 billion mark. In 1969 television took in nearly $3.6 billion.

THE STRUCTURE OF THE MOVIE INDUSTRY

The motion-picture industry, because of its peculiar relationship to the mass markets of an industrial culture, early developed most of the familiar characteristics of publishing and broadcasting. Its techniques and products were standardized, its policies mass-oriented, and it was characterized by bigness, costliness, and concentration of facilities both vertically and horizontally. However, in one important respect the Hollywood film industry was different from its rivals in the contest for the time and money of American consumers. Like book publishing and some notable exceptions in magazine publishing, it was distinguished by its independence from advertising for direct support. Film industry policies were determined largely by marketing considerations, and the industry made extensive use of the marketing apparatus to merchandise its products, but the Hollywood film was not a component of the marketing system in the sense that it sold products other than its own to consumers.

The first motion picture exhibited in the United States was shown on April 23, 1896, in New York City. Thomas Edison, after perfecting the earlier peep show, or kinetoscope, abandoned his original plan to exploit the commercial possibilities of movie exhibition because he believed that showing films on a large screen to many persons simultaneously would exhaust the market too quickly to be profitable. But the success of the first movies changed motion pictures from a novelty to a business, and aggressive entrepreneurs replaced the inventors to seek maximum profits. Almost immediately production, distribution, and exhibition practices were introduced that would characterize the industry half a century later.

Size and Expense

Today most motion pictures are geared to a mass market; size and expense have become typical of the industry. In the early days a film could be produced with relatively little capital. In time, however, a single feature-length film came to represent an investment of anywhere from half a million to $10 million—even as much as $40 million. In the early 1970s, with the near collapse of the Hollywood film industry, new and businesslike executives took over most of the major studios and introduced practices that reduced costs by many millions. A major studio once made as many as fifty pictures a year. In 1970 the average was fifteen. Also some of the younger film-makers demonstrated that profitable movies could be made on budgets that were low by Hollywood standards.

Some studios are now setting budget limits of $2 million a film, because the rule of thumb in Hollywood is that a picture must gross two and a half times its cost just to break even. Few films costing more than $2 million in the early 1970s promised to break even. Stars who once commanded $500,000 to $1 million a picture now are offered small salaries and a percentage of the return.

Entry and Survival

For the first dozen years of the motion-picture industry, almost perfect competition prevailed among numerous small companies. Since demand for equipment depended on the popularity of the pictures shown, movie-equipment manufacturers began to produce films to attract large audiences. Exhibitors began to cultivate industrial workers in large cities. Five-cent tickets fitted wage-earners' pocketbooks, and visual appeal overcame immigrants' language difficulties. Profits depended on quick turn-over of customers which, in turn, relied on short programs with frequent changes in pictures. The demand for films was so increased that the production of movies became the most important branch of the industry. And, as might have been expected, the leading equipment manufacturers—Edison, Biograph, and Vitagraph—joined in an effort to monopolize production through their control of United States patents. But their efforts were unsuccessful. Entry was too easy for new entrepreneurs. Cameras were legally available from abroad and illegally at home. And, as W. F. Hellmuth points out, the prospect of large profits was so alluring that it "overwhelmed the fear of lawsuits over patent rights."

With the eventual lifting of restrictions on equipment, distribution and marketing problems became more important. By 1908 the movies had become a serious competitor of the stage, churches, newspapers, and saloons for the leisure time and money of the public. Demand for better films forced increases in production costs. These in turn required more effective distribution to increase the return on films. This was made possible at first by national organizations of independent distributors, but later the major producers assumed distribution of their own products. Thus, horizontal consolidation for exhibition took place almost immediately after the reorientation of the industry to the mass market. And this was followed in the battle royal for control before and after World War I by vertical integration of the industry as a whole.

The Patents Company

In 1909 the ten leading domestic and foreign producers of film and equipment combined in the Motion Picture Patents Company to maximize profits from their pooled patents. The patents trust organized its own nationwide distribution system, the first vertical integration in the industry, which absorbed or forced out all other distributors except William Fox. But, like the previous efforts of Edison, Biograph, and Vitagraph to monopolize production, the patent trust's attempt to monopolize both production and distribution failed. The independents were far from extirpated, even after several years of bitter competition. To counter the trust's low-cost productions, the independents tried to raise the quality of their films by technical improvements and to enhance their salability by introduction of the star system.

As the independents sought to avoid attacks—both legal and physical—by the Patents Company, the production center shifted from New York to Los Angeles. The independents also countered the Patents Company with production of feature, or long-story, pictures. The first multireel films shown in the United States were foreign importations, but their immediate success led independents to produce feature films while the trust continued to produce one-reelers. The long-story film gave prestige to the independents' movies, appealed to the upper classes, and made higher admissions feasible. By 1914 there was only a minor market for one-reel films. Thereafter the Patents Company was unimportant, being displaced by an increasing number of independents, who reverted to the behavior of those they had overthrown by engaging in a battle for control of exhibition as well as of production and distribution.

Vertical and Horizontal Integration

The introduction of the star system and the feature film necessitated large capital investment. To make large investment profitable, production had to be continuous. This meant exhibition facilities had to be increased to consume the products of continuous production. Producers, seeking to acquire distribution and exhibition facilities, started a wave of theater building that continued unabated until the Depression of the 1930s.

In 1917 Paramount (the leading distributor) and Famous Players-Lasky (the leading major producer) and twelve lesser producers combined under Adolph Zukor to monopolize talent under the star system and to dictate terms to exhibitors. The resultant block booking, not a new trade practice, was ruthlessly used by Zukor to guarantee sales of the combine's less spectacular merchandise. Rivals countered by creating the First National Exhibition Circuit to act as purchasing agent for twenty-six of the largest first-run exhibitors in the country. This threatened not only Zukor's control of the star system, but the combine's domination of production. In retaliation Zukor went into the theater business and became an exhibitor, producer, and distributor.

The giant rivals, Zukor and First National, were not the only menaces to small independent exhibitors. By 1923 Loew's and Fox also had expanded their holdings considerably; the independently owned first-run theater rapidly became extinct through absorption either by major producer-distributors or by unaffiliated circuits.

The Big Five and Wall Street

By the 1930s the so-called Big Five—Paramount, Loew's, Warner Bros., Twentieth Century Fox, and Radio-Keith-Orpheum—dominated production, distribution, and exhibition. They remained in oligopical control of the industry until after World War II. Below them in importance were the Little Three—Universal, Columbia, and United Artists, the last a distributing company only. At mid-century, the Big Five and the Little Three were producing 95 per cent of American motion pictures. Those same eight companies also distributed about 95 per cent of the total films and controlled about 70 per cent of the first-run theaters in cities with populations of more than 100,000 and nearly 60 per cent of the first-run theaters in cities with populations between 25,000 and 100,000.

During the period of vertical integration by the Big Five, producers were forced to turn to Wall Street for financial backing, a move necessitated by several factors: competition for expensive exhibition palaces, the spiraling costs of the star system, the burdens of publicity and other marketing methods, and the high cost of sound equipment introduced in 1926. All the major companies established alliances with leading banks and investment houses. To oversee the use of funds and get maximum profits, the financiers installed their representatives in important positions throughout the industry. Thus, although the producing facilities were in Hollywood, the nerve center of the industry became New York City.

Entering the field when the production cost of the average feature was approaching the half-million-dollar mark, as against one-fifth of that amount for the same length film a few years before, the financiers quickly established a policy of getting maximum profits from every picture produced. Advertising budgets were increased enormously. The public was encouraged to demand star personalities, mammoth and expensive sets, stories based on famous books or plays, and well-known directors. Producers and directors were instructed to produce pictures to meet these specifications, sacrificing initiative and originality to the demands of the market place. Will Hays, former guardian of the public morals and apologist for the film industry, always maintained that making movies is an art rather than a business. But even artistic commodities require a financial and marketing apparatus when they are produced for mass consumption. The Hollywood end product was exhibited in theaters, but the basic character of the product and its packaging was determined by the chief executives in New York.

Antitrust Action

The motion-picture industry was founded six years after passage of the Sherman Anti-Trust Act. But, despite the statute, the major companies uninterruptedly pursued a policy of restraining competition, with monopoly and maximum profits as their goal. Many factors facilitate monopolistic practices in the movie industry. For example, the intangible nature of picture properties, the star system, and the fact that individual theaters are limited to offering one, two, or three pictures on a single bill. Such factors are inherent in the industry and beyond control. However, ownership and trade practices are subject to control; and as a result of occasional brushes with the Sherman Act, certain obvious monopolistic practices were enjoined. But it was not until 1938 that the long-run trend toward concentration in the industry was in any significant way retarded by legal action. The Department of Justice filed suits against eight film companies on the charge that they were engaged in monopolistic practices and in illegal restraint of trade in producing, distributing, and exhibiting motion pictures.

After about a week of opening skirmishes, the trial was adjourned to permit negotiation between the Department of Justice and the defendants for settlement by decree. Five companies reached an agreement with the department in 1940, but three refused to be parties to the decree. After eight more years of irregular testimony, intermittent negotiation, two lower court decisions, and one appeal, the Supreme Court held that the five fully integrated companies were parties to a combination that had exhibition monopoly in larger cities as its goal. There was no finding of monopoly or illegal practices in film production.

RKO and Paramount, apparently tired of the effort, expense, and uncertainty of continued negotiations, sought a consent decree. The Department of Justice insisted on divorcement of theaters from production and distribution interests, and early in 1949 Paramount and RKO agreed to the terms of the decree. Loew's, Twentieth Century-Fox, and Warner Bros. strongly disapproved. But after the Supreme Court upheld a district court's divorcement of theater holdings from the business of production-distribution of the three remaining majors, Warners and Twentieth Century-Fox in 1951 and Loew's in 1952 entered into consent judgments similar to those of RKO and Paramount.

At the time of the final consent decree in 1949, Professor Robert Brady, an economist, described the movie industry as a "small coterie of vertically integrated, horizontally co-ordinated, and monopolistically inclined corporations." He said they were "compacted" by contracts, agreements, and "understandings of one sort or another," and submissive to a trade association possessing "cartel-like powers over various activities of its constituent membership." According to Brady, members compete with one another in much the same way that the divisions of General Motors do. Industry policy and operations are governed by a selected management group "responsible to banking and real estate powers," whose interests in turn are interwoven with other monopoly or semi-monopoly groups "having little to do with the movie industry directly."

The Industry Fights Back

According to Hellmuth, since the "initial outburst of enthusiasm which greeted the decrees, delays and backsliding which may emasculate the effectiveness of the anti-trust decrees in the long run have developed." The backsliding has occurred on three fronts. Stockholders in divorced theater groups have maintained stock interests in production-distribution units. Exhibitors and distributors (United Artists, for example) have moved into production. Producer-distributor units have begun to collaborate with their enemy, the television industry, substituting television stations for the traditional exhibition houses.

After a period of consternation and uncertainty in which competition from television was almost wholly blamed for the decline of movie attendance, the motion-picture majors moved vigorously not only to reassert their dominance over the industry, but also to counteract the influence of the new electronic medium. Evidences of their aggressiveness are theater TV, which appeals to exhibitors as well as to producers, and direct affiliation of movie interests with television organizations. As Hellmuth points out, the 1953 merger of United Paramount Theaters, the largest theater company, with ABC, the third largest radio-television network, into American Broadcasting-Paramount Theaters is "only the most spectacular affiliation." Among the Big Seven nearly all turn out filmed shows for television, and all have sold film stocks to the networks.

CROSS-MEDIA OWNERSHIP

Until about 1960 the communications businesses stuck rather single-mindedly to their specialty of communicating. A magazine publisher wishing to expand might bring out a new magazine or add a line of paperback books. A newspaper publisher might add another daily to his chain or buy a broadcasting station. But it was usually low-key and had little effect on the large world of mass communication.

Today the scope, style, and substance of media ownership has changed. Many communications businesses are expanding into other areas, and others are being taken over by the huge conglomerates. Esquire, Inc, publishes magazines and owns Wide-Light Corp., Rig-a-Lite, Inc., White Night Company, and other outdoor lighting firms. *Saturday Review* and *McCall's* magazines are in the same corporation bag as Hunt's tomato sauce, Canada Dry gingerale, the TV program-packing firm of Talent Associates, Ltd., and the printers of dozens of magazines for other publishers.

When Briton Hadden and Henry Luce started Time in 1923, they were simply in the magazine business with an oracular weekly, which they filled with rewrites from the newspapers, mainly *The New York Times*. Today the company publishes newspapers, magazines, trade books, and textbooks; runs a book club; has a stake in community-antenna systems; is in the phonograph-record business in Germany; and holds a substantial bloc of stock in Metro-Goldwyn-Mayer.

Or consider the Columbia Broadcasting System. Its interests include Holt, Rinehart and Winston, which publishes trade books and textbooks; W. B. Saunders, publisher of medical works; production of feature-length motion-pictures for theaters and instructional films for classrooms; production of phonograph records; development of Linotron, an electronic typesetter; and the New York Yankees baseball team.

In 1968 there were more than 130 mergers and acquisitions involving communications properties. They included Litton Industries' acquiring Chapman-Reinhold, publisher of trade and technical publications; Xerox's acquiring Ginn and Company, textbook publishers; and Harcourt, Brace, Jovanovich taking over several farm and trade magazines.

The reasons for this development are various. One obviously is to broaden the financial base. Since magazine publishing is rarely a highly lucrative enterprise, for instance, some publishers would like alternative sources of income. Another is to capitalize on the swiftly expanding educational market by providing the textooks, teaching aids, programmed learning materials, and other elements of the curriculum from kindergarten through college. Yet another is recognition of the revolution in communications technology, which is already blurring the distinctions between the printed media and the electronic. The pairing-off of the print media firms with the electronic—Time Inc. with General Electric, for instance, and RCA with Random House and Harcourt, Brace, Jovanovich—has been a characteristic of recent years. When Time Inc. acquired $17.7 million of M-G-M stock in 1967, it did so on the basis of a 200-page staff report titled *Information Technology: An Overview of the 70s.* Time Inc. was attracted to M-G-M not only by its movie-making potential but also by its diversified holdings in such fields as TV programming, music, and recordings. Said the executive in charge of corporate development: "Such new and soon-to-come electronic techniques as satellite communications, CATV, pay-TV, video tape and video disc are part of the new world of communications, and this is what Time Inc. is interested in."

All this is profoundly disturbing to a number of thoughtful observers, including Commissioner Nicholas Johnson of the FCC. In a notable article titled "The Media Barons and the Public Interest," which was published in the *Atlantic* in 1968, Johnson reviewed the conglomerate record of mass communication and concluded:

In general, I would urge the minimal standard that no accumulation of media should be permitted without a specific and convincing showing of a continuing countervailing social benefit. For no one has a higher calling in an increasingly complex free society bent on self-government than he who informs and moves the people. Personal prejudice, ignorance, social pressure, and advertiser pressure are in large measure inevitable. But a nation that has, in Learned Hand's phrase, "staked its all" upon the rational dialogue of an informed electorate simply cannot take any unnecessary risk of polluting the stream of information and opinion that sustains it. At the very least, the burden of proving the social utility of doing otherwise should be upon him who seeks the power and profit which will result.

Whatever may be the outcome, the wave of renewed interest in the impact of ownership on the role of the media in our society is healthy. All will gain from intelligent inquiry by Congress, the Executive, the regulatory commissions—and especially the academic community, the American people generally, and the media themselves. For, as the Supreme Court has noted, nothing is more important in a free society than "the widest possible dissemination of information from diverse and antagonistic sources." And if we are unwilling to discuss *this* issue fully today we may find ourselves discussing none that matter very much tomorrow.

The Media
as Informers
and Interpreters

A people without reliable news is, sooner or later, a people without the basis of freedom.

HAROLD J. LASKI

Until the early 1930s the work of the average reporter was structured. His job was to fashion a clear and concise straight news story, starting with the who, what, when, and where of an event and proceeding toward the end, placing factual details in descending order of interest and importance. He was to hold a mirror up to an event to show its surface. Explaining why it had occurred and brooding over what should be done about it were left to the editorial writers and columnists. A few reporters, primarily foreign correspondents and Washington correspondents, had been given license to interpret the news and explain and clarify complex events. But ninety-five per cent were limited to straight news reporting.

Then came the New Deal, and suddenly the old forms seemed inadequate. Some correspondents say they can fix on the exact time when "the old journalism" failed: the day in 1933 when the United States went off the gold standard. Vainly trying to report that cataclysmic and baffling change, they appealed to the White House, and a government economist was sent over to help. Then the correspondents tried to explain the new facets of economic life to the American people in the economic specialist's idiom—almost disastrously.

The gathering complexity of public affairs during the New Deal days, and later when the Cold War began, made it increasingly difficult to confine reporting to the strait jacket of unelaborated fact. Reporting exactly what a government official said, or what Congress did, was often misleading; the facts by themselves didn't always speak the whole truth. Correspondents began, somewhat hesitantly, to build the structure of interpretative reporting. Behind the pioneering of some foreign correspondents and a few columnists whose forte was explanation rather than opinion, newsmen began to explain *why* events occurred and what the facts *meant*.

Interpretation did not come into being full-blown—its structure, in fact, is still developing—and so many editors and reporters resisted so fiercely that even today some of its proponents gingerly avoid the term, preferring to call it "depth reporting." For a time a debate split the top level of the great Louisville *Courier-Journal*. Editor Barry Bingham argued: "The need for interpretative reporting becomes more insistent week by week." At the same time Executive Editor James Pope attacked the interpreters, maintaining that "by definition, interpretation is subjective and means 'to translate, elucidate, construe . . . in the light of individual belief or interest . . . ' Interpretation is the bright dream of the saintly seers who expound and construe in the midst of the news." To Pope and other proponents of straight news reporting, interpretative reporting was simply an abandoning of objective journalism.

The most insistent advocate of interpretation, Lester Markel of *The New York Times*, attacked the notion that any form of reporting could really be defined as "objective":

> The reporter, the most objective reporter, collects fifty facts. Out of the fifty he selects twelve to include in his story (there is such a thing as space limitation). Thus he discards thirty-eight. This is Judgment Number One.
>
> Then the reporter or editor decides which of the facts shall be the first paragraph of the story, thus emphasizing one fact above the other eleven. This is Judgment Number Two.
>
> Then the editor decides whether the story shall be placed on Page One or Page Twelve; on Page One it will command many times the attention it would on Page Twelve. This is Judgment Number Three.
>
> This so-called factual presentation is thus subjected to three judgments, all of them most humanly and most ungodly made.

The debate is sometimes no more than a question of explicit definition. Reporting exactly what a Presidential candidate said in Oregon is clearly straight news. But how does one classify a story that matches what the Presidential candidate said in Oregon against what he said in California and points out that he was emphasizing different aspects of his policy and his program in each state? The interpreters call this interpretation; advocates of straight news say that such matching is entirely consistent with the concept of objective reporting.

Actually the fine distinctions matter little, for today's correspondents are carrying political reporting to a level that is clearly interpretative. The leading correspondents inquire around, dig in, think through—then explain that the candidate changed the pitch of his oratory in moving from one state to the other because his private polling organization had discovered that his anti-Communist image was weak in California and advised him to play up in Los Angeles the belligerence of his tone when last he faced the Soviet Premier.

One of the sharpest interpreters, Karl Meyer of the Washington *Post*, captured in the spoof quoted below the omniscient tone of the most exaggerated interpretations.

> WASHINGTON, Feb. 29—The feeling in this city is that the President has given a new twist to the tired formulas of foreign policy by his bold proposal to exchange the state of Alaska for the East German People's Republic.
>
> But despite the predictable outcry that has followed the President's carefully worded statement, the move is neither so ruinous as opponents contend nor as inspired a masterstroke as the administration's publicists insist.
>
> There would be gains and losses for both sides. Although the area of freedom would be extended to East Germany, the swap would also mean that the Soviet Union would acquire bases near our defense perimeter, absorbing in the process the people of Alaska.
>
> To an objective observer, the controversy over the President's proposals clearly provides another melancholy example of how the methods of diplomacy lag so sadly behind the needs of the atomic age. Surely such complex negotiations might best be carried on quietly by skilled specialists. At the same time, the necessity for secrecy—and the failure to brief the press—has meant that the public has been caught unawares, and a controversy damaging to unity is likely to follow.

Press Associations

The extent to which interpretation pervades political reporting today is indicated by a memo designed to warn Associated Press reporters against it. AP and UPI are generally considered the last bastions of straight news reporting and, in fact, much of each news report filed is as straight as fallible human beings can make it (although UPI is proud of its role in the development of interpretation). AP General Manager Wes Gallagher sought to emphasize in his memo that "the AP man is not a participant in the news. He is the recorder of it." But in spelling out the wire-service mission, Gallagher unwittingly revealed how far interpretation has penetrated the AP report, not to mention his own concept of reporting. He cited disapprovingly an AP story that began "Few Latin American military leaders have won such quick support from the grassroots as the one led by Col.———," and cautioned, "How could any reporter know this for a fact a day or two afterward? Nothing in the article gave specific support for the statement. It was just incomplete reporting." This surely suggests that AP reporters can make such judgments—and thus participate in the news—by waiting long enough and developing support for judgments they care to make. This is somewhat different from dispassionately holding a mirror up to an event.

Gallagher went further, citing with approval the work of James Marlow, a specialist in interpreting the decisions of the Supreme Court. Marlow, Gallagher wrote, "has read countless books on the subject and has accumulated over 100 reference books. When writing about the Court, he is in a position, therefore, to cite specific cases and instances to prove the point he wants to make." This is hardly reprehensible (and, in fact, Marlow is highly respected), but it is quite different from merely recording facts. Gallagher seems to be suggesting that the AP reporter is free to make points, not just make note of actions, provided he first develops some expertise.

Gallagher's memo had the tone of a warning that interpretation had just begun to creep into AP stories. In fact, the AP report had long been colored by occasional interpretative writing. On January 15, 1955, this story was widely reprinted by AP members:

> President Eisenhower at midterm is a changed man—a man of increasing political awareness, with a firmer grip on the problems of world leadership . . . . He has devoted nearly half a century of service to his country. As soldier and as President he has carved for himself a secure niche in history, but now he hears an increasing volume of criticism, mainly from Democrats . . . He evidences a determination to mold the GOP to the "progressive moderate" pattern he has designed for it. . . . In spite of ups and downs his goals have remained unchanged—peace for a trouble world and a "dynamic progressive, forward-looking" program to lead America down a "middle road" to greater strength and prosperity. . . . The President still exposes that sweeping infectious grin in all directions but there appears in his eye a glint of steel that seems indicative of a new kind of Eisenhower. . . .

Proponents of interpretation—or news analysis, as some call it—insist that interpretation is not opinion, that the interpretative reporter *explains* while editorial writers and columnists, who produce opinion pieces, *advocate*.

Many other developments have shaped the character of information and interpretation. News coverage was greatly improved nationally by the expansion of communication facilities, especially those of the press associations.

Founded in 1848, the Associated Press, by extending its franchise beyond New York, had become the main source of national and international news by the turn of the century. The rise of the press association was one of the most important developments in the history of journalism. AP expanded in the twentieth century, with strong competition from United Press and International News Service—these two news services in 1958 merged to make United Press International. While contributing to the increasing uniformity of American journalism, the press associations also improved newspapers by providing editors and readers with a continuous coverage of domestic and world events better than any previously available.

The Associated Press now serves more than 5000 newspapers and radio stations around the globe. It produces more than one million words a day—the equivalent of seven or eight novels of average length. Its communication system of leased teletype circuits, submarine cables, Morse wireless channels, and radio-teletype channels circles the world. Both AP and UPI spend more than $50 million a year to provide information. AP has more than 3000 employees; UPI, about 2500. Both services have trouble breaking even, but both attempt to cover the world.

MAGAZINES AS INFORMERS AND INTERPRETERS

By magazine standards, newspapers and press associations came quite late to interpretative reporting. Interpretation and its forerunner, the essay, have been at the center of magazine interest for centuries. Many trade and technical magazines are devoted primarily to *news* affecting their readers and thus may be considered informers more than interpreters. But even these specialized magazines usually carry some interpretative content, and a great many magazines are devoted almost exclusively to interpretation. To clarify, to explain, to place facts in a meaningful context—these are the *raisons d'être* of thousands of magazines.

As a continuing publication the magazine can serve as a forum for discussion by carrying responses from its readers. It can sustain campaigns for indefinite periods and work for cumulative impact. Its available space enables the magazine to cover subjects at length, and thus to appeal to the intellect more than to the emotions. It is neither as transitory as broadcasting nor as readily discarded as the newspaper.

Many magazines meet the stringent requirements for media of instruction and interpretation. John Fischer, former editor of *Harper's,* called the magazine article "the characteristic literary medium of our generation."

From the viewpoint of many critics, however, magazines have basic shortcomings that negate much of their value as interpreters. For example, although some magazines speak to and for little publics within the larger population, it is certainly true that the commercial magazine is essentially conservative and inclined to support the status quo. Despite strains of variety, it is also true that magazines are imitative. If a writer becomes popular, magazines compete for his work. If a topic catches the public fancy, magazines will explore it—and soon exhaust it. And magazines must share with other media the blame for creating a pseudo-world—one that may be especially dangerous because it is so nearly in focus that some readers confuse it with reality.

Against these shortcomings must be weighed some striking achievements in interpretation. Magazines have borne a real share of responsibility for social and political reforms. Magazines place events in a national perspective. Without national newspapers, magazines were for a long period almost alone in looking at issues with national and international implications in view. Indeed, some magazines have fostered a sense of national community and furnished Americans across the nation with a common fund of subjects for discussion.

For millions the magazine has long been an inexpensive instructor in daily living. It counsels on all the necessities of modern life: nutrition, child-rearing, marital and financial problems, home furnishing and redecorating.

Perhaps most important, interpretative reports in magazines may be the chief educator beyond college. Historical articles that explore the nation's past, biographical articles that recall the men who shaped that past and those who are shaping the present, foreign reports on the accomplishments of other peoples—these are the substance of many magazines. Magazines have introduced the American people to the best in architecture, painting, sculpture, and thought. *Life* is almost certainly the greatest disseminator of art in the history of mankind.

All in all, it is probable that the greatest value of magazines is interpretation. It is likely that of all the media the magazine is the best interpreter.

So far, we have been discussing information from a large, general perspective. To make this more meaningful, let us now consider the spread of information in detail. Consider first the operations of three fairly typical newspapers which receive press association reports and which were studied by a Stanford research team.

A SUBURBAN AFTERNOON DAILY

Virtually all this daily's state, national, and international news is received from an Associated Press wire and two United Press International wires. This news is processed by a news editor and his two assistants. In addition to making decisions on more than 100,000 words that come over these wires every day, these three men also edit and place all local news, which may run as high as 10,000 words a day, and select a dozen or so news pictures from approximately 100 provided by a wirephoto machine every day. Except for the society, sports, business, editorial, and comic pages, the three editors fill all the news columns.

The news editor does much of the work himself, discarding large quantities of wire copy and dividing the remaining stories among his assistants and himself. Because all wire copy is received on punched tapes as well as on paper, editing consists largely of choosing between the AP and UPI versions of a story, checking for accuracy and typographical errors, and finding suitable cutting points for stories. The punched tape can be set into type rapidly and inexpensively if few changes are made. These are very strong arguments against thoughtful editing. There is little rewriting—there is little time for it.

When the news editor arrived one morning at six, he found approximately 50,000 words of wire copy. (The wire service cycle for supplying news to afternoon papers begins shortly after midnight. Thus, most news editors who start work during the dawn hours find many stories waiting for them.) He swiftly discarded all but about 8000 words. During the next seven hours, as the wires continued to spew stories, the news editor and his assistants used more than 20,000 words of wire copy (of a total of about 110,000 words available—much of the information duplicated because AP and UPI report many of the same events). They edited lightly, wrote headlines, placed stories on each page, and then sent the selected stories to the composing room to be put into type.

They also edited and placed about 6000 words of local news and selected and placed sixteen pictures. During the last hour of their working day, they prepared some material for the next day's edition—just as the day before they had devoted the final hour to preparing material for today's paper. During a single working day, then, they edited the rough equivalent of a small book. (In contrast, after a book manuscript is in hand, a publishing house customarily devotes at least six months, and often a year or more, to its editing and production.)

The news editor is regularly afflicted with doubts, for he knows that many of his readers will already have read elsewhere some of the stories he plays up and that other readers will have been satisfied with the top-of-the-news sketches of the same stories heard on their car radios or seen on television; but he is concerned to provide for those readers who want more than they are able to get elsewhere.

Other questions and doubts arise. How much serious news can his readers take? How many of them will read yet another report on Vietnam, another story on the indecisive Paris peace talks, another report on the interminable battle between President and Congress? On the other hand, is the editor adequately serving those who follow such matters intently—if he publishes 5-inch stories rather than 20-inch stories?

Is the editor furthering the causes of rioters if he emphasizes their actions? Can a community really be informed if an editor decides to play down all the news of conflict? If he answers the clamors of local critics and tries to balance stories of conflict with stories of cooperation, how many subscribers will actually read all the reports of constructive work? If he boldly headlines a story of conflict, his paper will be accused of sensationalism. Reports on the New Morality—and especially those using the language that is its hallmark—will offend some older readers; but failing to give adequate attention to it will persuade many younger readers that they were right all along in thinking that the Establishment press was stodgy. Such diverse demands are imposed by the effort to inform and entertain a heterogeneous audience.

Thanks to court decisions made years ago, the suburban dailies now receive the same basic wire services (AP and UPI) that are available to the metropolitan papers. But they cannot obtain all the special services that most metropolitans purchase. Some of the special news services and some of the syndicates that supply news and features draw contracts—or have "understandings"—with metropolitan papers that close out the suburban papers. The metropolitans argue that their survival depends upon their ability to provide features that are unavailable to their competitors.

This explains, for example, the dreary comic strips that appear in some suburban papers. They are not offered because the editors believe that their readers will be enthralled by "Priscilla's Pop" and "Fred Bassett," but because the metropolitan papers publish "Peanuts" and "Bobby Sox" and "Dennis the Menace," and because few metropolitan papers will permit their strips to appear in the suburban papers.

All metropolitan editors treasure the attractive comic strips, and some, who discovered quite late which ones are attractive, have used cash to wrest "Peanuts" and "Dennis the Menace" from the smaller papers, which accurately forecast the popularity of the strips when they were first offered by the syndicates. Small-town papers may be able to assert territorial rights in some cases, but their contracts with syndicates have a way of running out, whereupon syndicate salesmen draw up more profitable contracts with metropolitan dailies.

There are other hazards in the jungle of comic strip syndication. The editor who tries to jettison "Orphan Annie" because he and his staff are sickened by it soon has forty irate readers calling him regularly at 3 a.m. to protest.

Such are the problems of publishing suburban and small-town dailies. Like the metropolitans these papers serve such a variety of readers—the leading banker in town and the janitor who cleans the bank, the college professor and the high school drop-out—that this variety would seem to be problem enough. But the small daily editor must cope with the appeal of the metropolitan paper that looms next door, and with the local weekly that nibbles away in his own backyard.

A CITY DAILY

The pace in an office producing a morning paper is somewhat more relaxed than in office producing evening papers. This does not mean that editors laze through their working hours. In fact, the editor who was by far the fastest worker observed in the Stanford study processed world news for a morning paper. In general, however, deskmen for morning papers are able to work steadily rather than frenetically.

The pace is suggested by the operation of a city daily with a somewhat larger circulation than the suburban daily described above. Wire news is processed by the telegraph editor, who arrives shortly after 2:30 p.m. to begin work on the mass that has already accumulated. A copy girl who arrived earlier has stripped the copy from the wire machines and distributed it among the various desks (sports, society, etc.). Most of it goes to the telegraph editor, who has instructed the girl as to how he wants the news stacked and arranged. Disciplined and orderly, the editor becomes absorbed. He is seemingly unhurried, but he works almost mechanically, pausing only now and then for a cup of coffee. His copyreader comes in at 5 p.m., but the telegraph editor delegates relatively little of the work. He has developed his system, and he is pleased with it. He discards story after story with only a glance. Some of the stories he selects are pencil-edited and passed to the copy girl to send to the composing room by pneumatic tube. Others are set aside in neat piles, later to be discarded or pieced into another story with pencil, scissors, and paste. This paper does not use punched tape, so that the telegraph editor has the freedom to edit a story thoroughly rather than merely to print what the wire services provide.

The managing editor had arrived at 2 p.m. By 3 p.m. the news editor and the country editor are on hand. The paper tries to cover a far-flung county. During the next hour these three editors confer briefly with the telegraph editor. Then they go to their desks, and it becomes clear that, unlike the suburban daily described earlier, this is a decentralized operation. The managing editor is chiefly a supervisor who advises the sub-editors on important matters and devotes much of his remaining time to mail, syndicated columns, and administrative decisions. Nonetheless, on the evening his work was observed, the managing editor processed more than 6000 words of syndicated material and press releases.

The tempo does not seem to vary greatly during the evening. Everyone works steadily until about 9 p.m., then in a more relaxed fashion until 10, when the first edition must be locked up, printed, and transported nearly a hundred miles. At this time only the county editor and his copyreaders, who are still receiving stories from reporters in outlying cities and who must prepare pages for four regional editions, are still hard at work. The hours from 10 to 12 are relaxed for most of the others. Night baseball scores and a few other late items complete the day.

And yet the calm is deceptive. For there are more editors and copyreaders at work here than on the afternoon paper described above—twice as many, in fact—and their duties are spread across more hours. The effective hours of work for most of those who produce afternoon papers are 6 a.m. to 12, with the noon hour devoted to late-breaking items. The effective hours for the paper described, and for most other morning newspapers, are 2 or 3 p.m. to midnight, and sometimes later.

As a measure of the productivity of the editors of this morning paper, consider the volume of material handled by the telegraph editor and the news editor. In all, the telegraph editor and his copyreader processed nearly 18,000 words. From 3 to 10 p.m., the news editor and his copyreader (whose task was somewhat simpler because much of the material they considered was preselected by the telegraph editor) processed 23,600 words, about 90 stories. In addition, the news desk prepared 3200 words for the Sunday edition. Together the telegraph editor and the news editor edited and placed nearly 45,000 words and 14 photos.

A METROPOLITAN DAILY

"The larger the paper, the larger the staff" is a satisfactory rule of thumb, but it is not necessarily true that a huge staff reduces the pressures on deskmen. A metropolitan daily subscribes to many more services than does a suburban newspaper or a small-city daily, and it is likely to do much more with what comes in.

The editors of a metropolitan paper of nearly half a million circulation who were interviewed for this study scoffed at the papers that publish wire copy from punched tape (like the first paper described earlier) and had little more to say for those that piece together two wire reports (like the second). The metropolitan city editor, an acid man, said of wire reports: "They're like the symphonies you hear on recordings, with one movement coming from this performance, another from that one. The whole thing never really happened." He cited examples of wire reports that he had found to be lacking in details, riddled with minor errors, or simply wrong. (This editor is probably unduly negative in his total condemnation of the wire services. It is true, though, that many editors complain that they find wire service reports on events in their areas misleading.)

Some wire stories do find their way into this metropolitan daily without change, but most of these are reports from locales beyond the reach of the fifty-man city staff or the small staff of state capital, Washington, and foreign correspondents. The editors make a manful effort to check out everything. Trips to the sites of important stories are fairly frequent. Calls to California, Texas, and Cuba are common. At the very least, sub-editors will check the reports of one service against another; piecing together a story from several submitted by AP, UPI, and special-report services is routine.

Not only is there thorough checking and rewriting of wire service reports, as well as of the stories provided by special services—most of it by the city editor's staff—there is a constant and mind-rattling spewing of reports from 22 machines. The staff argues that all these services are essential to produce the five major editions and the three replates (editions with minor changes) that come out every day. The staff opposes producing so many different papers—the city editor holds that the hastily produced first edition is "the worst newspaper in the world"—but management believes that all of them are necessary to retain the slender circulation edge over the competing daily.

Tensions are produced by the processes of multiple editing. Stories are stripped from the machines by copy boys in the wire room, and most of the stories are handed via a pass-through to the wire editor in the newsroom. Appropriate stories are carried directly from the wire room to the sports and business editors; those that originated in the state go directly to the city editor.

From the wire editor's desk, much of the copy goes to the foreign-national desk and to the city desk. Because the foreign-national editor is aided only by one rewrite man, while the city editor may command as many as twenty reporters and rewrite men during peak periods, some of the foreign and national stories go to the city desk for checking and rewriting.

From the various desks rewritten copy goes to the news editor. He makes final decisions as to publishing it, then passes the stories he has selected to the make-up editor, who assigns each a place in the paper. The stories then go to the copy editor, who parcels them out to the copyreaders on the rim of the universal desk for final editing and headlines. The stories are returned to the copy editor, who sends them to the composing room via pneumatic tube. The complexity of the operation promotes jurisdictional disputes and ragged nerves.

Although there are slack periods, editing this metropolitan daily—which is an afternoon paper even though one of its many editions is available at almost any time—is virtually a 24-hour operation. Observation began at 6 p.m., when the work was relaxed. During the next seven hours until 1 a.m., fewer than 50 stories were sent to the composing room. From 1 a.m. to 11 a.m. was the high point: 20 to 30 stories an hour moved for nine hours, with 41 moving between 10 and 11. The pace slowed during the afternoon and dropped off sharply at the beginning of the new publishing cycle at 6 p.m.

Because the city desk and the foreign-national desk handle wire copy and the rewritten stories that spring from it, they process substantially more copy than does the wire desk, which does little more with most stories than to pass them along to the appropriate desk. On the day the operation was observed, the city desk handled more than 150,000 words (almost 900 items) and used about 12 per cent of them. The foreign-national desk handled nearly 90,000 words (more than 400 stories) and used less then 10 per cent of them.

In all, the metropolitan daily handled nearly 2500 wire items made up of more than 400,000 words. (This figure, like the figure for the other papers, does not include sports, society, business, and editorial pages.) The staff used more than 40,000 words in a total of approximately 300 stories.

FEATURE SYNDICATES

Also important to newspapers was the development of feature syndicates, which supply on a contract basis articles, columns, poetry, fiction, serial stories, garden news, recipes, dress patterns, photographs, illustrations, and comic strips. The syndicate springs from an innovation in 1861 by Ansel N. Kellogg, the editor of a small Wisconsin paper. He supplied small country papers with "insides," commonly known as "boiler plates"—that is, whole papers with the inside pages already printed, or inside page-fillers that could be inserted into the regular edition. After 1875, when the first stereotype plate was introduced, he syndicated the plates in various lengths—column, half-column, half-page, full-page and, so on.

In 1884 Irving Bacheller began a similar service for metropolitan papers. By 1920 the syndicate was a well-organized business and an integral part of American journalism. Today there are nearly 200 syndicates of various kinds in the United States. Perhaps the best known is King Features, organized in 1896 by Hearst to sell features he was using in his own papers and to devise new ones for the Hearst chain. In its time King Features has syndicated such writers as William Jennings Bryan and George Bernard Shaw.

Newspaper Enterprise Association (NEA), another giant, sells a complete feature service, including a women's page, a sports page, a comic page, a page of canned editorials with cartoons, one or more pages of general news features, and numberless pictures sometimes presented as a "picture page." This canned material may be seen in the content and make-up of newspapers throughout the country—and may result in a paper in Maine so closely resembling one in Texas as to be scarcely distinguishable. Most syndicate copy is "soft," as compared with "hard" news stories, and it is superficial or intellectually innocuous. While encouraging lazy editors to substitute prefabrications for locally produced news, syndicated material does make available information and interpretation that costs hundreds of thousands of dollars to produce and that few single papers could afford to develop themselves. Thus, millions of readers are exposed to ideas and events they might otherwise not encounter. In many cases the syndicates and the press associations have virtually made metropolitan papers out of small-city dailies.

BROADCASTING AS INFORMER

The possibility that broadcasting would ever become a medium of information seems to have occurred to few observers during the early days of radio. Through the years of technical development that followed Marconi's first brief transmission of a wireless message in 1895, radio was considered a future competitor with the telegraph—an instrument to be developed for point-to-point communication—and a scientific novelty. Hobbyists assembled their own receiving sets, listened, and proudly reported distances. "How far" was the status symbol as listeners compiled logs with lists of the distant stations they could receive.

Nonetheless the possibility of making radio an information medium seems to have been inherent from the beginning. Donald E. Brown of Arizona State University has traced the development of broadcast news through four stages.

Sarnoff's Vision

In 1916 David Sarnoff, a twenty-five-year-old with a bent for science, wrote a memo to a superior in the company in which he was employed: "I have in mind a plan of development which would make radio a 'household utility' in the same sense as the piano or phonograph. The idea is to bring music into the house by wireless."Sarnoff also spoke of the possibility of transmitting lectures, baseball scores, and events of national importance.

From the vantage point of today, it seems incredible that no one followed through immediately on Sarnoff's proposal. But there were two handicaps: The primitive radio sets were not widely distributed, and World War I diluted the interest in broadcasting. News was almost incidental. It is true that Presidential election bulletins reporting the Wilson-Hughes race were read over Dr. Lee de Forest's experimental station in New York in 1916, but they excited little attention. Only in 1920, when two stations reported Presidential election returns, was there any real hint of the future.

The Press—Radio War

Radio grew phenomenally during the early 1920s, setting the stage for bitter warfare with the nation's newspapers. Fearful that the new medium might take over the news function, some publishers brought pressure; the Associated Press warned its member newspapers, some of which owned radio licenses, that broadcasting AP news was contrary to the association's bylaws.

Actually the radio stations of that time had little interest in public affairs. In the fourteen months beginning in January, 1922, the number of stations increased from 30 to 556, but the increase was in entertainment. Few broadcasters even attempted serious news reporting. They were eager for the new and different, to feed the millions who had suddenly become intrigued with the novelty of radio. But the focus was on special events, not on the ordinary run of the news.

Then, in the late 1920s, a few stations began to consider themselves competitors with newspapers. By 1933 the competition between press and radio had become full-scale war. One network news executive organized what he called the "Scissors and Paste-Pot Press Association" to combat the withholding of press-association news from broadcasters. Eventually radio won the right to share the reports of worldwide news-gathering systems, first through United Press in 1935. The importance of radio as a news medium was emphasized in 1936 with one of the most dramatic broadcasts in history—the announcement by King Edward that he was renouncing the British throne for "the woman I love."

The Zenith of Radio News

Radio news reached its zenith beginning in 1938. Americans listened tensely to detailed, on-the-spot coverage of the Munich crisis. War clouds gathered over Europe; millions were made instantly aware of the troubled present by reporters, and of the disturbing future by commentators. In Europe Paul White and Edward R. Murrow of the Columbia Broadcasting System were fashioning a great reportorial staff. At home Lowell Thomas, Boake Carter, Elmer Davis, H. V. Kaltenborn, and a host of other authoritative voices suddenly became national celebrities.

By the time the United States entered World War II, radio was firmly established as a major medium of information and interpretation. Surveys indicated that broadcast news ranked very high with listeners and that the American people had confidence in radio reporting and commentary. Then, into the postwar world came television.

The Rise of Television News

The development of television, which had been halted by World War II, came rapidly during the late 1940s. Television newsmen, many of them trained in radio, borrowed radio techniques—and cut heavily into radio listening. News remained one of radio's primary assets, but the nature of news programs changed considerably. Many small communities got their first radio stations, and local news was emphasized. In fact, most radio stations cut back significantly on national and international events and issues, trying to find a formula that would enable radio news to survive in the age of television. Newscasts became shorter; the traditional fifteen-minute news program was down to five minutes; mere headline reports became common. By 1969 eight radio stations were trying an all-news format, a few with a degree of success. But nearly all offered such heavy repetition that listeners would not stay with an all-news station for long periods.

Because of the nature of the medium, television news emphasized features—especially the human-interest stories—at the beginning. Gradually, as TV newsmen developed competence and confidence, daily news programs grew from fifteen minutes to half an hour. By the beginning of the 1960s, newscasters—Howard K. Smith, Edward P. Morgan, Walter Cronkite, Eric Sevareid, and the team of Chet Huntley and David Brinkley—had achieved greater celebrity than the radio commentators of the 1930s. News and commentary over television had become so important by the mid-1960s that NBC News was producing a quarter of the network's broadcast hours: straight news programs, documentaries, discussions, and programs such as Senate hearings, national elections, and political conventions.

How television news works has been studied by Frank Allen Philpot of Stanford, who has worked for newspaper and broadcasting operations. He has written of the operations of KGO-TV, an ABC affiliate in San Francisco:

> The KGO news department produces four newscasts a day but only the 6 p.m. local report is really important. Ninety-five per cent of the station's local news effort goes into this program. At 7 a.m. and again at 8:25 a.m. a reporter reads a five-minute newscast torn directly off the wire. Essentially radio newscasts, although the reporter is visible on camera, these reports use no film or tape and require virtually no preparation. After the hour-long local program at 6 p.m. comes the half-hour national news program from the network. At 11 p.m. the station carries another news program, but it is little more than an edited version of the local and national 6 to 7:30 news block.
>
> KGO has a sizable audience for news although this depends to some extent on which rating service one believes. A. C. Nielsen puts KGO news in a strong second place behind KPIX. The American Research Bureau has KGO and KRON almost tied for second.
>
> There are three primary sources for the news operation:
>
> *Wires:* The station subscribes to six wires: both the AP and UPI "A" wires, both radio wires (each of which has a regional split), the UPI sports wire and the UPI "B" or state wire. This combination obviously produces immense duplication. When the assignment editor was asked why the station took this combination of wires, he said, "That's all there are." The same question put to the news director drew this response, "That's all we need." Apparently no one has given any consideration to the possibility of dropping one of the radio wires and substituting one of the supplementary services such as the New York Times wire, the L.A. Times/Washington Post service, the Dow Jones Business Wire, the Reuters wire or some of the functional wires such as the local business wire or the weather wire. The assignment editor doesn't seem to know that these exist.
>
> *DEF:* The ABC network news department collects more tape and film reports each day than it can use on the national half-hour "Frank Reynolds Report" so the out-takes—or extra stories—are offered as a syndicated service to all the ABC affiliates. ABC calls this service "DEF" because those letters come after "ABC."

The producer of the KGO evening news leaves a certain number of holes for DEF material when he first puts together the rough schedule early in the afternoon. At 3:30 he receives a summary of the material, but the actual feed does not come over the network lines until 4:30. On the basis of the summary, he chooses two or three items to include in his program and gives directions to the tape editors to take these out of the feed when it comes. He does not look at this material until the program goes on the air. The producer of the 11 p.m. news may come in late in the afternoon and look at the DEF feed and he will warn the producer of the 6 p.m. show if any of the material is technically bad (fuzzy sound, bad picture, etc.). But basically the decision as to which items to include from the DEF feed is made by the producer without seeing the material itself. The analogous situation on a newspaper would occur if a wire editor chose his stories on the basis of the wire service budgets and did not read them before they went into the paper. His only check on the quality would be an occasional call from the press foreman informing him that some of the type was garbled.

Staff reporters: KGO-TV has seven street reporters plus two full-time trainee reporters. They almost always work as a team with one of the station's six film cameramen. (The two-man team is probably the most common arrangement, but it is by no means universal. In very small markets—particularly where the staff is not unionized—a reporter may act as his own cameraman. Union contracts in Los Angeles require that a separate soundman go with each reporter and cameraman and in New York a driver must be added to each crew.)

The nine reporters are divided over seven days and two shifts so that at any one time there are no more than five reporters available. Outside of New York and Washington almost 100 per cent of television newsmen are general assignment reporters. This has a number of important implications. On a newspaper a beat reporter often comes to the city editor and tells him about a story or brings in a story that developed in his area. In television, a reporter goes out to cover a story only when he is specifically assigned to do so by the assignment editor. Since no single editor can have as many contacts as a dozen reporters, the number of stories that a TV station can develop on its own is greatly reduced. A TV station is just not organized regularly to scoop the newspaper in its community. Second, the television reporter is usually much less informed than the newspaper reporter. Because he does not work in the same area over a long period, he usually does not have the background to ask perceptive questions. The secondary sources of news are:

Newspapers: Three newspapers are examined by the assignment editor each day—the *San Francisco Chronicle,* the *San Francisco Examiner* and the *Oakland Tribune.* These are used primarily as sources of leads; normally, stories are not rewritten directly out of the papers, as is the practice at small stations.

UPI Unifax: The station subscribes to the UPI picture service and receives approximately 100 pictures per day but these are very seldom used on the air. The importance of "live" action is so ingrained into the thinking of the staff that they seldom think in terms of still pictures.

KABC News: KGO receives the second half-hour of the KABC (Los Angeles) local news. The network lines are free for only an hour and the feed of the "Frank Reynolds Report" takes the other half of the hour. In special situations KGO can ask KABC for a special piece of film.

Other stations: News film is occasionally exchanged with KXTV, Sacramento, and KJEO, Fresno.

ABC Network news: The "Frank Reynolds Report" is fed by the network at 5 p.m. but delayed by KGO until 7 p.m. Often actualities from this show are used on the 11 p.m. news and occasionally also on the 6 p.m. program.

Other Network feeds: During special events such as a space shot, a national funeral, etc., KGO tapes the network feed and edits excerpts to use on its news programs.

Analyzing the news practices and presentations of television and newspapers, Philpot concluded that, in addition to the difference in legal standing, three other factors are important:

True Technical Differences:
Television is not indexable—at least in our present technology. This means that the longer the program the more material a viewer must sit through to get to the items that interest him. The practical effect is that most newscasts are limited to an hour.
Television can transmit news instantaneously. TV news can be "live" in a way that no newspaper ever can be. Most critics would agree that television is at its finest when it is covering live events: space shots, national conventions, presidential funerals, etc. There are two implications from this. First, television is able to create a sense of national community at certain times. Newspapers lack this capacity. Second, because it is "live" and involves pictures, the public sometimes falsely assumes that it is not mediated by human judgment.
One does not have to be able to read to use television. It is true, of course, that we have reduced functional illiteracy in this country to an extremely low level, but there are still millions of people who

do not read well or who do not enjoy reading. Implication: Television news is a more important news source than are newspapers among the old, the poor, and the black.

Given our present technology, television equipment is very bulky and obvious. People are more aware of the presence of a television news team—consisting in some instances of four people with cameras, bright lights and recorders—than they are of a newspaper reporter with a pad and pencil and a photographer with a 35 mm camera shooting with natural light. Implication: Television is more likely to influence the events it is reporting than are other news media.

Because television transmits pictures and sound instantaneously it gives the illusion of transmitting reality. This seems to have two effects. First, in major elections voters may feel they have personal knowledge of a candidate even if this feeling is based on only a few minutes of television exposure. Second, television can transmit information about an event that would be filtered out by the written process. The civil rights revolution, the campus student revolutions and the anti-war movements have all benefited because television has spread the feeling and style of these activities.

No one has ever developed a way to file newsfilm or video tape the way news clippings can be filed. The result is that even long-established TV stations do not have the complete files or morgues that newspapers have. Therefore, television reporters have less background information to work with when preparing a story.

Economic Factors:

Reporting the news is the principal business of a newspaper and no publisher would ever consider abolishing his news department. But television stations are primarily in the entertainment business. They broadcast news programs because news wins points with the FCC, because it helps the station's public image or because the management has a sense of obligation to the community. (Some local news programs do make money but most stations could make more money with different programming. The result is likely that when the financial problems become serious, a television station may simply close down its news department.)

Most newspapers in this country are in a monopoly position. Most television stations are not.

If we assume that most television sets are purchased for their entertainment value—a safe assumption for a major portion of the society—then television news is free while newspapers cost money, perhaps a significant amount for a person on welfare.

Most local television news programs are 30 minutes long. This is partially a result of tradition, partially because news is not as profitable as other kinds of programs and partially because of the indexing problems discussed earlier. By the time commercials, weather and sports are subtracted from the half hour, only about 15 minutes are left for hard news—perhaps time for 3,000 words. Result: Television reports fewer stories than do newspapers and the stories it does report are covered less fully.

Preconceived Ideas:
Television stations invest considerable amounts of money in film equipment and go to considerable trouble to get film for their programs. As a result, stations give more time to stories that lend themselves to film coverage. (For some reason, very few stations have made creative use of still pictures or cartoons, despite the fact that these are legitimate visual techniques.)

Many television news reporters are former announcers or entertainers. They get their jobs, ordinarily, not because they can think, write or interpret events, but because they are attractive and have good voices. Many are never socialized into the news ethic that young reporters pick up in a newspaper city room.

Television news is delivered by a person who is recognized by the public—by a star. This tends to increase the credibility of the news—the national stars and their local counterparts become friends of the viewer. When these on-camera personalities cover stories, they can alter the news. They are celebrities and their presence can be news in itself.

TV stations get most of their news from newspapers and the wire services. They react to news, they very seldom do background pieces or investigate reports.

Newspapers use reporting specialists—beat reporters—but almost all television reporters are generalists. They do not develop as many informal contacts and they are frequently less informed on a story than their newspaper counterparts.

Newspapers have more available manpower than TV stations. Most city editors would not be reluctant to assign a reporter to work on one story for three or four days. TV reporters, on the other hand, are expected to cover several stories every day.

BROADCASTING AS INTERPRETER

Survey after survey shows that television is the news medium most relied upon by most Americans. As informer, broadcasting is pre-eminent. This disturbs many of the more thoughtful television journalists because, as interpreter of the news, broadcasting is a failure. Walter Cronkite of CBS speaks of a "genuine crisis in communications" because most cities now have only a single newspaper, and "these monopoly survivors are not doing the thorough job of coverage that they should." He points out that there isn't time in a broadcast to develop the essential arguments on all sides of an issue.

One of the central problems is that when broadcasters have the time, they will not devote it to depth reporting. Even the all-news radio stations, some of which are on the air around the clock, dote on headline news and seldom let a single report run more than a minute or two. It sometimes seems that radio and television newsmen think that *any* story can be told in 58 seconds.

Distinguished exceptions are the "Newsroom" programs presented in several cities on educational television channels. They began almost by accident. In January, 1968, employees of San Francisco's two major newspapers, the *Chronicle* and the *Examiner,* went on strike. When the commercial television stations in San Francisco continued to deal primarily in headline news and did little to fill the void left by the struck newspapers, the educational channel, KQED-TV, developed a new program. Called "Newspaper of the Air," it featured reporters from the striking papers. For an hour each evening, KQED cameras were trained on them as they gathered around a table and reported the news and tried to fathom its meaning. For thousands of residents of the San Francisco Bay Area, the program was a refreshing intellectual change from the stylized headline reporting of the commercial stations. When the strike ended, KQED executives asked the Ford Foundation for a grant to develop the concept. The result was "Newsroom," which features reporters, nearly all of them former newspapermen, who cover events and can present them knowledgeably. Although some commercial television journalists cover and understand the news, it is still true that many are "talking heads"—personalities whose looks and tones are pleasant; they are put on camera to read stories written by reporters. Ford executives were so impressed with KQED's program that they awarded grants to educational channels in Washington, D.C., and other cities to develop "Newsroom" programs.

The great value of "Newsroom" is that reporters can explore the news rather than merely touch on it in the manner of commercial television. There are, of course, reporters in commercial television, especially with the networks, who are fully qualified to clarify, explain, and explore the meaning of the news. Unlike "Newsroom" reporters, however, they seldom have the opportunity except in documentaries.

THE VARYING ROLES OF THE MEDIA

In their fierce competition for advertising dollars and public attention, the media have developed varying roles. As *information* media, radio and television are primarily useful in signalizing events, making the immediate—and usually sketchy—reports that announce a happening. When broadcasters give full attention to an important subject or a momentous event, as in the case of documentaries and special-events reports, they must scant other news. This leaves an important role for the newspaper, which supplies many more details than the newscast and covers many more stories than the broadcast documentary or special report. In turn, newspaper reports leave a role for magazines, which are chiefly devoted to fleshing out the information that has been shown only in silhouette through broadcasting and newspapers and to reporting matters that the faster media have missed in the rush of meeting deadlines. Magazine writers also take advantage of their wide-spaced deadlines to fashion articles more graceful and unified than most writers for TV, radio, or newspapers have time to achieve. As a consequence the interpretative writing used to discuss the meaning of events is more advanced in magazine journalism. The writers of books of nonfiction are a step farther; they have the leisure to draw full-bodied portraits and to set their writing in a full context. Much the same point can be made regarding some informational films; at least a few of them aim at establishing themes with timeless relevance.

The media do not always work within the boundaries of these roles, and it must be obvious that they seldom take full advantage of their best qualities. Broadcasting is swift, but it sometimes misses important aspects of quick-breaking events. Newspapers are large, but they sometimes ignore significant stories. The long periods that go into the writing of magazine articles, books, and documentaries do not prevent the worst of them from exuding a helter-skelter, thrown-together quality. All in all, though, each medium has a clear and substantive role in supplying information and interpretation.

The Media
as Persuaders

There are more muckmakers than there are muckrakers.

DREW PEARSON

Wherever he turns today, the American is surrounded by sales talk—subtle, slick, and shrill. The editorial in his evening paper, sandwiched between the sales messages of department stores, urges him to vote for the incumbent mayor. His favorite dramatic program on television is interrupted by a vocalist singing the praises of a shampoo. Perhaps 50 per cent of the pages in his favorite magazine coax him to buy compact automobiles, gleaming refrigerators, decay-fighting toothpastes, astringent mouthwashes, and detergents that clean whiter than white. His automobile rushes him past billboards extolling this brand of motor fuel, that brand of salt.

Much of the persuasion comes from advertisers, public-relations specialists, and other special pleaders, who use all of the mass media to make their sell, hard or soft. Some of the persuasion comes from the media as advocates in their own right. Some comes as a by-product of content intended primarily to inform or entertain.

THE GROWTH OF PERSUASION

The American has become the target for all sorts of special pleading: he is called on to make manifold decisions, some of them trivial, some of them important, in his various roles as citizen, consumer, and member of many little publics.

His opinion in politics is important. The growth of population, extension of the franchise, and women's suffrage all helped to expand the electorate. Popular education gave to the great majority of citizens the opportunity of acquainting themselves with the issues and problems of government, of observing the gaps between the actual and ideal in society. The direct primary and the increased number of elections added to the responsibilities of the individual citizen.

The functioning of the economic system has come to rest in large measure on the behavior of the consumer. As John Kenneth Galbraith points out in *The New Industrial State:*

> From early morning until late at night, people are informed of the services rendered by goods—of their profound indispensability. Every feature and facet of every product having been studied for selling points, these are then described with talent, gravity and an aspect of profound concern as the source of health, happiness, social achievement, or improved community standing. Even minor qualities of unimportant commodities are enlarged upon with a solemnity which would not be unbecoming in an announcement of the combined return of Christ and all the apostles. More important services, such as the advantages of whiter laundry, are treated with proportionately greater gravity.

The complexity of twentieth-century existence; the advances in transportation, which shrank the world; the growth of the mass media, which broadened the horizons of the average man—all have widened the area of opinion. Should parents be strict or permissive? Should we discontinue testing atomic weapons? Should a Communist be allowed to teach? What policy should our government take toward Egypt? Should we have a high tariff or a low one? What should the government do to help the farmer?

As the American has been called upon to make an ever-larger number of decisions, more and more people have become anxious to help him make what, from their point of view, is the correct one. Reformers urge him to support their causes. Editorial writers and publicists ask him to share their opinions. Charitable organizations want him to support their work. Advertising men and public-relations specialists want him to favor their clients. Politicians want his vote. Every one of them wants a decision favorable to himself.

TYPES OF PERSUASIVE CONTENT

The mass media carry three broad types of persuasive content. One is advertising, which is treated, along with public relations, in the next chapter. Second is intentional advocacy—editorials, editorial cartoons, columns, and interpretive articles, which are intended to lead the reader to a conclusion. Third is content intended primarily as entertainment or information, with persuasion as a possible by-product.

The informational content of the media probably has more influence on public opinion than the avowedly persuasive. That is, news stories may be a greater force in shaping public attitudes than editorials and political columns. They record events, and the events a paper reports probably change more minds than what it advocates. In *Gauging Public Opinion* Hadley Cantril has generalized: "Opinion is generally determined more by events than by words—unless those words are themselves interpreted as an event." In addition, events tend to solidify changes in public opinion produced by words. Without some bolstering event, the change in opinion may be short-lived.

However, as Bernard Berelson has pointed out, those generalities call for two comments. First, it may be hard to distinguish between "events" and "words." Is a major speech by the President an "event" or just "words"? Second, many events exert their influence not of themselves but with the aid of words. That is, the importance of an event in persuading the public may be sharpened considerably by the interpretations given it by television commentators, editorial writers, and political columnists.

The relative emphasis given to information and entertainment on the one hand and frank advocacy on the other has varied with the time and with the medium. Newspapers, for example, have changed over the years from organs of political warfare to organs of information and entertainment. Some publications today by their very nature are organs of advocacy, even though they may be heavy with other content. The labor press is one example. The company publication is another. And, of course, the underground press may be the most conspicuous example of advocacy journalism.

Consider how the media have been deliberately used to shape public opinion.

Newspapers

Since 1890 at least, observers have been speaking of the declining influence of the newspaper on public opinion. They point, among other things, to the failure of newspapers to get their candidates elected to public office. In the 1940 Presidential campaign more than two-thirds of the newspapers in the United States supported Wendell Wilkie, who was defeated; in 1944 and 1948 a high proportion of the dailies supported Thomas Dewey, who was defeated both times; in 1960 Richard Nixon won the support of most newspapers and lost the Presidency. (But in 1964 Lyndon Johnson had most of the newspaper support, and won. In 1968 Richard Nixon was again supported by most of the nation's newspapers, and won.)

What these figures show is not that the newspaper has lost in influence, say its defenders, but that it has gained in fairness. True, newspapers have supported candidates who have been defeated. But their defeat, the defenders say, simply underscores the fact that other candidates have been treated so fairly in news columns that readers could make up their own minds. We cannot know, of course, whether the winning candidates might have won much more decisively with newspaper support.

Perhaps more important is the question of salience. In high-salience elections like those for President and Senator, newspaper endorsements may be unimportant. But in low-salience elections—for a complicated bond issue or local office—newspaper endorsements may be decisive.

The change of most newspapers from partisan persuaders to chroniclers was recognized by the Canons of Journalism adopted by the American Society of Newspaper Editors in 1923: "Promotion of any private interest contrary to the general welfare, for whatever reason, is not compatible with honest journalism."

To promote the general welfare as they see it, newspapers have continued to crusade through editorials, cartoons, photographs, and interpretive articles. The catalog of their causes is long. Silas Bent has summarized hundreds of campaigns up to and through the 1930s in his book *Newspaper Crusaders*. Newspapers have used their influence to promote traffic safety, parks and playgrounds, new and improved city charters, diversification of farm crops, fluoridation of city water supplies, recreation centers for young persons, pardons for the wrongly convicted, community hospitals, smoke-abatement measures, reduced utility rates, municipal auditoriums, mental health programs.

Periodically newspapers have flushed out crime and political corruption, which often overlap one another. Shortly after 12:30 on a July night in 1926, Don Mellett, the young crusading publisher of the Canton, Ohio, *Daily News*, went out to park his automobile while his wife put on a pot of coffee for some visitors. A volley of shots were heard. When his wife reached him, Mellett was dead, shot through the head from an ambush.

Mellett died fighting two things. One, some newsmen still say, was the three-to-two circulation lead of his opposition, the *Repository*. That fight led to the second—which pushed his circulation closer to that of his competitor—a campaign against public officials in Canton who were in league with criminals. The city seemed in need of reform:

wanted criminals could hide out in safety, gangland murders went unsolved, a policeman held a monopoly on the sale of perfume to prostitutes.

Under Mellett the *Daily News* hounded the police, attacked their chief, reported crimes prominently and at length. Mellett was presumably shot by enemies made during his crusade, but a mystery still surrounds his death. Although three men went to prison for their part in the murder, no one but the killers knew who the murderer was. Nor is the exact motive known; other editors have gone unharmed for crusades at least as fiery as Mellett's. One explanation is that he was shot for what he was about to publish, not for what he had published. However, for a short time, at least, Mellett's campaign cleansed the city. A more lasting memorial is a series of lectureships bearing his name. Each year for more than a quarter of a century, a distinguished lecturer has spoken on some aspect of the press to keep Mellett's crusading spirit alive in other newspapermen.

Over the years many Pulitzer Prizes for reporting have gone to crusades. In 1970 *Newsday* of Long Island won its second Pulitzer for public service, for a three-year campaign exposing secret land deals and zoning manipulations by politicians and office-holders in eastern Long Island. The campaign led to three convictions, four suspensions from official or political party positions, and four resignations. It also resulted in passage of the first state law requiring full disclosure of all zoning applications. The Pulitzer announcement stated: "By digging into a maze of land records and other documents and presenting their findings, *Newsday's* reporters and editors displayed both tenacity and courage in the face of threats and hostile acts by some of the politicians whose wrong-doing they attacked."

Also in 1970 Harold Martin of the Montgomery, Alabama, *Advertiser* and the *Alabama Journal* won a Pulitzer Prize for special local reporting for exposing the commercial use of Alabama prisoners for drug experiments. The program, which was brought to a halt by Martin's exposé, also merchandised blood plasma taken from prisoners until a hepatitis outbreak brought three deaths.

In fact, 1970 was a banner year for rewarding newspaper crusades. William J. Eaton of the Chicago *Daily News* won the Pulitzer Prize for national reporting for investigating the qualifications of Judge Clement Haynsworth to become a member of the United States Supreme Court. Eaton's stories helped to defeat the Haynsworth nomination—after his own paper had argued editorially for Haynsworth's appointment. Seymour Hersh of Dispatch News Service won the 1970 Pulitzer Prize for international reporting for his series of articles on the mass murder of Vietnamese civilians at My Lai.

Advocacy Journalism

By the early 1970s the journalism of advocacy had a firm hold on only a small part of the newspaper world. Although the underground press was offering prime examples of it, and although many reporters on conventional newspapers were angrily denouncing objectivity and fighting over it with their editors, another kind of newspaper affords a better view of the future of advocacy. This is the investigative paper, which is usually published weekly or monthly. One of the most valuable is the San Francisco *Bay Guardian.* Editor Bruce Brugmann explains its purpose:

> I aim my derringer at every reporter and tell him, by God, that I don't want to see an objective piece of reporting. . . . But this is not dishonest journalism; it is "point of view" journalism. Our facts are as straight as we can make them! We don't run a story until we feel we can prove it or make it stick; we always talk with the adversary and try to print his side as part of the story; he always gets the chance of reply in the next issue (rarely do they, even when I offer in letter or by phone). We run almost all the critical reaction we get to stories; but the point is we don't run a story until we think it is in the public interest to do so.
>
> How do you talk about our major stories, environmental pollution, Vietnam, the Manhattanization of San Francisco, saving the Bay, unless you do some "point of view" reporting? We're not just covering meetings. We're not just checking in with the official sources. We're going after stories, hopefully before they become certifiable facts. . . . Along with this come different forms of the new journalism; letting participants write their own stuff, using experts with special knowledge, more literary writing, the use of irony, poetry, impressionistic writing—everything really, that has relevance, and merit, and readability—and goes for the jugular.

Whatever one thinks of "point of view" journalism, the stance of Brugmann's paper—and others like the *Texas Observer* and *Cervi's Journal* in Denver—suggest a missing dimension in conventional newspapers. Much of the conventional press will take an adversary stance toward government, at least on occasion. The *Bay Guardian* and its counterparts look deeper into American society and recognize that rather than a relatively simple military-industrial complex, the United States is a military-industrial-labor-education complex—and it is eager to make an ally of mass communication. The little journals strike an adversary stance toward all the powerful institutions. And if it sometimes seems that they develop conspiracy theories where they are not warranted, no one who seriously investigates the work of these journals can fail to be favorably impressed. And even those who were nurtured on conventional reporting may grant that a publication that is issued only once a month (as the *Guardian* is) probably cannot contain all its fervor within the bounds of the editorial page.

Columnists and Editorial Writers

It is a curious fact that in a period when many knowledgeable observers agree that most locally written newspaper opinion columns are weak and watery, we may be experiencing a high point as well. For certainly it is clear that journalism in the United States may never have produced three political satirists as deft as Russell Baker of the New York *Times*, Syndicated Columnist Art Buchwald, and Art Hoppe of the San Francisco *Chronicle*.

Hoppe, whose columns appear in nearly a hundred papers, is less widely known than Buchwald or Baker. Nonetheless he may be the best of the three. Buchwald has greater celebrity—he is a genuinely funny man in person as well as in print—but his writing is blander than Hoppe's. Baker is probably the most gifted writer of the three, but he sometimes has trouble finding themes that will carry his wry commentary. Hoppe has more and richer ideas than either of his rivals. It is easy to suspect, too, that Hoppe is much more the political animal than Buchwald or Baker. There is an acid quality in much that he writes.

In essence, however, all three columnists follow precisely the same method. They observe the foibles of men, especially those in government, focus on one of their more dubious enterprises, and then imagine in print that it has been carried to its absurd conclusion. It is political commentary of a very high order.

It can be argued that political commentary *is* the opinion writing of newspapers today. There was a time when the term "columnist" was almost automatically associated with Walter Winchell or Leonard Lyons, Louella Parsons or Hedda Hopper. Today, however, even those who do not experience high political passions are likely to associate "columnist" with Buchwald, James Reston, William Buckley, Jr., David Lawrence, or some other political columnist.

Indeed, this may be one of the chief reasons for the general low state of local newspaper opinion writing today. When a local political columnist or editorial writer had little competition from syndicated political columnists, *he* was the oracle. With the widespread syndication of men like James Reston, the local man could no longer pretend to eminence.

There have been other changes. During recent years many publishers and editors have become concerned, if not nervous, about the monopoly power inherent in the single-newspaper-town situation. Accordingly even their editorial pages have become less partisan. Some of those with liberal leanings are now careful to publish at least a few syndicated columnists who lean the other way. Some with conservative leanings seek liberal columnists. And, of course, some of those with strong political passions of one kind or the other publish a columnist of the opposite persuasion for window dressing—even these lend a semblance of balance. But many editorial pages are still frankly partisan.

Does the effort by some publishers to balance syndicated columnists, right and left, please readers? Not all of them. The problem begins with defining terms. Doctrinaire liberals—especially those on the fringe of the radical movements—doubt that there *is* a consistently liberal columnist outside the underground newspapers. On the other hand, the devout conservative who holds to the tenets expressed by Russell Kirk in *The Conservative Mind* would probably doubt that American syndicates have offered a consistently and devotedly conservative columnist since the late Westbrook Pegler. From such perspectives there are no syndicated columnists who can be used to balance an editorial page because there is no one who can be placed at either end of the spectrum. Placing Nicholas von Hoffman at the left end and William Buckley, Jr., at the right does not seem adequate.

The problems of liberal-conservative balance are complicated by other factors. An editor who decides on a policy of balance may find that acceptable columnists are unavailable to him. Metropolitan papers often buy up the right to publish syndicated columnists in their areas, foreclosing publication by other metropolitan papers and smaller papers in the same territory.

Moreover, the editor who would like to publish James Reston's column, or Russell Baker's, finds that he must buy the entire *New York Times* News Service in order to get them. Any newspaper of consequence should use the *Times* News Services, but it is expensive, and it is often monopolized by those territorial-right contracts so dear to metropolitan dailies.

There is more to the philosophy of balance of opinion in many of today's newspapers. Certainly, the growing reluctance on the part of editorial writers (or their superiors) to say much that is pointed weakens many an editorial page. Some editorial writers argue, rather defensively, that they do not have all the answers and that there is room on their pages for interpretation as well as advocacy. The point is well taken; interpretation and analysis are useful tools. Yet there is a strong suspicion that this statement is more often an excuse than an explanation. Certainly it does not explain all the editorial salutes to Flag Day, Mother's Day, and Fourth of July.

With some notable and notorious exceptions, then, this is an opinion-writing era when most newspapermen believe that their freedom must be flavored with responsibility. It is not very exciting, especially if measured against the era of personal journalism, when the editor and his most responsive critic might carry horsewhips. Only the underground newspapers, the new college dailies, and the radical sheets—and only a *few* of these—reach the level of passion and invective that characterized some of the old thunderers. Only such outstanding papers as the Washington *Post* and the St. Louis *Post-Dispatch* offer editorial pages that approach greatness.

The Editorial Problem

An editorial should reflect grace of expression, clarity of writing, singularity of theme and purpose, and vigorous opinion. If an editorial advocates, it should do so unmistakably. If it explains or interprets or analyzes, the writer should present more than a reporter can in the news columns.

Perhaps above all, editorial writers should not waste their time and their readers' by presenting an issue in the manner of a news story, and then tacking on a short paragraph praising or vilifying the principal figure in the case. If a reader has any independence of mind, such an editorial means almost nothing to him. If he is swayed by a sentence or so of flimsy judgment, he is persuaded for a very poor reason: because an editorial writer says so. Such editorials are little better than salutes to Flag Day: they fill space.

The problems of the editorial writer are sticky. He may be given full instructions, usually by the editor, before he goes to work. But the editor is probably not available at the moment of composition, when the writer is putting thoughts into words. Moreover a publisher probably looms behind the editor, and perhaps a board of directors behind the publisher. These figures are not always threatening, but they can be.

Even when the system allows an editorial writer to submit his work for clearance, removing the ultimate responsibility from him, he is not really his own man doing his own work. But this is a far better system for most writers than sending their editorials directly to the composing room. Such a system is almost certain to produce a number of cautious editorials; the writer tries to *imagine* what the objections from on high might be.

Whatever the system, if two or three figures do not loom behind the writer, the newspaper as an institution does. Such a presence inhibits some editors-in-chief, and even some publishers who write their own editorials.

The newspapers and their editorial columns begin with a heavy handicap. The institutions of American society are under attack, and newspapers are substantial institutions, to which other institutions look for leadership in preserving the status quo. During this period of unprecedented institutional challenge, it is not surprising that even the great newspapers have only a hazy and obscured vision of the future. They are understandably slow to admit the deep fissures of hypocrisy in American culture and rhetoric, and they are quick to focus on the clearly reprehensible tactics of the militants who are trying to effect changes.

MAGAZINES

In crusading and in the original reporting that is sometimes its substitute, newspapers in recent years may have lost ground to magazines. Certainly magazines since the end of World War II do seem to have given greater emphasis to what might be called public-service articles, many of which have overtones of advocacy.

Public-service articles take many approaches, and they cover a great many topics. They include, on the one hand, *Life's* exposés of politics and *McCall's* revealing stories about water purity. They include, on the other hand, *Look's* efforts to gain understanding for mentally handicapped children and its articles on vocational education.

No really suitable term fits all these articles, although some of them bear a kinship to the muckraking articles of the turn of the century. Among themselves editors of one magazine call them "exposés," but the staff is not entirely satisfied with that term, for the authors try to present the case, if one exists, for whatever they are exposing.

Even in public-service articles, magazines generally have engaged in comparatively few outright attempts at persuasion. Rather they have tried to arouse the public's awareness or its conscience by reporting controversial situations. Only infrequently since the days of the muckrakers have large-circulation magazines sounded clear calls for action to correct abuses. *Sports Illustrated* did this in the opening article of a two-year campaign to clean up "boxing's dirty business." Its subtitle called the welterweight championship fight "one of the most brazen frauds of modern times" and asked for "a federal investigation of the hoodlums" controlling the ring. One of the longest and most persistent of magazine campaigns was waged by *Argosy* to improve the administration of justice. Members of its Court of Last Resort, created in 1948, included a former prison warden, a famous private detective, an expert on lie detection, and an authority on the medical aspects of crime. They thoroughly investigated the cases of persons thought wrongfully convicted of crimes, and the magazine gave full publicity to the board's findings. In its first six years the Court of Last Resort obtained the release from prison of twenty-one innocent people.

More often, magazines expose abuses and leave the action to authorities. Even the notable articles Richard Harris wrote on the Department of Justice for the *New Yorker* in 1969 did not call for reform. They simply exposed a situation. Rachel Carson's book *Silent Spring,* which was in part responsible for the environmental crusades of the early 1970s, first appeared as a series of articles in the *New Yorker.*

Business publications and trade and technical magazines generally have championed only the interests of their constituencies. But even they on occasion have reported conditions needing correction. Thus *Fleet Owner,* a monthly for operators and managers of motor vehicle fleets, once devoted 16 pages to reporting the dangerous extent to which truck drivers were using amphetamines—"stay-awake-pills"—and the resulting hazards to highway safety. In 1968 thirty-four McGraw-Hill business publications carried a special 16-page insert, "Business and the Urban Crisis," which focused on three critical problem areas—jobs, housing and education.

The Muckrakers

Today articles seeking to reform, even by interpretation instead of advocacy, comprise a relatively small proportion of total magazine content. The great age of reform was the period of muckraking, which began in 1902. Rapid industrial expansion after the Civil War had created many evils and injustices. Trusts were a matter of public concern, and some observers saw an unhealthful alliance between business and politics. By coincidence *McClure's* magazine for January, 1903, carried three articles similar in theme and treatment, all social criticism: Ida Tarbell's third article in her history of the Standard Oil Company, Lincoln Steffens' "The Shame of Minneapolis," and Ray Stannard Baker's "The Right to Work." Although magazines had carried other articles about the trusts and corruption in politics, that issue of *McClure's* officially established the era of muckraking.

Magazine after magazine called public attention to conditions requiring correction. *America, Arena, Collier's, Cosmopolitan, Everybody's,* and *Hampton's* joined the muckraking crew. Even the *Ladies' Home Journal* took time out from its efforts to improve the American woman's taste in art and architecture to give the muckrakers a hand in exposing the patent medicines. Its campaign included an article on phony testimonials, a full-page editorial demanding federal regulation of the manufacture and sale of patent medicines, and one especially telling feature—a reproduction of an advertisement for Lydia Pinkham's Compound showing "Mrs. Pinkham's tombstone in Lynn, Massachusetts." The slums, the importance attached to college athletics, the inequities and injustices of divorce laws, immorality in the theater, our interests in Mexico—these and others caught the muckrakers' attention.

Some subjects were treated with more rhetoric than fact, more sensationalism than sincerity. More often the articles were not advocacy but probing reportage which drew on official documents and which was subjected to scrutiny by experts. C. C. Regier, a historian of muckraking, has concluded that the general reliability of the articles was high. Significantly, although the magazines and authors were often threatened with libel actions—Will Irwin at one time had six pending—few ever paid out any damages.

An important force by 1906, the muckraking movement ebbed two years later, hit another high point in 1911, and had spent itself by 1912. The public had tired of it, financial pressures had discouraged certain magazines from continuing it, and some of the evils it had assailed had been corrected. Regier credits muckraking with playing a part in a number of reforms, among them a federal pure-food law, child-labor laws, workmen's compensation acts, a tariff commission, and congressional investigations.

Journals of Opinion

Perhaps the most forthright attempts at persuasion in magazines have appeared in such journals of opinion, comment, and controversy as *Ramparts, The Nation, National Review, New Leader, New Republic,* and *Progressive;* their emphasis is on ideas rather than on reportage, and their positions are rarely neutral.

Most of the journals since the turn of the century have been organs of liberal thought, although a few, like the *National Review,* founded in 1955, have been spokesmen for conservatism. In their agitation for political reform and social justice, the magazines often have been far ahead of popular thinking. For that reason and others, their way has always been difficult; their circulations have been counted in the thousands instead of in the millions of the general-interest magazines, their advertising volume has been lean or non-existent, and their financial position has ever been precarious. Yet they seem to have wielded an influence all out of proportion to their circulations, for they have aimed at opinion leaders instead of the great mass audience. Frank P. Walsh once remarked that he had written an article about railroads for the *Nation* in the days when its circulation was about 27,000 and a series on the same subject for the Hearst newspapers when their total circulation was around 10 million. No one ever commented on the newspaper series, he said, but as soon as the *Nation* article appeared, his phone jangled with calls from persons of importance. Charles Beard has credited the journals of opinion with contributing to such reforms as women's suffrage, old-age pensions, social-security legislation, wages-and-hours laws, public housing, and public ownership of hydroelectric sites.

More recently Consumer Crusader Ralph Nader has excited attention in liberal circles with articles in the *New Republic* on food dangers.

COMPANY PUBLICATIONS

A few years ago, the executives of a manufacturing company were honoring Joe Zipotas—the name is fictional, but the incident is true—for twenty-five years of loyal service. A curious investigator decided to find out just how much Zipotas had learned about the company in his quarter-century with it. He discovered that Zipotas did *not* know the year in which the company was founded; the number of plants it had; more than two of the company's products, which exceeded 200; the name of the president, who had held that office for three years; the location of the company's headquarters; the source of a single raw material going into the company's products; the operation that preceded his or the one that followed it, except in a very general way; and what free enterprise means (he did not even recognize the expression).

On the other hand, Zipotas could give the name and number of his local union; the names of three of five union officers; four direct benefits that, he thought, the union had obtained for him, although it actually had obtained only two of them; and a reasonably accurate definition of collective bargaining.

Terminology

It is in part to combat such ignorance that many companies publish magazines or newspapers for their employees. The term *company publications* is one of several used to describe the periodicals issued by big and little businesses to tell their stories to employees, salesmen, dealers, stockholders, customers, potential customers, and opinion leaders. For years the publications have been called *house organs*, a designation that company editors object to as having undeservedly shabby connotations. Some editors prefer the term *industrial publications.* Some use the term "employee publications" when speaking of periodicals issued primarily for employees.

Size and Scope

By any name company publications have become a permanent part of the publishing scene. Nor are they an inconsequential part. Their number, circulation, and expenditures are impressive. Estimates of their number range from 6000 to 10,000. Their combined circulation has been estimated at more than 150 million.

Company publications include magazines, newspapers, and newsletters. They range in size from two to sixty-four pages an issue. In quality they vary from crudely mimeographed collections of news notes to slick magazines, which compare favorably in technical execution with the top commercial magazines. *Think,* which is published by the International Business Machines Corporation, runs articles by well-known authorities on the arts, current affairs, education, and so forth for 100,000 leaders in business, the professions, and government around the world. It makes no references to I.B.M. in its editorial copy, carries no company advertising.

Some publications have full-time staffs of six or more. However, the typical company publication is the work of a single editor, sometimes aided by a secretary and a part-time photographer. The editor gathers the material and writes the copy, supervises a crew of volunteer correspondents, prepares the copy for the printer, and lays out the issues.

Types of Publications

In general, company publications are of three types. The *internal* type circulates within the company. It is exemplified by *Caterpillar Folks,* a biweekly tabloid "by and for the folks at Caterpillar Tractor Co., Peoria," and by *Hiltonitems,* a magazine for employees of the Hilton chain of hotels. The general aims of the internal publications are to bring about mutual understanding between management and employees as a means of effecting cooperation; to present management's policies, programs, and attitudes; and to help increase employee efficiency. The *external* type circulates outside the company. Examples include Nationwide Mutual Insurance's *Minutes,* John Deere's *Furrow,* and Kaiser Steel's *Westward.* The aims of an external company publication depend upon the specific reader group of the publication and the character of the issuing company. However, they often include improving business relations with customers and potential customers, telling the company's story to opinion leaders, or both. The *internal-external*, sometimes called the combination publication, goes to persons both within and without the company. Its aims combine those of the internal and external. A fourth type, the sales organ, is actually either an internal or an external, but its specific aims may be so sharply different that it is sometimes put in a class by itself.

Persuasive Functions

Some company editors would argue heatedly that their publications are not organs of persuasion. They may admit to editing organs of information or even education, but they find persuasion too akin to propaganda to be palatable. A former newspaperman who edits an employees' magazine for a public-utilities company insists that his publication is strictly informational, since he covers the company as he used to cover his newspaper beat.

True, the best of the company publications are long on information, mercifully short on exhortation. The casual reader, for instance, might mistake *Friends*, a monthly distributed free by Chevrolet dealers, for a regular general-interest picture magazine. The magazine carefully avoids references to Chevrolet in its editorial matter, which covers gracious dining, hobbies of readers, scenic attractions across the land, and similar features; the few Chevrolet advertisements are carefully separated from the editorial features. Some internals seem edited on the assumption that employees will accept the policies and attitudes of management if they but have the facts. One company editor in Chicago admitted that he had looked sharply down his nose on industrial editing until he had become a part of it. "I considered the field narrow and extremely biased," he said. "It is conservative, admittedly. But its limits are being swept away so quickly one can hardly keep abreast of the advancement. And I am less certain each day that it is more conservative than the daily field."

Yet the aims of company publications require that they be persuasive organs, even if the persuasion is not always blatant. Company publications are not issued for philanthropic reasons. They are issued to build, modify, or change attitudes toward the company. The internal seeks to gain acceptance for company policies; the external seeks to increase sales, either by a direct bid for them or by building good will and prestige. One of the topics current in industrial shop talk is how editors can document the worth of their publications to management. This worth is inevitably measured by some change in reader behavior—by an improved safety record, by a reduction in waste, by an increase in sales. As the director of publicity and public relations for one major company put it, "The sooner managements and editors alike stop all the prattle about the philanthropic reasons behind their externals, and admit to themselves and to their readers their objectives . . . which, in plain words, are to sell merchandise, the better off everyone will be." True, the publications may seek to persuade by information, by fact, by figures, by entertainment; but they are persuasive in intent, for all of that.

Causes of Growth

Not long ago a company editor—who should have known better—credited World War II with the swift proliferation of company publications in the United States. Certainly the war brought a rapid increase in their number. In 1940 there were perhaps 2400, to judge from the shaky data available; today there are probably 10,000. During the war there were good reasons for their growth. They were useful in building and maintaining employee morale, in acquainting the flood of new employees with company jobs and routine, in keeping in touch with employees in the service. Tax policies, which in effect permitted employers to deduct the cost of company publications, no doubt also contributed to their growth. But to credit the war with being anything more than a stimulant to their development is to misread the history of the twentieth century.

The company publication in America seems to have had its birth in the nineteenth century. One of the first true employee publications was the *Triphammer* of the Massey Manufacturing Company, begun in 1885. Another early one was *Factory News,* started at the National Cash Register Company in 1891. Some of today's commercial magazines were in effect house organs in their early days in the nineteenth century. *McCall's* for instance, was begun to promote the sale of ladies' dress patterns; *Harper's Magazine,* to promote the sale of books published by the four Harper brothers.

When cash came to business with relative ease during World War I, there was a blossoming of publications aimed at employees. Many of these war-born publications died with the peace, perhaps because of the recession of 1920–21. Thereafter the development of the publications seems to have been slow until World War II. Of 6500 publications surveyed by the International Council of Industrial Editors in 1952, for instance, about 70 per cent came into existence after 1938.

Five conditions seem to have fostered the development of company publications. One was the increased sense of public relations with which business became imbued after World War I but especially in the late 1930s. A second was the rise of the labor unions. In the 1920s inertia characterized the labor movement generally, and membership dropped off abruptly and significantly. In the 1930s, encouraged by federal legislation, the unions began their climb to power. Between 1933 and the end of 1937, membership in the hotel and restaurant employees' union had quadrupled, that in the teamsters' union had tripled, and that in the electrical workers' union had doubled. Perhaps a third influence on the development of the company publication was the labor press, which gained importance as the unions did. As organized labor strengthened its own press for reaching its members, management no doubt felt the need for some counter-voice.

Fourth, certainly the increased regulation of business and industry since the advent of the New Deal in the 1930s—a trend that some segments of management have seen as a threat to the free-enterprise system—has contributed to the growth of the company publication. Although editors disagree on the extent to which they should try to sell employees on the benefits of the free-enterprise system, they are in strong agreement that one of their purposes is to give him an understanding of how the economic system operates.

Finally, the growth of the company publication no doubt was fostered by the emergence of the giant corporation. The large company developed mass-production techniques that often reduced individual jobs to almost incomprehensible specialties. The plants came to be scattered over wide geographic areas, and management become remote from employees. It became increasingly difficult for the individual employee to see his contribution to the finished product, to take any craftsman's pride in his work, to see his place in the company and the industry, to feel any bond with management and his fellow employees. The company publication became one tool for orienting the employee to company and industry, for acquainting him with his employers and fellow workers, for assuring him of his importance to the production scheme.

THE LABOR PRESS

In the 1930s, in the decade before the great surge in the growth of company publications, the labor press underwent a somewhat similar revitalization. Those lean years of widespread unemployment made workers feel keenly the economic struggle for existence, and the general climate under the New Deal was one favorable to unionism. In their great organizing drives after 1933, labor leaders saw the need for the mass dissemination of trade-union persuasion if they were to combat opposition to unions and if they were to win and hold members. Between 1932 and 1938 more than 150 new labor and progressive periodicals joined those already in existence. Reliable figures on the scope of the labor press are hard to come by, for labor journalism, strangely, has rarely attracted scholars. In the early 1950s there were, according to one estimate, about 800 labor periodicals with a combined circulation of 300 million. The directory of the International Labor Press Association in 1957 mentioned 301 member periodicals with a total circulation of 20 million. Today there are nearly 300 labor publications.

Labor periodicals fall into several categories. They include organs of national and international trade unions, of state and national federations, of city and county federations, of locals, and of institutes and fraternal orders.

Content and Control

Just as company publications are the spokesmen for the interests of business and industry, labor periodicals are the house organs of the trade-union movement. Both readers and editors evidently want them to concentrate on labor materials and to leave other types of information to the general-circulation media. According to a limited study made a number of years ago by Manny Schor in Toledo, what readers want in the labor press is articles about their own trade or industry, shop columns, editorials and background articles about affairs affecting labor, letters from union members, and news stories about labor activities. Only a few of the editors surveyed thought that their periodicals should attempt to present the beliefs and objectives of labor to the community at large. Fewer still thought that their papers should run material not dealing with labor.

The several systems of control that are intended to keep the publications responsive to the wishes of union members probably help to perpetuate their house organ character. Many are controlled by boards of union members and elected officers whose primary responsibilities are in other areas. Some unions control their papers by electing the editors.

Despite such inhibiting factors the labor press has changed in some ways over the years. Perhaps the greatest change has arisen from a transformation in the ideology of the labor movement. At one time, especially from about 1873 to 1886, labor sought to accomplish its objectives by modifying or scrapping the existing political and economic order. The radical labor press of that era, varying in tone from moderate to anarchistic, lacked a unity of purpose, since the periodicals often represented factions that had lost sight of a common goal.

Today, with few exceptions, the labor press tries to achieve its purposes within the framework of the free-enterprise system. While it tries to improve the lot of the individual worker and of organized labor, it does not advocate an end to the system itself. Consequently the labor press now has a unanimity of purpose it lacked in the nineteenth century.

Another change has been a technical improvement of the newspapers and magazines. On some publications, especially the national and international ones, experienced journalists have replaced amateur editors whose chief qualification was zeal. Facilities for news-gathering have been expanded, and the physical appearance of the publications has been improved. Despite those improvements and despite considerable editorial enthusiasm, a good many labor papers, particularly local ones, are still below professional standards of technical competence.

BROADCASTING

Until very recently the overt persuasion of radio and television was largely in advertising. As a result of covering such events as the hearings of Senator Estes Kefauver's committee investigating crime and the hearings involving the late Senator Joseph McCarthy, broadcasters may have modified their attitudes on specific issues. But both radio and television were exceedingly slow to attempt to influence opinion by outright editorializing.

The Mayflower Decision

There were both legal and practical reasons for that reluctance. One inhibition was the Mayflower Decision. Radio station WAAB in Boston, owned by the Mayflower Broadcasting Corporation, had supported various causes and candidates for some years before 1941 without making its facilities available to those with opposing viewpoints. After investigating complaints about that practice, the Federal Communications Commission in 1941 issued what came to be known as the Mayflower Decision. In effect, the FCC ruled that "a licensee shall not be advocate" because the channel he holds is public property. Broadcasters were uncertain whether the FCC meant that a licensee could not advocate under any circumstances or only if he did not allow counter views to be heard. They interpreted it to mean that they were enjoined from editorializing altogether.

Although they never challenged it in the courts, broadcasters resented the Mayflower Decision. When a cross section of AM station managers was surveyed in 1947, 85 per cent said that they thought they should have the right to editorialize, and 55 per cent replied that they were sure they would do so if they had the right. The National Association of Broadcasters made the Mayflower Decision a part of a larger movement to abolish FCC concern with all program content.

Supporters of the decision contended that the station owner held his channel in the public interest. The right to editorialize would give him a preferred status over other members of the community, who did not have access to the airwaves. Editorializing, then, was quite a proper subject of regulation. They also contended that the editorials of broadcasters would be likely to have a sameness and conservatism not representative of the opinions of the public at large.

Broadcasters, on the other hand, used two major arguments against the decision. Regulation, they said, was originally justified on the grounds that the number of channels was limited. But the postwar expansion of AM channels and the advent of FM had ended the scarcity. Second, they argued that restrictions on editorializing infringed the First Amendment and even the Communications Act, which barred the FCC from censorship. Broadcasting could never achieve full stature, they said, unless it had the right to editorialize.

In June, 1949, after months of public hearings, the FCC redefined its position, ruling that a licensee could broadcast his own opinions on controversial subjects, provided he gave opportunity for the presentation of conflicting viewpoints. The FCC stated:

> Only insofar as it is exercised in conformity with the paramount right of the public to hear a reasonably balanced presentation of all responsible viewpoints on particular issues can such editorialization be considered to be consistent with the licensee's duty to operate in the public interest.

Extent of Editorializing

Despite that clarification few broadcasters hurried to use the new privilege. Even those who most vigorously protested the Mayflower Decision did little editorializing. Some news directors of local stations explained that impartiality in news coverage was their greatest asset. They argued that listeners think local newspapers carry too heavy a load of opinion in their news columns and therefore trust the broadcast media because they do not dilute news with views. Taking almost an opposite line, others said that they do editorialize, inevitably, in selecting their news, in preparing it for the air, in broadcasting it, even if they do not devote time to editorials as such.

Sig Mickelson, former general manager of CBS News, gave four reasons for the small amount of network editorializing. One involves the difficulty of meeting the FCC's requirements of fairness and balance in issues involving controversy. Another is the undesirability of the network's setting an editorial policy for its affiliated stations, which are autonomous units. Third is that broadcasting historically has had little precedent for editorializing. Finally there is the problem of how to editorialize. Should regular newsmen express opinions during regular newscasts, for instance, or should the network employ a number of commentators of differing opinions and permit each to speak his mind freely? Or should network management reserve for itself the right to editorialize? Nonetheless Mickelson thought broadcasters should seriously consider using their right to comment.

Not until the Mayflower decision was a decade old was there a strong sign that broadcasters would firmly grasp their editorial privilege. Led by pioneers like WTVJ-TV in Miami, broadcasters began to break away from the straight news format. By 1963 *Broadcasting Yearbook* was reporting that 40 per cent of radio and television stations were editorializing—1231 of 3780 AM radio stations, 212 of 561 television stations. Today well over half of all radio and television stations broadcast editorials. Many critics, observing the blandness of most of the editorials, wonder why. Radio and television remain media that usually avoid controversy, that carry entertainment primarily, interspersed with some information and interpretation, and that are still exploring the effects of overt persuasion.

MOTION PICTURES

Motion pictures are regarded as a medium more of entertainment than of deliberate persuasion. Yet they are beyond dispute an influential force on customs, habits, manners, ways of thinking and doing. Indeed, the assumption of influence underlies the widespread legal censorship and public pressure.

Because the motion picture requires a mass audience, because the foreign market has been a major source of revenue, and because government control has hung over the industry as a perennial threat, producers long tried to oblige their critics by offending no one. They did produce a few films dealing with such social problems as juvenile delinquency, segregation, racketeering, and mental health. The House Committee on Un-American Activities in 1947 conducted a number of hearings to determine whether the movies had been used by the Communists for subversive purposes. Although several witnesses spoke of writers' attempts to inject pro-Communist material into several films, the hearings failed to point up any convincing evidence. So for many years the Hollywood movie with an overt message of any sort was relatively rare. When film producers had a message, they usually tried to convey it through entertainment at worst or through art at best. In recent years, movie-makers have been bolder about making films of social concern. Although many of the messages have been obscured by sex and violence, message films are clearly on the increase.

POWERS OF PERSUASION

It is easy to overrate the efficacy of the mass media as persuaders. Many people see them as operating in simple terms of cause and effect, of communication stimulus and individual response. Some think, for example, that if an editor runs a blistering editorial calling for some action, his readers scurry like puppets to perform his will. A growing body of research evidence shows, however, that the persuasive effects of the media are neither that direct nor that simple. A single communication usually has little direct impact on attitudes or behavior. It is only after constant exposure that the media, little by little, affect us. Then they are more likely to modify attitudes than to change them.

Individual Response

The reason for this lack of direct persuasive effect is that much intervenes between the communication stimulus and individual response. Some uncertainty over the response to persuasion lies deep in human nature itself. How each of us reacts to a communication depends on our attitudes, values, needs, motivations—the whole complex of our personalities.

People tend to choose among and within the mass media. In general, they choose materials that do not challenge the opinions and values they already hold. They tend, in short, to select that with which they agree, to avoid that with which they disagree—and to remember that which will leave them in uninjured possession of their whims and beliefs.

Confronted with material they disagree with, people tend to interpret it in such a way that it will bolster their existing beliefs and attitudes. Consider what happened when an organization set out to diminish racial prejudice through a series of satirical cartoons featuring Mr. Biggott, a ridiculously prudish character with exaggerated feelings against minority groups. The organization thought that the cartoons might reduce prejudice in this way: Readers would see that Mr. Biggott's ideas were similar to their own, that Mr. Biggott was an absurd character, that it was absurd to share his ideas. What really happened was far from the intent. Strongly prejudiced readers tapped several mental devices to misunderstand the point of the cartoons, and they misread into the cartoons meanings that left their prejudices intact or even strengthened.

Some people will remain uninformed and unpersuaded no matter what the level or nature of the material directed at them. They are probably quite numerous; in one study they were estimated to comprise about one-third of the population being surveyed. People often suspect the new, since it requires effort to comprehend it and since there are no established patterns to govern the response. After a large-scale campaign to inform the people of Cincinnati about the United Nations and to create favorable attitudes toward it, researchers discovered that the effort had been ineffective. Only those who already knew about the United Nations were interested. Others were uninterested or negative; they resisted the efforts made to inform them.

Personal Influence

Personal influences also stand between a communication and the individual's response to it. Personal contacts with people "who know what they're talking about" have a strong influence. Each person has many authority points—acquaintances, friends, relatives—whose opinions he seeks or accepts on politics, movies, fashions, shopping, and so forth. One usually goes to opinion leaders on his own level in the social hierarchy, but he does not go to the same person for advice on all topics.

These opinion leaders are dispersed throughout the population. Their influence may be great with some individuals, nonexistent with others. Likewise they wield great influence in connection with some subjects, none with others. These opinion leaders, in turn, have their own authority points. Personal influence, then, runs a twisting, turning course throughout the population, and all the way it is important in shaping opinions and actions.

Personal contact has several advantages over the mass media. Our mental guard is down; we may be strongly affected by an offhand remark in casual conversation. We know our sources, and we trust them. They operate in the most intimate of circumstances. If they do encounter resistance in us, they have the opportunity for conversational give-and-take, a two-way process of communication lacking in the media. Furthermore they can reward or punish us by granting or withholding their approval.

The media, of course, exert influence through these opinion leaders. The leaders may get some of their information and ideas from the mass media and transmit them to others. For example, E. A. Wilkening tried to find out what had influenced farmers in adopting certain farm practices. One of the mass media was cited as the chief influence by about one-fourth of the early adopters but by fewer than one-twentieth of the late adopters. Other farmers were the main influence mentioned by three-fifths of the late adopters. It seems apparent that some of the farmers who had learned of the practices from the media influenced others who had not. There are indications that opinion leaders make greater than normal use of the media. In his study of Erie County, Lazarsfeld found that the opinion leader exposes himself to newspapers and radio about twice as much as the ordinary citizen, to magazines almost three times as much.

More recent research has shown that the mass media play the major role in disseminating news of average importance (such as a candidate's position on an issue) and that interpersonal sources are most important in spreading news of important issues (such as President Nixon's decision to invade Cambodia in 1970). Of course, those who spread important news nearly always get it from the mass media.

In attempting to persuade, the mass media also encounter a network of interpersonal relationships that may deflect or negate their messages. Each person is a member of small groups—families, circles of friends, work teams, clubs—which influence and support the opinions, attitudes, decisions, and actions of their members. Individuals conform to the opinions and attitudes shared by the group, the so-called group norms. When one reads or listens to the mass media, he checks what he learns against the norms of his group. If the message runs strongly counter to group norms, it rarely wins. However, a message from the media may make some headway in influencing the individual if group norms do not apply, if the reader or listener thinks that the group has altered its norms, or if he is about to leave the group. It may also be effective if it helps one to meet the norms of his group. Suppose, for example, a person becomes a member of a group with taste in music more advanced than his own. The media may be influential if they help to raise his tastes to those of the group.

How the Media Influence

Research workers generally agree that the media are much more likely to modify attitudes than to change them. When a group opposing the Tennessee Valley Authority was subjected to propaganda favoring it, less intense opposition was far more frequent than conversion.

The media are not only powerful reinforcers, but they can also slightly redirect existing behavior patterns or attitudes into new areas. Some observers believe that the power of advertising lies in its almost exclusive concern with such "canalization," as this redirection is called. Most Americans, for instance, are accustomed to cleansing themselves with soap; but the particular brand they use concerns them little, and advertising can influence the choice of brand.

In summary, then, what can we say about the influence of the mass media as persuaders? Wilbur Schramm has put it this way:

> Any given communication that comes to an adult enters into a situation where millions of communications have come before, where group norms are already ingrained, and where the mind is already made up and the knowledge structured on most subjects of importance. The new communication is therefore usually not an earthshaking event, but merely another drop in the long slow process that forms the stalactites of our personalities.

The Professional
Persuaders

⏎

I'm a professional. This is a professional job
[preparing TV commercials for Richard Nixon]. I was
neutral toward Nixon when I started. Now I happen to
be for him. But that's not the point. The point is, for
the money, I'd do it for almost anybody.
                                        EUGENE JONES

      Since every major enterprise with a shred of sensitivity now engages experts to build a favorable image through public relations or advertising or both, it was probably inevitable that image building would become a large and sensitive enterprise and that the experts would set about constructing a favorable public image for themselves. So it is that most of the 110,000 public-relations men in the United States have been turning ever more assiduously to developing general respect for their craft, and most of the approximately 400,000 men and women in advertising are equally concerned with promoting their own calling.

      A few advertising and PR men have confessed in their memoirs that they did work they detested for money they didn't earn to buy things they didn't need to impress people they didn't like. With most of them, however, to ask for a definition of public relations or advertising is tantamount to hearing a lofty response. When one advertising trade paper asked a number of the leading public-relations firms to define their role, the typical answer was: "Public relations is the skilled communication of ideas to the various publics with the object of producing a desired result." The most widely repeated definition, which was offered by Cyril W. Plattes, manager of the department of public services for General Mills, ran:

Public Relations is that responsibility and function of management which (1) analyzes public interest and determines public attitudes, (2) identifies and interprets policies and programs of an organization, and (3) executes a program of action to merit acceptance and good will.

Perhaps the most widely accepted definition of the role of advertising was written by Frederick R. Gamble, former president of the American Association of Advertising Agencies:

Advertising is the counterpart in distribution of the machine in production. By the use of machines, our production of goods and services multiplies the selling effort. Advertising is the great accelerating force in distribution. Reaching many people rapidly at low cost, advertising speeds up sales, turns prospects into customers in large numbers and at high speed. Hence, in a mass-production and high-consumption economy, advertising has the greatest opportunity and the greatest responsibility for finding customers.

Gamble's insight is valuable, but it fails to point up the essential similarity of public relations and advertising. Although advertising certainly does accelerate distribution, and it is most obviously at work in pushing particular brands, like public relations it is centrally concerned with winning acceptance and good will—for products, for people, for companies, for ideas. The only real difference between advertising and public relations is in method, and this difference dictates a different use of the mass media. Martin Mayer, author of *Madison Avenue, U.S.A.,* makes the distinction:

Advertising, whatever its faults, is a relatively open business; its messages appear in paid space or on bought time, and everybody can recognize it as special pleading. Public relations works behind the scenes; occasionally the hand of the p.r. man can be seen shifting some bulky fact out of sight, but usually the public relations practitioner stands at the other end of a long rope which winds around several pulleys before it reaches the object of his invisible tugging. . . . The advertising man must know how many people he can reach *with* the media, the public relations man must know how many people he can reach *within* the media.

Essentially public relations and advertising are selling devices. Their basic aims are so alike that they are, in fact, often linked—some advertising agencies have public-relations departments, some public-relations firms have advertising departments, many corporations placed advertising and public relations in a single department—and they are linked, too in the public consciousness.

PUBLIC RELATIONS

To increase the sale of garbage cans for a client, one public-relations firm drew up a model ordinance ostensibly designed to protect public health by preventing or controlling the spread of diseases carried by rats. Among other things the ordinance provided that all garbage must be deposited in containers of galvanized steel or other nonrusting material. After the ordinance had been approved by the United States Public Health Service, the public-relations firm sent copies of it, along with promotional kits, to every city and county health officer in the United States. Within a year more than 300 cities had adopted the ordinance. The sales of substantial garbage cans multiplied.

Edward J. Bernays, noted public-relations expert, used a different approach to stimulate the sale of bacon for a client: he got physicians to advocate hearty breakfasts. To promote the sale of luggage, he arranged for society leaders to come forth with the statement that a woman should take at least three dresses along on even the most informal weekend visit. The public-relations department of the Pan-American Coffee Bureau once set out to make the employees' coffee break, which had become common during World War II, an American institution. It surveyed top management on the benefits and drawbacks of the coffee break, then publicized the findings. It sent forth a flood of publicity about companies that had found that the coffee breaks improved morale, increased efficiency, and reduced employee fatigue. And in the 1960s, when coffee sales slumped, one public-relations firm tried to increase consumption among soft-drink-conscious young people by encouraging the establishment of coffee houses.

The difference between these approaches and a national advertising campaign to promote sales is obvious. And Martin Mayer's point, quoted above, about the PR man who "stands at the other end of a long rope which winds around several pulleys" should be equally obvious.

But the public-relations practitioner is often concerned with much more than the sale of products. His objective may be to change the public image of an individual or corporation or to alter public attitudes toward company policies. The Illinois Central Railroad, slicing North to South across mid-America, was once stigmatized as being controlled by Wall Street. In 1938 the company made three changes to remove conditions that contributed to that impression. It moved its financial offices from New York to Chicago, replaced its directors from the East with businessmen from along its route, and began to hold its monthly directors' meetings in Chicago instead of New York.

Objectives

Our public relations are those aspects of our behavior that have social consequences. As Harwood L. Childs puts it:

> Our problem in each corporation or industry is to find out what these activities are, what social effects they have, and, if they are contrary to the public interest, to find ways and means of modifying them so that they will serve the public interest.

What is the public interest? In effect, says Childs, it is what the public says it is.

But in practice only a few corporations subscribe to those objectives of public relations. Nugent Wedding of the University of Illinois studied 85 representative business firms to learn how they carried out their public relations. Only about 35 per cent of these regarded public relations as consisting of forming proper policies and then interpreting those policies to the public. Almost 11 per cent regarded public relations as solely a publicity activity.

Because American business persists in emphasizing words rather than deeds, it is wasting enormous sums of money on ineffective efforts to convert the public, according to Bernays. Public relations, he believes, must emerge as a form of social statesmanship. Its practitioner, with the full cooperation of his clients, must attempt, as his four objectives:

> To define the social objectives of his client or to help him define them.
> To find out what maladjustments there are between these objectives and the elements in our society on which his client is dependent. These maladjustments may be distortions in the mind of the public due to misinformation, ignorance, or apathy, or they may be distortions due to unsound action by the client.
> To attempt to adjust the client's policies and actions to society so that the maladjustments may be resolved.
> To advise the client on ways and means by which his new policies and actions, or old policies and actions, if it is deemed advisable to retain them, may be understood by the public.

Apart from the 35 per cent that had a concept roughly equivalent to Bernays', the firms surveyed by Wedding had narrow views of the objectives of public relations: to create favorable public opinion and good will, 29.4 per cent; to perform one aspect of the selling job, 10.6; to interpret business to the public and the public to business management, 8.2; and to whitewash business when business is under fire, 1.2.

History

The term public relations seems first to have been used in its modern sense in the closing years of the nineteenth century. One of the first to use it was Dorman Eaton of the Yale Law School in 1882 in an address, "The Public Relations and Duties of the Legal Profession." In 1906 and again in 1913 it turned up in talks by executives of the Baltimore and Ohio Railroad about railroads and their problems of "public relations." It was fairly common by the 1920s, when Bernays coined the expression "public-relations counsel," although it was ridiculed as an absurdly pompous synonym for the use of press agents.

Shortly before World War II the term became imbedded in the vocabulary of American business. In its issue of March 1939, *Fortune* observed:

> The year 1938 may go down in the annals of industry as the season in which the concept of public relations suddenly struck home to the hearts of a whole generation of businessmen, much as first love comes mistily and overpoweringly to the adolescent. Indeed, during 1938 there was scarcely a convention that did not feature an address on public relations, scarcely a trade magazine that did not devote some space to the subject, scarcely a board of directors that did not deliberate weightily on the powers of the new goddess. And they found that the sphere of this Mona Lisa was all of industry and that she presided over its most bewildering and least tangible aspects.

But if the term is fairly recent, the practice is certainly not new in this country. Some historians say that public relations in America expanded after the Civil War, gained ground as a result of the onslaughts on big business at the turn of the century, emerged as a new profession in the 1920s when it began to tap the techniques of the social sciences, and came of age in the 1930s when the Depression convinced management of its need.

Publicists in the early days were press agents for politicians, stage shows, and circuses, and later for hotels, railroads, and shipping interests. They tricked, cajoled, and bribed newspapers into giving them space in the news columns. Some of them used techniques and tools employed by present-day public-relations counselors. P. T. Barnum, that master promoter, had a fine talent for creating events that became legitimate news. Thus he arranged for one of his major attractions, General Tom Thumb, to have an audience with Queen Victoria. Here is an example of creating news on the one hand and of obtaining the testimonial of a prominent figure on the other. But Barnum's public relations went beyond mere words. To build good will for himself, he gave lectures for charity and contributed to welfare societies. To overcome church opposition to his shows, he emphasized their Christian character and admitted clergymen and wives free.

Several historical developments sharpened the interest of business and industry in public relations. One may have been the reaction to the robber barons who dominated the period of headlong industrial expansion after the Civil War. As they felled their forests, took their oil and ore from the earth, and built their railroads and factories, they held labor in close check, squeezed out their competitors, manipulated corporations and stocks, and bought legislation for their own benefit. They took the view that what they did and how they did it were their own concerns. Their attitude was exemplified in the public mind by Vanderbilt's phrase, "The public be damned!"

As abuses mounted, so did public criticism. Critics and reformers shouted against corruption in business and politics. Muckraking magazines exposed the evils perpetrated by the railroads, packing companies, oil companies, insurance firms, patent-medicine manufacturers, and political bosses. The government investigated antilabor practices and passed legislation regulating lobbies, monopolies, and the food and drug trade. For a time the individualistic entrepreneur passed from public hero to public villain.

Business and industry seem to have begun showing a conscious—perhaps a self-conscious—regard for the effects of their policies on the public in the last years of the nineteenth century. The acknowledged pioneer was the Bell Telephone Company under Theodore Vail, who saw as early as 1883 that sound policies were as important as pious words. That year, requesting a report from an affiliate in Iowa, he asked, "Where there has been any conflict between the local Exchange and the public, what has been the cause of the difficulties, and what has been the result?" When Vail saw that male telephone operators lacked the necessary tact and patience, he replaced them with women. In 1908 the company launched a campaign, which has continued down to the present in its basic approach, to give the public facts about the telephone system, to tell how calls should be made, and to urge subscribers to answer their telephones promptly. The company schooled its employees in dealing politely and sympathetically with the public. Sensitive to charges of monopoly, the company recognized that the impressions people got about it were from contacts with its employees. As one vice president of the company said in 1909, "They know us as a monopoly, and that creates hostility at once because the public does not like monopolies. They have no opportunity to see us or know us . . ." It is probably significant that the telephone companies, leaders in public relations, have emerged virtually unscathed from governmental investigations. In fact, telephone companies have had an amazing record. Not until telephone service became erratic in many urban areas in 1969 and 1970—a consequence of inadequate forecasts of needs for service—was there widespread dissatisfaction.

A second cause of the interest in public relations no doubt was World War I, in part because the war itself was charged by many to the influence of Eastern business, especially Wall Street. Then the vast outpouring of war propaganda on an unprecedented scale demonstrated the efficacy of words in shaping public attitudes. This intensified a general concern with the whole broad subject of public opinion on the part of scholars and laymen alike. And it gave experience in opinion manipulation on a large scale to some men who, with the peace, were to use their skills on behalf of business.

A third factor affecting the course of public relations was probably the Depression of the 1930s. Public faith in the free-enterprise system declined, and thousands of Americans listened attentively to new prophets with their share-the-wealth plans and other cures for economic ills. Besides selling products, American business had to resell itself to the public. Its task was complicated by labor troubles and unrest. Words might still be an indispensable tool of public relations, but policies in accord with the public interest seemed even to the less public-spirited to take on an increased importance.

By 1949, according to *Fortune*, 4000 corporations had public-relations departments or programs; in addition, there were 500 commercial public-relations firms, supported mainly by business. Today churches, schools, colleges, medical associations, philanthropic organizations, social-welfare agencies, and government bodies all have public-relations departments. Many of them, perhaps most, put greater emphasis on the dissemination of information than on Bernays' ideal twofold task of forming sound policies and interpreting them to the public. In 1957, according to a vice president of Carl Byoir and Associates, there were about 100,000 persons working in all aspects of public relations in America and annual expenditures on it were approximately two billion dollars. By 1970 the number had increased to 110,000, according to the Public Relations Society of America.

Criticisms

Public-relations men—who helped transform robber barons into benign philanthropists in the public image—ironically have never enjoyed good public relations themselves. Today newspapermen, from whose ranks many public-relations specialists are recruited, tend to look down on them—perhaps a little in envy of their higher salaries, perhaps much more in disdain of their "selling out to the special interests." Intellectuals scorn them as insincere hired manipulators, sometimes sinister, sometimes no more than offensive. The very term "public-relations counsel" suggests the status-seeking that led undertakers to call themselves morticians, janitors to call themselves maintenance engineers, and garbage collectors to call themselves sanitary haulers. The fact is that today's public-relations worker has inherited a legacy of criticism. The criticism goes back to the press agents of the nineteenth century, whose tactics aroused the enmity of editors, publishers, and just plain casual observers. From 1908 through the 1920s, the American Newspaper Publishers Association conducted a campaign against free publicity and free advertising. The trade press repeatedly denounced press agents, with which public-relations men were regarded as synonymous. In 1913 there were even attempts to make the use of press agents a legal offense.

Recognizing some criticisms, the Public Relations Society of America stated in its 1969 booklet *An Occupational Guide to Public Relations:*

> Because it is a young field which does not enjoy full understanding, public relations is sometimes not as well accepted as most other basic functions of management. This may detract from the status and security of its workers. While the work is allied to professionalism, it suffers from the absence of standards and definite boundary lines. Because it is concerned with influencing public opinion, it is often difficult to measure the results of performance, and, therefore to "sell" the worth of public relations programs. In the consulting field, competition is keen and if a firm loses an account, some of its personnel may be affected.
>
> Because of the dangers inherent in the exercise of persuasion and because of questionable tactics of fringe operations, all public relations has received considerable criticism. Public relations involves much more hard work and less glamour than is popularly supposed. The demands it makes for continual tact and for anonymity will be considered by some as less inviting features.

Modern Public Relations

Public relations is a large umbrella that covers many specialists, and the great majority of them protest that they should not be equated with the press agents who follow in the Barnum tradition. Indeed, they contend that publicity is only one facet of modern public relations—one among many tools used in many media. A news story, a speech, a film, a photograph—each is a tool of public relations. The channels that carry the tools—a newspaper, a club meeting at which a film is shown, a magazine—are media.

There is much more to the modern concept of public relations than the simple creation of publicity. Bernays and a few others began bringing a degree of respectability to a much-maligned craft by promoting the Total Program. They argued that public relations must run deeper than mere publicity. In *The Engineering of Consent* Bernays pointed out:

> The (company) president's acceptance of membership on advisory boards of national importance—indicates corporate interest in the national welfare. Speaking engagements of plant managers before local service groups highlight management's civic mindedness. . . . All of these symbol-projected themes—civic mindedness, interest in education and youth and the like—gradually form a composite and favorable picture in the public mind.

How the Total Program works and how it has been developed over the years is illustrated by the experiences of Paul Garrett, who was the only public-relations employee of General Motors when he joined the company in 1931. When Garrett arrived at company headquarters in Detroit, he was asked, "How do you make a billion dollars look small?" Acutely sensitive about the company's size and visibility in troubled times, the management's chief aim was to grow inconspicuously. Garrett said not only that he could not answer the question; he did not think providing an answer was part of his job. Public relations is the practice of winning confidence, he argued, not putting on an act. As a consequence of his prodding, General Motors has engaged over the years in a wide-ranging permanent program calculated to win acceptance and good will. The program resulted eventually in the company's setting up related departments known as Plant City and Field Relations, Educational Relations, Speakers Bureau, and Institutional Advertising—all designed to persuade everyone that General Motors is a desirable, if huge, concern. When Garrett retired as a vice president after twenty-five years, General Motors was spending more than one million dollars a year on a public-relations program that involved more than two hundred employees. The strength of this program may help to explain how GM was able to resist so successfully the challenges to its policies that developed in 1970. Part of a movement against destruction of the environment, the campaign was primarily devoted to convincing institutional owners of GM stock, especially universities, they should help reform the company.

It is a measure of the importance of PR in modern economy that public-relations specialists are holding scores of corporate vice presidencies and that many are serving as company directors. The atmosphere has proved so heady that PR men speak increasingly of their "profession" and its fast-developing "prestige." One leading counselor, E. Edward Pendray, even holds that "To public-relations men must go the most important social engineering role of them all—the gradual reorganization of human society piece by piece and structure by structure."

There is reason to doubt this sweeping role, and even more reason to question some of the methods of modern PR. This became especially clear when the firm of Carl Byoir & Associates undertook to defeat a bill that would have allowed increased size and weight limits for trucks on Pennsylvania roads. Byoir was paid $150,000 by the Eastern Railroads Presidents Conference. The firm earned the money in devious ways, primarily by setting up front organizations—the New Jersey Citizens Tax Study Foundation, the Empire State Transport League—to feed publicity unfavorable to truckers into Pennsylvania. The governor vetoed the bill, but the truckers brought a suit that eventually disclosed methods the presiding judge summed up as "the big lie." He commented, "This technique, as it appears from the evidence in this case, has been virtually adopted *in toto* by certain public-relations firms under the less insidious and more palatable name of the third-party technique."

Perhaps more important is the case of the attempted takeover of the American Broadcasting Company (ABC) by the International Telephone and Telegraph Company (ITT). It was a friendly takeover in that ABC wanted to merge with ITT, a huge conglomerate with 433 separate boards of directors which operates in more than forty countries. But some Senators and Congressmen, the Department of Justice, and especially three members of the FCC—Commissioners Robert Bartley, Kenneth Cox, and Nicholas Johnson—feared the takeover. Commissioner Johnson explained:

> The merger would have placed ABC, one of the largest purveyors of news and opinion in America, under the control of one of the largest conglomerate corporations in the world. . . . Consider simply that the integrity of the news judgment of ABC might be affected by the economic interests of ABC—that ITT might simply view ABC's programming as a part of ITT's public relations, advertising, or political activities.

Events of 1967 indicated that Commissioner Johnson's fears were justified. He has written:

> During the April, 1967, hearings, while this very issue was being debated, the *Wall Street Journal* broke the story that ITT was going to extraordinary lengths to obtain favorable press coverage of this hearing. Eventually three reporters were summoned before the ex-

aminer to relate for the official record the incidents that were described in the *Journal's* exposé.

An AP and a UPI reporter testified to several phone calls to their homes by ITT public relations men, variously asking them to change their stories and make inquiries for ITT with regard to stories by other reporters, and to use their influence as members of the press to obtain for ITT confidential information from the Department of Justice regarding its intentions. Even more serious were several encounters between ITT officials and a New York *Times* reporter.

On one of these occasions ITT's senior vice president in charge of public relations went to the reporter's office. After criticizing her dispatches to the *Times* about the case in a tone which she described as "accusatory and certainly nasty," he asked whether she had been following the price of ABC and ITT stock. When she indicated that she had not, he asked if she didn't feel she had a "responsibility to the shareholders who might lose money as a result of what" she wrote. She replied, "My responsibility is to find out the truth and print it."

He then asked if she was aware that I (as an FCC Commissioner) was working with a prominent senator on legislation that would forbid any newspaper from owning any broadcast property. [*The New York Times* owns station WQXR in New York.] In point of fact, the senator and I had never met, let alone collaborated, as was subsequently made clear in public statements. But the ITT senior vice president, according to the *Times* reporter, felt that this false information was something she "ought to pass on to [her] . . . publisher before [she wrote] . . . anything further" about the case. The obvious implication of this remark, she felt, was that since the *Times* owns a radio station, it would want to consider its economic interests in deciding what to publish about broadcasting in its newspaper.

To me, this conduct, in which at least three ITT officials, including a senior vice president, were involved, was a deeply unsettling experience. It demonstrated an abrasive self-righteousness in dealing with the press, insensitivity to its independence and integrity, a willingness to spread false stories in furtherance of self-interest, contempt for government officials as well as the press, and an assumption that even as prestigious a news medium as the New York *Times* would, as a matter of course, want to present the news so as to serve best its own economic interests [as well as the economic interests of other large business corporations].

Leading spokesmen for public relations argue that only a small percentage of the practitioners use devious methods and that the entire profession should not be tarred with the same brush. It is nonetheless significant that the standard-setting association, the Public Relations Society of America (PSRA), which is proud that it licenses PR men, did not ask Byoir or the ITT men to withdraw from the society. Several years ago *Tide* surveyed one hundred "top counselors" for their opinions on the use of front organizations of the sort employed by Byoir. Some simply responded with the suggestion that "front" is a loaded word; "allied interest group" would be better. Others seemed to miss the ethical point entirely, replying that fronts are ill advised because the opposition can blow up a campaign by exposing the deception. Only a small minority would approve legislation requiring the public disclosure of fronts.

In a candid speech to the Society of Magazine Writers, one spokesman described the problem of the wide assortment of "problem people" in public relations:

> We're struggling to find a way to protect ourselves. We haven't found it yet. . . . We have no firm code on malpractice for weeding out these people. But gradually we'll find some way of establishing standards of ethics so that you can tell us apart.

POLITICAL PR

As the mass media have moved to a pivotal position in elections, political public relations, which includes political advertising, has grown important. This became especially apparent in 1968, when Richard Nixon won the Presidency primarily because of shrewd use of television. The three men who guided Nixon—Roger Ailes, Harry Treleaven, and Al Scott—were soon besieged with other offers.

In 1970 Treleaven was the chief strategist for Senatorial campaigns in Florida, Tennessee, Michigan, and Texas. In some cases the fee for this kind of management can range as high as ten per cent of the campaign advertising budget—a budget close to a million dollars in a big state.

Men who know how to use the mass media have been working in political campaigns for decades, but they became the central figures only in 1952. The election of Dwight Eisenhower marked the grand entrance into politics of public relations and advertising specialists. Today, as Dan Nimmo has pointed out in his book *The Political Persuaders*, "we are approaching the time when all candidates and all proposals in all elections at all levels will be professionally managed." The task of reaching the electorate has become so complex and technical that politicians must recruit communications specialists to wage a campaign that will achieve significant exposure.

The campaign audience, Nimmo points out, consists of two groups. The members of one group use and believe the print media, although they are likely to attend to television as well. They are concerned and informed about issues and already have moderate to strong loyalities to one of the parties. They are more likely to vote than are others, probably for a candidate they decide upon early in the campaign. The aim of the candidate in appealing to them is to reinforce the commitments of those who favor him. He is unlikely to be able to convert the others.

The second group, which is larger—and growing—relies primarily upon television and radio. The members of this group command most of the attention of the professional persuader, for they are not very well informed. Although people of all backgrounds are represented, within this group are large numbers of those of low to moderate income, little education, little interest in politics, and much more experience with TV, film, and recording personalities than in deciding public issues. This is the audience that Robert MacNeil described in his book *The People Machine* as "moderately more sophisticated and somewhat better informed than that of a generation ago, but it is basically conservative and, from its reading habits, passive and incurious about the world. Because it is not particularly interested in many subjects and issues, it will apparently accept what it is told about them more or less trustingly." Such an audience is made to order for the political persuader.

ADVERTISING

In 1923 Claude Hopkins wrote a book titled *Scientific Advertising*, which began, "The time has come when advertising in some hands has reached the status of a science." Hopkins, who was reputed to be the best of the copywriters, was referring only to mail-order advertising, which involved printing coupons in ads that consumers could clip and send in with a dollar or so to receive a product. It was possible to gauge roughly the effectiveness of mail-order advertising by the number of returns, as Hopkins demonstrated in his 20,000-word book and in hundreds of mail-order campaigns.

Mail order is still an important facet of advertising, but, as the mass media show every day, there are many other kinds, and it is seldom possible to measure the effect of each with any real precision. Nonetheless, the methods of the behavioral sciences are so evident throughout the structure of the advertising world that it is clear that modern merchandising is attempting to make Hopkins' prescription apply to all advertising. Nearly every major agency spends a large share of its annual budget on research and on continuous efforts to take some of the guesswork out of appealing to masses of consumers.

Research in advertising is far too complicated to discuss in detail, but some understanding of the broad aims is available through considering the four major kinds of appeals, which have been described by Albert Frey in his book *Advertising:*

> Primary: those aimed at inducing the purchase of one *type* of product.
> Selective: those aimed at inducing the purchase of a brand.
> Emotional: (sometimes termed *short-circuit* and *human-interest* appeals): those aimed at the emotions rather than the intellect.
> Rational: (sometimes termed *long-circuit* and *reason-why* appeals): those directed at the intellect.

Advertising specialists who work for *Reader's Digest* have developed a detailed list of appeals, which they call an "Index of Human Emotions Which Will Actuate the Greatest Number of Prospects to Buy." It is a useful list, but there is, of course, a distinct limit to the value of analyzing appeals, in part because selling depends on so many other influences. Garrit Lydecker of J. Walter Thompson Company has pointed out: "I once made a list of all the factors that can influence sales. I had forty-five of them written down before I got bored with it. I'm sure there are more. Advertising was one of the factors."

General analysis is limited, too, by the fact that leading figures have some highly individual notions as to how advertising should be presented. One example is Rosser Reeves, chairman of the board of Ted Bates & Company, a sometimes frenetic and always enthusiastic proponent of technical authority. Reeves describes the doctor who advises the Bates agency on drugs as "the man we believe to be the world's greatest pharmacologist." Another doctor, who offered advice on a soap campaign, Reeves says is "conceded to be one of the three leading experts in the United States on dermatology."

Reeves' chief contribution to advertising theory is known as USP, outlined in detail in his book *Reality in Advertising*, which was briefly a best-seller. Reeves describes his agency's method:

> We can't sell a product unless it's a good product, and even then we can't sell it unless we can find the Unique Selling Proposition. There are three rules for a USP. First, you need a definite proposition: buy this product and you get this specific benefit. Pick up any textbook on advertising and that's on page one—but everybody ignores it. Then, second, it must offer a unique proposition, one which the opposition *cannot* or *does not* offer. Third, the proposition must sell. Colgate was advertising "ribbon dental cream . . . it comes out like a ribbon and lies flat on your brush." Well, that was a proposition and it was unique, but it didn't sell. Bates gave them "cleans your breath while

it cleans your teeth." Now every dentifrice cleans your breath while it cleans your teeth—*but nobody had ever put a breath claim on toothpaste before.*

Nearly every advertising man agrees with Reeves about the necessity for keeping everlastingly at it, for continuing the repetition. One agency man holds, "When the client begins to tire of an ad, you know it's beginning to catch on with the public." But there is considerable difference of opinion about Reeves' basic philosophy. This is emphasized by David Ogilvy of Ogilvy, Benson & Mather, who acknowledges the value of USP for advertising some products but holds that it is limited. Ogilvy is the high priest of brand-image advertising, specializing in building an aura of sophistication. A booklet he gives new employees points out: "It pays to give your brand a *first-class ticket* through life. People don't like to be seen consuming products which their friends regard as third-class."

Ogilvy is noted for choosing models who reflect elegance. He hired Baron George Wrangell of the Russian nobility to pose, black eye-patch prominently shown, as "the man in the Hathaway shirt." Commander Edward Whitehead became the symbol of Schweppes. In a speech at a meeting of the American Association of Advertising Agencies, Ogilvy pronounced his major theme: "Let us remember that it is almost always the total *personality* of a brand rather than any *trivial product difference* which decides its ultimate position in the market."

Still another approach is promoted by Norman B. Norman of Norman, Craig & Kummel. Although most agencies rely to some degree on the power of unconscious suggestion, Norman, who was trained as a social psychologist, has a distinctively Freudian orientation. His agency aims at empathy, seeking to involve consumers at deep levels; motivational research is basic. Some of the ads are highly suggestive—notably those for Maidenform bras and Veto deodorant—but the key is often subtlety. An ad campaign for Ronson lighters was built on research showing that flame is a sexual symbol.

One of the most admired agencies, Doyle Dane Bernbach, shuns all rules, relying instead on originality. In effect, William Bernbach simply hires the most creative copywriters and artists he can find, then encourages them to work together. He is one of the few agency presidents who think little of market research, holding that advertising is not a science but an art. Speaking to other advertising specialists, he has said:

Why should anyone look at your ad? The reader doesn't buy his magazine or tune in his radio and TV to see and hear what you have to say . . . What is the use of saying all the right things in the world if nobody is going to read them? And, believe me, nobody is going to read them if they are not said with freshness, originality, and imagination.

Few of the other large agencies promote anything that can be properly described as a philosophy, but there is general agreement on the goal: to reach the maximum number of users or potential users of a product at a minimum of cost. One authority, Otto Kleppner, has outlined three basic plans for using the mass media: the zone campaign, the cream campaign, and the national campaign. With the zone plan the advertiser puts his maximum effort into a definite and restricted geographic area—a city, state, or recognized trading territory—gets what business he can there, then passes on to another. With the cream plan he goes after the best prospects first, no matter how widely scattered, then goes after the next best, and so on down the scale. The national campaign combines the others on an enormous scale to get maximum sales from all possible prospects.

SELECTING MEDIA

Whichever sales strategy the advertiser selects, he chooses media carefully. Long books have been written about media selection, but it is possible to set forth here the general guidelines.

Geographic Selectivity

Selecting prospects geographically involves several choices of media for reaching them. Newspapers can carry a message to the cities the advertiser is most interested in reaching. He can limit advertising to the cities where his product has adequate distribution, where he thinks it has the greatest sales potential, where weather or seasonal conditions promise demand for it, where employment is high and the economic picture bright. Furthermore, the speed with which newspapers are produced allows flexibility.

Radio and television, through their spot commercials and through programs the advertiser can sponsor in cooperation with local dealers, also enable him to reach prospects on a geographical basis. Even with network facilities he need buy only a part of the entire national market.

Magazines also enable an advertiser to seek out customers and potential customers in definite regions. Some magazines concentrate their circulations in specific areas. *Sunset* circulates primarily in the western states, for instance, and *New Hampshire Profiles* has chosen a single state for its major concentration. *Successful Farming* draws the bulk of its audience from the rich agricultural heart of the midwest.

Some magazines circulate nationally and offer the advertiser a widely scattered but homogeneous body of readers sharing common tastes, interests, or even occupations. They are ill suited for geographical selectivity. In recent years especially, however, a number of large-circulation national magazines have given advertisers the option of buying either their entire circulation or a part of it. In 1959 *Look,* with a total circulation of nearly six million, inaugurated a Magazone Plan, under which advertisers could use any one or any combination of editions reaching seven standard marketing areas. Now magazines as diverse as *Sports Illustrated* and *Farm Journal* also are published in several editions.

Prospect Selectivity

But what of the advertiser who wants to reach only the most likely prospects for his product or service?

If his products are found in most households—as, for example, soaps, detergents, cigarettes—and especially if they are comparatively inexpensive, he may feel that he is reaching his market without undue waste if he gets his sales message before as many persons as possible. Sheer numbers may suit his purpose, then, and he can use the big-circulation national magazines, network television shows, Sunday supplements and a combination of dailies. But if his product appeals to some distinct body of purchasers or if it is relatively expensive, then he must carefully screen the audience for his sales pitch.

Magazines, because of their high selectivity of readers, are an excellent medium for such an advertiser. There are magazines for people with similar concerns, such as rearing children, protecting health, or homemaking; with similar hobbies, such as stamp collecting, skin diving, hunting, fishing, yachting, or driving a hot rod; with similar interests, such as music, literature, science, fashions, or foreign affairs; and with similar occupations. There is scarcely a vocation, an interest, a facet of the personality that is not appealed to by some magazine.

The screened audience attracted by editorial content is the magazine publisher's stock-in-trade. Condé Nast once likened the magazine publisher to a name-broker: The publisher baits his pages with reading matter intended to attract either a large number of readers or a special class of readers, sells those pages at less than cost, and makes a profit by charging advertisers for the privilege of addressing the distinctive audience he has assembled. Nast's own magazines reached a wealthy, sophisticated few, and Ilka Chase in *Always in Vogue* repeats the allegory Nast used to explain his publishing rationale:

> If you had a tray with two million needles on it and only one hundred and fifty thousand of these had gold tips which you wanted, it would be an endless and costly process to weed them out. Moreover the one million, eight hundred and fifty thousand which were not gold-tipped would be of no use to you, they couldn't help you, but if you could get a magnet that would draw out only the gold ones what a saving!

Obviously Nast regarded his magazines as just such a magnet.

Network broadcasting and newspapers, attracting large, heterogeneous followings, do not permit the degree of audience selectivity that magazines do. Nevertheless they can give the advertiser a coarsely screened audience—and more and more advertisers are looking for affluent, educated audiences. By the type of television program he sponsors and the time at which he schedules it, the advertiser can engage an audience with some of the characteristics he is looking for. He should know that about twice as many men as women watch televised boxing matches, for instance; that about seven times as many women as men tune in on daytime serials; that men constitute only 7 per cent of the total television audience in mid-morning but nearly one-third between eight and nine in the evening. By his choice of newspapers, he can reach populations that are predominantly rural or predominantly suburban. One metropolitan newspaper may give him an audience different from that of another. *The New York Times* is addressed to quite a different segment of the population than the New York *Daily News*, although each offers a good market for a specific purpose.

DEFENDING THE PERSUADER

Selling has always carried a stigma. Anarchus said, "The market is the place set aside where men may deceive each other," and there have been echoes of that statement ever since. It is a curious fact, however, that two authorities who have conducted searching examinations of professional persuasion through public relations and advertising have fashioned cogent defenses.

Robert L. Heilbroner, a respected writer on economics, wrote an exhaustive study of public relations for *Harper's* magazine. While Heilbroner did not overlook the chicanery characteristic of some PR, he summed up by quoting a public-relations specialist who holds that the large corporation gets nervous unless people say what wonderful public relations it has: "So it has to *have* wonderful public relations.

It has to *act* lovable. It has to *be* progressive." Heilbroner concluded:

> Hence, by an unexpected twist, public relations has become a weapon whose recoil is greater than its muzzle blast. Good Public Relations has come to be something very much like the corporate conscience—a commercial conscience, no doubt, but a conscience nonetheless.

Martin Mayer, author of *Madison Avenue, U.S.A.*, is also unstinting in criticism of advertising, but he, too, finds a value not generally recognized:

> Any realistic approach . . . ought to start with the premise that successful advertising *adds a new value to the product.* . . . A lipstick may be sold at Woolworth's under one name, and in a department store under another, nationally advertised name. Almost any teen-age girl will prefer the latter, if she can afford to pay the difference. Wearing the Woolworth's brand, she feels her ordinary self; wearing the other, which has been successfully advertised as a magic recipe for glamour, she feels a beauty—and perhaps she is.

Perhaps more important, a study reported in *Advertising in America: A Consumer View* revealed that 78 per cent of Americans consider advertising essential, 74 per cent say that it encourages the development of better products, and 71 per cent think that advertising contributes to higher living standards.

These defenses do not, of course, negate garish and false PR and advertising. No defense is possible, but an explanation is in order: Clearly, like the mass media themselves, public relations and advertising are shaped largely by the American milieu. In the end it is fruitless to ask that they be much better than the industrial economy to which they owe their existence.

13

The Media,
Entertainment,
and American Culture

> When books or pictures in reproduction are thrown on
> the market cheaply and attain huge sales, this does
> not affect the nature of the objects in question. But
> their nature is affected when these objects themselves
> are changed—rewritten, condensed, digested, reduced
> to kitsch in reproduction, or in preparation for the
> movies.
>
> HANNAH ARENDT

In February, 1933, over station WXYZ in Detroit, George Trendle began broadcasting a half-hour radio program in which a masked avenger called the Lone Ranger galloped about the West correcting injustices. Listeners were so pleased that Trendle started looking around for other stations to help bear program costs. After a good deal of work, he signed up WGN in Chicago and WOR in New York. Then a number of New England stations wanted the program, and later so did the Don Lee broadcasting system in California. In 1934 the stations that had cooperated in broadcasting the show banded together into the Mutual Broadcasting System. The Lone Ranger, among his countless other noble deeds, could take credit for helping to create a major broadcasting network.

The Lone Ranger was responsible for a multitude of other accomplishments in the next quarter-century. He became a big business, the Lone Ranger Enterprises, for which a Texas industrialist paid $3 million in 1956. By then the Lone Ranger had brought the Whitman Publishing Company some $20 million from the sale of books about his exploits. He performed his missions in a comic strip carried by 144 daily and 89 Sunday newspapers. He was the inspiration for a series of phonograph records issued by Decca. He was a busy endorser of guns, holsters, masks, and other paraphernalia for youngsters. He undoubtedly encouraged boys and girls to stow away millions of bowls of breakfast cereal for his sponsors, and the passage from Rossini's "William Tell Overture" that was his theme became perhaps the most widely heard bit of operatic music of all time.

One can draw a number of conclusions about the entertainment content of the mass media from this story, and there is considerable additional evidence to support each of them. One is that through entertainment the media are capable of creating folk heroes. Matt Dillon, Superman, and Dick Tracy, like the Lone Ranger, all are endowed with virtues larger than life, making certain that good triumphs over evil.

Another conclusion is that the media are parasitic. Whatever succeeds in one medium is often taken over by the others. Characters who have first appeared in books later turn up in films or on television. Magazine short stories and serials often form the basis for subsequent movies or television programs. Max Shulman, a successful author of humorous short stories, deliberately set out a few years ago to write a quantity of them for a women's magazine so that he could resell them as a television series starring his central character, Dobie Gillis. He succeeded in getting his television series—and a book for good measure. Hollywood has long looked to best-selling novels for movie plots, and in recent years some book publishers have reversed the process by bringing out novels based on film scripts. Book publishers and moviemakers recognize that they can mutually profit from the public interest generated when one of them has a success. When M-G-M released a new screen version of Lew Wallace's classic *Ben Hur,* book publishers issued eleven new editions of the work in addition to those already in print.

APPEAL OF ENTERTAINMENT

Perhaps the most obvious conclusion of all, however, is that entertainment has a powerful appeal. Although newspapers have become much more informative in recent years, it is beyond dispute that some newspaper content is intended simply to divert its readers. Studies of newspaper readership show that adults give greater attention to human-interest articles, comics, and illustrations than to information about public affairs or advertisements. According to one research report, about half the readers of a daily read the banner story on page one, yet about two-thirds read the comics, and more look at the picture page than at anything else in the paper. Consider the readership of an issue of one California daily. Researchers found that 30 per cent of the men and 18 per cent of the women read the major news story from Shanghai in the top right-hand corner of the front page. But 60 per cent of the men and 66 per cent of the women read a feature on page 21 about how the heroes who had rescued a little girl were still unemployed. It is clear, too, that much of the content of many of the underground papers is designed primarily to titillate readers.

Even before 1895—the year the records of best-sellers became somewhat systematized—entertainment items bulked large among the books with the widest sales in America: the novels of Sir Walter Scott, James Fenimore Cooper, Charles Dickens, Alexander Dumas, Nathaniel Hawthorne, and a number of other authors now almost completely forgotten. Since then books of entertainment, along with self-help volumes, have captured high and frequent positions on the best-seller lists. According to a study by Alice Payne Hackett, the authors who have most consistently appeared on the best-seller lists over the years since 1895 have been purveyors of entertainment: Mary Roberts Rinehart had eleven titles on the lists; Sinclair Lewis, ten; Zane Grey and Booth Tarkington, nine each. This tendency toward entertainment persists, even though recent years have seen serious books occasionally lead the best-seller lists.

Although magazines, since the advent of TV, have become increasingly serious, some are still essentially purveyors of diversion, and parts of serious magazines are frankly entertainment. In the 1920s and 1930s general magazines carried a high proportion of sudsy light fiction. In the 1940s they gave increasing space to nonfiction. In the 1950s and especially in the 1960s, recognizing that they could not compete with TV as a medium of escape and that their audience had become better educated and more sophisticated, they largely abandoned fiction, and in their nonfiction took to topics that would have been regarded as too serious even a decade earlier.

Movie-making and broadcasting are commonly referred to as entertainment industries, and amusing the public is their acknowledged primary function. The magnet that draws people into theaters may be a particular star or the promise of the story. Yet at bottom the appeal is entertainment; people go to the movies to enjoy escape from care and routine, to feed their daydreams. In the late 1960s and early 1970s, movie-makers were focusing heavily on social issues—and they were losing the huge audiences of another era.

Many of the greatest movies of all time in terms of box-office gross— among them *Gone With the Wind, The Robe, The Greatest Show on Earth,* and *The Sound of Music*—made no pretensions beyond giving large numbers of persons good stories, lavish spectacles, or both.

True, commercial television and radio have a potential for education, and both have devoted a little time to edifying their audiences. NBC-TV has proudly announced that the number of persons Dr. Harvey E. White was able to reach with his physics lessons on "Continental Classroom" would have taken him 1300 years to teach in the conventional classroom. Yet the great majority of the broadcast audience expects television and radio to entertain. The television set is an electronic door to the land of enchantment—and there are more sets in American homes than there are bathtubs.

We have been referring so often to entertainment as though it were a negative element that it may be important to consider its beneficial effects. Few have defended it more pointedly than Charlene Brown of Stanford:

> Entertainment is necessary to provide the relief to enable human beings to face the demands of modern life—or maybe just life in general. Not all of us have the same sensibilities. The highbrows prefer their entertainment in different forms from the lowbrows, but it's still entertainment no matter how arty or how heavy with message. People need to relax. The sad scene is the culture vulture who feels compelled to seek out art but doesn't enjoy it. In fact, he's punishing himself. He's miserable but he feels he's accomplished something. The experience has been good for him, he tells himself. I recognize that when I go to the movies I want to be entertained. I don't need to go to the movies in order to be depressed by the cares of the world. Even from that point of view, most of what is on television does not entertain me. But I don't want to let television give entertainment a bad name.

Difficulty of Definition

Few would deny that the mass media carry an enormous amount of pure diversion. Perhaps half of all media content is avowedly entertainment of some sort. Actually the proportion is immeasurable, for no one is quite certain what constitutes entertainment. The newspaper editor might argue that his column of advice on readers' personal problems is instructional, but many subscribers would contend that it is entertainment. A television producer might hold that his quiz show is educational, but a good many viewers would argue that the show simply amuses the audience and that education is the most accidental of by-products.

One way of deciding what is and what is not entertainment is to bypass the content itself and to consider its effect, which a number of social researchers have done. Some of them think that content is escapist if it relieves tensions by affording the media user respite from his personal problems. Joseph T. Klapper in *The Effects of the Mass Media* has reviewed the different meanings that social scientists have given to the term "escapist," and fashioned a common-denominator definition: "that communication which provides emotional release by diverting the reader from his own problems or anxieties."

What is escapist for one person, then, is not necessarily so for another. If one uses media content primarily for pleasure, it is escapist no matter what else it is. Thus a businessman who relaxes with a magazine article about science or a scientist who takes refuge in the sports page of his newspaper is using the mass media for diversion. Under that concept all media fare is potentially entertainment. Whether it is or not depends upon the use to which the reader, viewer, or listener puts it.

Difficulties of Presenting Quality Entertainment

The entertainment function of the media was intensified and in other ways affected as the media changed from a comparatively restricted audience to a broad-based popular one. In the nature of the communications system, one can find an explanation for critics' complaints that the mass media at best have made small contributions to art and at worst have debased popular culture on the one hand and have blurred the line between enlightenment and entertainment on the other. Both art and education are predicated upon a critical and discriminating reception; the conditions under which the mass media operate make such a reception difficult.

Intended for mass consumption, the media usually strive for mass appeal. Few find it economically feasible to consider the tastes of the individual members of their audiences, and must play to the average tastes of large numbers. Nor can the owner of a medium often indulge in the luxury of satisfying his individual tastes. He must produce whatever it is profitable to give great numbers of other people.

With the object of momentarily engaging the busy masses, the transient products of the media issue forth in an endless torrent, the significant cheek by jowl with the trivial, the good and the substantial emphasized little more than the bad and the shallow. The media must compete with themselves, with other claims on the individual's time and attention, with the individual's own lethargy. Somehow they must get through to their readers, listeners, and viewers. The nature of their task dictates their approach to content, and the approach to content contributes to their blending of entertainment with enlightenment. To capture and captivate their audiences, the media generally try to enliven and simplify their messages.

Newspapers have done so since the days of the penny press. According to the sociologist Robert E. Park, newspapers exist in their modern format only because a few publishers discovered in 1835 that people prefer news to editorial opinion and that they prefer being entertained to being edified. "This, in its way, had the character and importance of a real discovery," he says. "It was like the discovery, made later in Hollywood, that gentlemen prefer blondes. At any rate it is to the consistent application of the principle involved that the modern newspaper owes not merely its present character but its survival as a species." In short, the newspaper came to emphasize the interesting rather than the important, to use William Randolph Hearst's distinction.

This is not to say that newspapers ignore serious content seriously presented. They are certainly doing a better job on that score than they were when Park made his comment in 1940. It is true, however, that in undertaking serious discussion or in presenting information newspapers must always reckon with their reception. Because of the heterogeneous nature of the readers, reporters must not only translate complex issues and complex subjects into terms intelligible to the masses but must do so interestingly. The chief aim of the reporter, after all, is to get his stories read. The aim of the deskman is to arrest attention with a headline. If the handling of a story and the headline that surmounts it attract readers to serious fare, that in itself is justification.

Especially among the magazines leading in circulation, the pressures to find and keep a large audience have sometimes contributed to a fusion of the functions of entertainment and enlightenment. Since World War II many magazines have shortened nonfiction articles on the assumption that readers no longer have the patience for long ones. But it is difficult to treat some subjects more than superficially in the allotted space and a few magazines—notably the *New Yorker, Esquire, Harper's* and *Atlantic*—have devoted some of their columns to longer and more serious presentations. Although some magazines have found valuable substitutes for the conventional article form, many writers still develop their articles not by straight exposition but by presenting a few generalities, each illuminated by numerous anecdotes and dramatized examples. Quite often the net result is a little information surrounded by a copious gilt-wrapping of entertainment. Having discovered that readers are more interested in people than in ideas, a number of magazines use personalities as a peg on which to hang treatments of general topics. A news magazine may review current problems of organized labor in a cover story centering on a well-known union official or may discuss the economic health of Great Britain in a personality sketch of its chancellor of the exchequer. The technique, while a perfectly legitimate one to sustain reader interest, is often in danger of subordinating information to entertainment.

Network broadcasters feel obliged to offer something for everybody. As CBS executive Richard S. Salant expressed it:

> For the fact is that broadcasting is a truly mass medium; it has to be. Unless it can enlist and hold the interest of most of the people a good part of the time, it is just too expensive to survive. It must, in its spectrum of programming, have something—even the great majority of its material—that will appeal not just to the thousands or hundreds of thousands but to millions and tens of millions.

A medium that is compelled to interest the tens of millions, one that counts most first-graders among its regular users, usually finds its common denominator in entertainment. Television's preoccupation with providing mass escapism lay behind this remark of the late Edward R. Murrow: "If television and radio are to be used to entertain all of the people all of the time, then we have come perilously close to discovering the real opiate of the people."

In its entertainment fare, broadcasting must make certain compromises in subject matter and treatment as a result of the demands of the market. Paddy Chayefsky, who earned a reputation as a television playwright before he concentrated on writing for the movies, once said that he had never encountered sponsor or network interference with his television dramas, thanks to a producer who took a firm position. But he added:

> On the other hand, every one of us, before we sit down and write a television show, makes that initial compromise of what we're going to write. We don't sit down and write for television or conceive a television idea that we know is going to be thrown out the window. That's the compromise. I have never, never written down in television in my life, but I never aimed very high . . . You make that same compromise in the movies, and you make it on the stage too, but in a relatively less degree.

What Chayefsky recognized was that the television playwright must accommodate himself to a mass audience and to an advertiser who regards any controversy in the shows he sponsors as bad business. Limitations on dramatic subject matter arise partly because the advertiser does not wish to offend anyone. Several advertising-agency executives who testified at hearings conducted by the Federal Communications Commission agreed that programs that displease a substantial number of viewers represent a misuse of the advertising dollar. Because the sponsor wants to leave his audience with a favorable impression, he usually avoids dramas that treat socially taboo subjects, portray extremes of misery or desolation, leave the viewer sad and depressed, or deal with politics—politics being controversial and capable of alienating customers. An aspirin manufacturer would never permit a drama in which a person committed suicide by an overdose of aspirin, an advertising executive told the FCC. He also said the manufacturer of filter cigarettes wanted the villains in a television drama to be shown as preferring nonfilter cigarettes, whereas the maker of nonfilter cigarettes wanted the villains in his shows to smoke filter cigarettes.

EFFECTS OF ENTERTAINMENT

When a sponsor is concerned about what the characters in his television drama say and do, he is recognizing that entertainment may have effects beyond mere diversion. One effect is persuasion, but social scientists have hypothesized several others. While these by-products of entertainment are still largely surmise, they deserve some attention.

Persuasive Powers

As other chapters show, entertainment is capable of affecting the way people think and act. Indeed, the assumption that entertainment can influence the minds of men underlies a good deal of censorship. Fear of the persuasive and corruptive possibilities of entertainment lies behind much of the public concern over comic books, paperback novels, violence on television, and sensation in newspapers.

Convinced that entertainment is subtly forceful in propaganda, men have been using it for centuries. During the Revolutionary War newspapers, almanacs, and broadsides sought to lighten the burden of battle with anecdotes, jests, parodies, satires, and songs, which were also designed to promote the cause of freedom. The popular novel has been a widely used form of social protest, and cartoons have been a frequent weapon of crusaders at least since *Harper's Weekly* ran pictures by Thomas Nast to break the political power of the Tweed Ring in New York in 1870–71. The underground press has used cartoons to point up what it regards as the dangerous absurdities of the Establishment.

Some of the findings of empirical research involving the persuasive powers of entertainment are contradictory. Studies do show, however, that certain types of entertainment—the soap opera, for example, and magazine stories—are effective. It is reasonable to suppose that entertainment has some effects similar to those of informational and avowedly persuasive content. That is, entertainment works outright conversion only rarely; more often it slightly modifies existing attitudes. Little by little, over a long period, it probably contributes to the attitudinal prism through which people perceive their environment and with which they interpret the multitudinous messages reaching them.

Much magazine fiction in the 1930s and 1940s emphasized the conventional virtues and idolized the little man, according to a study by Patrick Johns-Heine and Hans H. Gerth. While ostensibly preaching racial equality, it subtly perpetuated discrimination against minority groups and glorified the white Protestant American of Anglo-Saxon stock, according to another study by Bernard Berelson and Patricia Salter. The "Orphan Annie" comic strip helps to reaffirm the accepted values of the broad middle class. Lyle Shannon, who analyzed "Orphan Annie," summarized his conclusions in this fashion: "The strip emphasizes reliance on 'providence,' faith, hope, and charity—but not too much charity . . . Orphan Annie is for the church, truth, hard work, and pressure when necessary to get what she wants. She opposes crooks, politicians, slowness in government, and foreigners who would like United States military secrets."

Emotional Release

In a comprehensive study of the effects of the mass media, Joseph T. Klapper reported that people sometimes use entertainment to escape from feelings of inferiority and insecurity by identifying themselves with successful characters in stories, articles, films, and broadcasts. By enabling them to share vicariously in the good life and triumphs of others, identification provides a sense of prestige. At worst this is harmless, Klapper concluded; at best, helpful.

Some observers think that media entertainment offers a safety valve for pent-up aggressions and aberrant impulses and consequently performs a useful social function. While many people have become agitated about comic books, for example, some authorities contend that they may serve the emotional needs of children. Dr. Lauretta Bender, Associate Professor of Psychiatry at New York University Medical School, has written:

> When the aggressive threat to society, or the immediate family, is so overwhelming as to be unbearable, the comics can present the problem symbolically and repetitively so as to allay anxiety. During

the war when Superman and Wonder Woman could protect our ships at sea from Nazi submarines through their quick seeing eyes and lightning feet and magic strength—they were a great help to children whose fathers were in the service.

Material heavy in sex may serve a similarly useful purpose. One authority has concluded that "contrary to popular misconception, people who read salacious literature are less likely to become sexual offenders than those who do not, for the reason that such reading often neutralizes what aberrant sexual interests they may have."

By enabling people to work off their impulses and hostilities vicariously, then, the media may help to quiet disruptive forces in society. This basic argument is at least as old as John Milton's *Areopagitica*, in which, to be sure, it took a somewhat different cast. While Milton no doubt would be appalled at being cited to justify comic books, he nevertheless argued that reading is the best way to learn of evil. No man can be virtuous without a knowledge of evil, he said, and it is far better to learn vicariously through reading than through experience.

The relatively scanty available research evidence does, in fact, suggest that well-adjusted children take violence in the media in their stride—indeed, use it as an emotional outlet. Katherine M. Wolfe and Marjorie Fisk discovered that comics contribute to the development of the normal child who reads them moderately by amusing him and strengthening his ego. They may satisfy the emotional needs of the maladjusted child as well. The great danger is that they may postpone correction of the maladjusted child's basic troubles by allaying the symptoms. Television programs of crime and violence help children who are well adjusted and secure in their peer groups to vent their aggressions, according to a study conducted by John and Matilda Riley. For secure children these programs probably do no harm. But for maladjusted, insecure children they build up rather than release tensions and create a world of unhealthful fantasy. There is the possibility, too, that all children may learn antisocial behavior patterns from the mass media and that children may imitate in situations in which social norms are weak or not in operation.

Possible Dangers of Escapism

Some perceptive students of mass communication, albeit with little research evidence to back them up, have expressed concern over the misuse or excessive use of entertainment. They fear that overexposure to escapist material, by diverting people from the problems of daily living and by encouraging their retreat into a dream world, may promote individual and group apathy and thus inhibit social progress.

Klapper has argued against that viewpoint. He sees little reason for believing that escapist material diverts people from serious media fare. True, some people overindulge, he concedes, but they might be more dangerously preoccupied if the media were not so readily available. He grants that those who make heavy use of the media for escape probably have little interest in serious social problems, but he submits that their lack of interest is more likely to be the cause rather than the result of their tastes.

Other observers are concerned because some users of the mass media depend upon entertainment for information and advice. This can work harm in any of several ways. For one thing the advice is usually so superficial or impractical that it is certain to be futile. For another it can lead people to a passive acceptance of whatever ills and misfortunes befall them in the confident hope that everything will work out all right sooner or later.

It seems evident, too, that television gives no sense of the patience necessary for accomplishment in a democratic society. Both commercials and programs, largely because of the time restrictions, imply instant resolution of all problems.

Still other authorities believe that certain types of media entertainment can seduce the weak-willed and the immature into lives of crime or immorality. The codes of performance for the comic-book, motion-picture, and broadcasting industries all recognize this danger by urging that criminals never be glorified, crime never be portrayed attractively, and sin never be glamorized. Stated simply, the fear is that some people, especially children, may imitate the worst of what they are exposed to in the media.

Herbert W. Case, former police inspector in Detroit, has been quoted as saying, "There hasn't been a sex murder in the history of our department in which the killer wasn't an avid reader of lewd magazines and books."

Yet equally competent authorities are as quick to discount imitative effect. As early as the 1930s, psychologists were showing that delinquents and criminals were prone to blame the movies for the crimes they committed. In evaluating those studies, Klapper has concluded, "The evidence they adduced, however, cannot substantiate any cause-and-effect relationship, and can be easily accounted for by the more established thesis that mass media material tends to further the development of already existing personality traits." Authorities sharing Klapper's view contend that the media do not teach the transgressor his bad impulses, which arise from a complexity of causes; at worst, they may teach him the methods of carrying out those impulses.

Despite this distinction, leading researchers are now convinced that entertainment directly affects behavior, especially with children. Eleanor Maccoby, professor of psychology at Stanford, summarized several studies:

> The nature of the effects depends upon many limiting conditions . . . But the impact of the media is real. What the child absorbs while he is being 'entertained' he uses in the interpretation of his real-life experiences, and in preparing himself for roles that he will play in the future, as well as for immediate action. And the media may influence moods (e.g., produce moods of pessimism) or transmit persuasive beliefs (e.g., that the world is a threatening place), as well as present bits of information or bits of action for imitation.

ENTERTAINMENT AND LIBERTARIAN THEORY

Traditional libertarian theory has given little attention to the entertainment functions of the mass media. True, entertainment is one of the six social functions ascribed to the press, but entertainment has no rationale, as does servicing the political system or making a profit; it seems to have been included as a function merely because the press has virtually always entertained. In neither England nor America has entertainment ever been considered important to the successful functioning of political institutions, as it has been under certain modern totalitarian regimes. Quite the contrary, it has often been suspected of threatening allegiance to the state, corrupting morals, and debasing the natural good taste of the public.

Therefore, entertainment has never been allowed the freedom accorded informational content. As Fred Siebert has pointed out, the entertainment media have been subject to strict government control and supervision, in theory if not in practice, from the earliest period to modern times. The theater in England fell under government control centuries ago when it turned from religious to secular drama; even today all public theaters in England must be licensed and their offerings submitted for censorship before they are performed. Only in recent years have there been indications that the courts in this country may be at last willing to free the motion picture from the legacy of state control it inherited from the stage.

However, there is another reason for stricter control over the movies—and over radio and television, as well—than over the printed media. It lies in their very nature.

Motion Pictures

The motion picture has been presumed to have a power over its audience that the other media do not possess. Although research on the effects of movies is scanty, numerous critics have speculated on the power of film to gain its viewers' uncritical acceptance of what it portrays. Some observers ascribe this supposedly unique power to two things: the conditions of film showings and the techniques and content of the films themselves.

The condition of mass film showings, some authors contend, are similar to those for inducing hypnosis. Hugh Mauerhofer, in *Penguin Film Review No. 8*, has described what he calls the "cinema situation." Reactions of the viewer include a change in the sense of time ("the course of ordinary happenings appears to be retarded") and a change in the sense of space, which may endow the unconscious with a larger than normal role. Results of the cinema situation are "continually imminent boredom, intensified power of imagination and voluntary passivity." The spectator thus gives himself voluntarily and passively to the action on the screen, according to Mauerhofer, and to an uncritical interpretation supplied by the unconscious mind. Further, the anonymity of the film experience prevents a "community" from being formed in the theater, so that the individual is thrown back on his most private associations. His personal participation is intensified; he identifies himself uncritically with the figures on the screen.

Broadcasting

Just as tradition and the nature of the medium have worked to give movies a narrower scope of freedom than the printed media, those same forces have helped to restrict the freedom permitted to the broadcaster.

Despite perceptive excursions into the treatment of public affairs, both radio and television are primarily entertainment media. Moreover, they transmit programs directly into the living room, where they are attended by both adults and the very young. As the television code of the National Association of Broadcasters holds, "It is the responsibility of television to bear constantly in mind that the audience is primarily a home audience, and consequently that television's relationship to the viewers is that between guest and host." And yet radio and television are more than mere entertainment. They combine aspects of the theater and motion picture with those of the magazine and newspaper. They focus on events with authenticity and an almost terrifying immediacy. By their very nature they raise a host of moral and legal problems that the printed media do not.

That point became apparent when in 1957 the Columbia Broadcasting System televised an hour-long interview with Nikita Khrushchev, First Secretary of the Communist party of the Soviet Union, over 105 affiliated stations. Herbert Mitgang, who analyzed the aftermath for the Fund for the Republic, wrote:

> If a newspaper had published an interview with Khrushchev, no responsible person in any communications field would have thought of questioning the propriety of the publication. But when a television network, after great precautions to protect the integrity of the performance and after making its intention known to the highest level of government, telecast an interview with the Kremlin leader, the propriety was seriously questioned. The President of the United States made a statement which at least implied criticism. Important members of Congress openly challenged the wisdom of the presentation. The press was ambivalent.

This reaction to a serious broadcast intended to enlighten the public clearly indicates that television is seen as deserving far less than full freedom. Given the common view that television is an electronic amusement device, it is not surprising that even such a traditionally liberal journal as the *New Republic* can discuss censoring it without raising an outcry from its readers.

THE CULTURE DEBATE

What effect does all the emphasis on entertainment have on American culture? No final answer is possible, but a clear focus on the question can be derived from an interesting debate between Bernard Rosenberg and David Manning White, the editors of *Mass Culture,* a book which carries many articles on the popular arts. To introduce their book, the authors wrote essays on culture in America.

Rosenberg's beliefs about the effect of mass communication on the fabric of culture are nicely summarized in these sentences:

> There can be no doubt that the mass media present a major threat to man's autonomy. To know that they might also contain some small seeds of freedom only makes a bad situation nearly desperate. No art form, no body of knowledge, no system of ethics is strong enough to withstand vulgarization.

The center of Rosenberg's argument is that mass culture is made to seem effortless. Dumping Shakespeare on the market along with Mickey

Spillane, Rosenberg argues, places a master of world literature on the same level with a lickspittle—and suggests to readers that the same preparation is required for each.

White is almost equally vehement on the other side:

> The xenophilic critics who discuss American culture as if they were holding a dead vermin in their hands seem to imply that in some other, better age the bulk of people were fair copies of Leonardo Da Vinci. No critic shudders more audibly when discussing the vulgarities of American life than T. S. Eliot. Yet it is only realistic to note that in the England which became Eliot's haven, one of the most popular of diversions for nearly 700 years was bear-baiting. I do not cite this to demean the contributions to our world culture of a Chaucer, a Reynolds, a Thomas Tallis, or any English artist who added to the world's treasury, but only to draw the point that art was no more important to the mass of the people of their day than the goings-on at Paris Garden in Southwark, the chief bear-garden in London.

White is not a blind defender of the media. He admitted that there are aspects of mass culture that are "banal, dehumanizing, and downright ugly." But he also pointed out that even though the media are Big Business and must show a profit, they bring valuable fare to millions. He cited the NBC presentation of Richard III, starring Laurence Oliver, which was seen by more than 20 million people.

Alexis de Tocqueville's View

The response of the critics to such defenses of the media is often to recall the observations of an insightful foreign visitor, Alexis de Tocqueville. If his gloomy analysis was accurate, there is little reason to speculate about culture in the United States; a democracy cannot develop a culture of high quality and unquestioned merit. In a closely argued section of Democracy in America, which was published in 1835, De Tocqueville began by discussing artisanship. Aristocratic nations, he pointed out, gradually segregate workmen until each craft forms a distinct class. Within each class the workers are known to each other and reputations are built on quality of workmanship. The aim of the artisan is to stand high among his colleagues, only secondarily to create rapidly at a high profit, and the aristocrats prize the lasting and the well-made.

In democracies, De Tocqueville argued, no such pride of workmanship is possible. The classes and professions are ever shifting. Every craft is open to everyone; the artisans are not necessarily known to one another; the artisan stands in relationship to his customer rather than to his craft. The customer, unlike the privileged classes in aristocratic nations, is himself a creature of mobility. If he is rising on the social scale, his desires are likely to grow faster than his fortune, and he tries to acquire the objects of wealth before he can afford them, usually by short cuts that create a demand for objects of synthetic value. The customer who is sinking on the scale retains the desires that were nurtured in the days of his affluence, and he, too, satisfies himself surreptitiously. The artisan, too, wishes to rise on the scale, and he perceives that wealth derives from selling many items at relatively low cost. Quality deteriorates.

De Tocqueville believed that the effect of democracy runs still deeper:

> Something analogous to what I have already pointed out in the useful arts then takes place in the fine arts; the productions of artists are more numerous, but the merit of each production is diminished. No longer able to soar to what is great, they cultivate what is pretty and elegant, and appearance is more attended to than reality.
>
> In aristocracies a few great pictures are produced; in democratic countries a vast number of insignificant ones. In the former, statues are raised of bronze: in the latter, they are modeled in plaster.

Dwight Macdonald

"The conservative proposal to save culture by restoring the old class lines," Dwight Macdonald has written, "has a more solid historical base than the Marxian hope for a new democratic, classless culture, for, with the possible (and important) exception of Periclean Athens, all the great cultures of the past were elite cultures." But Macdonald adds that the conservative solution "is without meaning in a world dominated by the two great mass nations, U.S.A. and U.S.S.R., and becoming more industrialized, massified all the time."

Macdonald sees three different cultures in America: High Culture, Mass Culture, and Folk Art. He is actually as gloomy about American culture as De Tocqueville was. For the appeal and the rewards of Mass Culture (which the Germans derisively term *Kitsch*) have been gradually affecting High Culture and Folk Art:

> If there were a clearly defined cultural elite, then the masses could have their *kitsch* and the elite could have its High Culture, with everybody happy. But, the boundary line is blurred. A statistically significant part of the population, I venture to guess, is chronically confronted with the choice of going to the movies or going to a concert,

between reading Tolstoy or a detective story, between looking at old masters or at a TV show: i.e., the pattern of their cultural lives is "open" to the point of being porous. Good art competes with *kitsch,* serious ideas compete with commercialized formulas—and the advantage lies all on one side. There seems to be a Gresham's Law in cultural as well as monetary circulation: bad stuff drives out the good, since it is more easily understood and enjoyed. It is this facility of access which at once sells *kitsch* on a wide market and also prevents it from achieving quality.

Macdonald thus argues that Mass Culture is not just bad in and of itself; it homogenizes all culture and debases the entire spectrum. Clement Greenberg agrees, holding that *kitsch* "predigests art for the spectator and spares him effort, provides him with a shortcut to the pleasures of art that detours what is necessarily difficult in genuine art."

It is a curious commentary on the validity of these criticisms that Dwight Macdonald's own career seems to bear out his chief contention. Writing in 1953, Macdonald listed the *New Yorker* among the magazines that debase High Culture. Its short stories, he wrote, are "smooth, minor-key, casual, suggesting drama and sentiment without ever being crude enough to create it;" *New Yorker* editors developed the style by skillfully selecting in the same way a gardener develops a new kind of rose. Then, a few years later, almost as though he were proving his point that High Culture is gradually enveloped in Mass Culture, Macdonald became a writer for the *New Yorker.*

Walt Whitman

If one accepts the premises of these critics, it is extraordinarily difficult to avoid their conclusions. But there is, of course, another side of the coin, which is not likely to be seen without looking at the conditions that obtained in the last century. As they were presented by Walt Whitman, the conditions set forth entirely different premises.

Much of the acclaim for Whitman springs from his poetry celebrating The People—the great, ill-defined masses that were beginning to loom on every side after the middle of the nineteenth century. A similar contribution may have come with the writing of *Democratic Vistas* in 1871, in which he argued for a clean break with the art of artistocratic nations:

I should demand a program of culture, drawn out, not for a single class alone, or for the parlors or lecture rooms, but with an eye to the practical life, the west, the workingman, the facts of farms and jack-planes and engineers . . . I should demand of this program or theory a scope generous enough to include the widest human area. It must have for its spinal meaning the formation of a typical personality of character, eligible to the uses of the high average of men . . . and not restricted by conditions ineligible to the masses. The best culture will always be that of the manly courageous instincts, and loving perceptions, and of self-respect—aiming to form, over this continent, and ideocrasy of universalism.

Gilbert Seldes

The rapid development of urban life in the twentieth century has, of course, dictated quite different conditions from any Whitman could have imagined. Whitman's appeal for a democratic culture to reflect the pioneer spirit seems quaint in these times. But some modern observers have provided modern echoes of the original call for a democratic culture. In *The Great Audience* Gilbert Seldes laments that the artist in America has often gone abroad to seek recognition:

> . . . from the time of James Fenimore Cooper to the day of Sinclair Lewis, writers have found some way to attack the average American, not in loving correction but in contempt. In all that time perhaps two dozen men and women have been artists so great that they were misunderstood; the rest were good, but not good enough to separate themselves from their fellow men; they made little effort to understand what was happening in America, were incapable of helping or guiding or comforting . . .

The "misunderstood" artist of the past has given way to the one who no longer cares whether

> he is understood or not, since he is not trying to communicate anything in the traditional sense of the word.

Although there are stark differences between the critics who argue that only an aristocratically oriented culture is viable and those who contend that there is a deep need for democratic culture, they are united in criticism of the mass media. This is entirely understandable: Aspects of art—some drawings, paintings, and music, for example—exist quite apart from the modern instruments of communication, but the great bulk of Mass Culture is carried by the mass media. In fact, the most severe criticisms of American culture from both factions center on the world of newspapers, magazines, radio, television, books, and films. Were they not so pervasive, the critics argue, Mass Culture would not be so overwhelming. And were the rewards of the mass media not so alluring, Mass Culture would not find it so easy to subvert High Culture and Folk Art.

It must be obvious, however, that those who argue for an aristocratic culture are the more caustic critics of the mass media: The very existence of instruments that can reach everyone is antithetical to the notion of a cultural elite. Ernest van den Haag dismisses them contemptuously:

> The circumstances which permit the experience of art are rare in our society anyway and they cannot be expected in the audience of mass media. That audience is dispersed and heterogeneous, and though it listens often, it does so intermittently and poised to leave if not immediately enthralled and kept amused. . . . And the conditions and conditioning of the audience demand a mad mixture of important and trivial matters, atom bombs, hit tunes, symphonies, B.O., sob stories, hotcha girls, round tables and jokes.

What can be claimed by defenders, clearly, is that the level of Mass Culture has risen perceptibly even as the mass media have become more powerful. Dwight Macdonald admits this, saying that Stephen Vincent Benét has replaced Edgar Guest, Walter Lippmann has replaced Arthur Brisbane, and that "There are no widely influential critics so completely terrible as, say, the late William Lyon Phelps." Typically, Macdonald holds that the seeming improvement is simply a corruption of High Culture: "There is nothing more vulgar than sophisticated *kitsch*." But it must be obvious that one who does not approve the advance from Guest to Benét and from Brisbane to Lippmann is simply dedicated to negativism.

McLUHAN AND CULTURE

Marshall McLuhan is concerned about the effects of the mass media on quite another level. His theories argue that the media change the very nature of a culture, root and branch. We are indebted to David Fagen of UCLA for many of these insights into McLuhan's thought.

McLuhan is primarily concerned with examining the physical mechanisms of communications media. Since a child in a book culture is taught reading as the primary act of formal learning, he gradually comes to identify acquiring knowledge with the sequential and continuous movement his eye makes as it scans the uniform line of alphabet symbols. This is quite a different sensory operation from the bombardment of the passive eye by the tidal wave of flashing dots that make up the fuzzy television image. And it is totally different from the acquisition of important information by ear in a preliterate society. Thus, according to McLuhan, since different cultures rely primarily on different senses, or on using the senses in different ways, these cultures structure their perceptions of the world differently.

In addition, television involves more senses than just the visual. McLuhan holds that the image is projected not only at the viewer, but *on* the viewer, which causes a tactile sense of involvement with the play of lighted images that is clearly not present in reading. Perhaps the most substantial difference is that television's effect is greatly modified by the diffused and kaleidoscopic nature of information that comes from the nonfocused, nonlinear world of the ear.

Significantly McLuhan's stress on the effects of the media of communication themselves clearly differentiates him from most communication theorists, who tend to concentrate on the effects of media content. McLuhan does not deny that the content of the information communicated has an effect, but he holds that changes in technology are the root causes in change of cultural perspective: The medium is the message.

To justify this assertion, it is necessary to understand the broad sense in which McLuhan construes the word medium. For McLuhan, a medium is any implement or vehicle used as extension of man—including not only the communications media, which extend man's senses, but also the mechanical media, which extend his manual capability, and the environmental media (clothing, for example), which extend his skin. These media are powerful: they functionally amputate the part of man that they extend, they limit and define possible modes of thought and action in their sphere, and once established as working media, they structure the environment in such a way that they become less visible as they grow more powerful.

The idea that the most influential media in the environment are invisible is not original with McLuhan, of course, but he does employ it to demonstrate forcefully that the media of communication are systems of conventions that must be learned, but that, once learned, are taken for granted. The only people who could describe with any degree of accuracy the conventions of a communication medium would be those totally unacquainted with it; the conventions would be the things they did not understand. For example, a sophisticated moviegoer might not list the limitations of the screen as one of the conventions of film; he is too accustomed to the screen as part of the film communication process. One study cited by McLuhan, however, reported that Africans who had never seen a film were dumbfounded when an actor disappeared off the side of the screen—they had never even imagined such a visual event.

In effect, McLuhan says, it is possible to perceive the conventions of the media only if one is outside their sphere of influence, since the only people within a culture who are aware of them are those who, because of physical or cultural defects, cannot share in the common mode of perception.

Not all scholars agree with McLuhan. In one of the best and most widely quoted critiques of McLuhan, James Carey challenged his basic assumptions:

> Unlike the traditional scholar, McLuhan deals with reality not by trying to understand it but by prescribing an attitude to take toward it. McLuhan is a poet of technology. His work represents a secular prayer to technology, a magical incantation of the gods, designed to quell one's fears that, after all, the machines may be taking over. Like any prayer, it is designed to sharpen up the pointless and to blunt the too sharply pointed. It is designed to sharpen up the mindless and mundane world of popular culture which consumes so much of our lives and to blunt down the influence of modern technology on our personal existence. The social function of prayer, I suppose, is to numb us to certain gross realities of existence, realities too painful to contemplate, too complex to resolve. Ultimately, McLuhan himself is a medium and that is his message. As a medium, he tells us we need no longer ask the imperishable questions about existence or face the imperishable truths about the human condition. The fundamental problems of existence are to be solved automatically and irreversibly by the subliminal operation of the machines on our psychic life.

14

The Audiences
of the Mass Media

My whole trick is to keep the tune well out in front. If
I play Tchaikovsky I play his melodies and skip his
spiritual struggles. Naturally I condense. I have to
know just how many notes my audience will stand for.
If there's time left over I fill in with a lot of runs up
and down the keyboard.

LIBERACE

On September 3, 1919, President Woodrow Wilson
climbed into his dark-blue private railroad car and set out on a campaign
to convert the American people to their country's participation in the
League of Nations. Most Senators opposed the League, but Wilson had
faith that the citizens themselves would support it if he could but present
his case to them. In the next twenty-two days, he traveled more than
8000 miles in 17 states and made 40 formal speeches. Hugh Baillie,
who covered the tour for United Press, remarked thirty years later in
his memoirs, *High Tension:* "If he'd had radio and television to carry
his message and personality to millions rather than to thousands, the
history of the world might have been different. With television, I am
convinced, Wilson would have carried the country for the League."

As recently as 1919, then, a speaker could talk to only as many
persons as could assemble within range of his voice. Today broadcasting
enables him to reach farflung millions simultaneously. Before World
War I virtually no American homes had radio receivers; today nearly
99 per cent of all American homes have sets and so do about 90 per
cent of all automobiles on the road. In recent years television has enabled
millions to see events that could once be witnessed by a mere handful.
Very few American homes had television sets in the late 1930s, and

not many more in the late 1940s. More than 95 per cent of all American households have them now, and as many as 54 million persons may be tuned in at the same time to a top-rated program.

The printed media, too, as a result of technical improvements, have come to count their audiences in the high thousands or millions instead of in the hundreds. At one time the book, patiently hand-lettered in the monks' scriptorium, was available only to the few who had access to the table to which it was chained. Today books reach more than 30 per cent of the population of the United States. Paperback editions are as available as razor blades and cigarettes—and are seldom much more expensive. Newspapers, which in the early nineteenth century sought out the cultured few, now reach almost everyone in the United States except the very young. Today daily circulation is almost 63 million—a copy for every household. Magazines are read regularly by at least two-thirds of all Americans. *Life* alone reaches about one in four adults.

Within the memory of persons still living, motion pictures have developed from a curiosity, which could be viewed by only a few who could peek into a cinescope, into a medium that reaches about half the population.

AUDIENCES ATTRACTED TO THE VARIOUS MEDIA

Figures showing the sizes of the various media audiences are dramatic and impressive, but they can also be misleading. They can easily give the impression that each newspaper, each magazine, each book, each broadcast program tries to reach all the people. But newspapers are restricted by geography. With rare exception, they concentrate their circulation within the trade area served by the community in which they are published. The audiences of individual radio and television stations are also restricted, their boundaries being limited by the station's wavelength. And all the media are restricted by the tastes, interests, and motivations of the public.

Therefore, mass communication does not mean communication for everyone. On the contrary, mass communication involves a selection of *classes*—groups or special publics, which might be quite large numerically—within the *masses*. The media and their audiences come together through a process of mutual selection. The media tend to select their audiences primarily by means of content. The audiences also tend to select among and within the media primarily on the basis of content. As noted above, geography is also important; some media are simply not available where prospective users live. And, of course, other factors help to determine selection, including literacy, habit, age, and costs. Researchers are now trying to fathom the influence of personality traits.

The audience attracted to one medium may be quite different from that attracted to another, although obviously there will be a great deal of overlapping. Television counts among its fans many who would never leaf through a book, let alone own one. Newspapers have readers who rarely attend a movie. Even within a single medium, the audience may differ widely in composition from one unit to another. The typical magazine, for example, is aimed at some homogeneous body of readers within the total population, readers sharing a common profession, common interests, common tastes.

Newspapers

Reaching all but the very young, newspapers attract a highly heterogeneous audience. About 98 per cent of all readers read something on the front page; about 58 per cent, some item on any other given page. But after the front page, subject matter is more important than page number in determining what is read, for different readers seek out different things.

Age, education, sex, and socioeconomic status are all factors in determining what will be read, according to studies conducted by Wilbur Schramm and David Manning White. In general, young people are likely to use the paper for entertainment, older readers for information and views of public affairs. Adults do more news reading than young people, who seem to be introduced to the paper by its pictorial content and then branch out to crime and disaster news. The more educated a person is, the more likely he is to use the paper for information; the less educated, for entertainment.

The amount of newspaper reading also tends to increase with education. Men tend to read newspapers at greater length and with greater intensity than women, and they are more likely to use papers for information than entertainment. Higher economic status is generally accompanied by an increase in the reading of public affairs news as well, and by an increase in the reading of sports and society news. Higher economic status, however, does not bring with it decreased attention to pictures and cartoons.

Broadcasting

Before the advent of television, radio ranked with the newspaper as the most universal of the media. The most distinctive characteristic of its audience was that it had no distinctive characteristic; radio appealed to all types, although tastes in programs and extent of listening varied. About 95 per cent of all American adults listened at least fifteen minutes a day, with the heaviest listening after 6 p.m. Now television has become a medium as universal as radio was in its heyday. Like radio it has so broad an appeal that it reaches all segments of the population—although, of course, with different programs.

The great popularity of television has been largely at the expense of radio. Radio listening has dropped off sharply since the television set became a fixture in the American living room. In 1949 the typical American family played its radio an average of about four and half hours a day; the average is now approximately two hours a day. In that same period—when the television set was becoming a fixture—the family's television viewing time increased from almost nothing to more than four hours a day—a figure that increased to about six hours and is now approximately five hours and a half a day.

Since television came along, the circumstances under which people listen to radio and their purpose in listening to it seem to have changed. Out-of-home radio listening apparently has increased, to judge from the sales of automobile and portable sets. Unlike television, which requires fairly close attention, radio can be heard with a so-called third ear. There is some evidence that people now use radio as a personal companion while driving to work or doing the housework or reading, whereas they usually watch television as a member of a family group. Having lost to television its pre-eminence as an entertainment medium, radio has become somewhat more selective in seeking its audience. It now beams its programs at little publics within the population, as with disc-jockey shows aimed at teen-agers.

Motion Pictures

Television has hit motion pictures only a slightly lighter blow than it has dealt radio. Since television made the living room a private theater, movie attendance has dropped precipitously. More than half of a national sample reported that their moviegoing had declined in the previous few years, and they mentioned television more often than any other reason. One in three said that television had kept him from attending movies in the previous month. Projecting those figures, survey statisticians estimated that television was costing theaters as many as 89 million admissions a month. There was also a decline of movie-making. The industry made 344 major feature films in 1953. Ten years later production was cut in half. Today, were it not for movies made for television, movie production would be at its lowest point in four decades.

Despite higher ticket prices, movie admissions also represent a declining percentage of total U.S. amusement expenditures. Americans spent 80 per cent of their amusement dollar on movies in 1947, 68 per cent in 1957, and 51 per cent in 1967. They now spend less than 50 per cent on movies.

Today, as has been the case almost from the beginning, movies depend largely upon youth for their support. The emphasis on youth is much stronger today, however, in part because movie-makers see that they have a youthful audience and lure even more young people by catering to those they have. According to a study made by the Opinion Research Corporation, the great majority of moviegoers are under thirty, more than half are under twenty, and almost a third are under fifteen. Adults of fifty or older seldom attend at all. Whatever their age, the unmarried attend movies more regularly than married people.

Even aside from content, it is not difficult to explain why movies are chiefly a medium for the young. The mere act of going to the movies, which is a social activity, may be as important to them as what is on the screen; groups of two or more account for four-fifths of all admissions. Then, too, the young are barred from some types of recreation—night-clubbing, for example—and have not become involved in activities like lodge meetings, bridge clubs, and P.T.A., which eat into the time of settled adults. In many communities there are few places a young couple on a date can go besides the movies. The lure of the movies for the unmarried can be explained by the fact that many of them find the social experience of moviegoing preferable to the solitary use of other media.

Books

Books attract people who are above average not only in education but also in their heavy use of the serious content of the other media. They are the "culturally alert," to use Bernard Berelson's phrase. Books are more likely to attract young adults than older ones, people living in urban communities rather than rural ones, people of high income rather than low. Readers of books are more likely than people who do not read books to be critical of other media.

Studies have shown consistently that book reading and education go hand in hand. As the level of formal education declines, so does the extent of book reading. Some of the other characteristics of the book audience can be explained partly by this one factor of education. For instance, while young adults read more books than old ones, age may not be the governing consideration, since the older the population group, the less formal education it has had. Similarly the great amount of reading by urban dwellers may be explained by the higher level of education in urban areas. Obviously, however, more than education is involved. The resident of a rural area has less ready access to books than a city dweller. And the person with a low income cannot easily spare money for books.

GENERAL PRINCIPLES

Although their audiences overlap considerably, each of the mass media has a general tendency to draw its most devoted following from a somewhat different sector of the population. From the many studies made of audiences, four general principles of communication behavior have emerged. While they are subject to exceptions, as generalities are, these principles are nevertheless valuable.

All-or-None Principle

Paul Lazarsfeld and Patricia Kendall have remarked on what they call the all-or-none aspect of communication behavior, the tendency for the person who is above average in exposure to one medium to be above average in exposure to all. They found that a radio fan was also likely to be a movie fan; on the other hand, people who seldom went to the movies were not likely to use their radios very often. Lazarsfeld and Kendall found, too, that regular book readers were more likely than other people to be frequent moviegoers.

Investigating magazine readership, Lazarsfeld and Wyant found that anyone who reads one magazine is likely to read several—another aspect of the all-or-none principle. An audience study made later by the Magazine Advertising Bureau underlined the same point; about half of all magazine readers read four or more magazines, 32 per cent read two or three, about 18 per cent read only one.

Studies since the advent of television seem to emphasize the all-or-none principle, indicating, for example, that pioneer set-owners tended to be more media-minded than non-owners. Those who first acquired television had read the most magazines, listened to the most radio, gone to the movies most frequently. Studies also suggest that after the initial novelty of television wore off, only the movies and radio suffered seriously because of declining attention. Television did seem to affect the *reasons* for using other media. People apparently used television primarily for entertainment and escape, which meant that the entertaining and escapist qualities of the other media became less important. Thus, television seems to have displaced the printed media as a source of entertainment and escape, but it does not seem to have affected them as a source of serious, useful information.

Lazarsfeld and Merton see the all-or-none principle as springing from interest and opportunity. That is, a person interested in escapist material may find it in books, in magazines, or on the air. Similarly one interested in public affairs will probably seek information in newspapers, books, and magazines. In short, one can best satisfy his interests by using more than one medium. And one who has little opportunity to use a medium—because of the demands of his job, hobbies, or other activities—will probably have little opportunity to use any.

Education Principle

In general, studies indicate that the better educated a person is, the more use he will make of the media, although this principle has more exceptions than the others. The amount of newspaper reading tends to increase with education, as does serious use of the paper. The typical magazine reader is likely to have well over five years' more schooling than the person who does not read magazines. Moreover, the number of magazines read by each one hundred persons in the population rises swiftly as the level of education goes up. The better-educated read more books than the rest of the population.

Education, however, is not a sure guide to the use of the electronic media. This seems a safe generality: Most reading is done by the college-educated, and the greatest fans of television, radio, and movies come from among the high school-educated.

Economic Principle

Another general principle is that use of the media increases as income increases, although this seems to apply more strongly to the printed than to the broadcast media.

Not only does newspaper reading increase with economic status, but so does attention to serious content such as editorials or material about public affairs, social problems, economics, and science. People with high incomes are more likely to read magazine than those with low incomes: about 90 per cent of those in the high-income group are magazine readers; only about half of those in the low-income group are. Those with large incomes tend to read more magazines as well. And the number of books read also increased as income rises.

Age Principle

As Americans become older, they tend to use the media more for serious purposes and less for entertainment. Older newspaper readers are more likely than younger ones to read letters to the editor and public affairs reports, less likely to read comics and sports news. They are great readers of editorials; for those over sixty, editorials rank second only to news pictures in readership, whereas scarcely anyone under twenty reads editorials. In radio listening, older adults seem to favor such serious fare as newscasts, discussions of public issues, classical and semiclassical music, religious programs, and quiz shows—the last perhaps because they are considered educational. On the other hand, older readers apparently have little interest in drama, comedy, mysteries, and popular music. The pattern is only slightly different in television. Older viewers are more likely than the young or those in their middle years to favor newscasts, forums, music, and quiz shows; less likely to favor dramatic programs, whose greatest appeal is to those between thirty and fifty; and less likely to favor mysteries. The elderly do like televised comedy-variety shows, sports, and films on television.

The extent to which people use the media does not increase steadily with age. Rather, it tends to drop off in the later years. The amount of news reading, rising swiftly through the teens, hits its height between the ages of thirty and fifty and then tapers off gradually. Older adults read fewer books and magazines than young adults. Movie attendance, at its peak in a person's late teens, drops off sharply after age thirty.

VERIFYING SIZES OF AUDIENCES

Advertisers have become increasingly interested in the audiences they are paying to reach. To assure himself that he is getting his money's worth, the advertiser needs many answers. Does the newspaper or magazine actually reach as many readers as the publisher says it does? How intensely are the readers interested in the publication? How strong is their loyalty to it? Are they really the best possible prospects for the advertiser's products or services? How many sets are tuned to a given radio or television program? How many people are clustered around each set? Under what conditions do they watch or listen and with what degree of absorption? What programs were they watching before this one? How desirable are they as prospective buyers?

Printed Media

In the nineteenth century advertisers looked to circulation as the measure of the audience of newspapers or magazines. One of the first attempts to verify circulation claims was made in 1847, when a neutral publisher and a paper dealer were called in to settle a dispute between the New York *Herald* and the New York *Tribune.* After checking the number of copies issued and the amount of paper consumed by each newspaper, the referees adjudged the *Herald* the circulation leader, 28,946 to 28,195.

But that was unusual. Ordinarily an advertiser was fortunate if he learned even the claimed circulations. Some publishers regarded circulation as a business secret, never to be shared with advertisers. Others made outrageous circulation claims. Rather than endorse possible exaggerations, the issuer of one directory of periodicals in 1870 simply omitted circulation figures. At about that time George P. Rowell, the pioneer advertising agent, was working painstakingly to get accurate figures for a directory he published. He gave special recognition to publishers who supplied affidavits certifying their circulation data.

Even fairly reliable circulation figures were subject to several interpretations. They could refer to all copies distributed, including those given away and those sold in bulk, or they could refer only to those copies sold at regular prices. Nor could the advertiser tell much about the quality of the circulation—how it was obtained, and how willing the subscribers were to pay for the publication.

The Association of American Advertisers in 1899 made the first effort to verify circulation claims on the basis of uniform standards, but it quickly encountered a host of difficulties, among them the reluctance of publishers to cooperate, a shortage of funds for operation and experimentation, a lack of standardization in the publishers' bookkeeping and auditing methods—and even the lack of an accurate definition of "circulation." The attempt ended in failure in 1913 with the association in debt to some of its backers.

But other advertising groups were proceeding with parallel programs, and the Audit Bureau of Circulations emerged in 1914. The ABC has for decades provided advertisers with essential circulation data about a lengthening list of newspapers, consumer magazines, business publications, and farm papers. By listing such points as methods by which circulation was obtained, authorized prices for subscriptions, premium offers, and market zones, the ABC helps the advertiser assess the quality as well as the quantity of a publication's audience.

Broadcasting

In February, 1953, the water commissioner of Toledo reported that he could rate the popularity of television programs by fluctuations in water pressure. Pressure stayed high while people remained close to their sets; it plummeted at program's end as viewers walked out on the closing commercial to go to the bathroom. By applying what he called the Program-Popularity-Through-Pumpage-and-Pressure-Index, the commissioner concluded that "I Love Lucy" was the most popular television show.

This intriguing but crude rating system did not, of course, lure many advertisers. Some of the other methods—not all of them more refined—have captured the advertisers' attention. When radio was in its infancy, broadcasters urged listeners to send in postcards. This yielded only the sketchiest information about how many people received the programs. Then researchers applied statistical techniques to obtain representative samples of the population and devised methods for gauging audience size. Four methods that were born in the days of great radio popularity have been adapted to television: the recall, the coincidental, the mechanical recorder, and the diary.

The *recall* method was first used in 1929. Interviewers ask a carefully selected sample what programs they have heard or viewed during a stated period. The researchers also try to learn the listening or viewing patterns of other members of the household. They may refresh the respondent's memory with a printed list of programs.

The *coincidental* method involves telephone interviews. While a program is on the air, interviewers call a sample group of people in various cities to ask whether they are listening or viewing, and if so to what program. The researchers can then estimate the size of the audience attracted to a given program or some part of it. Obviously this can cover only listeners or viewers with telephone service, but the researchers take the ratio of telephone service to set ownership into account.

The *mechanical recorder* method uses devices attached to receiving sets to enable researchers to learn the listening or viewing habits of those in rural homes and those without telephones. Special instruments installed in a number of representative households tell when the set is on and to what station it is tuned. One disadvantage, apart from the high cost of the research, is that the audimeter tells only when the set is tuned to a particular station, not how many are watching or listening, if indeed anyone is. Proponents of the method say, however, that actual listening and viewing correspond closely to the number of sets in use.

With the *diary* method individuals chosen to comprise a representative sample are asked to keep a record of all listening or viewing over a specified period. They may be asked to include information about which other members of the household watched or listened to the programs. They record all these data on a standardized diary form, then send it periodically to a central agency for tabulation.

These surveys can disclose two types of information: the average number of listeners or viewers for the duration of the entire program, and the total audience of the program, including those who tuned in for only part of it.

BASES OF SELECTION

Why do people make the selections among the media that we know they make? Wilbur Schramm of Stanford has offered a tentative answer to this basic question. He has advanced two general principles—least effort and promise of reward—as being in accord with existing research even if not yet proven conclusively.

Least Effort

By least effort Schramm means just what the term implies: that the reader, viewer, or listener takes the route of least resistance in his choice of communication offerings. George Zipf of Harvard has written a book to document what he calls the "principle of least effort." Simply stated, Zipf's principle is that in solving immediate problems a person looks at them against a background of what he believes to be his future problems. He tries to minimize the work he must do in order to solve both his immediate and his future problems. Least effort, Zipf believes, is fundamental to all human action. In communication behavior Schramm sees several factors contributing to least effort.

One is availability. All other things being equal, one helps himself to whatever communication medium is most readily at hand. A family is more likely to watch television in its own living room than to get out the automobile, drive to a far-off theater, hunt for a parking place, pay admission, and attend a motion picture. That same family will choose a program with a sharp picture over a program with a blurred or wavy one, of course. Moreover, some members of the family will not be especially interested in the picture on the screen but will watch it because it is less effort to watch than to leave the room. A patient waiting in the dentist's office will pick up a copy of *National Geographic* from the end table instead of walking to the corner drugstore for a newspaper.

Expense is also related to least effort. A family that has just spent $300 for a television set may not be able to afford a membership in the Book-of-the-Month Club, a subscription to *The New York Times*, and to half a dozen magazines, all at once. College students on limited budgets are more likely to buy inexpensive paperbacks than hardcover editions.

Time is another factor involving least effort. Leisure time comes at different periods for different people. Some men find the commuting train a good place to read the newspapers. Others consider the automobile ride to and from work a good time to listen to the radio. Daytime hours when the family is away are a good time for many housewives to listen to the radio or watch television. The television set is an electronic baby sitter in many households just before the evening meal.

Role, habit, and custom may also influence media choices, according to Schramm, for it is easier to continue behavior patterns than to change them. Communications behavior, in fact, becomes a part of social behavior, and some selection of media fare is really just a habitual social act. For example, a young man may take his date to the movies simply because going to the movies is what the young people in their group do.

Promise of Reward

Schramm interprets promise of reward to mean that a person chooses from the available communications whatever he thinks will give him the greatest reward. Schramm classifies rewards into two general types: immediate and delayed. Content that pays its rewards at once may relax tensions or help in problem solving. It usually includes stories dealing with accidents, corruption, crime, disaster, society affairs, and sports, all of which provide a vicarious thrill without the strain of actual participation. Content that pays its rewards in the future may promise information useful for social effectiveness. Instead of reducing tensions, it may increase them. But it prepares one for meeting needs and problems. This may include material about economic and public affairs, health, and social problems.

REASONS FOR USING THE MEDIA

Why do people pay attention to the media at all? A cynic might answer: because there is no escape. A more accurate reply is probably that the mass media satisfy certain needs. In recent years there has been a growing amount of research—still unfortunately small—which provides some clues to these gratifications.

As one would expect, different people make different uses of the media. Age, sex, education, socioeconomic status—such things tend to influence the reasons for which people turn to the media. So do much more subtle factors—attitudes, aspirations, hopes, fears. Not only do these predispositions affect the use a person makes of the media; they also affect what he finds there.

Newspapers

To say that people read newspapers to become informed is true, but it oversimplifies. They want to become informed for varying reasons: to achieve prestige, to escape boredom, to feel in contact with their environment, to find reassurance for their behavior, and to adjust to their roles in society.

Some insights into readership were developed when the delivery-men of major newspapers in New York City went on a strike that lasted for more than two weeks. While most New Yorkers were without their papers, Bernard Berelson and a team of researchers moved in to determine what doing without the newspaper means.

To some readers the paper is important in its traditional role as a source of information and ideas about serious public affairs. They use it not only for the raw facts of current events, the researchers found, but also for the interpretations of editorial writers, background writers, and columnists. Yet other readers are apparently less interested in the content itself than in the use to which they put it—that of bolstering their own egos. They read the newspaper because it enables them to appear informed about issues and events in conversation with others. It is a source of prestige.

Some readers find the newspaper an indispensable tool in the routine of daily living. They feel a little lost, sometimes almost helpless, without its advertisements for local stores, entertainment schedules, financial information and stock market reports, weather forecasts, recipes, and fashion tips.

Readers also use the newspaper for social contact. It gives them, through its gossip and advice columns and its human-interest stories, glimpses into the lives and problems of others. A small-town reader knows many of his neighbors; in a large city, as one reader expressed it, the newspaper "makes up for the lack of knowing people."

Then, too, readers use the newspaper to escape from their every-day world. It is an inexpensive vacation away from the cares, problems, frustrations, and boredom of daily routine. More than that, it is a socially acceptable form of escape.

Reading has value *per se* in American society, Berelson concluded, and the newspaper shares in that value as the most inexpensive and convenient purveyor of reading matter. The newspaper is a source of security in an insecure world to some, and reading it has become for many people "a ritualistic or near-compulsive act."

When newspapers suspend publication because of a strike, New Yorkers have an almost universal feeling of loss, according to a survey conducted by the Department of Journalism at New York University. Though their daily routine is scarcely disturbed by the lack of papers—they turn to radio as their chief source of news and to television as a poor second—no other medium has really taken the place of newspapers; without them, New Yorkers feel "out of touch with the world" and have "a distinct feeling of loss." The survey questionnaire returned by one Manhattan housewife neatly summarized the findings of the entire survey. After the question asking if the absence of newspapers had affected her daily routine, she wrote, "No." Alongside it in large letters, she added, "I JUST MISS THEM."

Broadcasting

Radio and television content affords a variety of lures. Social contact, counsel in daily living, self-glorification, escape from boredom—all are served by broadcast fare.

Herta Herzog of McCann-Erickson sought to learn what gratifications listeners found in daytime serials. For some women, she found, the programs were a source of emotional release. Listeners welcomed the chance to cry over the misfortunes of others or to share in their triumphs, to compensate for their own troubles, or to magnify their own problems by identifying them with those of the heroes and heroines. Secondly, women liked the opportunities for wishful thinking that the programs afforded. By identifying themselves with the fictional characters, listeners could compensate for their own inadequacies and failures.

Finally, for many women the serials were a source of advice on meeting life's problems and on proper modes of behavior. The less formal education women had had or the more they regarded themselves as worriers, the more help they found in the serials. They were aided in social relationships—getting along with other people, handling husbands or boyfriends, rearing their children. Said one listener, "Bess Johnson shows you how to handle children. . . . Most mothers slap their children. She deprives them of something. That is better. I use what she does with my children." Listeners also learned how to meet the threats of a hostile world. They learned to adjust to such tragedies as a death in the family or a son's going off to a war. They learned how to react when trouble came. "When Helen Trent has serious trouble, she takes it calmly," one listener commented. "So you think you'd better be like her and not get upset." Some listeners considered the programs so valuable that they sometimes referred friends seeking advice to specific programs.

It is easy to find fault with this sort of help. Basically the listeners learned to cope with adversity in three ways: by wishful thinking, which promised that everything would work out all right; by projecting blame to others; or by applying some convenient formula. Whether or not those measures are adequate for solving one's problem's is certainly questionable, but thousands of listeners evidently thought that they were.

According to Miss Herzog, people tune in on quiz shows because of four major appeals: the competitive, the educational, the self-rating, and the sporting. The listener can satisfy his competitive urge by pitting his knowledge against that of the actual contestant or that of someone who is listening with him. He may show off by simply displaying his knowledge before others clustered around the set. If he fails to answer some questions, he is more than compensated by his correct answers to others. What listeners regard as the educational aspects of the quiz program have greater attractions for them than the competitive aspects. They see the answers as contributing to diversified knowledge, more easily obtained from the quiz show than from reading, and useful in everyday conversation.

To attempt to explain the popularity of television Westerns, Dr. Ernest Dichter, a pioneer in motivational research, explored their psychological appeal in an article in *Broadcasting* magazine. Westerns are typical folk art with unchanging characters writ larger than life, he said. They provide rootless Americans an emotional identification with their country and its past. By having the hero single-handedly solve problems justly and with dispatch, they help to allay the frustrations that the viewer feels as an impotent individual in a complex and threatening society. They give him a sense of security by portraying a world of perfection and order, in which the wicked are punished and justice triumphs. For women they have an added appeal: They help to satisfy a craving for independence by picturing woman as sharing the decisions and hardships necessary to creating a good society.

Magazines

To learn what motivates women to read magazines, *Good House-keeping* commissioned Social Research, Inc., to conduct a study covering six women's magazines and two general magazines. The study, published under the title "Women and Advertising," pictures what it calls the "middle majority housewife." She moves in a small world, physically and socially, and her home is its center. Even in her own community, she seldom travels beyond her own neighborhood; her social circle consists largely of her family and a few close friends. She views the outside world with distrust and anxiety. She wants to hold it at bay, although she knows she cannot control it, for it can strike suddenly with disastrous effect. Whatever happens outside of her own little world she evaluates by its impact upon her home. Within that home she regards herself as the central figure, the one who primarily, and properly, manages the family. She wants nicer things and more security than her own parents had, although she is not impelled to alter the basic pattern of her existence. Her homemaking tasks are arduous, but she is compensated in part by praise and affection from her family. It is from them, not from outsiders, that she craves approbation. She does not care for the recognition that comes from participation in civic and charitable organizations. On the contrary, she does not think that women should be active in affairs outside the home, except possibly in those that impinge directly upon it, such as P.T.A.

What part do the women's magazines play in her life? According to the study, they are important in three overlapping areas of her existence: social orientation, realistic concerns, and personal experiences.

From stories, articles, and advertisements, she gets ideas for relating herself to the people in her world and for strengthening her position as the central figure in the household. She learns how to get along with her own family, her friends, and the outsiders she is likely to meet, such as teachers and doctors. She finds answers to a host of questions raised by her dealings with others: How much should her children watch television? How should she prepare them for a stay in the hospital? How should she entertain guests, and what should she serve them? What is a proper wardrobe for her husband?

The magazines also teach her how to do all sorts of practical things not closely involving other people—her "realistic concerns," to use the phrase of the study. They teach her the practical skills of cooking, sewing, and housekeeping. They help her to formulate her goals, and some give her an idea of what she can reasonably expect from life. They give her information about the ways and costs of attaining her goals, about her own world and that of other housewives, and about the outside world she fears and mistrusts.

The magazines also enter into her personal experiences, into her private set of values and judgments. They help her to ward off a feeling of loneliness. They provide her the stuff of creative daydreams, in which she explores ways of life unfamiliar to her. They bolster her self-esteem by underscoring the importance of her work and contributions. They assure her that the virtues and values she cherishes are the right ones.

By guiding their readers in daily living and by supporting their moral and ethical code, the women's magazines seem to afford gratifications similar to those of daytime radio serials. So do the confession magazines. Indeed, Herta Herzog noticed some overlapping of audience: "If a magazine is especially preferred by daytime serial listeners, it is of one of two types: either its content is noticeably similar to that of the daytime serial (the 'true story') or it centers about home life."

Perhaps the greatest similarity in audience and appeal is between the daytime serial and the confession magazine. Readers of the confession magazine ordinarily do not read the "white-collar" women's magazines. Indeed, according to the publishers of confession magazines, such women read little not written in their vernacular; apart from daytime serials, which can treat but one behavioral problem at a time and that only over a period of several weeks, only confession magazines deal in the problems, lives, and language of these women.

Who are the readers of confession magazines? According to the publishers, they are women who have been moved by the redistribution of income into a middle-class setting. They find their new setting and their roles in it strange and uncomfortable. They may live in the same general neighborhood as their white-collar sisters and share economic equality with them, yet they move in an entirely different social orbit and have an entirely different outlook on life.

There are hypotheses about the gratifications provided by other types of magazines. One sociologist has suggested that perhaps much of the attraction of *Playboy* is to young people moving up the socio-economic ladder because it depicts the attitudes and behavior patterns they expect to share once they have reached the next level. A writer has hypothesized that a reason for the popularity of such men's magazines as *Argosy* and *True* is that they reassure the readers that the individual is still a potent force in a world that seems to be governed largely by complex, bewildering, impersonal forces.

LIFE SPACE AND THE MASS MEDIA

The U.S. Bureau of the Census estimated in 1970 that one out of every ten Americans over twenty-five years of age is functionally illiterate. Harvard researchers contend that this is a gross understatement—that well over half of the men and women in this country are functionally illiterate. Richard Tobin, managing editor of *Saturday Review*, has written:

> It may be that we are drifting into two classes of adults, not divided by social position, income, religion, color, or background, but by those who can read and write and do so habitually and those who cannot. . . . One undeniable mark of the educated man is a flexible, versatile mind capable of dealing rationally with expansive new conditions. And this mind cannot be formed without the linear reasoning that comes only from habitual exposure to the printed word.
>
> Since democracy is the most complex, the most advanced, the most sophisticated of political ideas, the system requires a large and prosperous middle class, and it asks of that great middle class a certain minimum literacy. . . .

Wilbur Schramm has looked at the same problem in a different way. He points out that the more one's life space is enlarged, primarily through developing the skill of reading in school, the more possibilities one has to interest himself in the various media. The further enlargement of life space after the school years turns those with highly developed reading skills and an interest in policies and problems toward the printed media and the more serious aspects of the audiovisual media. Such people are the bulk of the audience for public television. Schramm writes:

> Clearly, there are other elements in the general patterns of mass media audiences. One of these is the changing role patterns that people are called upon to play throughout life; these patterns are clearly reflected in the selections made from the mass media channels. Still another is the declining vitality of human beings with age. A third is the procession of events and personalities through the media themselves. Certainly more Americans found themselves going to the mass media to learn about coronary thrombosis when President Eisenhower had his heart attack, to learn about Presidential history and Constitutional law when President Kennedy was killed, and to learn about astronautics and Newtonian mechanics at the time of the moon shots, than would ever have occurred without those spectacular events.

When we look at the complex skein of causes that determine what audiences will gather around what channels at what time, a program rating, a readership percentage, or the head count on a movie audience is not such a simple figure as it seemed.

Criticisms
of the Mass Media

Criticizing is easy, but reporting is a good deal harder
than I thought.

BYRON SKINNER

        Early in May, 1970, an incident occurred that perfectly illustrates the current dilemma of the mass media. The World Affairs Council of Northern California had scheduled a three-day conference on "The Mass Media, Public Opinion, and Foreign Policy." The keynote speaker was to be Vice President Spiro Agnew, who was then capturing large headlines and much news program time with attacks on the news media—attacks that expressed a point of view most conservatives considered accurate. As the conference began with a social hour, a large group of radicals came marching upon the scene. The splashiest sign they carried shouted: "The Media Lie!"

        There could be no more forceful reminder that both the right and the left are falling upon the media with shrill cries. The conservatives are certain that the media aid and comfort not only the liberals but the radical fringe as well. The radicals are equally certain that the media do the bidding of conservatives and reactionaries. And the large center element fears that the media give so much attention to extremists that the fabric of American society has been torn beyond repair.

        All this is understandable. The media as a system of human communication take on a new and greater significance in a world in which, as the late C. Wright Mills wrote, "primary experience" has been replaced by "secondary communications": the printed page, radio, television, and film. The media have played a major part in transforming the social order into a mass society. More than that, according to Mills, they are an increasingly important means of power for the elite of dominant institutional orders. They not only filter man's experience of external reality; they also help to shape his experience. They tell him who he is, what he wants to be, and how he can appear to be that way to others. They provide a rich fund of information about the world of events. But because they provide it in the language and images of stereotype and wishes, they often frustrate the individual in his efforts to connect his personal life with the realities of the larger world. Therefore, as man depends more and more on the media for knowledge and guidance, he becomes more and more vulnerable to manipulation and exploitation by the dominant orders of society.

So it is that in the twentieth century, as the press became a ubiquitous and pervasive institution, criticizing it became a popular indoor pastime. Early critics were for the most part much less perceptive than Mills; they adopted what we might call a conspiratorial theory of press malfunction. The press is guilty of the grave charges they tick off, the critics said, because publishers have conspired with big business to promote and to protect their mutual interests. Some publishers themselves are a part of big business; others are in league with it. In exchange for suppressing and distorting media content so as to keep big business powerful, publishers can share in such rewards as handsome advertising contracts, social position, and political prominence.

Over the years, critics have played variations on these general themes:

The media have used their great power to promote the interests of their owners. The owners have propagated their own views, especially in politics and economics. They have ignored or played down contrary views.

The media have been the tool of big business generally. At times advertisers have controlled policies and content.

The media have resisted social change; they have perpetuated the status quo.

The media, in reporting current happenings, have generally been more concerned with the superficial and the sensational than with the significant. In providing entertainment, they have been heavily weighted with fare lacking substance or artistic merit.

The media have endangered public morals.

The media without good cause have violated the privacy and debased the dignity of individuals. The inability of some who have been charged with crimes to receive a fair trial because of publicity is only one face of this problem.

The media have been controlled by individuals of a single socioeconomic class, the business class, and newcomers have difficulty starting new communication enterprises. Moreover, control is in the hands of very few people. As a result the free and open market of information and ideas has been endangered.

These general criticisms may seem to be a broad umbrella that will cover almost any specific case. And yet recent years have brought into sharp focus a number of other criticisms:

The media have helped to socialize readers, listeners, and viewers into consumer roles. The role and the act of consumption have been elevated.

The media have helped to make the American people a nation of spectators rather than doers.

The media foster a cult of immediate success, leading American youth to believe that their desires are instantly attainable and that the long, slow processes of democracy are unnecessary.

The media, by their presence at the scene of news events, create more news.

The media are often inaccurate.

The difficulty in assessing such charges is that examples can be found to support almost any of them—yet examples do not prove the case about all. Does anyone who has read the *Christian Science Monitor* or *The New York Times,* for example, really think that these papers are more concerned with the superficial than the significant? Does the *New Yorker* endanger public morals? Do the films directed by Mike Nichols perpetuate the status quo? The point is that we cannot speak of any medium as a monolith. How much more difficult is it to treat the *media* as though they were one, all equally flawed and at fault. Let us, then, look at the criticisms of the media singly—remembering as we do that newspapers, broadcasts, and movies are not all alike.

NEWSPAPER CRITICS

In 1911, in a series in *Collier's* magazine, Will Irwin set the pattern for much of the later criticism of the newspaper. Although a rash of articles praising or condemning the press had broken out in other periodicals in the preceding four or five years, his series and other articles springing from it were among the first attempts in the United States to assess journalism fully and candidly.

In exchange for its financial support of the newspaper, Irwin wrote, advertising demanded and often got suppression of certain types of news, biased news accounts, and similar concessions:

> Slowly at first, then with increasing momentum, advertisers learned their power. Indeed, in certain quarters, advertising solicitors helped to teach them. For the less conscientious and solidly run newspapers began offering comfort and immunities as a bonus to attract customers. Advertisers got into the way of asking for these special privileges; often, in communities where the newspapers were timid and mushy, for every privilege, even to dictating policies. The extent of their demands varies with the local custom of their communities. But finally . . . the system had grown so set that [the publisher] must make concessions or fail.

The concessions that advertisers asked for were sometimes a whole change of editorial policy, Irwin said, but most often the concession concerned insertion of publicity for, and the suppression of news harmful to, the advertiser, his family, or his business associates.

With more perception than most early critics, Irwin made a point that social scientists were to return to decades later: That many of the shortcomings of the press arise not just from the baneful influence of advertising but from the commercial nature of publishing.

> The advertiser pays more of the revenue, but he is paying for circulation. The greater the circulation, the greater the advertising rate, and the more eagerly advertisers will buy. This is a kind of double product. You must have circulation first, last, and all the time, though circulation pays you no profit, except as you turn it into advertising—as a stock-feeder gets his profits not from his hay and corn, but from his fattened steers.

Unlike some later students of the press, however, Irwin believed that over the long haul only a good product, a truthful product, could attract and hold a large circulation. Commercial and conscienceless, publishers persistently ignored that point, he said, and for a short-term advantage colored their product to the taste of the advertisers.

But Irwin also saw that the advertiser was not the only influence working on a publisher. He observed that newspaper publishers are businessmen and the newspapers they control will necessarily reflect the viewpoint of the businessman.

The newspaper field had become increasingly difficult for the newcomer to enter, Irwin noted, a perceptive observation since daily newspapers were only two years past their numerical peak. He noted also that the influence of newspapers had shifted from their editorial columns to their news columns.

Later Critics

Irwin was followed by a line of critics who reiterated his themes, although often without his acuteness of observation, and who in essence charged, "You can't believe what you read in the papers because the press is controlled by advertisers and big business."

One of the early critics was Upton Sinclair, who in 1919 published *The Brass Check,* a title emphasizing the analogy he saw between journalism and prostitution. Sinclair already had a national reputation as a reformer. In 1904, two years after he had aligned himself with the Socialists, he had written *The Jungle,* a novel exposing conditions in the Chicago stockyards. Written for a socialist paper and then published in book form, *The Jungle* was a best-seller in America and England and was translated into seventeen languages. Public indignation aroused by the book led to the Pure Food and Drug Act of 1906. Thereafter books streamed from Sinclair's pen, most of them with some sort of message, and on his eightieth birthday he could point to a book for each year of his life.

The Brass Check, like its author, proved durable. By 1926 it had gone into its ninth edition, and in 1936 it was reprinted in a revised edition. Half of the book deals with Sinclair's personal experiences with the press; the remainder calls on other witnesses to the prostitution of a free press.

"The Empire of Business," Sinclair wrote, controls journalism by four devices. First and most direct is ownership of many of the nation's periodicals. A second and most important means has been to achieve ownership of the owners. By playing on the ambitions of publishers, by applying pressure on their families, by club associations and gentlemen's agreements, big business has strengthened its hold on the press. A publisher is a member of the ruling class in his community, Sinclair noted, and by accommodating the right people he may become a senator, a cabinet minister, even an ambassador. Advertising subsidies are the third means by which business controls the press. They make publishers prone to suppress ideas inimical to advertising interests, news embarrassing or detrimental to advertisers. Finally, Sinclair said, business at times resorts to outright bribery to promote its views and censor antagonistic ideas.

Sinclair's belief that conspirators manipulate the press to their own ends was shared by George Seldes, a former head of the Berlin and Rome bureaus of the Chicago *Tribune* and war correspondent in Spain for the New York *Post*. One of the most diligent critics of American journalism, Seldes set the theme for much of his subsequent criticism in his book *Freedom of the Press* in 1935. He saw and tried to document the corrupting influences of the financial, political, social, and advertising worlds. These were responsible for such suppressions as that of news of an epidemic of amebic dysentery in Chicago during the Chicago World's Fair of 1933 and for such propaganda as that used by the utilities against publicly owned power.

The arch conspirators are the members of the American Newspaper Publishers Association, the house of lords of the press, Seldes argued in *Lords of the Press* in 1938. The publishers gather behind closed doors at their annual meetings, he said, because their conspiracies against the public welfare cannot bear the light of publicity:

> . . . in the closed sessions they defend the employment of child labor, they take united action against a Congressional measure which would keep drugmakers from poisoning or cheating the American people, and they gloat over their own strikebreaking department which offers scabs not only to members but to anyone who wants to fight the unions.

Both professional and amateur critics have complained that newspapers have reflected the biases of their owners and the viewpoints of big business in their coverage of major election campaigns since the 1930s. Newspapers were accused of giving unfair treatment to the Democratic candidate, Adlai Stevenson, in both the 1952 and 1956 Presidential campaigns. They did not confine their support of the Republican candidate, Dwight Eisenhower, to their editorial columns, critics charged; instead, many newspapers of the overwhelming majority that supported Eisenhower played down Stevenson's speeches and played up his opponent's.

Second thoughts began to grow in 1960. Most political reporters were clearly for Democrat John Kennedy in his Presidential race against Republican Richard Nixon, although publishers generally supported Nixon. Some Democrats admitted privately that the reporters had helped elect Kennedy. Researchers then began to reassess the easy and traditional assumption that reporters had to slant their stories in the direction of the publishers' leanings. Thoughtful observers now hold that some of the power of the late thunderers of the publishing world—the William

Randolph Hearsts and the Robert R. McCormicks—has passed to the reporters.

Many of the comfortable assumptions of decades were upset in 1964. Most political reporters were clearly for Democrat Lyndon B. Johnson in his race with Republican Barry Goldwater—but so were most of the committed newspapers. Johnson was supported by 445 dailies with an aggregate circulation of nearly 30 million; Goldwater was supported by 369 dailies with an aggregate circulation of less than 10 million. Even more striking was the lack of newspaper commitment; 60 per cent of United States dailies either declared themselves neutral or failed to support either candidate. This was, of course, an unusual election. But one should not ignore the fact that newspaper independence-neutrality has long been tracing a steep curve. Only one daily in twenty failed to take a stand in 1932. In the 1960 election one in three took no stand. In 1968 Republican Richard Nixon had more than three times the newspaper support that went to Democrat Hubert Humphrey. Again, about one paper in three took no stand.

Critics of News Values and Techniques

A number of critics, including some newspapermen, have found fault with current standards of news evaluation and with some techniques of news presentation. A familiar criticism, repeated over the years, has been that newspapers play up the sensational, the superficial, the silly, at the expense of the significant. Thus they give more space and attention to a torso murder in Cleveland, a marital entanglement in Hollywood, a nudists' convention in New Jersey, or a rape in Delaware than to an important session of the United Nations. Another familiar charge is that the technical presentation of the news—the headlines, the inverted pyramid structure of the stories, the fetish of objectivity—prevent the reader from seeing a coherent picture of current events.

To a large extent the citizen is deprived of necessary information and discussion because the press is preoccupied with reporting trivia and conflict, the Commission on Freedom of the Press charged in 1947. The compulsion to attract a large audience has led the press to emphasize "the exceptional rather than the representative, the sensational rather than the significant."

Many activities of the utmost social consequence lie below the surface of what are conventionally regarded as reportable incidents: more power machinery; fewer men tending machines; more hours of leisure;

more schooling per child; decrease of intolerance; successful negotiations of labor contracts; increase in participation in music through the schools; increase of sale of books of biography and history.

Instead of reporting such developments adequately, the commission said, the press gives disproportionate attention to riots, strikes, and murders.

Much earlier Walter Lippmann had questioned the technical ability of the newspaper to report the social conditions underlying news of consequence. Newspapers, he said in his *Public Opinion,* do little more that station reporters at points of record—at the police station, say, and the courthouse. Here they catch only what he called the obtrusions of social conditions. A reporter might note a businessman filing for bankruptcy, for instance, but he is not equipped to explore the conditions leading up to that situation until it actually happens. Thus, said Lippmann, what the reader gets is a somewhat distorted picture of social conditions, a picture much like a halftone made with an exceedingly coarse screen.

Newspapers have failed to give the reader a coherent picture of the news, several critics have charged. In 1939 Sidney Kobre called on newspapers to increase their amount of depth reporting. Their coverage of spot news needs little further development, he said; what is needed is an attempt to weld the findings of the rapidly developing social sciences to the newspaper so that the reader could understand not only the surface event but also what lay beneath. He quoted with approval a remark by Irwin Edman, a philosopher at Columbia University, who described the newspaper as "the worst possible way of getting a coherent picture of the life of our time . . . The mind of the newspaper reader, if it could be photographed after ten minutes of reading, would not be a map, but an explosion."

To give the reader an orderly and understandable picture of the life of our time, Herbert Brucker proposed a number of reforms in *The Changing American Newspaper.* In the old days before the world had become complex and the reader harried, he wrote, it was enough for a newspaper to run separate stories on the day's happenings and to scatter them helter-skelter throughout its pages. Today that practice often bewilders the reader. Brucker suggested that newspapers give more attention to background and interpretation, that their staffs rewrite wire stories for coherence and round them out with additional facts supplied by their own research departments. Moreover, he recommended that newspapers take greater care in organizing the news to make it comprehensible. The entire front page might be devoted to concise but adequate summaries of all major happenings, classified by subject matter, he said. Within the paper fuller accounts, sometimes combining several individual stories, might be departmentalized by subject matter, somewhat as the news magazines group stories.

Contributing to the chaotic portrayal of the day's events are misleading headlines, written to catch the lethargic reader and to fit a given space, with little regard for meaning, according to some critics. "As now employed by most dailies, the headline is a convenient device gone wrong," wrote nine Nieman Fellows in their blueprint for a better press. "Newspapers have converted its limitations—brevity and emphasis on the categorical imperative—into a commercial asset, a shabby trick to sell papers." Most readers shun the full account and read only the headline. Too often the headline is not warranted by the facts of the story. The reader then gets a distorted view of events, the charge runs. Even the reader who moves into the story may be misled. For, according to the Nieman Fellows, the impact of a bold, black headline may be greater than that of the story itself.

A number of newsmen, foreign and domestic, have complained that the five-W lead and the inverted pyramid form of newswriting, despite their practicality, make for dull, repetitious stories. "Perhaps this formula has become more important than the end originally sought," Herbert Brucker wrote. "At least one wonders whether its advantages in practice justify its strange results in newswriting." When the reader is hit in the face with the most important facts in the first sentence or paragraph, the logical sequence of events is destroyed, according to critics. The story is told piecemeal, with repetition, and all tension and interest vanish. That point was reiterated by Urs Schwarz, foreign editor of *Neue Zürcher Zeitung*. He noted that the Grimm brothers opened their story of Rumpelstiltskin in this fashion: "Once upon a time there was a miller; he was a poor man, but he had a beautiful daughter." In the hands of an American reporter, he said, the opening would have come out something like this: "A queen's success in pronouncing his name led a dwarf to tear himself to pieces, and saved a child's life."

Yet another criticism of newspapers is the fetish of objectivity. Newsmen are so afraid of editorializing in the news columns, so this charge runs, that they cheat the reader. By giving only the objective facts instead of interpreting those facts, they often turn out stories that are distorted, incomplete, even incomprehensible. By striving to present all sides in a controversial situation, they often give the same credence to a known liar and a known truth-teller. Hence the objectivity they cherish is far too often not objectivity at all but a form of distortion. Critics acknowledge that the reporter who interprets the news must walk a narrow line between fact and opinion, yet walk it he must if he is to put the facts into a context that gives them meaning.

CRITICS OF MAGAZINES

Magazines have shared in the criticisms directed against the mass media generally, but they have come in for remarkably little criticism on their own.

True, critics like Upton Sinclair have lumped magazine publishers with newspaper publishers as parties to the conspiracy with big business to keep the public uninformed or misinformed on certain issues. Advertising pressure has killed off the magazines that dared to tell the truth, Sinclair charged, and has made the survivors spineless; it has even corrupted the authors of magazine fiction, who tend to treat themes favorable to big business and the status quo.

True, too, individual publications have stirred the critic's pen. A number of authors, most of them disenchanted former employees, have found fault with Time Inc. and its magazines. The *Reader's Digest* has been the subject of a book-length dissection.

For the most part, perhaps because the magazine world is so varied, the charges against magazines have been those leveled against the media as a whole. Magazines have been accused of a general conservatism, inhospitality to significant new ideas, reluctance to change the status quo. They have been charged with overemphasizing the material side of life and with catering to a low common denominator of taste in their eagerness to give the public what it wants. Although these charges are true of some magazines, it is difficult to see how they can apply to *Ramparts, Commentary, Rolling Stone,* and others.

Most of the criticisms directed specifically against magazines seem to have been aimed at periodicals lurking in the dark shadows along the fringes of the industry—at the scandal magazines, the pornographic magazines, the comic books. Perhaps the shrillest criticism has been of the comic book, which some authorities consider a factor in juvenile crime, delinquency, and maladjustment. In his *Seduction of the Innocent,* Dr. Fredric Wertham, a psychiatrist and one of the most persistent critics, has summed up the eight specifications in indicting comic books:

> They invite illiteracy with their format.
> They create an atmosphere of cruelty and deceit with their heavy load of material about crime.
> They make readers susceptible to temptation.
> They encourage unwholesome fantasies.
> They suggest ideas which may lead to crime or sexual perversion.
> They provide a rationalization for the execution of those ideas.
> They give detailed information on criminal techniques and other undesirable practices.
> They may weight the scales in favor of delinquency or maladjustment.

CRITICS OF MOTION PICTURES

Ever since 1896, when an indignant public protested a shocking kiss in *The Widow Jones,* the motion picture has been attacked and ridiculed. Intellectuals have scorned the Hollywood product as entertainment fit only for a twelve-year-old mentality. The morally righteous have exerted pressure to stop portrayals of what they have regarded to be flagrant immorality on the screen. Minority groups of various kinds have protested the way in which the movies have depicted their members and treated their interests.

In the revolution of manners and morals after World War I, there was an erosion of the old taboos against public discussion of sex, a development that affected the various media. The confession magazine was born of this changing attitude and perhaps even contributed to it. Some movie-makers took advantage of this new freedom to film stories recognizing sex as a motivating force in human affairs. Theater marquees carried such titles as *Passion* and *Forbidden Fruit,* and movie advertising attracted customers with purple prose and suggestive illustrations. Off screen, a few movie stars became involved in widely publicized scandals. Hangers-on of the industry became involved in still more and contributed to a popular image of movie-making as a business characterized by loose living and shoddy morals.

Acceptance of Pressure

Religious, civic, and women's organizations spoke out in protest during the early years, as did many magazines, both secular and religious. After studying film content, the General Federation of Women's Clubs demanded state legislation. A precedent existed, since Chicago had set up a censorship board in 1909; between then and 1922, eight states passed laws providing for movie censorship.

Anxious to protect its investments in stars and studios, the movie industry in 1922 began to experiment with self-regulation. From those early attempts, in 1930 came a production code that outlined standards of performance. Four years later, under pressure from the Catholic organization National Legion of Decency, the industry set up machinery for enforcing the code.

The movie industry adopted its code in self-defense against the widespread charge that the movies endanger public morals. In exchange for its attempt to still that criticism, the industry acquired a new one—the criticism that the movies traffic in inanity. The real curse is conformity, according to film writer Robert Ardrey. And conformity came about when Hollywood gave in to the "puritan uproar," which culminated in the production code. "It was a mistake that the theater never made," he wrote. "Down the drain went the best and the worst, the fine and the wicked, the baby with the bath water. Public relations replaced private instinct; brains replaced glands: the cautious the courageous: the package the substance."

In decrying the inanity of the movies, Ardrey was by no means alone. Time and again the movies were attacked for creating a dream world of unrestrained fantasy. For the most part the critics conceded that a certain proportion of purely escapist films—the sentimental romance, the action-packed Western, the slapstick comedy, the star-studded musical—worked no great harm. What they objected to was that these films constituted the overwhelming bulk of Hollywood's offerings. They deplored Hollywood's reluctance to attempt serious drama, to base movies on themes with relevance to twentieth-century life. In recent years the criticism—and the critics—have changed. Whatever one can say about most movies today, lack of realism is not among their faults. Indeed, the chief complaint seems to be that there are few movies families can attend because scenes and dialogue have become so earthy.

The American Image Abroad

For years a strong criticism has been that Hollywood gives the rest of the world a false picture of American life, culture, and institutions. American movies have been immensely popular throughout the world, and the foreign market is important to movie-makers. In the ideological conflicts of the twentieth century, some authorities contend, it is especially important that the movies give a fair representation of American life.

Yet, these same critics asserted, the picture that the movies convey abroad is distorted, showing Americans as wasteful, extravagant, and insensitive; inordinately concerned with material gain and comfort; indifferent to social injustice; preoccupied with physical beauty, sex, and amorous intrigue; given to lawlessness and violence. As a member of the British Parliament once remarked, "Anyone who suggests that the American films portray the American way of living is an enemy of the United States."

It is important, of course, to recognize that no medium whose chief substance is fiction is likely to give a "fair representation of American life." The central problem is that many foreign audiences look at films as if they were representative.

Recently American movies have declined in popularity abroad, perhaps because of the change to an appeal to American youth, perhaps also because foreign films have improved.

The Image of Minorities

Another common complaint is that movies, in their failure to portray things as they really are, have often given stereotyped and even harmful pictures of members of racial, professional, and occupational groups. The typical reaction has not been criticism alone but pressure on the industry by groups believing themselves harmed by their treatment on the screen.

Movie-makers have been exceedingly sensitive about their portrayals of racial groups ever since D. W. Griffith's *The Birth of a Nation* was denounced by the National Association for the Advancement of Colored People in 1915. Negro and white leaders alike have been quick to object to movies showing Negroes in servile positions, as villains, in parts thought detrimental to the interests of their race. When Walt Disney adapted Joel Chandler Harris' Uncle Remus stories in *Song of the South,* certain Negro groups picketed theaters in protest against what they believed to be an unflattering picture. Others have complained that the movies usually show Negroes as servants, singers, and dancers, not in the representative positions they hold in their communities.

Physicians, lawyers, teachers, and others have objected when the movies have shown members of their professions as villains or have otherwise portrayed them unfavorably.

Sensitive to pressure, anxious to please, Hollywood has had difficulty in presenting an accurate picture of the many racial, religious, professional, and avocational groups that make up American society. Moreover, there seems validity in the charge that the movies have tended to depict some as stereotypes instead of individuals. In general, for instance, they have shown Negroes in subordinate positions; college professors as amiable, forgetful eccentrics; and newspaper reporters as offensively brash, hyperactive extroverts. Movie-makers have certainly sought to change some of their practices, especially those regarding racial minorities, but many of the stereotypes persist.

CRITICS OF BROADCASTING

Although the charges against radio and television have varied, most of them have fallen into perhaps a half-dozen categories.

A basic criticism of radio made during the 1930s and 1940s was that the advertiser had taken programming out of the hands of the broadcaster. The broadcaster sold the advertiser not merely the time for his commercials; he sold the program time surrounding it as well. The advertiser to a large degree decided what would be broadcast in the quarter-hour, half-hour, or full hour he had purchased. More than that, he and his agency packaged the show, hired the performers, supervised the entire production. The situation was far different from that of newspapers and magazines, which merely sell the advertiser space for his sales message and decide on the editorial content themselves.

This criticism has seldom been made of television. By the time television came along in the mid-1940s, the networks were keeping a much firmer hold on programming. Whereas advertising agencies had either produced or controlled the majority of shows when radio was at its peak, they have done comparatively little producing and supervising of today's television programs.

A second complaint is that the airwaves are filled with sales talk—obtrusive sales talk, much of it in questionable taste. The correct time is brought to the listener by courtesy of a watch manufacturer, the weather outlook by a feed dealer, an important news bulletin by a manufacturer of headache remedies. Programs are interrupted by pleas that the viewer or listener buy this soap or that automobile. In all this, critics complain, the broadcaster has lost sight of the important point that the airwaves belong to the public and not to the pitchman. But the pitchman dominates, say the critics, and a medium with extraordinary potential for educating the public has become a vehicle for vending cigarettes, laxatives, beer, and dog food. Perhaps most important, many newscasters are pitchmen as well as reporters. On radio, which has no visual props to cue the audience to changes of role, the quick switch from journalist to salesman is sometimes misleading as well as irritating. Even on the "Today" show on television, which is profitable enough to afford better, Frank Blair and Barbara Walters leap from news to salesmanship as though there were no difference.

Because radio and television broadcasters have become interested primarily in building huge audiences for advertisers, another charge runs, they have skimped on unprofitable serious educational programs but have dished out lavish helpings of entertainment. Addressing a convention of radio and television news directors, the late Edward R. Murrow lamented the reluctance of networks to undertake serious programs of news and public affairs, which are expensive to produce and which do not add to profits: "I am frightened by the imbalance, the constant striving to reach the largest possible audience for everything; by the absence of a sustained study of the state of the nation." He added:

> Our history will be what we make it. And if there are any historians about fifty or a hundred years from now, and there should be preserved the kinescopes for one week of all three networks, they will find there recorded in black and white, or color, evidence of decadence, escapism, and insulation from the realities of the world in which we live. I invite your attention to the television schedules of all networks between

the hours of eight and eleven p.m. eastern time. Here you will find only fleeting and spasmodic reference to the fact that this nation is in mortal danger. There are, it is true, occasional informative programs presented in that intellectual ghetto on Sunday afternoons. But during the daily peak viewing periods, television in the main insulates us from the realities of the world in which we live.

Not only does entertainment comprise an inordinate proportion of broadcast fare; much of it, critics say, is of low caliber at that. On television especially, they deplore the preponderance of programs involving murder, mayhem, violence of all sorts, and the inanitities exemplified by the quiz show.

A fourth charge is that the viewer or listener gets fictitious choice even in cities with competing radio or television stations. This springs from the imitativeness of broadcasters. Once the appeal of a Western or a domestic comedy has been demonstrated, other broadcasters hasten to put similar programs on the air. Consequently the viewer or listener does not have a real choice between the cultural and the commercial at a given hour; he has a choice between two Westerns or two domestic comedies or two variety shows, both pretty much alike.

Local stations have been accused of being scarcely more than mouthpieces for the large national networks. They generally have failed to develop local talent, critics say, and they have been sadly inadequate in providing an effective platform for the discussion of local issues.

CRITICS OF ADVERTISING

No less than the media that carry it, advertising has felt the sharp stab of the critic's pen. The cries of the critics, the threatening cloud of government regulation, the organized movements of consumers, the increased awareness of advertising leaders to their social responsibilities—all have influenced advertisers toward higher standards of performance, according to Willard L. Thompson of the University of Minnesota in a study of self-regulation in advertising.

Down to the end of the nineteenth century and in the first years of the twentieth, advertising that gulled the unwary consumer was perhaps what most frequently stirred critics. Jurists, essayists, reformers, some editors, and even some advertisers, from time to time decried the fraudulent and deceptive advertising that turned up in the press. As the nineteenth century closed, such critics were heard more and more frequently, perhaps in part because of the rapidly increasing volume of advertising, largely because of the blatantly misleading patent medicine advertising, which roused a number of magazines to attack.

In the years just prior to World War I, some critics found a new cause for anxiety—the social and economic effects of advertising. The high cost of living no doubt helped to focus attention on those aspects, for soaring prices were a subject of widespread concern. Congress heard proposals for investigating the high cost of living, and government agencies planned studies of distribution costs. Quite naturally, some wondered whether advertising added an extra and unnecessary burden to those costs.

Many critics thought it did. They contended that most advertising simply tries to persuade the consumer to buy a particular brand at a price inflated by advertising instead of an equally good product not so extensively extolled.

Criticisms of Advertising Summarized

The range of criticism broadened as the century grew older. Most of the charges that have been made against advertising were summarized in a ten-point indictment issued in a talk before the Advertising Club of Grand Rapids, Michigan, by Colston E. Warne, president of Consumers Union and professor of economics at Amherst College. Warne complained that advertising:

Stressed inconsequential values.

Brought a false perspective as to merit of products, often bewildering rather than informing.

Lowered our ethical standards by the all-too-frequent insincerity of its appeals.

Corrupted and distorted the news.

Wasted much good timber and chemicals, and spoiled much of the landscape and radio enjoyment.

Blocked the speedy use of correct medication.

Created many parental problems by "abominable" radio programs.

Turned our society into one dominated by style, fashion, and "keeping up with the Joneses."

Retarded the growth of thrift by emphasizing immediate expenditures.

Fostered monopoly through its large-scale use by only a few financially favored companies.

In 1970 Ralph Nader, who had by that time turned his major attacks to the food industry, blamed an advertising "bombardment" for a younger generation that knew nothing of good food. Nader attacked the "Pepsi Cola-Pretzel-Frito-Lay's Potato Chip syndrome," saying that "thousands of kids are growing up believing that Pepsi or Coke are prerequisites of a life of health and vigor."

Fosters Wastefulness

In *The Tragedy of Waste*, which appeared in 1928, Stuart Chase wrote that advertising is not only nonproductive; it is counter-productive, cutting into the economy by sidetracking a part of the working force. Other critics have lined up with Chase. What advertising does, they say, is to harness a good deal of potentially productive effort to the unproductive task of diverting consumables from one company or product to another, both usually of equal merit.

Moreover, critics hold, advertising creates an artificial obsolescence by making consumers dissatisfied with goods long before they have ceased being useful. A man is urged to buy a new automobile even though the present one has years of potential service—but even so obsolescence is built in; a woman discards last year's dress, with months of wear still in it, because advertising tells her it is outmoded. Such artificial obsolescence results in a tremendous waste of America's resources and productive effort, critics say.

Critics of the American penchant for destroying the environment argue that the wastefulness bred by advertising and conspicuous consumption require a complete reorganization of the American way of life. They have also pointed out that citizens of the United States represent a very small proportion of the world's population, but they consume an enormous proportion of the world's production. And, of course, the mass media play a crucial role in mass consumption.

Fosters Materialistic Attitudes

The loud voice of advertising, trumpeting the wonders of worldly possessions, has forced Americans, some critics have charged, to place undue emphasis on material values to the detriment of more enduring values.

In their own land Americans tend to measure their fellow man by the size of his income and automobile, by the elegance of his home, and by the number of possessions in it. Abroad they tend to judge foreign lands by the extent of such material comforts as modern plumbing and electrical refrigeration. They put the dollar above principle, the material above the spiritual. So say the critics; and while they do not put the sole burden on advertising, they insist that it must share a substantial part of the blame.

Fosters Monopoly

Advertising also has been condemned because it creates monopolies. The manufacturer has the power to raise the possibility of monopoly, according to a few critics, for, by an incessant barrage of advertising, he is able to convince consumers that his product serves them better than any similar product. Take aspirin, for a hypothetical example. Although all aspirin tablets are nearly alike, since they must meet certain minimum specifications set by the government, one manufacturer might so dominate the advertising picture that he convinces consumers that there is no really effective aspirin but his own. As his sales increase, so does his economic power. It becomes increasingly difficult for competitors to get a share of the market.

On the other hand, C. H. Sandage has pointed out that such a monopoly rests on control of human attitudes, not of supply, and that, because of consumers' shifts from brand to brand, it is highly uncertain. Moreover, he adds, the chief aim of such control is increasing sales rather than prices, since any significant price increase might send customers flocking to competitors' products.

A cooler and subtler analysis of advertising than that of most has been made by Professor David Potter of Stanford. In his book *People of Plenty,* he points out that advertising has become a powerful institution. And yet it is unlike other institutions of society in that its view of man is solely commercial. The church conceives of man as an immortal soul; schools conceive of him as a being guided by reason; business and industry conceive of him as a productive agent who can create goods or render services that are useful to mankind. But advertising conceives of man as nothing more than a consumer. In contrast with the other institutions, Potter has written:

> Advertising has in its dynamics no motivation to seek the improvement of the individual or to impart qualities of social usefulness, unless conformity to material values may be so characterized. And, though it wields an immense social influence, comparable to the influence of religion and learning, it has no social goals and no social responsibility for what it does with its influence, so long as it refrains from palpable violations of truth and decency. It is this lack of institutional responsibility, this lack of inherent social purpose to balance social power, which, I would argue, is a basic cause for concern about the role of advertising. Occasional deceptions, breaches of taste, and deviations from sound ethical conduct are in a sense superficial and are not necessarily intrinsic. Equally, the high-minded types of advertising which we see more regularly than we sometimes realize are also extraneous to an analysis of the basic nature of advertising. What is basic is that advertising, as such, with all its vast power to influence

values and conduct, cannot ever lose sight of the fact that it ultimately regards man as a consumer and defines its own mission as one of stimulating him to consume or to desire to consume.

CURRENT CRITICISMS OF THE MEDIA

One can detect a change in the nature of criticisms of the media since the early 1940s. In the 1920s and 1930s what we have called the conspiratorial theory of press malfunction was especially prevalent. Its theme was that business and advertising interests directly influence what the media carry and do not carry. Its assumption was that publishers and broadcasters are in covert league with big business to suppress or distort much information and opinion of social consequence. In short, the critics blamed men, not the system.

In *America's House of Lords,* which appeared in 1939, for instance, Secretary of the Interior Harold L. Ickes argued that newspapers would be all right if their editorial direction were left to editors and reporters; unfortunately, however, owners of even small newspapers are dominated by a big-business psychology that causes them to require a considerable amount of suppression, fabrication, and distortion. Criticism of that sort was quite common in the 1930s when faith in business and businessmen was at a low ebb. Publishers sat for a number of unflattering individual and group portraits. In 1936 Ferdinand Lundberg's *Imperial Hearst* painted William Randolph Hearst as a sinister press lord who had played a "great and ghastly part in shaping the American mind" and who had been able to make America accept "his deceptions and debaucheries of its political institutions" in regard to such issues as war with Spain, military preparedness, and sales and income taxes.

Some defenders of the press tried to show that what the critics called instances of suppression often simply represented differences in news judgment. Putting a story on page 32 instead of on page 1 was not necessarily burying it, as the critics charged; it appeared on page 32 because that was where it belonged under any standard of news values. Some news, which did not appear in newspapers at all, simply did not warrant space, they contended. And certainly some charges of bias sprang from critics who had clearly identifiable biases of their own.

From the early 1940s onward, critics seem to have shifted the blame for many of the shortcomings of the media from the individual publisher or broadcaster to the system. A common viewpoint today is that mass communications are influenced by social processes. Social and economic forces, our system of values, indeed the whole of our culture, have been at least as important as men in shaping our media and in affecting their performance. If we wish to alter the performance of our media, then, we may well have to make some rather fundamental changes in the order in which they operate.

There seems to be a growing awareness that many of the criticisms of the media are, at bottom, really criticisms of our society and its system of values. The critics dislike the materialism that is ingrained in our entire culture, not just in the mass media. Their protests represent their frustration that Americans, despite their system of free, universal education, prefer Popeye to Plato and the Beatles to Beethoven.

There seems to be a growing recognition that publishers, broadcasters, and movie producers are not necessarily evil men, conspiring to propagandize the public in their own interests. They are becoming accepted as men of honest conviction whose attitudes toward business are usually conditioned by the simple fact that they are businessmen. Their dilemma is becoming generally recognized: On the one hand, they are expected to perform an important public service; on the other, they are required to make a profit.

Joseph T. Klapper wrote in *The American Scholar:*

> The influence of big business on the content of mass media is probably not exerted in any large conscious Gestalt designed to perpetuate a social system. The conscious and manifest purpose of a radio program sponsor is primarily, and almost wholly, to sell his soap. Although the maintenance of the existing social and economic system may be a precondition of the sale, such social guardianship is, for the usual sponsor, at most a secondary and latent purpose—except in the face of direct attack.

Furthermore, there is a growing awareness that advertising may not be the prime evil it was once thought to be. After all, some of the shortcomings that have stirred critics are also found in media that do not carry advertising. What is now seen to be at fault is the commercial basis of the press, which exerts pressure for building large audiences. Seeking large audiences—in order to hold down their unit costs and to attract advertising—they must necessarily aim at a low common denominator, must avoid offending any sizable portion of their market, must traffic in what the majority wants and believes. Many contemporary critics take into account the changes that industrialization and other forces have wrought in the communication system.

Serious students such as Paul Lazarsfeld and Robert K. Merton have commented on the tendency of the media to reaffirm existing attitudes. "Since the mass media are supported by great business concerns geared into the current social and economic system, the media contribute to the maintenance of that system," Lazarsfeld and Merton remarked in *The Communication of Ideas.*

> This contribution is not found merely in the effective advertisement of the sponsor's product. It arises, rather, from the typical presence in magazine stories, radio programs, and newspaper columns of some element of confirmation, some element of approval of the present structure of society. And this continuing reaffirmation underscores the duty to accept.

The barrage of media content favoring the status quo has two advantages, according to Klapper. One is its static position. There is little counter-argument, little challenging of the sanctioned attitudes, few attempts to present the unaccepted view. Any effort to depart from the majority taste or attitude, he observed, would jeopardize the media's chances of amassing their essential large audiences. The second advantage is that the media implement existing drives and do not create new ones. With little resistance, they channel behavior one way or another after the basic behavior pattern or basic attitude has been established; they rarely try to instill significantly new behavior patterns or new attitudes. "For Americans who have been socialized in the use of a toothbrush, it makes relatively little difference which brand of toothbrush they use," Lazarsfeld and Merton noted; it is quite another thing, they remarked, to persuade them to overcome deep-seated prejudices against a racial or ethnic group. The media have been far more successful in rechanneling the existing system of values, they concluded, than in reshaping it.

If present-day critics are right in putting the bulk of the blame for the shortcomings of the media upon the system instead of on the men who run them, the task of improving media performance is large and complex. No longer can one assume that performance can be improved simply by wheedling, exhorting, or educating media personnel into a more serious acceptance of their responsibilities. No longer can one assume that a free trade in ideas can be achieved simply by breaking large communication units into a multiplicity of small ones. Before advancing any realistic solution, one must clearly understand the communication system in the context of its historical and contemporary setting. Only from that beginning can there emerge any solution that will not be anachronistic, ineffective, or both.

The Mass Media
and the Future

My interest is in the future, because I am going to
spend the rest of my life there.
                              CHARLES F. KETTERING

When a new managing director joined the London *Times* some years ago, he became curious about an obscure little man carrying a black satchel who entered the building every Friday and left on Monday morning. Old-timers had seen the man come and go every weekend for years, but no one knew who he was or what he did. One day the director noted a curious expenditure in the ledgers. Bookkeepers told him it was for meals that a nearby restaurant sent in to the little man on weekends. Eventually the director tracked down the intruder. The little man was from the Bank of England, and his little black satchel contained five thousand pounds in cash.

On a Saturday afternoon decades earlier, during the Boer War, the *Times* had wanted to send a reporter to cover a big story on the Continent. Boat traffic was halted by a storm, and the man could not charter a boat because there was no cash in the office and the banks were closed. To make sure it would always have cash on hand for such contingencies, the *Times* arranged for the Bank of England to send a representative each weekend with five thousand pounds in cash.

The story may be apocryphal, but it epitomizes how the mass media become set in their ways—ways they unthinkingly perpetuate long after the reasons for them have vanished. Newspapers have doggedly printed their news columns in 12 or 13 picas even though that is not the optimum width for easy reading but because that was about as wide as columns could be in the days of hand composition

317

if a press were not to scatter the type like confetti. As new technology has come along, the media have tended to try to adapt it to their established ways. Thus, when newspapers experimented with facsimile twenty-five years ago, they used it not to disseminate information in an entirely different way but to transmit their conventional pages.

It is true, of course, that there are sometimes good reasons for retaining old methods and equipment. Newspapers, for example, have usually invested heavily in the equipment they are using, and some must continue to use it because there is no market for it. Also, unions are often quite conservative about changing work practices in a way that would allow introduction of new equipment. Nonetheless newspaper executives themselves admit that they have been slow to change.

THE COMMUNICATIONS REVOLUTION

All this leads directly to a brutal fact: We are now in the midst of a communications revolution that has profound implications for the mass media, for their content and even for the sort of world we live in. Some companies now turning a regular profit may well become casualties of the revolution unless they adapt to it. Thirty years ago Joseph Schumpeter, the economist, said that the fundamental reason business firms do not exist forever is that most of them are founded for a definite purpose that is fulfilled or becomes obsolete. The natural cause of death, he said, is failure to innovate; and he added, in the dismal prose of his dismal science:

> No firm which is merely run on established lines, however conscientious the management of its routine business may be, remains in a capitalist society a source of profit, and the day comes for each when it ceases to pay interest and even depreciation.

The inventory of instruments of the communications revolution is long: Attachments that will enable TV sets to play prerecorded films and tapes or to convert broadcast signals into printed pages; computer-programmed tapes that enable printers to turn out a book-sized page every five seconds; space satellites that have made simultaneous, instantaneous global communication a virtual reality: holographic equipment that can produce three-dimensional pictures; personal two-way phones for communication and data processing; inexpensive home video recording and playback equipment; electrostatic printing, in which type never touches paper; cathode-ray tube composition of type; computerized information banks with telephone links; and many others.

No one can be certain when specific items of the new technology will move from the laboratory into widespread, everyday use. Some of them seem already in the anteroom; others seem to be knocking at the door or at least coming up the front walk. Yet communications technology often has a way of lying around for a long time before it gets put to use, often because there is a heavy investment in equipment already being used. It is also true, of course, that technological changes in broadcasting often depend upon government decisions. Certainly the development of UHF and CATV have been heavily impeded by the Federal Communications Commission. CATV was also impeded by broadcasters who had invested heavily in conventional stations. When the growth of CATV became inevitable, some of the broadcasters bought into CATV—and they oppose it no longer. Direct broadcasts from space satellites to home TV receivers seem technically feasible, but they would make every TV set in the country obsolete. Also, many of the items are parts of a system, and they cannot be adopted more swiftly than the entire system. Even when all of the components of a system are available, there must be a congruence of interests before adoption. Consider color television, which was technically feasible long before it was widely available. Broadcasters did not want to convert to color until advertisers were willing to use it. Advertisers were not willing to pay for color until enough home TV sets could receive it. And people did not want to invest in color sets until enough programs justified the expense.

On the other hand, some factors seem to be working for rapid adoption. Virtually all of the new technology is electronic; and for various reasons, economic and technological, the electronic media seem to have been more willing to scrap outmoded equipment than the printed media. (Local TV stations, for instance, have converted to color transmission much more rapidly than local newspapers have converted to full-color printing.) And in some cases the foundations for elaborate new systems already exist. (Telephone lines and community antenna systems, for instance, could well be the foundations for intricate new information networks.) Finally, there now seems to be a shorter period between basic idea and application, between invention and adoption, than in the past. Consider, for example, how rapidly business has accepted a wide variety of new communications tools—computers, closed-circuit television, copying machines, intercom systems, and so forth.

It is difficult to predict just when holography will enable Hugh Hefner to display his Playmates in generous three-dimension, and when a home video link to a central computer will enable a housewife to shop without leaving her living room. Yet that day may be close.

Impact on the Media

All of the present and forthcoming technological advances are certain to have a strong impact on our mass communication system and to affect our communications patterns. Let us consider some of the things that might well happen.

First and perhaps obviously, people will be getting their information and entertainment from a far greater variety of sources than ever before. Microcards are not likely to kill off the book, say, nor will computerized information banks kill magazines. When a new means of communication comes along, the old ones do not die, although they may change. Radio did not kill the phonograph or the magazine, despite predictions that it would, and television did not kill radio.

Certainly, each communicator will have fierce competition for his messages. Moreover he may lose some of the control that he now has over his messages—over the ways they are received, the times they are received, and so on. One professor, for instance, no longer subscribes to scholarly journals. Instead, he scans them in the library and has copies made only of the articles that especially interest him. Once home videotape recorders come into common use, a viewer will not have to be on hand at the scheduled time to see a program he is interested in; he can have it recorded for later viewing.

Second, it may no longer be useful to think of the media—books, newspapers, magazines, movies, radio, TV—as having entirely separate identities, for the distinctions among them are becoming blurred. For instance, some New York producers have used TV tapes as the basis for theatrical productions that fall somewhere between movies and closed-circuit television. And when a TV set can receive news and other information and print it out on a facsimile receiver, it is difficult to think of TV and newspapers as being unrelated entities. The fact is that a good deal of mass media content is pretty much interchangeable. The television networks have gone into motion-picture production as a way of getting program fare; their production will turn up both on the picture tube and in the neighborhood Rialto.

Third, it may no longer be useful to think of communications as just person-to-person or medium-to-person. It is also becoming increasingly machine-to-machine.

Fourth, the audience of the individual medium will become increasingly fragmented or stratified because the media have been aiming at more clearly defined audiences. Books, of course, have always been published for some specialized market. When a publisher brings out a volume on the themes of idealism and indignation in the writings of Louis Sullivan, as the Northwestern University Press has done, he does not regard every literate man, woman and child in the United States as a potential purchaser. The other media are now showing this tendency to address themselves to some like-minded constituency within the total population. Newspapers have defined their audiences geographically. Although the larger metropolitan dailies have been dying or merging, the suburban press, with its circumscribed constituencies, has been flourishing. While the suburban papers have appealed to geographically narrow audiences, the metropolitan dailies have remained omnibus products with something for everyone. At least one newspaper executive sees the end of that approach. Not long ago, W. D. Rinehart, assistant general manager of the American Newspaper Publishers Association, predicted that the large-city daily of the future may use technological advances to publish as many as twenty different versions of its final home edition. Each of the twenty would contain highly localized news and advertising for one particular sector of the community.

Magazines addressed to special interests have boomed since World War II, and there now seems to be no interest, taste, inclination or condition of mortal man too esoteric for at least one periodical. Even the mass-circulation magazines have seen the benefits of appealing to an elite. Since 1968 *Look* has given advertisers the chance to reach only its upper-income subscribers. Using census data and other information, the magazine has distilled the 40,000 Zip code zones into 1068 high-income areas. Advertisers can buy space in copies going to *Look* readers in only these affluent neighborhoods—about 14 per cent of the magazine's 6.5 million subscribers. More than 230 general and farm magazines, by offering split-runs and regional editions, allow advertisers to buy space in only a part of their total circulations.

Movies, at least in a very broad sense, have also become selective of audience. The producers of underground movies and the operators of art theaters that serve espresso at intermission are certainly not aiming at the rural trade.

Radio, once an almost universal medium, has become coarsely selective. Some stations devote themselves exclusively to news and public affairs, to ethnic programming, to good music, to country music or rock. To capitalize on this development, in fact, ABC Radio divided itself, amoeba-like, into four networks, each with different program fare. Television has not yet begun this drift toward audience segmentation. Yet it probably will not remain immune in the face of multi-set homes, portable receivers, the expansion of CATV systems and other developments.

The ultimate in this form of audience selectivity has been suggested by Carroll Streeter of *Farm Journal*. In a decade, he has speculated, his magazine might be able to tailor the content of each issue to the individual subscriber. Information about each subscriber's interests would be stored on electronic tape. As the copy for a given subscriber moved along the bindery, the tapes would enable a computer to drop in selected material of special interest to him alone.

The Receiver's Role

This individualization of content is coming not just from the sender's end of the communications process but from the receiver's end as well. Like a diner in a cafeteria, a person is becoming able to choose the particular items he wants from a wide array that others have prepared for him. He can choose what he wants when he wants it. In short, he is becoming his own editor and programmer.

David Sarnoff of Radio Corporation of America foresees a home communication center with these hallmarks,

> Today's console and table model furniture may be displaced by an all-purpose television screen, mounted on the wall. It would be coupled to a sound system and a high-speed electronic printer for recording any information the viewer wishes to retain.
>
> This means that the major channel of news, information and entertainment in the home will be a single integrated system that combines all of the separate electronic instruments and printed means of communications today—television set, radio, newspaper, magazine and book.
>
> The home will thus be joined to a new, all-embracing information medium with a global reach. This medium will serve a vast public of differing nationalities, languages, and customs and its impact will be profound.

All of this leads to a fifth point: that the distinction between individual communication and mass communication is being blurred. On the one hand, technology is making it possible to use mass-produced communication in highly personal, individualized ways. On the other hand, it has also helped to make personal communication public. Once letters were a highly personal form of communication, private and between individuals. But now copying machines threaten to destroy the private nature of correspondence; within an office, it is easy to give a personal letter mass distribution. Telephone conversations are ordinarily personal, but the conference call now enable large groups around the country to get a word in.

Sixth, it is doubtful that the traditional printed media will be killed off by the new technology, although they will certainly have to change to survive. One of the great fascinations of the printed media is that they permit a reader to browse. Often a reader does not know what he is interested in until an editor lays it out before him. As long as man retains any intellectual curiosity, he will want to explore little byways on his own; and it will be a long time, if ever, before automated information systems satisfy that human characteristic.

All of this suggests that much of the new technology may be best suited to providing highly utilitarian information—information catering to interests that can be readily profiled. It will be less suited to providing background and interpretation. True, the new technology may provide wonderful tools for analysis; the computer, for instance, has capabilities for processing data that can provide researcher and reporter with many new insights. But for the ordinary reader and viewer many of the new channels may have sharp limitations as interpreters.

To survive, the printed media probably will have to do a job that other means of communication cannot or will not perform as efficiently and as effectively. Printed media may find their role in providing assessment, evaluation, and interpretation on a scale they never have before.

That, in turn, may call for some serious readjustments in newspapers. It may call for a redefinition of news. Traditionally news has been a report of something that has happened. Thus the conditions in our society and in our institutions ordinarily do not get reported until some event calls attention to them. The student demonstrations have long been news, for instance, but the conditions that prefaced them were not—at least they were not until after the demonstrations. Given our traditional definition of news, the interpretation usually comes too late to do us the most good. If the news media are to improve their analytic reporting, they might have to report conditions before the inevitable eruptions.

KNOWLEDGE, POWER AND THE FUTURE

How the new information systems will develop—and how rapidly—is likely to depend less upon more technological advances than upon the intelligent exercise of power. This is suggested by the quiet but fierce battle that is now being fought in Congress. Some of the younger members of the House of Representatives are working for the development of computer information and data-processing systems for Congress itself. Congressman John Brademas of Indiana has reported that the young men are opposed by many senior Congressmen who fear that sophisticated information systems will spread knowledge so widely in the House that many of the advantages of seniority will be lost.

Certainly, knowledge is power—or at least, as Professor Edwin Parker of Stanford points out, the redistribution of knowledge threatens the existing distribution of power. But if the powerful are also shrewd, they may be able to manipulate the new system to serve themselves better than the generality of the people are served. For example, if the people are better informed because of improved communication technology, the powerful may be able to judge the limits of their power and exercise it more skillfully than ever. "Good information about public opinion," Parker notes, "may make it easier for officials to influence that opinion." He asks, "Are we developing an elite medium of communication that will further enhance the information resources of those segments of society already rich in information resources?"

Parker believes that such a danger can be avoided, especially if we begin immediately to spell out a national information policy. He envisions a time when important information will be as available to a militant Black Panther as it is to an oil lobbyist, and he holds out the hope that the Panther will then have more incentive to participate in politics nonviolently.

It is nonetheless true that certain human factors present dangers. There are people in every society who seek and use information. For some, especially the naturally curious, information is its own reward. For others, there are other rewards. Information may help them in problem solving, or it may mean advancement—economic, occupational, social. These are the people who learn how to seek and process information through whatever means exist at the time. And among these people, of course, are those who have and use power.

The danger, then, is that the segment of society that now uses knowledge to wield power will be in the same position with the new system. Certainly, to the extent that the system is operating today, these are the only people who make use of it because they are among the few who can afford the current high costs. The danger that their advantage will continue as costs decrease is acute; in the formative stages of the new system, this segment of society—like the senior Congressmen—can influence the legislation that will make wider applications possible.

It is now likely that most of the homes in the major metropolitan areas of the United States will have access to cable television by the end of the 1970s. Since cable TV will provide most of the transmission links for the new media of communication—with telephone lines serving others—the time for considering questions of knowledge and power is now.

Bibliography

1 THE MASS MEDIA AND THE CHALLENGE OF CHANGE

BERELSON, BERNARD, AND MORRIS JANOWITZ (eds.), *Reader in Public Opinion and Communication*, 2d. ed. New York: The Free Press, 1966.

PEPPER, THOMAS, "Growing Rich on the Hippie," *The Nation*, April 29, 1968.

SCHRAMM, WILBUR (ed.), *Mass Communications:* A Book of Readings, 2d. ed. Urbana, Ill.: University of Illinois Press, 1960.

————, *The Process and Effects of Mass Communication.* Urbana, Ill.: University of Illinois Press, 1954.

2 COMMUNICATION AND SOCIETY

BERELSON, BERNARD, AND MORRIS JANOWITZ (eds.), *Reader in Public Opinion and Communication*, 2d. ed. New York: The Free Press, 1966.

BOULDING, KENNETH, *The Image.* Ann Arbor, Mich.: University of Michigan Press, 1956.

CAREY, JAMES W., "Harold Adams Innis and Marshall McLuhan," *Antioch Review* 27, Spring 1967, 5–39.

CASSIRER, ERNST, *An Essay on Man.* New Haven, Conn.: Yale University Press, 1962.

INNIS, HAROLD, *The Bias of Communication.* Toronto: Toronto University Press, 1951.

————, *Empire and Communications.* Oxford: Clarendon Press, 1950.

JENSEN, JAY W., "A Method and A Perspective for Criticism of the Mass Media," *Journalism Quarterly* 37, Spring 1960, 261–66.

LIPPMANN, WALTER, *Public Opinion.* New York: Harcourt, Brace & World, Inc., 1922.

MCLUHAN, MARSHALL, *The Gutenberg Galaxy.* Toronto: University of Toronto Press, 1967.

————, *Understanding Media.* New York: McGraw-Hill, Inc., 1964.

SCHRAMM, WILBUR (ed.), *Mass Communications:* A Book of Readings, 2d. ed. Urbana, Ill.: University of Illinois Press, 1960.

3 THE MEDIA AND THEIR SOCIAL AND ECONOMIC ENVIRONMENT

CASEY, RALPH D., "Channels of Communication" in Bruce Smith, Harold Lasswell and Ralph D. Casey, *Propaganda, Communication and Public Opinion.* Princeton, N.J.: Princeton University Press, 1946, pp. 4–30.

FISH, CARL R., *The Rise of the Common Man.* New York: The Macmillan Company, 1927.

GALBRAITH, JOHN K., *The New Industrial State.* New York: New American Library, 1968.

LEHMANN-HAUPT, HELLMUT, in collaboration with Lawrence C. Wroth and Rollo G. Silver, *The Book in America: A History of the Making and Selling of Books in the United States.* New York: R. R. Bowker Co., 1951.

MOTT, FRANK LUTHER, *American Journalism: A History, 1690–1960,* 3d. ed. New York: The Macmillan Company, 1962.

NOSSITER, BERNARD, *The Mythmakers.* Boston: Houghton Mifflin Co., 1964.

PETERSON, THEODORE, *Magazines in the Twentieth Century,* 2d. ed. Urbana, Ill.: University of Illinois Press, 1964.

POTTER, DAVID, *People of Plenty.* Chicago: University of Chicago Press, 1954.

SCHLESINGER, ARTHUR M., *The Rise of the City, 1878–1898.* New York: The Macmillan Company, 1933, 1940.

SINCLAIR, UPTON, *The Cry for Justice*. New York: Lyle Stuart, Inc., 1964.

STEFFENS, LINCOLN, *The Autobiography of Lincoln Steffens*. New York: Harcourt, Brace & World, Inc., 1931.

4 *THE INTELLECTUAL ENVIRONMENT— LIBERTARIANISM*

BECKER, CARL L., *Freedom and Responsibility in the American Way of Life*. New York: Alfred A. Knopf, Inc., 1945.

————, *The Heavenly City of the Eighteenth-Century Philosophers*. New Haven, Conn.: Yale University Press, 1932.

BRINTON, CRANE, *The Shaping of Modern Thought*. Englewood Cliffs, N.J.: Prentice-Hall, Inc., 1963.

————, "Natural Rights," in *Encyclopedia of the Social Sciences*, Vol. II. New York: The Macmillan Company, 1935, pp. 299–302.

CHAFEE, ZECHARIAH, *Free Speech in the United States*. Cambridge, Mass.: Harvard University Press, 1948.

GURVITCH, GEORGES, "Natural Law," *Encyclopedia of the Social Sciences*, Vol. II. New York: The Macmillan Company, 1935, pp. 284–90.

LEVY, LEONARD, *Legacy of Suppression*. Cambridge, Mass.: Belknap Press of Harvard University Press, 1960.

LINDSAY, A. D., "Individualism," *Encyclopedia of the Social Sciences*, Vol. VII. New York: The Macmillan Company, 1935, pp. 674–80.

MOTT, FRANK LUTHER, *Jefferson and the Press*. Baton Rouge, La.: Louisiana State University Press, 1943.

PERRY, RALPH BARTON, "Liberty and the Limits of Government," in *Puritanism and Democracy*. New York: Vanguard Press, Inc., 1944, pp. 421–27, 512–15.

SIEBERT, FREDRICK S., THEODORE PETERSON, AND WILBUR SCHRAMM, *Four Theories of the Press*. Urbana, Ill.: University of Illinois Press, 1956.

5 *THE INTELLECTUAL ENVIRONMENT— SOCIAL RESPONSIBILITY*

BARRON, JEROME, "Access to the Press—A New First Amendment Right," *Harvard Law Review*, 1967.

CARR, EDWARD HALLETT, *The New Society*. London: The Macmillan Company, 1956.

COMMISSION ON FREEDOM OF THE PRESS, *A Free and Responsible Press.* Chicago: University of Chicago Press, 1947.

GERALD, JAMES EDWARD, *The Social Responsibility of the Press.* Minneapolis, Minn.: University of Minnesota Press, 1963.

HOCKING, WILLIAM, *Freedom of the Press: A Framework of Principle.* Chicago: University of Chicago Press, 1947.

JENSEN, JAY W., "Toward a Solution of the Problem of Freedom of the Press." *Journalism Quarterly* 27, Fall 1950, 399–408.

———, "Freedom of the Press: A Concept in Search of a Philosophy," in *Social Responsibility of the Newspress.* Milwaukee, Wis.: Marquette University Press, 1962.

JOHNSON, NICHOLAS, *How to Talk Back to Your Television Set.* Boston, Little, Brown and Co., 1970.

RIVERS, WILLIAM L., AND WILBUR SCHRAMM, *Responsibility in Mass Communication.* New York: Harper & Row, Publishers, 1969.

SIEBERT, FREDRICK S., THEODORE PETERSON, AND WILBUR SCHRAMM, *Four Theories of the Press.* Urbana, Ill.: University of Illinois Press, 1956.

6 THE MEDIA AND GOVERNMENT— THE EARLY EXPERIENCE

LEVY, LEONARD, *Legacy of Suppression.* Cambridge, Mass.: Belknap Press of Harvard University Press, 1960.

MOTT, FRANK L., *American Journalism.* New York: The Macmillan Company, 1962.

POLLARD, JAMES M., *The Presidents and the Press.* New York: The Macmillan Company, 1947.

RIVERS, WILLIAM L., *The Opinionmakers.* Boston: Beacon Press, 1965.

———, *The Adversaries: Politics and the Press.* Boston: Beacon Press, 1970.

ROSTEN, LEO, *The Washington Correspondents.* New York: Harcourt, Brace & World, Inc., 1937.

7 THE MEDIA AND GOVERNMENT— THE MODERN EXPERIENCE

CHAFEE, ZECHARIAH, *Government and Mass Communications.* Chicago: University of Chicago Press, 1947.

MOTT, FRANK L., *American Journalism.* New York: The Macmillan Company, 1962.

POLLARD, JAMES M. *The Presidents and the Press.* New York: The Macmillan Company, 1947.

RIVERS, WILLIAM L., *The Opinionmakers.* Boston: Beacon Press, 1965.

————, *The Adversaries: Politics and the Press.* Boston: Beacon Press, 1970.

ROSTEN, LEO, *The Washington Correspondents.* New York: Harcourt, Brace & World, Inc., 1937.

8 REGULATION OF THE MASS MEDIA

FRANKLIN, MARC A., *The Dynamics of American Law.* Mineola, N.Y.: Foundation Press, 1968.

GILLMOR, DONALD M., AND JEROME A. BARRON, *Mass Communication Law.* St. Paul, Minn.: West Publishing Co., 1969.

KAHN, FRANK J., *Documents of American Broadcasting.* New York: Appleton-Century-Crofts, 1969.

SIEBERT, F. S., "Communications and Government," in Wilbur Schramm (ed.), *Mass Communications.* Urbana, Ill.: University of Illinois Press, 2d. ed. 1960, 219–26.

9 THE ECONOMIC FRAMEWORK OF THE MASS MEDIA

"The American Media Baronies." *Atlantic,* July, 1969.

BAILEY, HERBERT S., JR., *The Art and Science of Book Publishing.* New York: Harper & Row, Publishers, 1970.

COWLEY, MALCOLM, "The Big Change in Publishing," *Esquire* 54, December 1960, 309–15.

HEAD, SYDNEY W., *Broadcasting in America: A Survey of Television and Radio.* Boston: Houghton Mifflin Co., 1956.

HELLMUTH, WILLIAM F., "The Motion Picture Industry" in Walter Adams (ed.), *The Structure of American Industry: Some Case Studies,* 3d. ed. New York: The Macmillan Company, 1961.

JOHNSON, NICHOLAS, "The Media Barons and the Public Interest." *Atlantic,* June 1968.

KREPS, THEODORE J., "The Newspaper Industry" in Walter Adams (ed.), *The Structure of American Industry: Some Case Studies,* 3d. ed. New York: The Macmillan Company, 1961.

MAYER, MARTIN, "Spock, Sex, & Schopenhauer (Soft Bound)," in *Esquire* 57, April 1962, 101-2, 137–41.

PETERSON, THEODORE, *Magazines in the Twentieth Century*, 2d. ed., Urbana, Ill.: University of Illinois Press, 1964, Chap. 4.

SCHRAMM, WILBUR, (ed.), *The Process and Effects of Mass Communication*. Urbana, Ill.: University of Illinois Press, 1954.

TEBBEL, JOHN, *Paperback Books: A Pocket History*. New York: Pocket Books, Inc., 1964.

10 THE MEDIA AS INFORMERS AND INTERPRETERS

CATER, DOUGLASS, *The Fourth Branch of Government*. Boston: Houghton Mifflin Co., 1959.

COHEN, BERNARD, *The Press and Foreign Policy*. Princeton, N.J.: Princeton University Press, 1963.

DAVIS, ELMER H., *But We Were Born Free*. Indianapolis: The Bobbs-Merrill Co., Inc., 1954.

FRIENDLY, FRED, *Due to Circumstances Beyond Our Control*. New York: Random House, Inc., 1967.

GRAMLING, OLIVER, *AP: The Story of News*. New York: Farrar, Straus & Giroux, Inc., 1940.

GREENBERG, BRADLEY, AND EDWIN PARKER, (eds.), *The Kennedy Assassination and the American Public*. Stanford, Calif.: Stanford University Press, 1965.

JOHNSON, GERALD W., *Peril and Promise: An Inquiry into Freedom of the Press*. New York: Harper & Row, Publishers, 1958.

LIPPMANN, WALTER, *Public Opinion*. New York: Harcourt, Brace & World, Inc., 1922.

MORRIS, JOE ALEX, *Deadline Every Minute: The Story of the United Press*. Garden City, N.Y.: Doubleday & Co., Inc., 1957.

RIVERS, WILLIAM L., *The Opinionmakers*. Boston: Beacon Press, 1965.

11 THE MEDIA AS PERSUADERS

BENT, SILAS, *Ballyhoo: The Voice of the Press*. New York: Boni & Liveright, 1927.

BERELSON, BERNARD, AND GARY A. STEINER, "Mass Communication" and "Opinions, Attitudes and Beliefs," in *Human Behavior: An Inventory of Scientific Findings*. New York: Harcourt, Brace & World, Inc., 1964.

GALBRAITH, JOHN K., *The New Industrial State*. New York: New American Library, 1968.

HOVLAND, CARL IVER, IRVING L. JANIS, AND HAROLD H. KELLEY, *Communication and Persuasion: Psychological Studies of Opinion Change*. New Haven, Conn.: Yale University Press, 1953.

KATZ, ELIHU, AND PAUL LAZARSFELD, *Personal Influence: The Part Played by the People in the Flow of Mass Communications*. New York: The Free Press, 1955.

KLAPPER, JOSEPH T., *The Effects of Mass Communication*. New York: The Free Press, 1960.

REGIER, CORNELIUS C., *The Era of the Muckrakers*. Chapel Hill, N.C.: University of North Carolina Press, 1932.

ROGERS, EVERETT, *Diffusion of Innovations*. New York: The Free Press, 1962.

12 THE PROFESSIONAL PERSUADERS

BENDINER, ROBERT, "The 'Engineering of Consent'—A Case Study." *The Reporter* 13, August 11, 1955, 14–23.

BERNAYS, EDWARD L., "American Public Relations: A Short History." *Gazette* (International Journal of the Science of the Press) 2, November 2, 1956, 69–77.

BOORSTIN, DANIEL, *The Image*. New York: Harper & Row, Publishers, 1961.

FREY, ALBERT, *Advertising*, 3d. ed. New York: Ronald Press Co., 1961.

HEILBRONER, ROBERT L., "Public Relations: The Invisible Sell," *Harper's Magazine* 214, June 1957, 23–31.

HILL, JOHN W., *The Making of a Public Relations Man*. New York: David McKay Co., Inc., 1964.

MAYER, MARTIN, *Madison Avenue, U.S.A.* New York: Harper & Row, Publishers, 1958.

MCGINNIS, JOE, *The Selling of the President, 1968*. New York: Trident Press, 1969.

NIMMO, DAN, *The Political Persuaders*. Englewood Cliffs, N.J.: Prentice-Hall, Inc., 1970.

PRESBRY, FRANK S., *The History and Development of Advertising*. Garden City, New York: Doubleday & Co., Inc., 1929.

PIMLOTT, JOHN ALFRED RALPH, *Public Relations and American Democracy*. Princeton, N.J.: Princeton University Press, 1951.

SANDAGE, CHARLES H., AND VERNON FRYBURGER, (eds.), *The Role of*

Advertising: A Book of Readings. Homewood, Ill.: Richard D. Irwin, Inc., 1960.

WOOD, JAMES PLAYSTED, *The Story of Advertising.* New York: The Ronald Press Co., 1958.

13 THE MEDIA, ENTERTAINMENT, AND AMERICAN CULTURE

BODE, CARL, *The Anatomy of American Popular Culture: 1840–1861.* Berkeley, Calif.: University of California Press, 1959.

CAREY, JAMES W., "The Communications Revolution and the Professional Communicator," *Sociological Review Monograph No. 13,* January 1969.

————, "Harold Adams Innis and Marshall McLuhan," *Antioch Review* 27, Spring 1967, 5–39.

GRIFFITH, RICHARD, AND ARTHUR MAYER, *The Movies.* New York: Simon and Schuster, Inc., 1957.

HALL, STUART, AND PADDY WHANNEL, *The Popular Arts.* London: Hutchinson Educational, 1964.

HOGGART, RICHARD, *The Uses of Literacy: Changing Patterns in English Mass Culture.* Fair Lawn, N.J.: Essential Books, 1957.

KLAPPER, JOSEPH T., *The Effects of the Mass Media.* Glencoe, Ill.: Free Press, 1960.

KAEL, PAULINE, *Kiss Kiss Bang Bang.* New York: Bantam Books, 1969.

LOWENTHAL, LEO, *Literature, Popular Culture and Society.* Englewood Cliffs, N.J.: Prentice-Hall, Inc., 1961.

MACDONALD, DWIGHT, *Against the American Grain.* New York: Random House, Inc., 1962.

MENDELSOHN, HAROLD, *Mass Entertainment.* New Haven, Conn.: College and University Press, 1966.

POWDERMAKER, HORTENSE, *Hollywood, the Dream Factory.* Boston: Little, Brown and Co., 1950.

ROSENBERG, BERNARD, AND DAVID MANNING WHITE, (eds.), *Mass Culture: The Popular Arts in America.* New York: The Free Press, 1957.

SCHRAMM, WILBUR, JACK LYLE, AND EDWIN B. PARKER, *Television in the Lives of Our Children.* Stanford, Calif.: Stanford University Press, 1961.

SCHUMACH, MURRAY, *The Face on the Cutting Room Floor.* New York: William Morrow & Co., Inc., 1964.

SELDES, GILBERT, *The Great Audience*. New York: The Viking Press, Inc., 1950.

————, *The Seven Lively Arts*. New York: Sagamore Press, Inc., 1957.

WARSHOW, ROBERT, "The Gentleman with a Gun." *Encounter* 6, March 1954, 18–25.

WHITE, DAVID MANNING, AND ROBERT H. ABEL, (eds.), *The Funnies, An American Idiom*. New York: The Free Press, 1963.

14 THE AUDIENCE OF THE MASS MEDIA

"The American Reading Public: A Symposium." *Daedalus*, Winter 1963.

DEXTER, LEWIS ANTHONY, AND DAVID MANNING WHITE, (eds.), *People, Society, and Mass Communication*. New York: The Free Press, 1964.

HANDEL, LEO, *Hollywood Looks at Its Audience*. Urbana, Ill.: University of Illinois Press, 1950.

SCHRAMM, WILBUR, (ed.), *The Process and Effects of Mass Communication*. Urbana, Ill.: University of Illinois Press, 1954.

————, JACK LYLE, AND EDWIN B. PARKER, *Television in the Lives of Our Children*. Stanford, Calif.: Stanford University Press, 1961.

STEINER, GARY A., *The People Look at Television*. New York: Alfred A. Knopf, Inc., 1963.

WILENSKY, HAROLD C., "Mass Society and Mass Culture: Interdependence or Independence?" *American Sociological Review* 29, 1964, 173–97.

15 CRITICISMS OF THE MASS MEDIA

BAGDIKIAN, BENJAMIN, "The American Newspaper is Neither Record, Telegram, Examiner, Observer, Monitor, Mirror, Journal, Ledger, Bulletin, Register, Chronicle, Gazette, Transcript nor Herald of the Day's Events—It's Just Bad News." *Esquire*, March 1967.

COMMISSION ON FREEDOM OF THE PRESS, *A Free and Responsible Press*. Chicago: University of Chicago Press, 1947.

ERNST, MORRIS L., *The First Freedom*. New York: The Macmillan Company, 1945.

GERBNER, GEORGE, "Press Perspectives in World Communication: A Pilot Study," *Journalism Quarterly* 38, Summer 1961, 312–22.

IRWIN, WILL, *The American Newspaper*. Ames, Iowa: Iowa State University Press, 1969.

JENSEN, JAY W., "A Method and a Perspective for Criticism of the Mass Media." *Journalism Quarterly* 37, Spring 1960, 261–66.

LIEBLING, A. J., *Mink and Red Herring: The Wayward Pressman's Casebook.* Garden City, N.Y.: Doubleday & Co., Inc., 1949.

——, *The Press.* New York: Ballantine Books, Inc., 1961.

——, *The Wayward Pressman.* Garden City, N.Y.: Doubleday & Co., Inc., 1947.

LIPPMANN, WALTER, *Public Opinion.* New York: Harcourt, Brace, & World, Inc. 1922.

MEHLING, HAROLD, *The Great Time-Killer.* Cleveland: The World Publishing Co., 1962.

PACKARD, VANCE, *The Hidden Persuaders.* New York: David McKay Co., Inc., 1957.

PETERSON, THEODORE, "Why the Mass Media are that Way." *Antioch Review* 23, Winter 1963-64, 405–24.

RIVERS, WILLIAM L., AND WILBUR SCHRAMM, *Responsibility in Mass Communication.* New York: Harper & Row, Publishers, 1969.

ROWSE, ARTHUR, *Slanted News.* Boston: Beacon Press, 1957.

RUCKER, BRYCE, *The First Freedom.* Carbondale, Ill.: Southern Illinois University Press, 1968.

SELDES, GEORGE, *Freedom of the Press.* Garden City, N.Y.: Garden City Publishing Co., Inc., 1937.

——, *Lords of the Press.* New York: Julian Messner, Inc., 1939.

SINCLAIR, UPTON, *The Brass Check: A Study of American Journalism.* Pasadena, California: The Author, 1931.

SVIRSKY, LEON, (ed.), *Your Newspaper, Blueprint for a Better Press, by Nine Nieman Fellows 1945–1946.* New York: The Macmillan Company, 1947.

16 THE MASS MEDIA AND THE FUTURE

CAREY, JAMES W., AND JOHN J. QUIRK, "The Mythos of the Electronic Revolution." *American Scholar* 39, Spring 1970, 219–41; Summer 1970, 395–424.

"The Communications Revolution." Special Issue, *Science and Technology* No. 76, April 1968.

FIELD, ROGER KENNETH, "Tomorrow's Communications: A Special Report." *Electronics,* November 24, 1969, 73–104.

GOLDHAMER, HERBERT, (ed.), *The Social Effects of Communication Technology*. Santa Monica, Calif.: The Rand Corporation, 1970.

NEW YORK TIMES, "The New York Times Information Bank." Unpublished, undated release made available in 1970.

PARKER, EDWIN B., "Information Utilities and Mass Communication." Paper delivered at the Conference on Information Utilities and Social Choice, University of Chicago, December 2, 1969.

RUCKER, BRYCE, *The First Freedom*. Carbondale, Ill.: Southern Illinois University Press, 1968.

"Information." Special Issue, *Scientific American* 215, September 1966.

SARNOFF, DAVID, *New Dimensions in Mass Communications*. RCA reprint of address at Advertising Council Annual Dinner, New York, December 13, 1965.

Index of Names

Adams, John Quincy, 108–109
Agnew, Spiro, 136, 138–39, 141, 296
Ailes, Roger, 246
Allen, Frederick Lewis, 43, 48
Allen, Wallace, 1
Anderson, Paul Y., 119, 122
Ardrey, Robert, 304–05

Bacheller, Irving, 199
Bagdikian, Ben, 6, 10, 100
Baillie, Hugh, 277
Baker, Ray Stannard, 219
Baker, Russell, 131, 215–16
Barron, Jerome, 2–5, 94
Bartlett, Charles, 134
Bartley, Robert, 244
Beard, Charles, 68, 71, 221
Bender, Lauretta, 263–64
Bennett, James Gordon, 45, 58, 61, 111, 114
Bent, Silas, 212
Berelson, Bernard, 211, 263, 281, 289
Bernays, Edward J., 237–38, 241, 243
Bernbach, William, 249
Bingham, Barry, 188
Blackstone, William, 76
Blair, Francis P., 109–10
Bok, Edward, 49
Boorstin, Daniel, 26
Boulding, Kenneth, 21, 24
Bradford, Andrew, 48
Bradford, William, 104
Brady, Robert, 183
Brandt, Raymond "Pete," 121
Brown, Charlene, 258
Brown, Donald E., 200
Brucker, Herbert 302–03
Brugmann, Bruce, 214
Bryan, William Jennings, 199
Buchwald, Art, 215
Buckley, William F., Jr., 168, 215–16
Burch, Dean, 158
Bush, Chilton R., 99
Butt, Archie, 117
Byoir, Carl, 241, 244, 246
Byrd, Harry, 127–29

Camden, Lord, 76–78
Campbell, John, 104

Canham, Erwin, 97
Cantril, Hadley, 211
Carey, James, 29–30, 275
Carter, Boake, 201
Carter, Douglas, 128
Catledge, Turner, 122
Caxton, William, 15
Chafee, Zechariah, 155
Chandler, Robert W., 100
Chapin, Charles, 12, 14
Chase, Ilka, 251
Chase, Stuart, 311
Chayefsky, Paddy, 261
Childs, Harwood L., 238
Clapper, Raymond, 126
Clark, Tom, 147–48
Coolidge, Calvin, 199ff., 122
Coughlin, Father, 35
Cox, Kenneth, 4–5, 244
Craig, Daniel, 61
Cranston, Alan, 142–43
Cronkite, Walter, 21, 201, 206
Curtis, Cyrus, 48

Daniel, Clifton, 5
Dann, Mike, 163–65
Davis, Richard Harding, 11, 115
Day, Ben, 45, 47, 84
de Tocqueville, Alexis, 269–70
Dewey, John, 28
Dewey, Thomas E., 129, 211
Dichter, Ernest, 291
Dreyer, Thorne, 10
Duane, William, 108
Dunn, Arthur Wallace, 116

Earley, Stephen, 127
Eaton, Dorman, 239
Eaton, William J., 213
Edison, Thomas A., 52, 178, 180
Edman, Irving, 302
Eisenhower, Dwight, 95, 129ff., 133, 134,
    138, 190, 246, 294, 300
Erskine, Thomas, 76–78
Evans, Rowland, 134

Fagen, David, 273ff.
Field, Marshall, 55

Fischer, John, 192
Fischer, Paul, 14
Fisk, Marjorie, 264
Force, Peter, 108–09
Fox, William, 180–81
Frank, Reuven, 1, 140
Franklin, Benjamin, 48
Franklin, Marc, 145, 147, 149–150
Freneau, Philip, 107
Frey, Albert, 248
Fulbright, J. W., 3–4

Galbraith, John Kenneth, 210
Gallagher, Wes, 189–90
Gamble, Frederick R., 236
Garett, Paul, 243
Gerald, J. Edward, 99
Gerbner, George, 33
Gerth, Hans H., 263
Gould, Jack, 139
Greeley, Horace, 90, 112–14
Green, Duff, 109
Greenberg, Clement, 271
Griffith, David Wark, 53, 307

Hackett, Alice Payne, 257
Hagerty, James, 130–31, 133
Hamilton, Alexander, 106
Hand, Learned, 148, 186
Harding, Warren G., 119ff., 122
Harris, Benjamin, 103
Harris, Richard, 219
Hays, Will, 182
Hearst, William Randolph, 44, 47, 63, 199, 221, 260, 301, 313
Heilbroner, Robert L., 252–53
Hellmuth, W. F., 180, 183–84
Hennock, Frieda B., 177
Hersh, Seymour, 213
Herter, Christian, 129–30
Herzog, Herta, 290–92
Hocking, William T., 92
Holmes, Oliver Wendell, 80–81.
Hoover, Herbert, 121ff., 127, 176
Hopkins, Claude, 247
Humphrey, Hubert, 27, 137, 301
Hutchins, Robert M., 92
Hyde, Henry, 125

Innis, Harold Adams, 29, 31–32
Irwin, Will, 220, 297–99
Isaacs, Norman, 94

Jackson, Andrew, 61, 109–11
Jefferson, Thomas, 76-78, 82, 106ff.
Johns-Heine, Patrick, 263
Johnson, Lyndon, 60, 95, 134ff., 212, 301
Johnson, Nicholas, 160, 185, 244
Kellogg, Ansel N., 198
Kendall, Amos, 109

Kennedy, John F., 131ff., 134ff., 294, 300
Kennedy, Robert, 87, 95
Klapper, Joseph, 32, 34, 259, 263, 265, 314–15
Kleppner, Otto, 250
Kobre, Sidney, 302
Krock, Arthur, 125, 133–34

LaPiere, Richard T., 34
Lasch, Robert, 154
Lasswell, Harold, 28–29
Lawrence, David, 119, 215
Lazarsfeld, Paul, 33–34, 232, 282, 314–15
Lehman, Ernest, 65
Lehmann-Haupt, Hellmut, 49–50
Levy, Leonard, 68
Lewis, Ted, 136
Lincoln, Abraham, 42, 60, 103, 111ff.
Lindsay, Vachel, 53
Lippmann, Walter, 25–26, 67, 134, 273, 302
Locke, John, 74–75
Lydecker, Garrit, 248
Lyons, Leonard, 215

MacArthur, Douglas, 130
McCarthy, Joseph, 138, 156, 227
McClure, S. S., 48
Maccoby, Eleanor, 266
McCormick, Anne O'Hare, 133
Macdonald, Dwight, 270–71, 273
McGinnis, Joseph, 27
McKinley, William, 115
McLuhan, Marshall, 30–32, 273ff.
MacNeil, Robert, 247
McRae, Milton, 63
Madison, James, 105, 107–08
Mallon, Paul, 121–22
Mansfield, Lord, 76
Markel, Lester, 188
Marlow, James, 190
Martin, Harold, 213
Mauerhofer, Hugh, 267
Mayer, Martin, 236–37, 253
Medill, Joseph, 112
Mellett, Don, 212–13
Mellett, Lowell, 100
Mergenthaler, Ottmar, 14
Merton, Robert K., 33–34, 283, 314–15
Meyer, Karl, 189
Michelson, Charles, 123
Mickelson, Sig, 228–29
Mill, John Stuart, 79–80, 82
Mills, C. Wright, 295–97
Milton, John, 72–81, 264
Mitgang, Herbert, 268
Monroe, James, 108
Morgan, Edward P., 201
Mott, Frank Luther, 47, 172
Mungo, Ray, 9, 10
Munsey, Frank, 48–49, 57, 63

Murrow, Edward R., 201, 261, 308–09

Nader, Ralph, 152, 221, 310
Nast, Condé, 251–52
Nast, Thomas, 262
Nelson, William Rockhill, 90
Newton, Isaac, 74–75, 87, 294
Nimmo, Dan, 246
Nixon, Richard, 27–28, 95, 132, 136*ff*., 158, 211–12, 232, 235, 246, 300–01
Norman, Norman B., 249

Ochs, Adolph S., 172
Ogilvy, David, 249
Osgood, Whitman, 127

Page, Walter Hines, 64
Palmer, Volney, 59
Park, Robert E., 260
Parker, Edwin, 324
Pendray, E. Edward, 244
Pepper, Thomas, 8, 10
Phelps, Richard, 145
Philpot, Frank Allen, 202*ff*.
Plattes, Cyril W., 235
Pope, James, 97, 188
Porter, Edwin S., 53
Potter, David, 164, 312–13
Pulitzer, Joseph, 44, 46–47, 90

Rankin, William H., 57
Raymond, Henry, 90
Reeves, Rosser, 248–49
Regier, C. C., 220
Reston, James, 21, 97, 134, 136–37, 139, 215–16
Reynolds, Paul, 20
Riis, Jacob, 115
Riley, John and Mathilda, 264
Rinehart, W. D., 321
Roosevelt, Franklin D., 60, 100, 123, 125*ff*., 129, 133, 154
Roosevelt, Theodore, 115–18
Rosenberg, Bernard, 268–69
Rosten, Leo, 120, 125–26
Rotha, Paul, 54
Rowell, George P., 56, 285
Russell, A. J., Jr., 170

Salant, Richard S., 261
Salinger, Pierre, 134–35
Salter, Patricia, 263
Sandage, C. H., 84, 312
Sapir, Edward, 22
Sarnoff, David, 167, 175–76, 200, 322
Scherr, Max, 8
Schor, Manny, 226
Schouler, James, 109
Schramm, Wilbur, 9–10, 29, 101–02, 233, 279, 287–88, 294

Scott, Al, 246
Scripps, E. W., 63
Seldes, George, 299
Seldes, Gilbert, 272
Sennett, Mack, 58–59
Serling, Rod, 171
Shannon, Lyle, 263
Shero, Jeff, 10
Shulman, Max, 256
Sidis, William, 147
Siebert, F. S., 81, 266
Sinclair, Upton, 299–300, 304
Smith, Adam, 74–75, 83
Smith, Samuel Harrison, 107–08
Sokolsky, George, 83
Stanton, Frank, 94–95
Steffens, Lincoln, 44, 115–16, 219
Steiner, Gary, 29–30
Stewart, Potter, 157
Stone, Melville E., 172
Streeter, Carroll, 321–22
Sullivan, Mark, 122
Suydam, Henry, 121

Taft, William Howard, 116–18, 122
Tarbell, Ida, 219
Thompson, Charles Willis, 116
Thompson, Willard L., 309
Tobin, Richard, 293
Townes, William, 99
Treleaven, Harry, 246
Truman, Harry, 128*f*., 130, 134
Tucker, Ray, 119

van den Haag, Ernest, 273
van Hoffman, Nicholas, 216

Wallace, DeWitt, 64
Walsh, Frank P., 220–21
Warne, Colston E., 310
Washington, George, 78, 105*ff*., 121
Weed, Thurlow, 114
Wertham, Fredric, 304
White, Byron, 6, 7
White, David Manning, 268–70
White, Paul, 201
Whitman, Walt, 271–72
Whittemore, Reed, 10–11
Wicker, Tom, 139–40
Wilson, Woodrow, 115, 117*ff*., 120, 127, 277
Wirth, Louis, 34
Wolfe, Katherine M., 264
Wright, Charles, 29

Zanuck, Darryl F., 156
Zenger, John Peter, 104
Zipf, George, 287
Zukor, Adolph, 53, 181

Index of Subjects

Advertising, 55ff., 59f., 90, 174, 235ff., 247ff.; criticisms of, 309ff.; as economic basis for mass communications, 164ff.; influences, 169; radio, 176; regulation, 151f.; selecting media, 250ff.; selective vs. mass audiences, 165ff.; television, 178

American Association of Advertising Agencies, 236

American Broadcasting Co., 177, 202, 204

American Newspaper Guild, 8, 13, 100

American Newspaper Publishers Association, 176, 300, 321

American Society of Newspaper Editors, 91, 97

Antitrust action in movie industry, 182ff. (see also Sherman Anti-Trust Act)

Areopagitica, 72–74, 264

Audiences, 282ff.

Bill of Rights, 1, 67, 68, 80

Birth of a Nation, The, 53, 307

Blow-Up, 157

Book-of-the-Month Club, 20, 287

Book publishing, condition of, 20

Books, dependence on periodical press, 49f.; newsbooks, 51; paperbacks, 51, 52; readership, 50f., 281f.

Boston News Letter, 104

Broadcasting, audiences, 279–80; audience-supported, 168; competition with press, 200ff.; editorializing, 227ff.; interpretive reporting, 206f.; newscasting, 199ff.

Broadcasting industry, structure, 175ff.

Brass Check, The, 299

Canons of Journalism, 91

Censorship, 71ff., 153ff.; "clear and present danger," 81; of movies, 155ff.; of radio, 158ff.

Changing American Newspaper, The, 302

Citizens' advisory councils, 99f.

Codes of performance, 91

Columbia Broadcasting System, 1, 94, 95, 139–40, 163–65, 177, 206, 228, 261

Communication(s), defined, 22ff.; and society, 21ff.

Company-sponsored publications (see House organs)

Constitution, 2ff., 87, 89; Alien and Sedition Acts of 1798, 68; First Amendment, 2ff., 89, 100; Fourteenth Amendment, 2ff.; Hutchins Commission, 6; libertarian basis, 78ff.; Red Lion decision, 6, 7

Copyright restrictions, 149f.

Corp. for Public Broadcasting, 169

Cross-media ownership, 184ff.

Declaration of Independence, 74

Defamation, 146

Educational broadcasting, 168f.

Effects of the Mass Media, The, 259

Engineering of Consent, The, 243

Equal-time policy, 95

Fairness Doctrine, 4, 159–60

Federal Communications Commission, 4, 158–62, 177–78, 205, 227–28, 261

Ford Foundation, 102, 169, 207

Foreign-language papers, 46

Four Theories of the Press, 81

Free and Responsible Press, A, 92

Freedom of expression, 74ff., 87ff. (see also Freedom of the press)

Freedom of Information Act, 138

Freedom of the press, 2ff., 145; and *Areopagitica*, 72ff.; Commission on, 92, 301; as function of economic interests, 67ff.; and *laissez-faire*, 75; legislative safeguards, 76ff.; and protection of minority rights, 79f.; redefined as responsibility, 89ff.; and safety in diversity, 80 (see also Constitution, and Mass media, regulation of)

Freedom of the Press, 300

Freedom of the Press: A Framework of Principle, 92

Gauging Public Opinion, 211

Gazette of the United States, 106

Great Audience, The, 272

Great Train Robbery, The, 53

House organs, 16, 221ff.

Interpretative reporting, 187ff.

Interstate Commerce Act, 42
Journalism, as a business, 144: corporate ownership, 63, and economic structure of industry, 172–73; newspaper chains, 171–73; defined, 14; history of, 11*ff.*; redefined, 15, 16
Journalists, autonomy of, 7, 8

Labor press, 225*ff.*
Lady Chatterley's Lover, 157
Legacy of Suppression, 68
Libel laws, 79
Liberation News Service, 9, 10
Libertarianism, 67*ff.*; Areopagitica, 72*ff.*; economics and the press, 82*ff.*; philosophy, development of, 69*f.*; social functions of a free press, 81*ff.*; theory of government, 69*f.*; theory of the press, 70*ff.*; tyranny of the majority, 79*f.*
Linotype, 14, 43, 60
Lone Ranger, 255–56
Lords of the Press, 300

Madison Avenue, U.S.A., 236, 253
Magazine industry, current condition of, 18–19; structure of, 173–75
Magazines, audiences, 284–85; criticisms of, 304; as crusaders, 218*ff.*; as informers and interpreters, 191*f.*; journals of opinion, 220*f.*; modern, emergence of, 48; reasons for using, 291*ff.*
Magazines: *Argosy*, 218; *Atlantic*, 48, 260; *Business Week*, 18; *Century*, 48, 56; *Collier's*, 18, 219, 297; *Commentary*, 304; *Esquire*, 260; *Harper's* 48, 56, 170, 192, 252, 260, 262; *Ladies' Home Journal*, 49, 219; *Life*, 18, 166, 169–70, 175, 192, 218, 278; *Look*, 19, 175, 218; *McCall's*, 218; *McClure's*, 49, 219; *Munsey's*, 49; *The Nation*, 8, 55, 220–21; *National Review*, 220; *New Leader*, 220; *New Republic*, 10, 55, 220–21, 268; *The New Yorker*, 17, 147, 170, 219, 260, 271, 297; *Newsweek*, 27, 121, 137; *North American Review*, 90; *Ramparts*, 220, 304; *Reader's Digest*, 21, 64, 166, 168, 170, 248, 304; *Rolling Stone*, 175, 304; *Saturday Evening Post*, 49, 165–66; *Scientific American*, 18; *Scribner's*, 44, 48; *Sports Illustrated*, 18, 218; *Successful Farming*, 17, 251; *Sunset*, 18; *Time*, 21, 175; *True*, 169; *TV Guide*, 18; *Yachting*, 18
Mass communication(s), characteristics, 16*ff.*; defined, 14*ff.*
Mass culture, 270*ff.*
Mass Culture, 268–69
Mass media, as affected by: democracy, 38*f.*, 44*ff.*, Industrial Revolution, 39*ff.*, mass production, 40*f.*, urbanization, 43*f.*; audiences of, 277*ff.*; commercial support

of, 55*ff.*; criticism of, 1*f*, 295*ff.*; and cultural change, 29*ff.*, 35; as entertainment, 255*ff.*; future of, 317*ff.*; and government, 103*ff.*: Congress, 110*f.*, the party press, 111, the Presidents, 26*ff.*, 105*ff.*, 125*ff.*; as informers and interpreters, 187*ff.*; as persuaders, 209*ff.*; and pseudo-environment, 25*ff.*; regulation of, 87*ff.*, 145*ff.*; social responsibility, 83*ff.*; and society, 21*ff.*; Soviet system, 33
Mayflower Decision, 227*ff.*
Media councils, 98*ff.*
Media publications: *Broadcasting*, 161–62; *Editor & Publisher*, 99–100; *Printer's Ink*, 57, 167; *Radio Broadcasting*, 57; *Variety*, 19, 65
Mellett Fund, 100
Miracle, The, 157
Motion Picture Patents Company, 180*f.*
Movies, antitrust action 182*ff.*; audiences, 280*f.*; censorship, 155*ff.*; codes, 91; condition of industry, 19; criticisms of, 305*ff.*; history of, 52*ff.*; specialization of function, 58*f.*; standardization of, 64*f.*; structure of industry, 178*ff.*
Muckrakers (*see* Magazines)

National Broadcasting Co., 1, 65, 140, 163–65, 177–78, 202
National Gazette, 107
National Intelligencer, 108
National Journal, 108–09
National security and secrecy, 148*f.*
News management in Cuban crisis, 132
Newspapers, advocacy journalism, 214–15; autonomy of journalists, 7–8; birth of, 15; chains, 171–73; city daily, 195–96; in Colonial America, 37*f.*; columnists and editorial writers, 215–19; comic strips, 194–95, 198–99; condition of, 18; and constitutional guarantees, 2*ff.*; corporate ownership, 63; criticisms of, 1*f.*, 89, 297*ff.*; as crusaders, 212–13; economic structure of, 172–73; European, 7; as informers and interpreters, 187*ff.*; metropolitan daily, 196–98; militant, 8*ff.*, 214*f.*; as political persuaders, 211–12; readership, 279, 284*f.*; Red Lion decision, 6–7; right of access to, 5–6; specialization of function, 58*ff.*; standardization of, 62*f.*; suburban afternoon daily, 193–95; syndicated features, 173, 198–99, 215–16
Newspapers: Baltimore *Patriot*, 61; (Berkeley) *Barb*, 8, *Tribe*, 8; Brooklyn *Eagle*, 121; Canton, Ohio, *Daily News*, 212–13; Chattanooga *Times*, 134; (Chicago) *Daily News*, 172, 213, Sun, 154, *Tribune*, 112, 114, 154; *Christian Science Monitor*, 297; Cleveland *Plain Dealer*, 172;

Denver *Post*, 8, 12; Detroit *News*, 154; Kansas City *Star*, 90, 153–54; London *Times*, 317; (Louisville) *Courier-Journal*, 188, *Times*, 94; Minneapolis *Tribune*, 1; *Newsday*, 213; (New York) *Daily News*, 17, 136, 154, 252, *Herald*, 45, 58, 61, 285, *Herald Tribune*, 134, *Journal*, 47, *Sun*, 45, 47, 116–117, *Tribune*, 117, 285, *World*, 12, 46, 47, 117, 123, *The New York Times*, 5, 17, 52, 61, 90, 116, 122, 131, 133, 139, 145–46, 172, 184, 188, 252, 287, 297; *The Rat*, 10; (St. Louis) *Post-Dispatch*, 119, 121, 217, *Republic*, 53; (San Francisco) *Bay Guardian*, 173, 214–15, *Chronicle*, 203, 207, *Examiner*, 203, 207; (Washington) *Daily News*, 100. *Globe*, 109–10, *Post*, 10, 189, 217

Newspaper Crusaders, 212
"Newsroom" programs, 207

Objectivity in reporting, 188
Obscenity laws, 79, 150f.

Permissible Lie, The, 170
Photojournalism, 43; photoengraving, 43, 61f.; wirephoto, 61
Political Persuaders, The, 246
Press agentry, Congressional, 127; government, cost of, 141ff.; in photographs, 126f.; Presidential, 125ff.; Press Secretary, 133; public-information departments, 127–30
Press associations, 189ff., Associated Press, 19, 63, 116, 119, 153–54, 167, 189–91, 193–94, 197, 200, 202; United Press International, 63, 120–21, 140–41, 176, 189, 191, 193–94, 197, 202, 204, 277
Press Fair Practices Commission, 98–99
Printing presses, development of, 60
Privacy, invasion of, 146f.
Public Occurrences, 103
Public Opinion, 25, 302
Public relations, 170, 235ff., criticisms of, 241–42; history of, 239–40; objectives, 238; political, 246–47 (*see also* Press agentry)

Pulitzer Prizes, 213

Radio, advertising 176; codes of broadcasting, 91; concentration of ownership, 177; condition of, 19; criticisms of, 307ff.; history of, 54f.; regulation of, 158ff.
Radio Corp. of America, 167, 175, 322
Reality in Advertising, 248
Right of fair trial, 147f.

Schools of journalism and communications, 100ff.; for working journalists, 102
Scientific Advertising, 247
Sedition laws, 68, 79, 104
Selling of the President, The, 27
Sherman Anti-Trust Act, 42, 182
Six-penny papers, 45f.
Study of Four Media, 165
Symbols in communication, 23ff.

Tabloids, 47
Television, audiences, 279–80: verifying size of, 285–87; codes of broadcasting, 91; condition of, 19; criticisms of, 1f. 307ff.; educational, 168f.; Fairness Doctrine, 4, 159ff.; and Federal Communications Commission, 4–5; and freedom of expression, 2ff.; government regulation of, 158ff.; network competition, 163ff.; network domination, 177ff.; newscasting, 201ff.; Red Lion decision, 6–7, standardization of, 65

Underground press (*see* Newspapers, militant)
Universities: Columbia, 102; George Washington, 2; Harvard, 102, 287, 303; Illinois, 29, 102, 238; Michigan State, 102; Minnesota, 99, 102, 309; Northwestern, 102; Pennsylvania, 29; Stanford, 102, 145, 165, 192, 202, 258, 266, 324
University reviews: *Chicago Journalism Review*, 8; *Columbia Journalism Review*, 8; *Harvard Law Review*, 2–3; *Journalism Quarterly*, 14

Yellow Journalism, 46–47